AF228897

COLD SUN

Williams-Ford
Texas A&M University
Military History Series

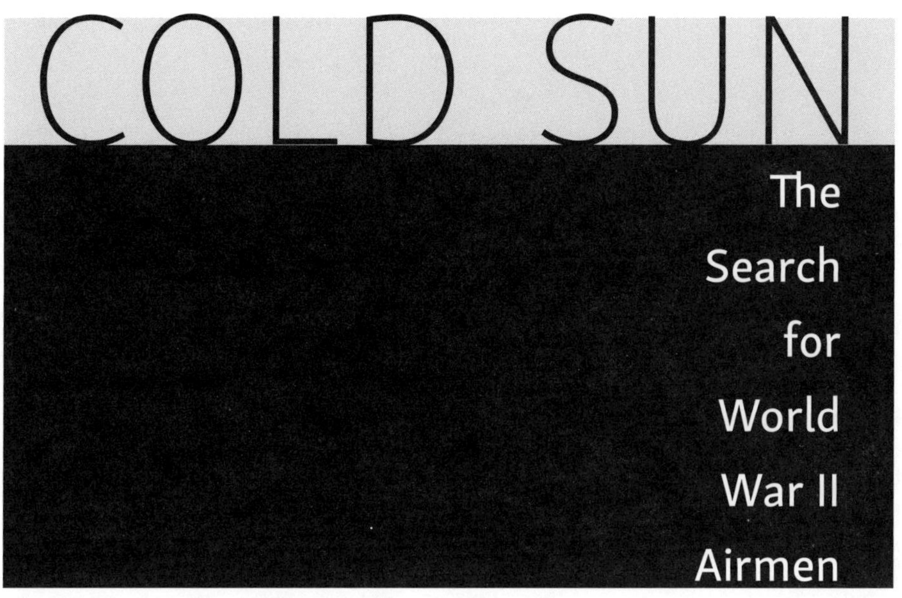

COLD SUN

The Search for World War II Airmen Lost in a Tibetan Glacier

William H. Jordan

Foreword by Mac Thornberry

Texas A&M University Press ▪ College Station

First edition

♾ This paper meets the requirements of ANSI/?NISO Z39.48-1992
(Permanence of Paper).
Binding materials have been chosen for durability.
Manufactured in the United States of America

Library of Congress Cataloging-in-Publication Data

Names: Jordan, William H., author.
Title: Cold sun: the search for World War II airmen lost in a Tibetan glacier / William H. Jordan; foreword by Mac Thornberry.
Other titles: Williams-Ford Texas A&M University military history series.
Description: First edition. | College Station: Texas A&M University Press, [2023] | Series: Williams-Ford Texas A&M University military history series | Includes bibliographical references and index.
Identifiers: LCCN 2022021563 (print) | LCCN 2022021564 (ebook) | ISBN 9781648430916 (hardcover) | ISBN 9781648430923 (ebook)
Subjects: LCSH: United States. Defense POW/MIA Accounting Agency—History. | U.S. Army Central Identification Laboratory. | World War, 1939-1945—Repatriation of war dead—United States. | World War, 1939-1945—Missing in action—United States. | Airplanes, Military—Accidents—Investigation—China—Bomi Xian. | Airplanes, Military—Accidents—Investigation—Himalaya Mountains. | World War, 1939-1945—Search and rescue operations—China—Bomi Xian. | World War, 1939-1945—Search and rescue operations—Himalaya Mountains. | Repatriation of war dead—United States—History—20th century. | Missing in action—United States—Identification. | Bomi Xian (China)—History, Military. | BISAC: HISTORY / Military / Aviation & Space | HISTORY / Wars & Conflicts / World War II / General
Classification: LCC D810.D4 J67 2023 (print) | LCC D810.D4 (ebook) | DDC 940.54/8—dc23/eng/20220601
LC record available at https://lccn.loc.gov/2022021563
LC ebook record available at https://lccn.loc.gov/2022021564

TO JOHN NELSON (1918–2016)
Seventy-seven flights over the Hump

"I'll teach you how to escape death.

. . . there is a raven in the eastern sea which is called Yitai ("dull-headed"). This dull-headed cannot fly very high and seems very stupid. It hops only a short distance and nestles close with others of its kind. In going forward, it dare not lead, and in going back, it dare not lag behind. At the time of feeding, it takes what is left over by the other birds. Therefore, the ranks of this bird are never depleted and nobody can do them any harm. A tree with a straight trunk is the first to be chopped down. A well with sweet water is the first be drawn dry."

—Taikung Jen, in a conversation with Confucius
From *Fate Is the Hunter: A Pilot's Memoir* by Ernest K. Gann

Contents

Foreword

On November 8, 2017, the leaders of Congress gathered in the Capitol's Emancipation Hall to unveil a commemorative chair honoring America's Prisoners of War and Missing in Action. The empty chair serves as a permanent reminder of the commitment of the American military and of the American nation not to leave any service member behind.

A lot of discussion in recent years has revolved around what obligations the nation owes to those who serve in the armed services. It certainly owes them the best training, the best weapons and equipment, and the best support that the nation is capable of providing for the missions they are assigned. If the country cannot fully support them for any reason, the country should rethink what it is asking them to do.

But for some time it has been clear that the country owes those who serve an additional obligation: to never forget about them and to never leave them behind, whatever their fate. The country promises to ensure, one way or another, that they are brought back to their loved ones.

The promise has been engrained in numerous creeds and mottos, including the Army warrior ethos and the Ranger creed. An individual service member makes this promise to his brothers and sisters in arms. And it is a promise made to each of them by the nation they serve, whether the situation calls for a rescue operation or for freeing prisoners of war. The promise extends beyond the life of the individual service member—to recover and return remains should a life be given in service.

A variety of new technologies, such as GPS tracking and satellite communications, has led to improved search and rescue capabilities, making it easier for the promise to be kept today than it was in earlier conflicts. For the fallen, DNA analysis has enabled bodies to be positively identified. But those remains still have to be recovered from wherever they are, and in some places that is an incredibly difficult job.

Colonel Bill Jordan provides us with an extraordinary account of recovering the remains of a World War II flight crew from one of the most inaccessible locations in the world. He actually weaves together two remarkable stories, one about the bravery of the World War II air crew and the other about the dedication of the team to bring them back home.

The Honorable Mac Thornberry,
Former Chair, US House
Armed Services Committee

PREFACE

The Hunter, September 1993

Sherap Chopel worked his way down a 17,000-foot-high ridge in northeastern Tibet. The wiry sixty-two-year-old Tibetan was hunting bharal, the elusive blue sheep of the Tibetan Plateau.

He went on long hunts every year in September, the best time of year in northeastern Tibet, although now he rested more often and turned into his thin woolen bedroll earlier each night, no longer a young man.

This was also a spiritual journey—his wife's father lay near death in his village of Yigon, seven days' walk away. Sherap viewed death, like most Tibetan Buddhists, as a continuum—the human form had lived before and will live again, so his father-in-law's imminent departure from this life was merely a passage in an endless journey. Nonetheless, this was still a melancholy event, and he decided to let his wife, an only child, suffer the grief privately with her father.

Although the rivers and streams were raging furiously from the summer rains and snowmelt, the days were mild and relatively windless, the passes largely free of ice and snow. But each night the temperature dropped a little, and he knew that in another three weeks snow would begin to fall; in six weeks, the landscape would be choked with it and the passes closed. Travel in the Himalayas would be hazardous, if not deadly.

Now, in September 1993, he often thought of the changes that occurred in his native Amdo region, the most restive part of Tibet. He was ten years old when World War II raged in neighboring India, Burma, and China.

Tibet was still a mysterious, xenophobic, highly secretive land in his boyhood, trying desperately to stay neutral, independent, and out of the conflict. His part of Tibet was the most contentious and volatile of all; eastern Tibet lay in the only viable invasion route from their openly hostile neighbor, China.

Entrances to Tibet from the north (Russia), south (India), and west (Xinjiang, China's mostly Muslim province) was ringed by mountains with narrow, easily controlled passes, watched over by Lhasa's soldiers and tax collectors. The east (China) was open and accessible through steppe-like grasslands ringed by mountains, from Chengdu and the rest of Sichuan.

In addition, many of the peoples of eastern Tibet's Amdo region were Khambas—nomadic tribesmen far enough from peaceful Lhasa to relax its Buddhist precepts of peace and engage in a little profitable brigandage and banditry. Another tribe, the Goloks, were worse—they were more along the lines of professional despoilers and marauders, but without the Khambas' physically intimidating tall, broad-shouldered presence.

Britain, China, and Russia continued to play a version of "the Great Game," the struggle to control the Himalayan Plateau that formed gateways to south Asia, Southeast Asia, and Northeast Asia. Even formerly isolationist America was interested in his country and had sent an American OSS officer, grandson of a famous Russian writer, to explore for a road through his country to China and Russia. But Captains Ilya Tolstoy and Brook Dolan found the passes were difficult or impassable to all but animal transport and only added an interesting American footnote to the history of his beloved country. Only China claimed suzerainty over Tibet when Sherap was a child, and it was tenuous at best.

He smiled as he remembered his first trip outside of his village, Yigon.

Sherap had been born and raised in this little village, and his life had been good, especially before the Chinese came. He had traveled to Lhasa on foot when he was a boy, a ten-day walk with his father, mother, and older brother. His grandmother and older sisters traveled the conventional way—walking and prostrating themselves every few feet. They arrived in the small capital city six days behind Sherap's party for the noisy and raucous Yellow Hat festival, but also a festival with considerable religious splendor.

Monks in golden robes sounded the four-meter-long rams' horns. He had seen the Boy King—the Dalai Lama, not much older than himself. He remembered the bruises on his grandmother's and sisters' foreheads and the hands that were severely torn and lacerated from prostrating themselves on the rock-strewn road through the mountains. They wore these wounds proudly—the sign of devout Tibetan Buddhists invoking their love and total immersion in their religion.

Then the Chinese came, many on horseback or in trucks, but most walking like all the people in his village. The villagers had never seen a motor vehicle before. In 1950–51 their 1949 reclamation exploding violently, Peoples' Liberation Army troops fresh from their victories over the Kuomintang forces of Chiang Kai-shek, swept over the border. They were infiltrating into North Korea also and by the end of November would have thousands of soldiers violently engaged with over-extended United Nations' forces. There seemed to be no limit to their soldiers, even though they were not always well-equipped or armed. But there were plenty of them. In Tibet they staged from areas to the east such as Chengdu in Sichuan and other routes out of Yunnan and Kwang Si provinces to the south. Although he had never seen these places, nomadic traders had spoken of them, talked of great vistas and warm, forested mountains, not like these of the high Tibetan Plateau.

Sherap was already a husband and father when red-turbaned Khamba tribesmen and the Goloks revolted in the winter of 1958, killing whole Chinese garrisons with their outdated weapons and their ubiquitous belt knives. They helped the young Dalai Lama escape on horseback to India in 1959, fighting the pursuing Chinese in desperate rear guard actions. Others spoke of some of their best warriors going to an island in the Pacific for training, then to a place called Colorado in America, more like Tibet, with snowy mountains.

He was resting and meditating on this when a flash of sunlight glinted on something a mile away, on the boulder field the glacier had spilled into a narrow valley.

Curious, he worked his way gingerly down the steep slope and discovered the wreckage of a large aircraft. The waning late summer sun had reflected off a huge round engine, otherwise he would have not noticed it.

Small pieces of unfamiliar metal, cloth, and obvious wreckage were scattered along several hundred yards of the glacier's boulder field. When he found mummified human remains, all thoughts of hunting vanished and he began the long walk home, carrying some distinctive parts of the aircraft in his pack.

Safely back in Yigon, he and other village elders examined the artifacts and gravely agreed—this was a government matter. They notified Peoples' Liberation Army authorities in the provincial capital of Lin Zhi, a day's drive from Yigon and 250 miles from Tibet's capital, Lhasa. The Chinese were alarmed—was this a recent crash that had gone unreported? Could there be survivors attempting to get out of the remote area?

Within a few days a hurriedly mounted Chinese military expedition was en route to the crash on foot, with pack animals. They recovered remains of the crew, pieces of wreckage, and they carefully videotaped the proceedings.

At that point the Peoples' Republic of China's Ministry of Foreign Affairs took over and called on the United States ambassador to the Peoples' Republic of China in Beijing.

COLD SUN

Reflections

A Retrospective Overview

Retrospective, indeed, but this work is in no way a memoir. It is merely a first person account and an observation from a ten-year vantage point. I spent thirty-two years enlisted and commissioned in service in the US Army; the last decade was spent almost totally (with the exception of the year at US Army War College) in the field of unaccounted-for US servicemen.

The major events depicted in this book occurred over my last decade of that service, the ten-year period beginning in July 1987, when I joined the largely stagnant Joint Casualty Resolution Center (JCRC) in Barbers Point, Hawaii, until I retired in December 1997.

During this decade I had three assignments in three different agencies or organizations, all dealing with POW/MIA matters: first, operationally in the JCRC; second, in the politico-military matter, initially in the East Asia Pacific Region (EAPR) then in the subsequent Defense Prisoner and Missing Office (DPMO) of the Office of the Secretary of Defense. Lastly, service as the commander of the Central Identification Laboratory, Hawaii (USACILHI), or usually just CIL, which was an unusual combination of operations and policy, plus a science that was also an arcane art, physical anthropology, so far advanced over my undergraduate degree in chemistry that I rarely alluded to it. But we had the finest anthropologists, archaeologists, and forensic dentists in their fields. Everyone in the unit, and all the offices and agencies I found myself in during that ten-year period, were absolutely first rate and thoroughly committed to the mission.

In July 1987 I was a slightly over-age in grade lieutenant colonel of Cavalry, coming from Korea where I had commanded a tank battalion. The JCRC's mission, not terribly popular and largely unknown at the time, was to maintain a tenuous contact with the Socialist Republic of Vietnam to keep the Missing in Action issue in focus.

The events in Tibet happened over a two-assignments-later, thirty-two-day period in September–October 1994 when we recovered (we thought) the last two crewman from a US Army Air Force aircraft that had hit a mountain in northeastern Tibet while trying to return to its home base in Jorhat, Assam, India. The C-87 cargo plane crashed January 31, 1944. It's interesting that Jorhat was situated at a scant few hundred feet in altitude; the mountain the aircraft hit the last day of January 1944, was over 20,000 feet high. Such is the nature of terrain near sea level river valleys adjacent to major mountain ranges. The crew, we thought anyway, was killed instantly in the crash, and the C-87 aircraft, and its enclosed crew, probably slid into a snowfield and was covered in an icy tomb over the ensuing years.

My last ten years in the Army, before my retirement in 1997, was a third of my military career, spent largely in southeast and northeast Asia and Hawaii when I was overseas (plus some time in Europe during the Cold War). During that near decade—1987–89 in the JCRC; 1990–93 in the Office of the Secretary of Defense in the Pentagon; and as commander, US Army Central Identification Laboratory, Hawaii—I dealt with the POW/MIA issue, both in Indochina and to a much lesser, and infinitely more frustrating and disappointing extent, Russia and North Korea. There was no distinction between possible POWs from Vietnam, Korea, or the Cold War and the Missing, for somewhere in that decade the operative term became "accounted for." Which, in this case, meant a near final resolution of the fates of the Missing. Thus, to be in the "POW/MIA issue," you understood that an aircrew gone "off the scope" in January 1944 was inextricably linked to wounded US Special Forces soldiers in Laos, reporting they were outnumbered, out of ammunition, surrounded, and destroying their radio and code books—and would not be heard from again. At that point, only the North Vietnamese or Pathet Lao could answer our questions and help us seek resolution for the families, the nations, and ourselves. The Russians had the most complete answers in the files of the GRU (Main Intelligence Directorate of the General Staff of the Armed Forces of the Russian Federation), and NKVD (People's Commissariat of Internal Affairs), KGB (State Security Committee), and subsequent FSB (Federal Security Service of the Russian Federation). The real secrets were never released, despite great efforts from Task Force Russia, a collaborative effort between the United States and the former Soviet Union. China, for the most part, was open and cooperative, from our airmen shot down and captured over Chinese territory during Vietnam (China "interned" them, though as POWs) to the World War II recoveries attempted. Those first two years spent in the Joint Casualty Resolution Center, the JCRC, in 1985, backlit the nearly two and a half years I spent in Vietnam in the 1960s and early 1970s, first as an artillery officer along the DMZ in the northern province of Quang Tri. I, like nearly a half million other Americans, weathered the Tet Offensive, the battles of Con Thien, and the siege largely of Marines during the fall and winter of '67 and '68. Khe Sanh also protectively encircled Vietnamese Rangers and their American Army advisors. The Air Force was also there coordinating air drops of supplies and helping direct rescue operations. There were a few US Army combat engineers, and Field Artillery as well as our on-direct-fire weapons. The Navy made their appearance overhead, with their ubiquitous flitting A4 Skyhawks, like so many nimble deadly ordnance-loaded fliers, and their lumbering Skyraiders.

The Special Forces ninjas and their Bru indigenous strikers sparred with the North Vietnamese Army (NVA) on their own playing field across the Xepon river in Laos from Forward Operating Base 3, Military Assistance Command, Vietnam Studies and Operations Group (MACVSOG) within Khe Sanh's perimeter. Our own Dusters of 1/44 Artillery with their fast firing twin 40 mm guns and Quad-50 caliber guns added to the fiery chaos of that outpost along Route Coloniale 9 on the border of Laos and far western Vietnam.

After a fast promotion to captain (which I remained for a decade) I took command of Mobile Advisory Team 51, designed like a split Special Forces team with an Infantry lieutenant executive officer, light and heavy weapons noncommissioned officers (NCOs), and a medic. We advised a largely ethnic Cambodian company (actually a battalion) with its 500 or so soldiers, nearly all complete with families accompanying them at our base camp, in the coastal Mekong Delta of Bac Lieu.

Following a temporary leave of absence and a meandering worldwide journey I returned to serve a second tour in Chuong Thien Province in 1971–72 as the Paramilitary Forces advisor; I learned the hard facts of a war beginning to unravel against us. Chuong Thien was in the center of the vast watery flatlands of the Delta, and North Vietnamese soldiers with their distinctive haircuts and more aggressive tactics had already stiffened the Viet Cong infrastructure that had largely been shot away from their mission three years earlier during Tet.

Every day in the military is an interesting adventure. None was more interesting—or fulfilling—than the work of bringing home those men who gave their lives to bring a modicum of peace and security to their families, citizens, and country.

The crew of C-87 862 who waited for rescue for a turbulent half century, deserved to come home to people who dimly remembered them, reawakening their love and grief acutely, but grateful for their return. The return of those five luckless heroic airman in a doomed plane wouldn't have been accomplished without the plucky and determined Joint Casualty Resolution Center (JCRC), and the US Army Central Identification Laboratory, who labored to keep the war going for some 2,000 missing Americans.

The JCRC, CIL, and the Defense Intelligence Agency (DIA) Special Office took their policy guidance from remarkably talented people in the Pentagon's East Asia Pacific Region of International Security Affairs as well as the Defense Prisoner and Missing Office (DPMO) where the officers, NCO and civilians, and I were not only the staff but also the researchers, historians, and frequent briefers for various professionals in government and out, such as veterans' organizations, reporters, and foreign correspondents. The office guided the process from policy direction from Richard Childress, the Asia expert of the National Security Council, to creating the public affairs swell with Ann Mills Griffiths of the National League of Families of the Missing in Southeast Asia. Initially, this effort was for US losses in the Indochina War, but eventually Americans realized and reaffirmed their respect for servicemen from all wars, particularly after the Gulf War ended successfully with everyone accounted for; those who lost in earlier conflicts were returned from years of isolated lonely deaths on barren formal battlefields and crash sites became as important.

All were lost sons of America.

The Defense Intelligence Agency's Special Office for POW/MIA Affairs analyzed the refugee reports and other intelligence, the National Security Agency trolled the airwaves for current Signals Intelligence (SIGINT), and the Central Intelligence Agency maintained their own intelligence and operational files. The State Department and the Office of the Secretary of Defense were partnered equally in this effort, although State had no operational role.

This was a large slice of the US government, perhaps not in manpower, but in agencies involved.

The JCRC and CIL, with their motivation and articulate briefings, formed the canvas of the new painting of the war. Thus the Department of State handling the diplomatic portfolio balanced the Office of the Secretary of Defense, with the aforementioned agencies part of the expansive DOD. The portfolio was the Democratic Republic of Vietnam, now the Socialist Republic of Vietnam, which won the war but lost all the battles and likewise the peace.

The wives and mothers of the missing punched well above their weight, particularly with Congress, like the tiny, forgotten JCRC buried on a naval patrol plane base in Hawaii, and their sister unit, the US Army CILHI, languishing like a forgotten child, on the rundown docks of Honolulu.

The history of that struggle has been described sparsely, but necessarily, because the reverberations moved all the presidents to account for, or at least honor, the missing. Including those scattered across World War II battlefields from the deadly Himalayas to the bloody atolls of the Pacific and blood-stained Europe.

President Reagan would be the first to regularize both the diplomacy and the operational portions with the appointment of a distinguished American military man. The Vietnamese cheered this silently, because they also recognized him not only as a distinguished military man but also as a seasoned diplomat.

General John Vessey, US Army, former Chairman of the Joint Chiefs of Staff (CJCS), stood in the pantheon of Pershing and Marshall. Both sides hoped there would be traction. It would depend almost solely on their cooperation in the POW/MIA issue—the first steps of their "Road Map" to normalization. The others, the pull-out from Cambodia was welcomed; they had fought a two-front war there, with the Chinese in the north and the Khmer Rouge in the south, and were now ironically fighting their own counterguerrilla campaign. The emptying of the "reeducation" camps was ongoing, although those inmates, once released, would not find they were peaceably integrated into the new Communist government. They would continue to have a hard time in their new country.

Regrettably, I was a poor diarist, so in the words of John Masters in his first volume of his soldier's trilogy: "so please do not pounce on me with scorn if there were seven, not eight platoons of Tochi Scouts on the [Iblanke] of May 11–12, 1937. For the purpose of this book, it does not matter."[1]

Now that I'm approaching my eighth decade on this earth I make the same claim. I hope some future historian will write the complete history, finishing the story that Paul Mather so thoroughly covered in his book on the JCRC, born in a war that virtually had no advocates and only families to welcome home those who were there.

There is a rich database thanks to the Senate Select Committee on the POW/MIA issue and the McCain Bill, where declassified information resides in the Library of Congress.

Finally, Desert Shield and Desert Storm wiped out the stigma attended to the military after the mercifully quick and victorious conflict ended with all the Coalition and US Prisoners of War returned, somewhat worse for wear, but safely home. This groundswell of approval helped staff and fund General Vessey's now virtually worn-out JCRC and CILHI, trying to man the recovery teams and identification process with the same small numbers it had when the first successful operations began haltingly in the fall of 1988.

But I served, and finally commanded, in all three branches of that trilogy, the JCRC, EAPR, and CILHI. What I describe did happen—as I remember and describe it. So any mistakes in this account are mine alone.

PART ONE

Legacy

CHAPTER 1

"Bring my Boy Home"

Americans' obsession with returning their war dead is a peculiar phenomenon, one not readily understood by some of our America's countrymen, let alone citizens of foreign nations.

America is largely an insular nation shielded by two large oceans east and west and two friendly (after a few skirmishes) nations north and south. Our geography shapes the foundation of our own collective identity, history, foreign policy and defense. We lacked the porous borders and principalities of the Hapsburgs' rule in seventeenth-century Europe. In Europe, monarchies and duchies moved like pieces on a chessboard, their progeny inheriting their titles, crown, and serfs.

By 1789, the revolution in Paris and revolt in the thirteen colonies led to the first American president and Continental Congress abandoning the Articles of Confederation. They adopted a Constitution instead.

George Washington warned us against foreign interventions as he prepared to leave office—the founding fathers' anathema to continued leadership beyond term limits was as distasteful as foreign conflict—they were deemed not in the best interest of our fledgling nation.

Despite our good intentions, foreign conflict was necessary to acquire additional territories and states. The Mexican-American War was the first of these (the incursions against the Barbary pirates at the turn of the eighteenth century were punitive in nature to prevent plundering of American ships and hostage taking). General Zachary Taylor, the commander of the Mexican incursion, was troubled by the losses of American dragoons in Mexico. He ordered the dead to be personally identified in order to inform the families and loved ones of the circumstances of their loss. He also wanted to ensure disinterment and reburial by their loved ones if they so desired. Unfortunately, the tactical situation in Mexico prevented this, and only the recording of their deaths was possible. America's first foreign deaths in combat are buried in Mexico.[1]

This type of rapidly moving mounted warfare provided valuable lessons to the junior officers of the Quartermaster Corps, and by the time of our Civil War, their Graves Registration Units. These recovery units scoured battlefields and buried and recorded hasty interments' locations. They also verified (as much as possible) personal identities. The various other factors associated with combat deaths or fatal accidents or illnesses were being refined by medical doctors or what passed for pathologists in the mid-nineteenth century.

A sizable war with combatants of largely the same racial makeup, using similar weaponry and tactics—like our Civil War—was tragic but provided a useful if macabre tutorial on death and identification of the dead. There were no official identity discs during the Civil War period, but many soldiers scrawled their names and hometowns on pieces of paper, cardboard, or wood and kept them in their pockets. The first identity discs appeared in World War I and were round. World War II discs were rectangular with rounded edges. Initially, they had "tooth grooves" to hold them in the mouth of the fallen or wounded. These eventually mutated into the Vietnam-era type of name, religion, and blood type and the same rounded rectangular shape—minus the tooth grooves.

In the twenty-first century, pantographs of teeth for specialized personnel such as pilots and special operators have been refined, and now every serviceman is swabbed for DNA identification. They are still issued identity tags, and they are still called dog tags.

Dying as an unknown and remaining unaccounted for was abhorrent to a Civil War soldier or his family from either the North or the South. Not coming home from foreign wars was worse; Americans were attached to their country and their land. They wanted to be buried where relatives and loved ones could visit their eternal resting place. To honor their sacrifice, to let them know they were still loved. Not forgotten.

Much of the successes of the post–Civil War accounting can be attributed to Brigadier General Montgomery Meigs, no lover of Robert E. Lee. Meigs, quartermaster general of the Union Army, visualized the Custis-Lee families' ownership of prime real estate looking across the river from its hilltop prominence at Washington as an ideal place for interment of the Union dead. Thus Lee's plantation holdings became Arlington National Cemetery.

After the war ended, and Meigs was no longer totally overwhelmed by the equipping, supplying, and servicing of the Union Army's military and combat needs, he stopped, took several deep breaths, and surveyed the situation of the dead, missing, and interred. There were 341,670 recorded losses of Union soldiers, but when the burial records were called in, only 101,736 individual burials could be accounted for. Meigs addressed this discrepancy by dispatching two large, well-equipped Graves Registration crews under the command of able quartermaster officers to the eastern and western sectors. Their mission was to find all burial locations and document as much information about the losses as possible. The Graves Registration soldiers were augmented by painters, carpenters, and lumber for markers.

Many of the hasty burial sites were turned into national cemeteries, and by the time the four-million-dollar program ended in 1870—longer than the war itself—there were seventy-four in existence, scattered from Maine to Texas.[2]

This was an enormous undertaking, but it exceeded expectations, accounting for over 315,000 of the 341,000+ Union soldiers.

More importantly, it *forecast* the mood of the average American citizen regarding its dead and missing. Americans wanted them accounted for. They also wanted them identified and buried with their wartime brothers or their families.

Meigs's staff kept a comprehensive effort going to collate all the reports of losses for a "roll of honor," which attempted to account for the individual, his rank, unit, and final burial location. When finished, this work encompassed twenty-seven paperback volumes. Even though there were errors and misspellings, this was the least the nation could do for its war dead and is a testimony to Meigs's diligence.

But this was a war fought on our own soil, both belligerents were American, and the South grieved for their lost just like the North. It would be decades before the Confederate dead were brought to light, even though there were organizations and guilds that sought the same information. Eventually, Confederate dead would come to Arlington and be interred side by side with their comrades.

The next conflict would be a foreign war, and for the first time, excepting the relatively small Mexican-American War, the families and the government had to examine the whole issue of American men lost in foreign lands and the disposition of its dead. Bring them home or leave them where they fell, tended well in a foreign cemetery among comrades, or home to families.

These were still troubling issues three decades after our own conflict that pitted different American polities against each other.

The Union said no slaves and no separate polities; the Confederacy said "let the states decide," thus the War of Southern Rebellion fought the War between the States, and both sides discovered that in spite of what you called it, War was a pathetically ignorant way to exist and conduct business and society.

But losers seethe, churn, and plot, whether they're Nazi Germany or the Reconstruction South who waged an insurrection against the carpetbaggers and blue-coated Cavalry administrators that barely skirted armed violence. Sometimes it did spill over into violence; torches and hoof beats broke out, leaving behind bodies, burning buildings, and more seething.

So, for much of the American body politic, the fighting was *largely* over, but the hostility was not. A prescient president would see that the only way to heal the rift was to have former Confederate soldiers incorporated into US forces to fight Spain—for both sides to channel their enmity to a new foreign enemy rather than each other.

More than three decades in the future the war with Spain would do much to mend the differences between the North and South. President McKinley, a Union officer who fought at Antietam, would shrewdly manage reconciliation by invoking our own Civil War. He appointed Alabaman "Fightin' Joe Wheeler" as a major general of the force that shortly would be facing Spain on deadly Cuban hilltops and the swamps of the Philippines. He was a former Confederate lieutenant general of Cavalry turned Alabama congressman who plagued the North during our bitter Civil War; he was also one of those Cavalry generals who led from the front. Reportedly, in Cuba after one engagement when the enemy fled their redoubt in the face of an American charge, his troops heard a piercing Rebel yell, "Go boys, we got the *damn Yankees* on the run!" Lee reckoned him the equivalent of Jeb Stuart, and many Union generals would likely agree.

After the routing of Spanish combatants and the seizing of Santiago, US divers recovered some of the bodies of the dead sailors and marines from the wreckage of the *Maine*. This saddened and enraged American citizens further. In total, 163 sailors and marines would be temporarily buried in Cuba and reinterred under the *Maine*'s main mast memorial in Arlington in December 1899. Sigsbee Street, running by it, was named for the *Maine*'s skipper, Admiral Dwight Sigsbee, the captain and *Maine*'s skipper at the time of the *Maine*'s sinking in February 1898.

It was—and is—a somber reminder of the "Splendid Little War," as a newsman labeled it. It wouldn't be the last time the loss of a ship was a tipping point that would tumble America into a foreign war.

CHAPTER 2

Foreign Shores, Global Conflict

When the news of the of British ocean liner *Lusitania*'s sinking was announced, with the loss of nearly two hundred Americans among the two thousand lives, World War I, the War to End All Wars, had seen a year of slaughter. The May 1915 sinking burst out in the newspapers and caused extensive heated American deliberation about it and the ultimate effects on the future it might have. This was a war of territorial aggression that might change the relatively peaceful world forever.

The news reports were right. The casualties in even our foreshortened entry into the conflict in 1917—three years after the blood-lettings of the Somme, Ypres, and other bouts of butchery to both sides—made the Spanish-American War pale in comparison.

While it's a *stretch* to label it a "world" war (very little of East Asia or Latin America was involved as in World War II), World War I was still a complex and bloody struggle, especially for the French, Belgians, British, and Germans. However, it did *stretch* to the gates of Asia where the British and the Australians fought the Ottoman Turks on peninsular Turkey's Dardanelles, hoping for an allied seizure of Constantinople (Istanbul). Success would facilitate a line of communication into Russia, but Gallipoli would be put into the bin of British bad military decisions alongside the Boer War and the war between them and their American cousins a couple of centuries before.

Besides fighting alongside French and British forces in mainland Western Europe, a smaller force of Americans wound up in Russia in an ill-advised military adventure.

When the Armistice cease-fire went into effect on the eleventh minute of the eleventh hour of the eleventh day and month of 1918, 53,400+ had been killed in action.[1]

Approximately 53,000 US servicemen perished in combat with another 63,700 listed as noncombat deaths (many had died in the devastating worldwide influenza epidemic that devastated the ranks of all troop concentrations).[2]

One of the 116,516 Americans killed in the war was the youngest son of Theodore Roosevelt, shot down and killed in his Nieuport 28 fighter near Chateau Thierry on July 14, 1918. The Germans, recognizing who he was, conducted a solemn and respectful funeral and burial, marking his grave with the propeller of his aircraft.[3]

All four of President Theodore Roosevelt's sons were fighting in France, but when General Pershing sent his condolences and offered to return his youngest son's body, Roosevelt demurred, replying to Pershing's offer: "Mrs. Roosevelt and I wish to enter a most emphatic protest against the proposed as far as our son Quentin is concerned. We have always believed that 'Where the tree falls, there let it lie.' We know that many good persons feel differently but to us it is painful and harrowing long after death to move the poor body from which the soul has fled. We greatly prefer that Quentin shall continue to lie on the spot where he fell in battle and where the foreman buried him."[4] General Pershing honored his request.

In 1955, Lieutenant Quentin Roosevelt, US Army Air Service, T. R.'s youngest son, was disinterred from his grave in a French cemetery and reburied next to T. R.'s oldest son, Theodore. Theodore was a brigadier general, an assistant division commander who died of a heart attack shortly after the Normandy invasion. They were interred at the national cemetery at Colleville-sur-Mer, France, and both still rest there. Quentin was twenty years old when he died. Theodore Jr. was fifty-six. T. R.'s eldest and youngest son, both wartime casualties from successive world wars, lay together.

The disposition of American remains killed in Europe in World War I became a burning postconflict issue. Despite T. R.'s choice of a foreign burial site for his youngest son, public sentiment largely went with the return of sons, fathers, and husbands. American soldiers would largely repose in American soil, either in Arlington, other military cemeteries in the United States, or in their family plots. In fewer cases, families would, like the Roosevelts, choose to leave them in the beautifully and gratefully tended overseas cemeteries.

And a compassionate Congress, reacting to an overwhelming outpouring of grief from families, relatives, and loved ones seeking the return of their fallen, accommodated them. Funding for the return of the dead would never falter, despite cold-eyed bureaucrats and fiscally minded government decision-makers' qualms about expense and logistical and administrative problems.

The families' spokesman, usually the next of kin, like their earlier generation and the Spanish-American War, would determine where their slain soldier rested through World War II and Korea.

Only for Korea, the cemeteries would be fewer in number and all established and maintained well in Asia and the Pacific. Korea was like that, an unusual conflict with an unusual outcome. The nation we defended remained free but autocratic. Democracy would evolve initially from violence but ultimately from democratic processes and the lessons we fostered on successive leaders of the Republic of Korea.

We went into Vietnam with those same hopes; the best we could do was a familiar sardonic refrain from those who fought there: "we were winning when I left."

Lieutenant General Walton Walker, commander of the Eighth US Army, was ordered by General MacArthur to rapidly continue his attack north up the west and east side of North Korea, the Yellow Sea on his left or west flank. With evidence of three Chinese armies lurking in ambush in the snow-covered mountains, intelligence MacArthur's staff denied, Walker wisely moved cautiously.

Tenth Corps was commanded by Army Major General Ned Almond, one of MacArthur's trusted friends, who also served as chief of staff to the powerful general, a rather unusual arrangement. His responsibility was the central and eastern sector, anchored on the latter by the Seventh Division, the Bayonets of the US Army and O. P. Smith's First Marine Division. It was a bleak, gray winter landscape, surrounded by the snowy mountains and ridges that concealed a formidable white-clad foe.

Nondivisional Army units were mixed in with most of the Third and Seventh Divisions under Almond's command. The bulk of the rest of the troops, including the Twenty-Fourth Division and the famed First Cavalry Division, were moving rapidly up to the Chinese border. The First Marine Division was moving more cautiously north on an axis of advance south and east of the bulk of the Army units, bounded on the mountainous left or landward side, with the Sea of Japan over their right shoulders.

The Marines. The easternmost forces were headed into a buzz saw of Chinese.

Marine commander Major General O. P. Smith also wisely slowed down to quickly construct an evacuation airfield and reset his Marines for a fighting retreat. Their fighting withdrawal out of the murderous mountains surrounding the Choisin Reservoir is another legend in the annals of Marine history.

As the western flank and central thrust faltered and fell back in disorderly confusion, Task Force Faith from the Seventh Infantry Division, fighting alongside a regiment from the Fifth Marines, conducted a fighting night retreat in below zero weather. The Task Force commander was mortally wounded and died in the freezing cold wind and blowing snow. His body wasn't recovered in the retreat that was becoming a rout.

Almond had plenty of warning from his subordinate commanders; he had too much faith in a five-star general who had enjoyed a spectacular successful amphibious reentry into the war in September and ran the campaign from Tokyo.

After the debacle of Chinese intervention in November and December 1950, MacArthur was eyeing Walker as the sacrificial lamb because he too prudently (in MacArthur's estimation) approached the Chinese in a maneuver likened to a reconnaissance in force. This was a more careful tactical technique that put fewer forces forward. One that General Smith was also pursuing, with the added component of a fixed-wing aircraft airfield at Hagaru-ri his engineers scraped out of the frozen earth.

This airfield, if secured, would be a quick back exit for the critically wounded and also a vital resupply airfield. The airfield was completed between bouts of scrambling off their bulldozers to return sniper fire.

It was a wise decision on the part of the quiet, pipe smoking, lover of classical literature, music and marines, Major General Oliver Prince Smith.

But now every American soldier and marine was in full retreat, pursued by Ned Almond's "Laundrymen," wearing their distinctive Russian winter white overgarments and clutching Soviet "burp" guns, Russian Moisin-Nagant rifles, and light and heavy machine guns. Many of them carried US Thompson submachine guns, lend-lease spoils captured from the Kuomintang in the civil war. In some cases, like the Marines on the right flank and Lieutenant Kingston's on the left, it was a no-holds-barred fighting retreat. The Marines were hacking their way back to the Hagaru-ri airfield where they would start their own concurrent return to Japan, C-47s crammed full of wounded, packed in tightly around the frozen dead.

The remains of Lieutenant Colonel Faith were recovered by CILHI in 2004 and identified in 2013, in one of the sporadic bursts of cooperation from the Democratic Peoples' Republic of Korea. Faith had lain there sixty-three years after disgustedly throwing into a snowdrift the Silver Star Ned Almond pinned on his parka before exhorting him to keep advancing to the Yalu with his decimated, scattered battalions.

He would never learn he'd been awarded the Medal of Honor for his rallying of his men to beat back ceaseless waves of Chinese before he was shot dead in the bleak winter snowscape of North Korea. And he would no longer be Killed in Action, Body not Recovered, probably the bitterest classification for loved ones.

Approximately eight thousand US soldiers, marines, sailors, and airmen remain unaccounted for from this war that wasn't labeled a war, a return to the status quo that had to be considered a victory of sorts. Now conflicts were being measured with different yardsticks.

By 1950, all remembered the two weapons of unimaginable destruction that had averted the bloody forecast destruction of an invasion of the fanatic Japanese homeland islands. In those intervening five years, all armed services—except the Strategic Air Command (SAC) of the US Air Force—had been hollowed out with few exceptions; one exception was the miniscule US Marine Corps. While the Army units in Japan and Europe struggled with diminished budgets, the United States maintained an uneasy peace with former Soviet allies that now were strangely hostile and spreading like a red stain over eastern Europe, the Balkans, and central Asia.

The national defense policy of the United States was "Massive Retaliation." Our nuclear weapons were now enough to cover any incipient conflict. All services except the nuclear services, primarily the Air Force's Strategic Air Command, languished without adequate funding, housing, or training. Army troops in now-occupied Japan and Europe tried to adjust to the austere funding and lack of interest in their mission, but soon gave up and enjoyed their vacations. You didn't need to clean your weapons when you had a nuclear arsenal, a sledgehammer to strike a fly. And about as effective. General Maxwell Taylor's *The Uncertain Trumpet* defining the Kennedy administration's new strategy to defeat Communist-inspired urgencies would come out in 1960, a decade after the beginning of the Korean War.

Senior NCOs pulled at their graying hair while they tried to hold on to the semblance of a tough, focused service with hardened combat soldiers maintaining their skills. But they knew they were losing their grip. Those soldiers were back on the farms or factories or in the classrooms, thanks to the GI Bill. The new soldiers had not seen combat, only boring occupation duty. Their first baptism of fire would be against Korean Peoples'

Army soldiers, who had some veterans of guerrilla operations against the Japanese, but most were as inexperienced as their South Korean allies.

Only the Marines, still drilling, training, tearing down their weapons and reassembling them, floated in amphibious-ready groups and maintained the toughest edge they could.

In June 1950 North Korea invaded their southern neighbors and the new United Nations responded mostly with American forces rushed from Japan. US nuclear weapons did not deter the North Korean attack and were not seriously considered until Chinese intervention became a reality. Russian and Chinese decision-makers realized there was a politico-military void they could slip through, and the "sledgehammer to kill a fly" nuclear weapons were still a dangerous consideration, but largely because of the unreality of a policy that said nuclear weapons should be the primary defense mechanism of the United States, even in rather small conflicts. It was unrealistic and unbelievable.

By 1956, Stalin's successor, Khrushchev, had announced support for "wars of national liberation," and Eisenhower and Kennedy had figured out a "flexible response" with the help of Maxwell Taylor's book *The Uncertain Trumpet*.

American servicemen still fought these confusing conflicts skillfully and bravely. They died honorably, and efforts continued to bring them home. These figures pale when contrasted to the 79,000 missing from World War II. Many of these were in planes disappearing over the oceans, ships going down, and even American prisoners of war on Japanese ships scuttling to the mainland from former Pacific bastions.

Papua New Guinea's formidable weather wreathed the Owen Stanley Mountains, and the Himalayas shielding northeast Asia hide a formidable amount of losses. American bones would continue to turn up on remote Pacific islands with nothing more than a few fields of coral. Those Americans also, whenever their crash or battle site was found, would come home. Even those airmen who had overflown or been blown by cyclonic winds into Tibet. Into mountains that defied belief. Into nothingness.

CHAPTER 3

On Their Shields

Child, either come home carrying your shield . . . or on it.[1]

Concurrent Return meant that the serviceman's remains would get home to the family immediately, generally a few days after notification of death. This became policy shortly after the Eighth Army Commander, Lieutenant General Walton Walker, was killed in a jeep accident. In World Wars I and II, the return of the dead would be at war's end; in some cases, years after the war's end. These battlefield searches and remote crash-site exploitations were still ongoing in June 1950, but with the Marines packing out their own and Army dead, with wounded packed carefully around and above them, virtually ending World War II.

Lieutenant General Walton Walker changed from Lamb to Lion in immortality. He was posthumously promoted to four stars, and his funeral cortege was led by beribboned flag officers and was a near state funeral.

After World War I, battlefields were scoured in Belgium and France, and in World War II, similar labor was undertaken in all theaters including Central and South America, wherever Americans fell in combat from the Aleutians to almost Antarctica. Small teams of quartermaster soldiers, sometimes accompanied by armed troops, host nation security forces, or, in most cases, serving as their own security, searched battlefields and crash sites for bleached shattered remains or hasty graves. Also, by World War II most servicemen had emergency address notification and locator cards for the soldier's primary next of kin or an alternate NOK with telephone numbers and addresses.

But three decades earlier, many of the US decision makers of World War I were grappling with this issue for the first time. They tended toward former President Theodore Roosevelt's sentiments of not returning American soldiers. This included General Pershing who maintained the French opposed returning American soldiers for fear of creating a desire for French families to want the return of their 4.5 million war dead repatriated to every village and town in France.

Pershing and his cobelievers pointed out the British didn't return their war dead—they were buried where they perished or in some of the tidy French cemeteries that would become permanent fixtures and be enlarged with more added for World War II casualties. Pershing also cited health risks and distraction from the important work of reconstruction and economic recovery for all of France, devastated by over four years of war. Finally, the return of the dead would seem an interminable wait for grieving families and loved ones. Sledge, in *Soldier Dead*, cites a wait of "two, three, four or five years and longer before they were able to bury their loved ones."[2]

The first and one of the most forbidding administrative problems was determining the desires of the families. From a twenty-first-century viewpoint, very accurate IRS records and digitized population statistics mask the challenges that military personnel offices had at the end of World War I with ledgers and paper files. After the armistice of November 1918 ended the bitter fighting, the Casualty and Memorial Affairs offices of the War Department had to communicate with the families of Great War fatalities in a country of 106 million men, women, and children. They lived in America's large cities and small hamlets (up some 15 percent of the previous decade's count). They had to find the person that could direct the final disposition of their sons and husbands, brothers, uncles, and nephews and in a few cases, grandfathers.

Who and where was their next of kin, or NOK? They called across desks and thumbed through filing cabinets and ledgers. These harried military clerks and civilian accountants, officers, and sergeants had to ensure this was done with respect and succor, and in a few cases, watching through mailed replies families disagreeing and becoming angry with each other, the war, and a harried bureaucracy trying to do its difficult job. The clerks, accountants, and field Graves Registration soldiers, undaunted, continued as best they could.

World War II would find many of the problems of World War I lessened by technology, established records, and a longer war duration, all of which enhanced learning the tasks of casualty management. In World War I the learning curve was almost circular. In addition there were many emigrant Americans that might have been literate in their native German,

Serbo-Croatian, Italian, or any other of dozens of languages, but their penmanship, spelling, and verbal communication might have been challenging when trying to transfer it to written English. Enlistment documents and records were done largely in longhand by individuals. As in the Civil War, records probably contained spelling and address errors, even down to the city and state.

The tired clerks in the cemeteries and memorial branches of the Adjutant General Corps were the last link between the telegram to the families, next of kin, and the mothers, wives, and every other loved one. The initial telegram informed these families of a solitary tragedy on some muddy, shell-chewed field far away. Now it was time to determine what they wanted to do with their mortal remains after a reasonable period of grief and mourning. This process fell to the one presumably closest to the deceased, thus the one who would choose how and where the mortal remains would spend eternity, a difficult task at best.

A soldier's widow had the highest priority in determining final disposition of remains (provided she had not divorced the soldier, separated, or remarried). If she was not able, deceased, unavailable, or unwilling, the duty fell to the children, oldest son first, and he had to be over twenty-one (a somewhat unrealistic requirement since frequently the deceased soldier wasn't even twenty-one). If the soldier was unmarried, then the father was the next of kin. In his absence, it was the mother, then right on down the line of sons and then daughters. By age of course, oldest first. But the clerks and young bureaucrats at the lowest levels set about the challenges of operationalizing the sentiment to "bring my boy home" at the highest levels.

As notifications to families and NOKs flowed in, pressure increased to return them from the charnel house that was World War I France and Belgium. There would be no returns until war's end, anyway, so the American proponents for leaving them in cemeteries abroad settled in for a projected long wait. They didn't count on the effects the US Army and Marines introduced into the war—no more lengthy crawling bloodbaths like the Somme or Ypres—the Americans, like the Australian Light Horse, would go straight at them.

In Washington, General Peyton C. March, Army Chief of Staff, reinforced his objections and echoed Pershing's concerns. As the controversy grew, he urged that "steps be taken to give publicity to the difficulties attendant on the return of bodies with a view to creating a sentiment in favor of having all America's dead left abroad."[3]

General Pershing's leeriness about returning the dead to their families reinforced his earlier arguments. He also highlighted the tremendous expense the task would incur and its effect on training and equipping the shrunken force after demobilization.[4]

What if the family wanted to view the remains? Hardly the thing the battle-hardened generals wanted for the family's last glimpse of the handsome young man they entrusted to the generals' training and care.

But American family and loved ones' traditions trumped all this. Nearly everyone realized the British returned none of their dead to Britain largely due to their imperial past, something Americans largely eschewed, despite the acquisition of the Philippines from Spain scarcely two decades earlier. Most wanted their boys home; some, like Theodore Roosevelt, wanted them buried on well-tended American soil in friendly countries like Belgium and France.[5]

The "thin Red Line" of English hegemony ran to many parts of the world, and where British servicemen lay interred, a "little piece of England" was marked by their blood. At least initially perhaps, but their final resting place was usually a well-tended French or Belgian cemetery; hardly part of the British Empire.

Doubtless one rationale for next of kin leaving their charges in overseas cemeteries was the belief they were undisputedly buried in "America," although they weren't. Photographs, however, did not do justice to the splendid, quiet beauty or the conviction of the host countries who kept the cemeteries in such good order. Americans who left their next of kin in these pastoral grounds could be content with their resting place.

In contrast to Theodore Roosevelt's bluff request to leave Quentin where he fell and spare the family public grieving, there was a famous Englishman's polar opposite view.

Rudyard Kipling's only son, John, a frail, nearsighted young man, enlisted in the Irish Guards (with his father's appeal to the elderly regimental commander) at barely eighteen years of age. He was lost in combat near Loos in the autumn of 1915, and his mortal remains were not identified; he was "unaccounted for" in contemporary American terms. Kipling's grief inspired him to become a member of the Commonwealth Wartime Graves Commission and write a history of the Irish Guards. But the most memorable thing he wrote was a poem, thinly disguised by making the protagonist a sailor named "Jack."

Kipling was a proud Englishman and fervent nationalist, (with more than a hint of racist imperialism in his makeup. He was never a soldier but had covered the conflict during the Boer War in Africa, 1898–1902, and early fighting in France as a war correspondent prior to his son's death in combat. He also became the literary advisor to the War Graves Commission. Like Theodore Roosevelt, he carried the grief of losing a son to his grave. The anguish intensified by the fact he was never found, although researchers found disputed evidence that placed his mortal wounding distant from where official records indicated he was killed in the early 1900s. A headstone bearing his name, disputed rank of first lieutenant, and date of death, now stands in France. Who is buried beneath that headstone now is anyone's guess.

CHAPTER 4

Known but to God

General Peyton March and "Blackjack" Pershing had diplomatically and politically yielded on the return policy, but there was another initiative March would also dismiss out of hand. Brigadier General William D. Connor, commander of Army forces in France, had been impressed with the French's honoring their unknowns by selecting one for burial in the Arc de Triomphe and suggested to March in October 1919, that America might want to do the same. March brushed it aside (although Pershing and General Lejuene, commandant of the Marines, liked and endorsed the idea). A year later, as Armistice Day passed, a New York magazine editor, Marie M. Melony, wrote to General March and made a pitch to reconsider—her rationale was, "it would bring patriotism home to men in a personal way."[1]

She also cited England, which had selected an unknown for interment in Westminster Abbey, as another good reason. March must have groaned when he read the letter; he wrote his reply citing no national memorials existed in the United States like the Arc de Triomphe or Westminster Abbey and the British had over 100,000 missing and unidentified British soldiers. Their unknown represented a missing class, and then perhaps presciently, he noted, the number of our missing and unidentified men was relatively small (then just over 4,200) by comparison.

It was possible with the Graves Registration's successful recovery and identifications the numbers would shrink further, perhaps making anonymity impossible for an unknown, he continued, again eerily prescient. Sensing defeat once the press and the public seized on the idea, he added that if Congress approved a memorial for the unknown, he'd support it.[2]

The bill, introduced by veteran World War I officer Representative Hamilton Fish of New York, ran smoothly through the House but hit a snag in the Senate Committee on Military Affairs when Newton D. Baker, Secretary of War, also raised the specter of the number of growing identifications and that soon there might be no Unknown Soldier from World War I.[3]

With Generals Pershing and Lejeune's championing it, and the American public supporting it, the proposal won out. America would have her unknown.

On November 9, 1921, the cruiser *Olympia*, Admiral Dewey's flagship in the violent clash that sent Spanish ships to the bottom of Manila Bay, nosed into the Washington Navy Yard. Her principal cargo, the World War I Unknown, were four soldiers selected from graves in French cemeteries that had sprung up like spring flowers—Aisne-Marne, Meuse-Argonne, Somme, and St. Miheil. All were near major battles or sectors where American soldiers fought valiantly and perished. The four caskets were identical and had been rearranged like peas under cups on the board game to give all the caskets anonymity, then laid out in the village sanctuary of Chalons on October 24. They were guarded all night by US and French sentinels. There were speeches, honors, flowers.

A French citizen who lost two sons in the war presented a bouquet of white roses to the US quartermaster major in charge, who passed them to Sergeant Edward Younger, twice-wounded and veteran of nearly every significant action involving US troops.

He would select the Unknown.

Sergeant Younger entered the room and stood before the four caskets. Backgrounded by a French military band playing a solemn hymn, Sergeant Younger laid the roses on the second casket and rendered a proper slow salute, then returned outside to the sunlight. All the records according the Unknown were burned by the American officer in charge.

The Unknown were then never left unguarded while in transit on the *Olympia*, waiting quietly at anchor at the port of Le Havre. There amid throngs of citizens, a man limped forward on a battle-shattered leg. He was Monsieur Andre Maginot, Minister of Pensions. He presented France's highest award for gallantry, the Cross of the Chevalier of the Legion of Honor, the first of many foreign national honors the Unknown would receive. Two decades later a Nazi blitzkrieg would go around an extensive, sophisticated obstacle system. These obstacles were attributed to him, now the Minister of War, as the Maginot Line.

The Unknown lay in state in the Capitol Rotunda and then proceeded in a stately parade to Arlington on November 11, officially proclaimed by

President Wilson as Armistice Day (now Veterans) Day, November 11, 1921. There the burial site was thronged with visitors, VIPs and ordinary citizens, and veterans poured into Arlington Cemetery. Among them Lord David Beatty, admiral of the British Fleet and commander in the Battle of Jutland; he presented an award that had never been bestowed on a foreigner—the Victoria Cross. Also present were Belgium's General Baron Jacques; former British prime minister Arthur Balfour; French premier Aristide Briand; General Armando Diaz of Italy; and Chief Plenty Coups of the Crow Nation, in ceremonial Crow regalia.

President Harding proclaimed an end to war then placed the Medal of Honor and the Distinguished Service Cross on the casket of the Unknown, already teeming with the highest awards for valor from France, Belgium, Italy, Romania, Czechoslovakia, and Poland. General Pershing picked up a handful of dirt from the soil of France that was brought over on the *Olympia* for the burial, threw it into the gravesite, and solemnly saluted. Chief Plenty Coups somberly placed his war bonnet and coup sticks on the tomb.[4]

The lonely echo of "Taps" sounded over the wooded hills, and twenty-one guns were fired in final salute. The crowd of citizens gradually began to flow back through the gates; a somber gray mass of humanity, tired of war and grieving for the detritus it left behind—memories and images of its fine young slain—like broken stone.

Despite the obvious reminders of the tragedy of human conflict, the Tomb of the Unknown Soldier became the National Monument of the United States, with its armed sentinel on duty twenty-four hours a day in all weather. The huge crowd removed any doubts about the mood of the people and their feelings for this lonely, Unknown Soldier or Marine. He was *their* missing one; *they had sent their boy home*. It was our Arc d'Triomphe and Westminster Abbey combined and consecrated with crypts of marble, their afternoon shadows sheltering remains that could have been anyone's son, brother, husband, or father that fell unrecognized on the battlefield.

And for many it was.

In 1956 two more unknowns were interred, this time from World War II and Korea, with the same healing, euphoric effect and enthusiastic crowds of citizens. One was a just war; the other a confusing police action, but America ignored these distinctions. Her men were lost in conflicts that were of vital interest to America, whatever they were called by politicians. Both were unknown heroes and both had earned the Medal of Honor.

On Memorial Day, 1984, a recognizable actor and popular American president presided over a military funeral at Arlington. America was going to inter and honor the Unknown from the Vietnam War. President Ronald Reagan described the deceased serviceman as "symbolic of all our missing sons." This unidentified loss was a symbol from a controversial and lengthy conflict (at the time America's longest war) and a loss that occurred in the waning days of the war twelve years earlier.

In an overreach by the Democratic Republic of Vietnam that would almost equal the Tet Offensive, North Vietnamese armored units rolled into the city of An Loc, some sixty miles northwest of Saigon. This was an enemy-initiated battle in a protracted campaign known as the Easter Offensive in April and May of 1972. A two-plane section of USAF A-37 "Dragonfly" fighter-bombers attacked the phalanx of enemy armor and mechanized infantry on May 11. The flight lead rolled in and released his ordnance; the second rolled in and was shot down. First Lieutenant Michael Blassie then began his journey to the Tomb of the Unknown Soldier, only now classified as Killed in Action, Body not Recovered (KIA/BNR).

In October 1972 an ARVN patrol at the direction of the Joint Personnel Recovery Center made its way to the crash site disguised as Viet Cong soldiers and removed the remains of the pilot, a few ribs, a humerus, and a pelvic bone, just a few of the 206 or so bones allotted to the human body. Material evidence from the crash included parachute scraps, a life raft, and components of a signaling device.

His personal identifying media was more important—his wallet and government identification card with a photo and remnants of his flight suit. The friendly patrol worked its way back to a rendezvous point with American advisors and turned over the two bags of meager remains and other evidence. His wallet, identification card, and money disappeared and were never seen again. Captain Richard Hess, one of the advisors, had the forethought to look at the evidence and note Blassie's name and physical description. From the laboratory in Samae San, Thailand, the remains took the long circuitous route to Hawaii when Saigon and the south fell to the Communists in April 1975.[5]

When the Commander in Chief wants something done, it generally happens. In this case in was going to be difficult, for there were just a few remains at CILHI that might meet the requirements of the Unknown. CILHI's objections brought Secretary of the Army John Marsh, the Secretary of Defense and president's point man, to the Hawaii laboratory to talk to the commander and scientists who had raised so many objections.

There were only four thinly suitable candidates when Marsh visited the laboratory in 1982 to break the logjam. One, labeled X-15, the X signifying currently unknown, had evidence of a claymore mine wound and was thought to have been an AWOL soldier slipping through a friendly perimeter—he was eliminated after long absent dental records were discovered matching his teeth. Another, X-32, turned out to be another soldier misidentified immediately after an action and mistakenly buried in Massachusetts. That was corrected when his dog tags showed up in another shipment of remains. These identified him as the previously mistakenly and interred soldier. After disinterment and burying the newly identified soldier, technicians focused on a unilateral turnover of single remains by Laos.

Major Johnnie Webb, the commander of the CILHI at the time, objected to this because of the lack of provenance, and "the pertinent law says it must be an American fighting man who died in combat during this time period . . . won that argument."[6]

"That brought us down to the fourth guy, the X-26 case . . . that one I lost."[7]

In the identification community there is also BTB—Believed to Be, a quasi-status associated with remains, particularly one with a name association or other indications that an identification might be possible. Blassie was also labeled BTB. The major factor in preventing his identification was, again, provenance; his wallet with the identifying Identification card had gone missing. Marsh recognized the tangled circumstances surrounding the "non-ID" while remaining very aware the president wanted an Unknown by Memorial Day.

When X-26 emerged as the likely candidate, Webb fired one last salvo, buttressed by the National League of Families and Richard Childress of the NSC. Since Blassie had name associations and the lack of provenance was the major obstacle, interring an Unknown who had been close to identification could fire a political back blast—interment for a political reason.

Both the League of Families and Dick Childress at the NSC opposed an Unknown from Vietnam, while the veterans of that conflict and the veterans' service organizations like the VFW and American Legion pushed for it. As did probably every Vietnam veteran, myself included.

At the time, despite the JCRC's efforts, the United States and Vietnam were still estranged but talking, albeit sometimes past each other or not on the same frequency. Normalization would not be possible until over a decade later.

But this was 1984, three years before the issue would gain positive traction. Both Ann Mills Griffiths's and Childress's thinking rested on the fact that only the question of missing Americans, some possibly alive but with certainty well over two thousand dead in unknown locations in Vietnam, or their surrogates, Laos and Cambodia, would be considered. These unaccounted for were their hole cards. Until the Vietnamese turned over as many as they could or agreed to US search and recovery teams, the war wasn't over.

Interring a Vietnam Unknown was the next step—in their view—to declaring the war over, and no reason existed to not get to serious negotiations concerning reconciliation and normalization. This may or may not have been a logical assumption, but it made sense to them. The "pro" argument would have made the case the symbol that would force greater cooperation based on the emotion of the American people.

But if that gossamer thread was all that stood between the Socialist Republic of Vietnam and normal relations with the United States, for Griffiths, Childress, and those in their camp, continued access and cooperation by the Socialist Republic of Vietnam was vital. Any manifestation or symbol that the war had ended was not in the best interest of the families or the nation. For them, and for many veterans, that war still raged. But, the president was serious, and with his powerful subordinates determined that X-26 was the Unknown from Vietnam.

Webb was told to forward the material evidence and anything written about the case to the Pentagon for destruction. He demurred, wrapped them securely and with the remains, and placed them in the casket. He also made a copy of the documents and locked them in his desk. They would remain there for over a decade, until a seismic shift occurred. On Memorial Day, 1984, America got its Vietnam War Unknown.

A decade later a POW/MIA activist told a revealing story. In 1994, Ted Sampley, longtime activist and Special Forces veteran of Vietnam, "rooted through his extensive files on POW/MIA cases, grilled sources . . . and pored over Pentagon documents . . . independently pieced together his own conclusions, publishing his findings in his publication *Veteran's Dispatch*, July 14, 1994, under the headline, "The Vietnam Unknown Soldier Can Be Identified."[8]

Before publishing, Sampley contacted Blassie's mother (his father had passed away) and shared his information.

Sampley had pieced together evidence that the Blassie family had allegedly never heard, that the Casualty Office had somehow never passed on since the young officer's 1972 shoot down. The remains of Vietnam's

Unknown had once been linked to their son by strong evidence that had disappeared. Sampley's allegations naturally stirred up old emotions, and Blassie's sister, Pat, now an Air Force officer herself, queried the Air Force Casualty Office in San Antonio. They informed her that Sampley's information "couldn't be authenticated" and expressed no interest for reopening the case.[9]

It lingered for another two years until a CBS News producer read Sampley's report and approached the family again. After a seven months' investigation, CBS *Evening News* broadcast the results: "Blassie *'almost certainly'* buried in the Tomb of the Unknowns." Two powerful Missouri senators, John Ashcroft and Christopher S. "Kit" Bond queried President Bill Clinton's Secretary of Defense William S. Cohen. The family wanted the tomb opened and mitochondrial DNA used to determine his identity.[10]

The Veterans of Foreign Wars and American Legion, the same groups that had supported President Reagan's initiative for a Vietnam Unknown, were outraged at the request. Cohen appointed a study under Rudy de Leon, the longtime respected Undersecretary of Defense for Personnel and Readiness. De Leon had no expectation of disinterment and DNA testing: "that was the last resort." Instead, he focused on three goals: to establish that the casualty, X-26, was the serviceman interred in the Tomb; to find a paper trail and evidence linking him to the 1972 crash at An Loc and to determine if the new mitochondrial DNA testing could provide a foolproof identity if the remains were exhumed.[11]

De Leon met privately with Webb, who revealed he had dropped the physical evidence in the casket prior to the interment. From Marsh, de Leon learned of the intense political pressures put on all the participants. De Leon would conclude: "in every other war there were so many sets of unidentified service members that you could just arbitrarily pick a set of remains and there was no history. With Vietnam, everything was different . . . we got Captain Hess's memo from the pre-interment period. We got information from all of the primary sources. When this [was] done, I felt that indeed all of the data we had on X-26 told us these were the remains at Arlington. Then the next question was whether the DNA testing could be conclusive . . . we were satisfied it could be." In April 1998, de Leon recommended that the tomb be opened.[12]

In mid-May, the tomb was cut open and the remains indeed were identified as Michael Blassie through mitochondrial DNA. Shortly after his reinterment at Jefferson Barracks, Missouri, Secretary Cohen stripped the Medal of Honor after pressure from the American Legion and the Medal of Honor Society.[13]

The rationale was irrefutable—the medal was presented to the Unknown by President Reagan, not the identified airman. It was accepted by the family, however; the lesson was clear—America wanted its boys brought home *and identified*.

Likely, very nearly all would be in the future.

CHAPTER 5

"Ain't Our Fight"

During the economically bleak 1930s, the Depression and World War I argued for isolationism. After all, the Great War had spawned both Japanese—who had joined the allies, albeit in a relatively minor role—and German expansionism scarcely a decade after its successful conclusion. American isolationists looked at the great oceans on the left and right flanks of the continental United States as a tremendous buffer. This, to them, meant no involvement in conflicts in Europe and Asia and little involvement in international politics. After all, the first president of the United States, George Washington, had advocated such in his farewell address in 1796.

Woodrow Wilson's internationalist views, that America should export democracy and engage in collective security arrangements espoused by the League of Nations, fell flat—Article X of the League of Nations charter provided for all members to assist in the defense of other member nations. This was embodied in the Treaty of Versailles. The US Congress wouldn't ratify the treaty.

The United States did not join the League of Nations.

Most Americans had no problem with small wars; General Pershing's Cavalry troopers could pursue Pancho Villa's bandits and experiment with their newfangled military airplanes until they were bowlegged blind, but conflicts of global scale were out of the question.

Going back to Europe or intervening in some Asian nation's cultural, socioeconomic, or political problems wasn't going to get a politician elected or reelected. Or provide jobs for Americans or food on the tables of our hungry citizens.

Accordingly, the decades of the 1920s saw few military adventures with the exceptions of US Marine expeditionary activities in Haiti, and in Nicaragua and other Latin American countries. These incursions were principally geared toward protection of American lives, properties, business interests, and putting down rebellions that figured to upset the principles of the Monroe Doctrine. This was a specific policy that recognized American economic primacy, at least in the hemisphere. At first the major players in the isolationist camp were American peace societies, many of them part of larger international movements. Their goals were large-scale disarmament for all nations and an international treaty to abolish war.

Their efforts were rewarded—the Kellogg-Briand Pact, the signing of a major agreement among the great powers to, inter alia, reduce their numbers of battleships. Battleships in the 1920s and '30s were almost akin to nuclear weapons today—strictly bellicose, offensive weapons.

Six years later most of the world's nations signed the Kellogg-Briand Pact, in which the signatories pledged never again to go to war with one another.

Japan, the primary maritime military power in Asia, signed the Pact but the battleship ban irritated them considerably; theirs was a new, offensive Navy, and capital ships (battleships and cruisers) had limitations among the allied powers (the United States, Britain, France, Italy, and Japan).

Capital ships, especially oil-burning battleships, were the *principal* weapons of the day. To war fighters they represented capability; to war resisters, they represented intent.

Japan was proud of its navy, having defeating both China and Russia with it, much as Dewey had sent the Spanish fleet to the bottom of Manila Bay just a few years earlier. When the Japanese defeated the czar's fleet, they were clearly a ranking power in the Pacific. They proved this by seizing Manchuria, an industrial prize in 1931–32. They attempted to reassert their image by waging a short and bloody series of air land battles with the Soviets near the Mongolian border. This time, they lost, to General Georgy Zhukov, one of the last major commanders left out of Stalin's maniacal and bewildering purges of the 1930s. He must have been very confident to purge his military (and much of his civilian) leadership just a few fighting seasons prior to the German invasion in the summer of 1941.

China, on the other hand, had an impressive fleet in the Ming dynasty's fifteenth century because of Zheng He, the admiral who sailed exploratory voyages with huge vessels almost a century before Christopher Columbus and Vasco da Gama were born. It wasn't an offensive navy, but an exploratory one, and it also had a little commercial bent since it was known as the Treasure Fleet, but it created more expense than profit. Some believed Zheng He might have touched America's shores; whether true or not, he did visit many of the important ports in the Indian Ocean.

That maritime expertise had slipped away. While Japan was being modernized, militarized, and was flexing its Bushido muscles, it dreamed of empire during the Meiji Restoration of the mid-nineteenth century. China moved in the other direction—nervous at the extent of the barbarian's world over the horizon. The *gweilos* (westerners) had virtually annexed the southeast Chinese ports in the nineteenth century and drenched the poor peasants with opium, largely from British India. The Chinese retrenched and turned inward, quarreling and fighting among themselves.

Competing Chinese interests and factions waged internecine warfare and schemed intriguing plots while European and American commercial bullying ran unchecked during the same time frame. The 400 million Chinese saw this as another foreign invasion from the barbaric states of Europe and America.

The twentieth century was only slightly past its first decade when it marked the end of the last Chinese dynasty, the Qing (pronounced Ching), or Manchu dynasty, dating from the mid-seventeenth century. With the death of the final empress dowager, Cixi, in 1908, China began anew, blinking into a new and frightening world as a nation emerging into modernity in 1912 with the birth of the nationalist, or then, revolutionary, movement.

However, Americans who read of the treaties, mutual defense pacts, and other diplomatic events in the early to mid-1930s led many to believe that such agreements were insufficient.

After all, they did not deter Japan from occupying Manchuria in 1931, or four years later they did not stop the German government from authorizing a huge new arms buildup, or Italy from invading Ethiopia. The US Congress responded by passing the Neutrality Acts, a series of laws banning arms sales and loans to countries at war, in the hope that this would remove American desire for international "meddling."

The isolationists in Congress were a powerful political bloc in the 1930s, when a significant jobless populace pushed foreign policy and intervention to the bottom rung on the priority ladder in the Roosevelt White House and the post–World War I Congress. Major General Smedley D. Butler, USMC, helped them by publishing a pamphlet in the mid-1930s titled "War Is a Racket." This apparently reinforced his Quaker beliefs despite having served in World War I, China, the Philippines, and various other hotspots and being one of the few who received two Medals of Honor.

The leading "pacifists" of the 1930s were Republicans, cautious about foreign involvement while trying to keep America free from starvation during the worldwide recession. Roosevelt was a Democrat whose liberal leanings led him to believe a new world order and spread of democracy would be furthered by the dissolution of worldwide empires.

The spread of American democratic precepts, including the Christian religion and economics—and the combating of both Fascism and Communism—would be key foundations.

Fascism and Communism, and their principal nationalist proponents, Germany and Italy for Fascism and the Soviet Union for Communism, were finely tuned in the Spanish Civil War of the mid-1930s.

Nonisolationist Americans and Europeans were largely drawn to the side supporting the soon-to-be ousted leftist incumbent government of Spain, the Loyalists or Republicans. They were advised, supplied, and serviced—at least somewhat—by the Russians and Russia's internal but allegedly international organ, the Comintern.

Hence, the "International Brigade" was largely looked on as Communist, but these shortcomings were muted and romanticized somewhat by the aerial atrocities of the Fascists. The leveling of Republican-sympathizing Guernica, a city in the Basque region, by the Fascist bombers of Italy and Germany was typical. Picasso immortalized the bombing of Guernica by the Luftwaffe in a complex modernist painting. Ernest Hemingway wrote a best-selling novel, *For Whom the Bells Toll*, and moviegoers across the nation and the world watched Gary Cooper woo Ingrid Bergman in the film with the same title.

Spain simmered; the very nature of it confusing to most Americans, who knew only Communists and Fascists, as the term Nazi was not quite in vogue, yet. But they knew the Japanese were tough and somebody needed to keep an eye on them. Thus, the simmering fire burst into conflagration in China in 1937 with a probably contrived military event at the Marco Polo Bridge, near Peiping.[1]

Americans had largely internationally "retrenched," while Japan, Germany, Russia, and Italy had gone to war. Admittedly, Ethiopia and Spain weren't major international conflicts involving many nations, although residents of Addis Ababa or Guernica might argue the point.

The years 1937 and 1938 would see increasing volunteers from many nations fighting on the Fascist, Franco's side, or the Republican's, commonly labeled Communist or Socialist depending on the observer's political leanings, supporting the leftist government that Franco opposed.

China, now a lend-lease client along with Russia and England, could be—would have to be—almost totally supplied by air. There was a notable American airline partnered with a long-standing Chinese airline that would be, as they said in Confucian times—fortuitous. American William Langhorne Bond, a World War I veteran, shipped out to Shanghai in 1931 to join a Chinese-American-affiliated airline as vice president and operations manager. The China National Aviation Corporation and the US airline, Pan American, was a joint operation with a chinese majority share and fealty to the aviation ministry's guidelines and Chinese law. Bond hired experienced US pilots, many of them Chinese American, and later native Chinese-born pilots and crewmembers, especially radio operators. He also was blessed with an excellent maintenance operation—versatile and responsive. The maintenance group would stand them in good stead, as Japanese depredations prompted quick pack-up and departures from major cities from the spreading war in 1937.

Until Pearl Harbor. CNAC and Bond were displaced from Shanghai in 1937 when the war started between the Japanese and nationalist Chinese.

Lufthansa was a seasoned competitor, and the German airline had recently supported Germany in the Spanish Civil War and was eager to earn a profitable commercial niche in China. German bombers and fighters of the Luftwaffe supported the Fascists of General Franco, and the Fascists were fighting to take control of the government and country from the Republican forces largely supported by the Russians. The Republicans were a leftist party that gained control of the elections with the flirtation of socialism in Spain as the worldwide depression of the 1930s worsened. In addition, the multinational western volunteers of the international brigade and other western nations also supported the Republicans.

The war turned against the Republicans as Franco's Fascist allies applied stronger and more technologically sophisticated weaponry and airpower against the Republican air force and the Russians. The Russians were also using the conflict as a testing ground.

When the war concluded, leaving General Franco in power for decades, Germany's aviation had been thoroughly immersed in a learning experience for the blitzkrieg. Lufthansa had honed its pilots during the conflict, also sharpening it's "rough service" air field expertise and parachute operations supporting the Luftwaffe. Bond knew they'd be formidable competitors in China for passenger and freight trade.

Stilwell wanted to press the China National Aviation Corporation (CNAC) into military service, but senior Army Air Force leaders, knowing of the shortages of transport aircraft across the entire US military spectrum, recommended that CNAC be contracted for the entire airlift. Stilwell, uncomfortable with a Chinese majority ownership of the airline, balked, but CNAC went into the air logistics mix and performed admirably with its few planes.[2] They punched above their weight, as they say in boxing. Even with a small contingent of aircraft, they delivered a disproportionately high percentage of freight for their size and personnel.

CNAC's first mission was back-hauling aviation fuel for the Doolittle Raiders, this time with American Airlines and Pan American pilots from North Africa in CNAC uniforms. Unfortunately, most of the raiders' aircraft were scattered wrecks along the coast of southeastern China.

Despite all the shortcomings and the theoretical and real-world obstacles—bases that didn't exist; navigation facilities that weren't installed; the absence of reliable weather forecasting to include the all-important winds aloft that shortened or lengthened an aircraft's useful time in the air . . . and one million militant and experienced Japanese who had made an example out of the Chinese along the coast they suspected of aiding the Doolittle Raiders—the CNAC had razed whole villages, and the people in them.

Seemingly unimportant, the commander in chief of US forces and the commander and potentate of China had decided: aircraft and American pilots were the key to this challenge.

There would be a virtual air bridge from bases extant and yet to be built in Assam, at the time the only reasonably safe haven for allied airfields.

The Air Plans Division, the operational and logistics staff officers, would have to make it work.

CNAC would play a significant role under contract to the Army Air Force. They would fly 12 percent of the cargo that ultimately made it over the Hump to China, an extremely enviable record considering their size.

To understand the reasons for these machinations, it is important to realize that in the Army Air Force during this period, there were only two types of pilots—fighter pilots and bomber pilots. There were no airlift pilots dedicated to that type of long-range flying and sometimes austere un-instrumented air fields. Reasons for the military's uncertainty are understandable—*airlift* as thought of in contemporary terms wasn't in its infancy, it hadn't been born.

At the time only two relatively small units were charged with the "logistics" of flying.

The Fiftieth Air Wing was responsible for flying parts and major items of equipment from the four major supply depots in Pennsylvania, Ohio, Texas, and California.[3]

The other, the Ferry Command, had been formed in May 1941 to deliver aircraft to ports of debarkation for overseas flights to England. It was a product of President Roosevelt's lend-lease, and General Henry H. "Hap" Arnold tapped pilots from all the major commands to fly the aircraft to build experience.[4]

Decision-makers in the Air Force were preoccupied with training young men to fly fighters and bombers—the aerial weapons of decision—and with fewer than three hundred aircraft capable of flying cargo (most of them flown by the Fiftieth Wing), airlift had been addressed only in passing.

Fortunately, President Roosevelt signed an executive order in December 1941 that "softly" nationalized the airlines of the United States. This would affect the lives of pilots everywhere in the Pacific and Asia, but especially in the China Burma India theater, an almost nonentity against the bloody operations just conducted by the Allies in North Africa and Italy. As such it was a theater with a blank screen and largely empty of seats, especially of pilot seats.

That was changing. A young veteran B-17E pilot of the southwest Pacific with the patriotic name of Fulton Pershing Lanier and a fresh-faced young man from Texas, Frank Ramos, married and a newly father, would shortly meet three young men at their new base in Assam. Unfortunate circumstances would impose a bonding for these five young men for a long time, and through many conflicts of their beloved country.

In effect, it focused their main objectives on supporting the war effort by leaving the individual companies intact in personnel and equipment but operating for the War Department under contract.[5]

CHAPTER 6

Operators

Jorhat, Assam, India, January 31, 1944, well before dawn

"Corporal Petrella . . ."

Corporal Joseph Petrella turned to see who was speaking to him in the dingy mess hall of Jorhat Army Airfield this predawn last day of January 1944. A slender, fit young airman in flight coveralls approached him.

"I was told to look you up this morning. I'm going along as the assistant radio operator on your flight."

Joe balanced his mess tray and peered at the name on his flight coveralls, sure sign of a new guy: Giacalone, then answered: "*Quale parte dell' Italia?*"

The young man flashed a slight grin, "*Mia famiglia è cresciuto in Sicilia, ma iosononatonel New Jersey.*"

"Ah, I'm from around Belleplain and Dennis Township in Cape May County."

"I'm from around Woodbridge, Middlesex County," the dark-haired young man replied with a grin, shaking hands.

"I'm Joe."

"Bart, but everybody calls me Benny."

Joe nodded and received one back, "I heard there was another RO going but I haven't seen the manifest. Always good to have another pair of ears under headphones up there," Joe remarked, pointing with his tray to a table where another airman was sitting.

"He's one of our crew, I'd guess . . . no one else up at this hour."

"I was just going to get a cup of coffee; I heard the food was better in China," Benny replied as they slid into their seats with the other airman.

"It is, but you never know when you're going to have to walk in this business," Petrella rejoined, sliding in beside the other lone airman.

Joe and Benny exchanged nods with Private Eugene Beebe, who acknowledged he was the flight engineer (sometimes called crew chief or loadmaster) on their aircraft. Joe had seen him around the base but had not flown with him. He was older—nearly thirty, he guessed—quiet and reserved with a gentle demeanor. Joe and Beebe talked for a moment in an almost unintelligible garble of acronyms, numbers, and some unfamiliar slang.

"We're carryin' the usual avgas; nineteen drums, seventy-seven hundred gross; two Pratts on skid pallets, a ton, plus packing and rigging so we'll be right at max gross takeoff weight, probably a little over," Beebe said, describing their cargo of aviation fuel and aircraft engines.

Joe shook his head, "Twenty-five tons . . ." and the other two airmen rhymed in "of flyin' fun!"

Benny made the sign of the cross, and his tablemates nodded.

Benny also noticed something unusual—a wedding band on Beebe's left hand, and the weather-beaten face of a man of more years than the average private. He wondered if Beebe had been a sergeant at one time, reduced in rank for some reason.

"How much fuel did the pilots want?" Joe asked. He had pushed his plate away, his hand curled around a smoking cup of coffee while Benny ate and mentally translated the conversation.

"Sixty-eight hundred, 'little over 1,100 gallons' . . . big wind outta 270 today," Beebe replied, blowing a smoke ring from a Chesterfield as he raised his coffee cup.

Benny understood that much—aviation fuel was six pounds per gallon and from what he'd picked up in his short time at Jorhat, winds were nearly always westerly. A wind from 270 degrees, three-quarters of a clockwise circle, was coming out of the west, pushing toward 90 degrees, due east, where nearby Burma lay, and east of it, China.

A wind pushing an airplane—nearly directly behind it anyway—would add its velocity to the airspeed to become speed over the ground. The reverse was true returning westbound to India, however. The wind on the nose of the airplane would cut the ground speed by a like amount—it would take more time, and more importantly, more fuel. Benny understood that could be a significant problem.

He also understood, at least the principle, of dead reckoning, or DR, as it was commonly abbreviated. The groundspeed of an aircraft in flight was diminished or increased according to the angle the winds ran across the craft. Accordingly, a wind going in exactly the same direction as an aircraft "pushed," or added, the entire component of its velocity to the speed of the aircraft. Thus a 50-knot[1] wind coming out of 270 degrees (blowing from due west to due east), "pushing" an aircraft indicating 180 knots airspeed would, in effect, be maintaining a 230-knot ground speed as it pursued its easterly heading. The reverse was also true. Benny enjoyed the radio work, but he really liked working the dead reckoning problems. They were like puzzles with pieces—wind direction and speed, aircraft speed over the ground, distance to the destination, and significant landmarks en route.

Beebe snubbed out his cigarette and picked up his tray and cup to turn it in through the window to the Indian dishwashers, and the Italian American airmen did the same. As they finished up giving their trays and cups back to the white-turbaned dishwashing crew, two pilots entered the mess hall and headed for the big coffee pot.

"Those are our pilots, I'll bet; let's drag our feet a minute and let them get settled then we'll go over and let 'em know who we are," Joe said to Benny in a quiet voice.

The pilots had pulled off their leather flight jackets, both with the colorful "Blood Chit's" sewn on the back. These were rectangular squares of silk with the Nationalist and American flag sewn on the back. A message in Chinese and Burmese with a couple of other languages described the owners as Americans, and if the rescuers helped the Americans, hid them from the Japanese, and returned them safely to friendly forces, they'd be rewarded. The insignia was colorful and covered about half the back of the jacket. Benny was supposed to get a blood chit when he in-processed, but the supply clerk's stock was exhausted, and he told him to come back next week when they should have a new supply.

Joe and Benny approached the pilots' table; Joe threw a salute, which the pilots returned, Lanier threw a friendly two fingers to the forehead gesture, since they were seated.

"Sir, if you're flying 862, we'll be your R/O's today. This is Corporal Benny Giacalone, and this is his first trip over the Rock Pile.

Both pilots smiled in appreciation; these two men—pilots called them "operators"—were invaluable. The operators (they called themselves "communicators" or "radio operators") also served in the navigation of the aircraft by skillfully identifying "beacons" scattered along the route like guttering candles in a breeze. Sometimes, just about as effective.[2]

In clear weather and daylight, the radio operators, like the pilots, looked for prominent terrain features where an electronic fix identified itself and pointed the plane in the next direction.

"Dead reckoning," the aerial science of flying a certain direction (heading, in compass-read degrees) at a maintained airspeed, with wind figured in for converting it to ground speed, to either a visual terrain feature or an electronic fix, was the predominant navigation used.

Of course, mountainous terrain or stratospheric phenomena could always make this problematic.[3]

As the aircraft passed over the "fix," the needle of the radio compass would swing around pointing to the departing station and guiding the plane and crew out on a compass heading to the next "fix," either a visual one, or in the more frequent event of instrument conditions, another navigation aid.

Navigation aids were valuable but often fickle, bouncing off mountainsides or thunderheads, sometimes pushing the needle erratically and uselessly around. Both the low-powered (perhaps twenty miles in optimum weather and terrain) "homing" beacon that identified a particular airfield and the more powerful "direction finding" beacon (200-mile range) could be used to triangulate a location if multiple beacon signals could be received.[4]

They were hostages to weather and terrain, however.

Wise pilots still relied on time, distance, and winds aloft—winds sometime so severe that aircraft flew cocked into the wind to stay on course—as their primary navigational aid.

The Japanese had on occasion used false radio signals to lure pilots off course into the deadly terrain that surrounded the routes. In modern military parlance, this tactic, called "meaconing" in modern parlance, was infrequent, but still cause for concern among crews.[5]

Reading the Morse code identifiers of the stations through the squealing static was a vitally necessary skill for the radio operator; tuning the radios to optimum reception and pitch was necessary to interpret what you heard—misidentification of the station could be disastrous.

"Sir, could I have both of your full names for my logbook. I like to record a few words about the flight and remember my pilots' names."

Both pilots grinned again, and Lanier gave him his name slowly in his slight drawl. He drew out his middle name, *Pur—sheng* and added, "yep my momma and daddy named me after the general. And this is my second tour in Asia; I toodled [*sic*] around in a B-17E in Southwest Pac for General MacArthur last year. Uh, year before last, 1942, forgot we've jumped into 1944, then instructed on our own planes in Texas for a while before coming over here."

Ramos also gave them his name, then added that he'd occupied the right seat of a DC-3 for an airline for a few months as part of his training and was waiting on a picture of his new baby boy, just born back in Texas. Joe glanced over at Benny and observed he'd noted the information in his own pocket notebook. They thanked the pilots then headed out to see if the loadmaster needed any help.

The loadmaster and/or flight engineer, Private Eugene Beebe, a quiet Minnesotan, kept the plane as harmoniously balanced as possible with the overloads of cargo now pouring over the Hump.

He had studied weight and balance and understood well the complexity of keeping cargo rigidly strapped down. Since a large portion of their cargo was volatile fifty-five-gallon drums of aviation gasoline, this was vital to keep the aircraft from turning into a blazing roman candle. Frequently, extreme turbulence would tear the cargo loose and send it careening around inside, leaking fuel in the case of gasoline, doubling the danger with deadly fumes filling the entire aircraft. In the case of an engine loss or another aerial emergency it was often necessary to jettison cargo quickly to lighten the load, and Beebe would be the principal architect of this hazardous undertaking. The loadmaster would unbind and roll or push cargo to the open door of the aircraft, assisted by the entire crew minus one pilot to keep the crippled plane airborne.

This harrowing undertaking was nearly always conducted in aircraft bouncing almost uncontrollably, with the shrieking wind screaming through the yawning cargo door as the crew fought to keep their footing and not plunge out of the aircraft themselves. His responsibilities were monitoring the hydraulic, mechanical, and electrical functions of the aircraft in flight and insuring it was safe to fly.

Before the war, particularly in commercial flight operations, flight engineers were trained mainly in assisting the pilots in monitoring fuel flow, power settings, and the other myriad systems that kept the plane healthy and functioning. Many flight engineers had started their career as Airframe and Power Plant mechanics. Although now the loadmasters weren't experienced mechanics like the airframe and engine specialists that repaired the aircraft, frequently under the blistering sun of India, they understudied and assisted these mechanics until they could carry out rudimentary repairs themselves.

The savvy flight engineer was infrequently without a box of vital spare parts—generators, starters, spare tires, fuses, and his trusty, battered toolbox. Aircraft that had broken down on remote airstrips for lack of these essential components might be there for a long time.

The crews were self-contained capsules of expertise—pilots to get them all to their destinations and return, radio operators to monitor their locations and call for assistance in emergencies. Loadmasters kept the aircraft loads distributed evenly and led the efforts to shove it out of the aircraft in an emergency. They doubled as flight engineers monitoring flight systems and making rudimentary repairs. Notably missing on these relatively short flights, by airlift standards, were navigators. They were deemed necessary to guide the bombers of the mighty Eighth Air Force to their targets in Europe, another indicator of the China-Burma-India operation was a vital—but still secondary—theater.

As the heavy airplane porpoised slowly up, the pilot flew north parallel to the Brahmaputra River—*"Brahmaputrid"* to the US airmen of Jorhat. Petrella leaned over to point out landmarks. Giacalone leaned back toward him, pulling one earpiece of his headset away as Petrella shouted out over the engines. Joe pointed out the distant rise of the Paktai Range and farther south some rolling hills stretching away to the south not far from the India-Burma border. Joe drew a finger across his throat and Benny—wide-eyed—mouthed "Nagaland." Joe nodded back. Headhunters were reputedly the principal occupiers of Nagaland, and all crews had heard stories of airmen forced down there meeting grisly fates, whether true or not.

They finally cleared the Sanstung Range, adjusting their path in a diagonal series of high terrain ascents reaching nearly 15,000 feet. The aircraft skirted the mountains in the clear weather, maintaining 12,000 feet altitude to preclude donning oxygen masks.

On takeoff, one portion of the Automatic Direction Finding (ADF) system had been tuned to Jorhat, tracked their outbound heading. The other ADF was tuned to Fort Hertz in Burma, about midway along their route. The code was barely distinguishable in the static, and Joe told Benny to retune it and also try "Tommy King," the Kunming beacon on the other radio.

Giacalone proved to have a good technique and good "ear." He managed to refine the two-letter identifier to where it was at least clearly identifiable as the Fort Hertz Morse letters, although the compass needle jerked and the static boomed and faded, indicating weather or terrain conditions interfering. Petrella shook his head in annoyance, shouting out that Fort Hertz was a very "iffy" signal.

The first tentative bumps of turbulence occurred, skittering Joe's canteen cup of cold coffee across the navigator's table.

"Remember what the surface winds were when we left Jorhat?"

Benny glanced at his notes, "25 knots from 290 degrees," he responded.

"Right, now multiply that by four and you've got the approximate winds aloft," Joe replied.

Benny was impressed. "Wow," he thought, "add that to our indicated airspeed of 180 knots and we're going over three hundred miles an hour."

"We'll be in Kunming in time for breakfast again," he grinned and yelled back at Petrella.

Joe flashed a return grin, but his mood darkened as he thought, "if the Jap fighters out of southern Burma don't get us, or the icing, or the mountains, or . . ."

Barely two hours after wheels up at Jorhat, picturesque Mount Dali appeared on the horizon, rapidly rising out of the cloudy morning sky. The copilot was flying, and although not as smooth as the experienced pilot-in-command in the left seat, he was proficient and careful. Again, Joe was impressed. Ramos and Lanier had discussed the vagaries of the approaches and aerial traffic into Kunming and kept a running dialogue about them as they approached. The pilot reminded him of the turbulence around the landmark mountain that overshadowed the 6,000-plus-foot city.

"Yeah, I almost got flipped on a five-mile final last week," the copilot murmured.

"Yep, Dali can bite you," the pilot agreed.

The copilot pulled up the approach and landing checklist and started reading it off, with the pilot dutifully completing the check and repeating the item: "Cowl flaps one through four open, check." Occasionally, the checklist item was the copilot's responsibility, and he went through the same procedure, responding to the pilot's recitation: "flaps set at 30 degrees, check . . ."

Joe and Benny both marveled at the copilot's dexterity on the controls mixed with the beauty of the snow-capped mountain off the left wing. Benny noticed the powerful roar of the 1830 Pratt & Whitney engines—his first ride in a four-engine airplane compared to the two-engine C-47s he'd flown in previously. He also noticed something else—the humid, fetid smells of the Brahmaputra River valley were missing as they descended. The smell was totally different, redolent of coal and wood smoke and a crisper tang as fresh air replaced the rubbery smells of the oxygen masks at lower altitude: It was the smell of China.

The radio chatter was incessant as planes of every description approached and departed. Benny thought he was in the loudest blender he'd ever heard. Joe called over the intercom: "keep an eye out for traffic on your side and sing out if you think someone's going to be a problem."

The pilot glanced over his shoulder at them with a confirming grin and thumbs up. The copilot's eyes were glued to the end of the runway ahead, intent on making a smooth landing. From the left seat the pilot leaned over to lower the landing gear when the copilot called for it. The copilot had already called for final flap setting, and the pilot had dropped it to 30 degrees, lowering the stalling speed and the aircraft for a softer, shorter landing. He also pushed the four fuel mixture levers to full rich and turned on the fuel boost pumps, settings used for takeoff power should the need to go around and again arise occur.

"The pilot and copilot have switched jobs," Benny thought. The copilot now making the landing, and in effect the aircraft commander had talked the pilot through the prelanding checklist when they approached Kunming. The pilot had taken the subordinate copilot role, working the radios, talking to airmen in the tower controlling their approach. When directed he switched the frequency to "tower," talking to operators who reported traffic and surface wind conditions as well as the runway they were assigned.

"Good for the pilot," Joe verified for Benny, leaning in to shout in his ear. "The copilot has to take a check ride before he can move to the left seat as an aircraft commander himself. Some pilots never let the copilot do anything but move the gear up and down, and it's a long time before they move up. The pilot let his guy do quite a bit of flying on this leg, even through that patch of turbulence back over Burma."

The engine RPMs and manifold pressures were reduced to approach speed, yet Joe and Benny still couldn't converse without shouting due to the noise. Benny nodded, deciding he was going to like this job and the men who flew and crewed these big four engine beasts.

"Heavy 862 five mile final for active," the pilot called, fluidly in his role as copilot. The "Heavy" indicated a loaded aircraft, and the tower would be informing the cargo reception center by telephone that they had business in the cargo staging area. Lanier, in his role of copilot, reached over and reset the altimeters to 29.96 in the small windows in the middle of the altimeter dial, ensuring the pressure altimeters were breathing the same air pressure as the field. Joe and Benny noticed the altimeters were just now winding down through 7,000 feet with the threshold of the runway only a few miles in front of them. For Benny, this would be the highest altitude of any airport he had ever landed.

"Heavy 862, Kunming tower, check gear down and locked and clear to land on active; altimeter 29.96; wind 280 gusting 15–25 knots."

Benny and Joe closed their eyes for a moment and visualized a mental picture far above the now lumbering C-87, which was turned on the runway heading just a little bit west of due north with a pretty good quartering crosswind hitting somewhere near the front of the left wing root and flowing over the fuselage to a few feet behind the right wing root. Essentially blowing the aircraft left to right. Accordingly, Ramos had lined up on the left edge of the runway and dipped his left wing tip slightly into the incoming wind. This allowed the fairly stiff wind to work them to the right and lined up almost perfectly in the center of the runway, the lowered wing tip blocking the greater effects of the wind on the whole aircraft. It squeaked down on the first fifty feet of runway, and Ramos expertly kept the nose up and the nose wheel off the runway, slowing the big C-87 even more.

"If possible take first taxiway to the ramp, contact ground when clear of active. Good day, sir, and welcome to China."

"Authoritative, concise, and courteous," Benny thought. "Everybody's a professional in this business."

The aircraft slowed on the main gear and then the nose wheel touched down with a barely audible squeak. Benny looked over at Beebe, who grinned back and circled a thumb and forefinger. Flight engineer/crew chiefs liked "their" airplanes to be handled gently. The lumbering aircraft taxied clear and moved to a revetment with Chinese handlers waiting to unload the fuel barrels and engines from the plane. As the engines wound down, Joe led Benny through the shutdown procedures of the radios, and then they finally removed the headphones. The silence was a stark contrast to the cacophony of sound they had endured for the last few hours.

Lanier grunted, "good landing, Frank."

Eugene Beebe was a blur of motion—he had primary responsibility for supervising the off-loading, getting the aircraft refueled, taking care of any minor maintenance "squawks" that occurred during the flight, and generally preparing the plane for the return trip to India.

Joe asked if he and Benny could assist in the postflight procedures or watch the aircraft while Beebe got something to eat, but the quiet flight engineer waved them off.

"Got a box lunch before we left," he explained, but he asked Joe to bring him some cigarettes while passing him a handful of colorful Chinese paper money. Joe and Benny also asked the pilots if there was anything they could help the officers with, but they also required no assistance, suggesting they get a "good breakfast" and then take a quick tour of Kunming, particularly for Benny, a first-time visitor to China.

"You guys go get some *eggies*," the pilot said flashing another engaging grin. He knew that Petrella had experienced the wonder of fresh eggs many times in cool Kunming rather than the powdered "gloop" in the sea level hot and humid Brahmaputra River valley base of Jorhat.

"But be back at noon," he continued. "We'll probably be getting out of here around then if we don't have any cargo," he added.

The copilot looked from the cargo manifest they were off-loading and added, "You guys have fun. Don't bring back any, uh, communicable diseases." Joe and Benny thanked the pilots, assured them they'd be back well before noon, and saluted the two officers.

The two officers returned the salutes and watched them scurry across the flight line to the mess hall. "Pretty good kids," the pilot mused. The copilot agreed. "Yeah, the corporal knows those radios and the new private seems sharp, too. Even though he was introduced as a corporal." They both grinned.

The pilot looked at the towering cumulus clouds building on the far horizon to the west of them. "Yeah, and we might need both of 'em to pick out the Hertz and Jorhat beacons with that junk building up behind us."

At the time of Pearl Harbor, there were only trainers, fighters, and bombers—and a few transports, chiefly the C-47, the C signifying Cargo or the militarized version of Donald Douglas's DC-3 airliner. This "militarization" consisted mainly of reinforced fuselage floors and a wider cargo door and paratroop door. Similarly, there were two services—the Army and the Navy, with the Army Air Force subordinate to the entire ground-based force, just as the Marines were to the Navy. The Curtis C-46, the much larger, more powerful and comfortably flying aircraft could almost double the useful loads of the C-47; additionally, they had hydraulic controls, which cut down considerably on the need to manhandle the controls. They arrived in India without full flight testing, and many of them had to be further maintained before letting them begin work as aerial packhorses.

The Douglas C-54 was clearly designed as a future passenger/cargo aircraft in civilian livery, as was the DC-4. It also came out in late 1943, but without the powerful superchargers, which robbed it of altitude and necessitated it to the lower Hump routes.

The only aircraft not designed as a cargo hauler was the C-87, built on the airframe of the B-24 bomber, but again without the powerful and much heavier supercharged engines of the B-24. Also, since a bomber shed its heavy loads, the nosewheel and landing gears were not configured to efficiently handle the heavy cargo loads, so pilots had to watch that, keeping the fragile nosewheel off the tarmac as long as possible, keeping the bulk of the aircraft on the main landing gear.

Deep snow and wooden saddles . . .

Shangri-La would swallow two crews, and probably more, of young men in two months; one crew would make it back to their base in Jorhat—on foot and horseback—after an incredible many-month trek of survival and adventure. The second crew—from the same base and also flying a C-87—would not be so fortunate.

Some of the mystery shrouding Tibet lessened when the Jorhat crew returned to their base months after bailing out over Tibet the last day of November 1943. The crew survived the bailout, landing on a mountain at an altitude of 16,000 feet. Even more miraculous was the linkup of the entire crew and their rescue by Tibetan nomads, internment in Lhasa as detainees of the political struggle, and eventual release to make their way by foot and on horses back to India.

C-87 862's crew knew nothing of this; Lanier and Ramos, undoubtedly reading the safety and search and rescue bulletins, knew only that one of their C-87s at Jorhat had gone "off the scope" two months earlier. He, Frank Ramos, and thousands of other airmen like them were keeping over a million troops of the Imperial Japanese Army, Air Force, and Navy tied down in China and not fighting American forces in other parts of Asia. The China Burma India theater (CBI) was a necessary backwater compared to the fighting in Europe and the Pacific Islands. What was one crew in one theater compared to hundreds of men dying while working their way up Italian mountains, or perishing during the fighting with Rommel's men in North Africa?

Even prior to hostilities, President Roosevelt recognized the value of China's role at keeping the Japanese tied up without massive commitment of US forces. But for the past year the Hump had grown more dangerous, thanks to Colonel Tom Hardin's famous "no weather over the Hump" decree that certainly drove up tonnage delivered to China.

Hardin, who arrived in India in March 1943, was one of the legions of airline moguls who had gone from pin-striped suits to senior officer, one foot in mufti the other in an Army flight suit. He now commanded the India-China wing of the Hump. The Clark Gable look-alike knew his directives were chewing up airplanes and young men, but his mission was getting more and more tonnage to China. Before long he would wear the stars of a brigadier general and go to another hotspot that needed correction.

The additional numbers came with a cost of more pilots and crews. Now, if you could see the end of the runway you could fly, and fly day or night; Hardin had also declared "airplanes don't need sleep."

Tonnage went up, but men and aircraft went down. For most, night flying wasn't a problem. Often it was always instrument conditions—dark anyway, and the only thing the two pilots saw were their airspeed indicator, artificial horizons, rate of climb indicators, and altimeters, usually from the rubbery confines of an oxygen mask. But more airplanes were being lost and crews killed because of terrain, weather, and the unreliability of en route navigational aids.[6]

Hardin was constantly on the move in his personal stripped down, fast B-25 bomber; he'd drop in on a base with problems, round up the base commander, and demand better results. Sometimes he would simply drop off another base commander and tell the incumbent to pack his B4 bag and come with him.[7]

An on-the-spot relief of a commander who failed.

Hardin, described by Plating, was not being maniacal but was demanding positive results, under difficult conditions.[8] "Feared and hated by the incompetent and slack but also loved and respected by the competent and aggressive."[9] Most experienced military men would argue Hardin's directives and guidance were needed or the president of the United States' guidance wouldn't be carried out.

But even Hardin's boss, Colonel Cyrus R. Smith, stated the obvious: "these 'boys," he lamented, "were asked to do what would be most difficult for men to accomplish; with the experience level here we are going to pay dearly for the tonnage moved across the HUMP."[10]

Smith was an airline executive-cum-general officer (Hardin had taught Smith to fly after the Mexican Expedition of 1916).

Somewhere above him the weather and terrain gods harrumphed agreement; the subgod gremlins of airframes and engines chortled concurrence.

CHAPTER 7

The Last "Peaceful" Season

A Pilot's Odyssey

North Carolina was, and is, a football state; the Piedmont region of it is particularly notorious for loyalty to its college gridirons.

After two years in Buies Creek, Fulton Pershing Lanier transferred to Lenoir Rhine College in Hickory, North Carolina, for a final year and a half of football, academics, and "running around" with his buddy, D. K. Stewart, a football teammate. Fulton and D. K. were typical young men of the era—shaking off the drudgery of the Great Depression in a world already at war, albeit without America. They assumed that they—and America—would soon be joining young men in the khaki drill of His Majesty's forces fighting in Africa or over the skies of London and Coventry. Stalingrad, Dieppe, Singapore, and Guadalcanal lay over the horizon.

In the early summer of 1941 Lanier temporarily abandoned football, college, friends, and family and enlisted in the Army Air Corps as a flying cadet.

By June 1941 he stepped into a cockpit for the first time and began primary flight instruction in the open cockpit PT-17 "Kaydet" biplane, at Turner Army Airfield, Albany, Georgia. Primary flight training was the first introduction of the air corps cadet to aviation and aircraft, and it was taught by civilian flight instructors. Carefully recorded in Lanier's logbook are 61.55 hours of flight time over the next three months for the 220-horsepower PT-17. This was followed by basic flight training taught by military instructors: seventy-two hours in the BT-13, a larger, low-winged aircraft with the characteristic greenhouse closed cockpit, at Barksdale Army Airfield near Bossier City, Louisiana, from September to December 1941.

Just before he graduated, America's political and societal argument about intervention or continued isolationism became moot on December

7, 1941, when forces of the Emperor of Japan leveled a great portion of the Pacific fleet at Pearl Harbor. The young pilot's aerial training accelerated as an uneasy, somnolent America awakened with a start. It now realized, in the blazing backlight of destroyed cruisers and battleships, it was finally, irrevocably at war.

After a brief Christmas reunion with family and friends in North Carolina, Lieutenant Lanier learned to fly multiengine aircraft at MacDill Army Airfield, Florida, again refamiliarizing himself in the PT-17 before moving on to the twin engine B-23, B-18, AT-7, and AT-8 aircraft. Later in January, only a month after Pearl Harbor, and a new, grim year shaping up, he would be at Seattle/McCord Airbase, Washington.

He was checking out one of the most formidable American bombers of World War II—the long range, four-engine B-17E. His logbook shows a lengthy ferry flight in the aircraft he checked out in through Portland, Oregon, to El Paso, Texas, and on to San Antonio.

A few days later, he began the journey to war: from Florida to Belem, Brazil, a refueling, rest, and a maintenance stop. He and his crew flew on to Natal, Brazil, the closest point to Europe—through Africa—in the southern hemisphere.

Shortly before, Natal was just a sleepy jungle town on the Potengi River, emptying into the vast Atlantic, but in July 1941, it became an important waypoint for US aircraft delivered to British forces in Egypt and Africa.

President Roosevelt's lend-lease program had edged America closer to war. Additionally, the disposition of Japanese air and naval forces in the Pacific was unknown in the months following Pearl Harbor, so many aircraft and crews destined for parts of Asia beyond Hawaii also used this safer, if much longer, route.

Now Natal was a bustling metropolis, and Brazilian entrepreneurs had cashed in on the steady stream of aircraft loads of *norteamericanos* with *dinheiro de yankee* in their flight suits. Everything from Brazilian rum to mosquito boots—the soft leather slip-on footgear favored by flight crews—was available.

January brought the usual end of the rainy season in east central Brazil, and clearing weather made their climb out of Brazil over the vast south Atlantic less worrisome. There is no record of who flew in the right seat as copilot, or of the other crewmembers. It is doubtful any of them had flown over a significant body of water. The next leg took them to Freetown, Liberia, over 2,000 miles of the South Atlantic Ocean. In January 1942 pilots with only a few hundred hours and generally no time over water climbed out of Natal eastward to the coast of Africa.

As Natal's outward bound radio beacon weakened, pilots depended on the previously discussed dead reckoning—flying a known heading for a prescribed time with corrections made for winds aloft and waypoints along the route. This is bread-and-butter navigation for all pilots over land routes, with airfields and places to put down an aircraft in relative safety. But when aircrews looked around after a few hours and the only thing in vision was hundreds of miles of angry ocean—even the relatively placid South Atlantic—it became problematic and disquieting to say the least, particularly to novice aircrews.

They also depended on the previously mentioned navigators, young officers trained in all aspects of moving an aircraft from point to point using, among other techniques, celestial navigation, a science and art that goes back to the time of Phoenician mariners. They were uneasily aware that navigators had about the same level of training and experience as they had. For shorter range aircraft—"short legged"—in pilot parlance, Ascension Island was a flyspeck in the mid-Atlantic, with a British administered airfield. This was the only respite for aircrews in case of emergency. Long range navigation at the time, particularly over oceans or when battered by high crosswinds at altitude, relied on celestial navigation—not easy to become proficient in without hundreds of hours of carefully supervised practice. Merchant marine officers were schooled in it for years and would never aspire to a mate or captain's rating without mastering it.[1]

Young wartime aerial navigators may have received a couple of weeks of training, by instructors who weren't terribly proficient in the arcane science themselves. But these were minor considerations to America's finest young men going to war.

Otha Spencer, a military pilot from 1941 until 1946, eloquently describes one flight when a newly minted B-25 ("short legged") bomber crew took off for Ascension one night after hearing German submarines were sending false radio signals to lure American aircraft away from the Island.

Spencer recalls: "Our navigator's fixes were great but, soon, common sense and a fading radio signal indicated we were far off course. The sun was about to rise and I suggested that he take a reading and plot our position.

"The navigator admitted that he had forgotten how to do that. The clear Automatic Direction Finding (ADF) system indicated that Ascension was far to the south, so sub or no sub, Foster turned south and flew for thirty minutes and found Ascension. After getting the sextant checked, we took off for Accra, on the African coast. Again the sun lines were off. With a sharp right turn and a radio beam, we found Accra. Suddenly, the navigator gave a whoop, 'I've found the problem. It's really simple. You won't believe it. All the time I was using a July instead of a June almanac.'"[2]

His readings had been precise to the second, but in the wrong month.

Despite thousands of similar occurrences attributed to inexperience, youthful American hubris, and expedited, hasty efforts to train young men to fight the Axis, young airmen and aircraft poured into the arenas of war.

Lanier's logbook documents the crew's journey from Natal to Freetown, Liberia, and on to Accra, Ghana. Kano, Nigeria, was followed by Aden, then off the African subcontinent into South Asia and Southeast Asia: Aden to Karachi, to Colombo, Ceylon, finally landing at Jogjakarta, Dutch East Indies.[3]

The weeklong odyssey found the stateside crew now in the Nineteenth Bomb Group, Ninety-Third Bombing Squadron, flying B-17E's. Some of the B-17s had landed in Hawaii in the middle of the Japanese raid and eventually wound up in Java, island hopping from the beleaguered and soon-to-be conquered Philippines. In the Philippines, there was a long-heated debate about bombing Formosa, origin of many of the attacks, but the debate sputtered out and many aircraft were destroyed on the ground on December 8.[4]

Survivors scattered like quail flushed by dogs, working their way south to Australia.

Lieutenant Fulton P. Lanier couldn't have come to a better—or worse—place for quick immersion in aerial combat. By now, British, Australian, and Dutch forces, already drained of personnel and materiel by two years of war with Germany, were heavily committed in the Middle East, North Africa, and elsewhere. They were unable to provide much more than token resistance to the battle-hardened Japanese.

The battle of Malaya began on December 8, 1941, hours after the Pearl Harbor attack. Indian forces of the British Army would shortly face Japanese troops. The Allies suffered many disastrous defeats in the first months of the war. The Japanese marauded almost unopposed, and the speed of the Japanese advance eclipsed even the German blitzkrieg. Two major British warships, HMS *Repulse* and HMS *Prince of Wales*, were sunk off Malaya on December 10, 1941.

Thailand, with its territory already serving as a springboard for the Malayan campaign, surrendered within 24 hours of the Japanese landing.

The Kingdom of Thailand formally allied itself with Japan four days before Christmas 1941.

Hong Kong was attacked and fell on Christmas Day after two weeks of attack by the Imperial Japanese Army and Marines, with newly arrived Canadian forces and the Royal Hong Kong Volunteers fighting savagely as an important part of the defense. US bases on Guam and Wake Island were lost at around the same time.

Following the January 1, 1942, Declaration of Hostilities by the United Nations (the first official use of the term United Nations), the Allied governments appointed the British General Sir Archibald Wavell to the patchwork American-British-Dutch-Australian Command (ABDACOM), a supreme command for Allied forces in Southeast Asia. This gave Wavell nominal control of a huge force, albeit thinly spread over an area south of Burma and the Philippines to northern Australia.

Other areas, including India, Hawaii, and the rest of Australia remained under separate local commands. On January 15, 1942, Wavell moved to Bandung in Java to better control the forces of the four nations.

In January, Japan invaded Burma, the Dutch East Indies, New Guinea, the Solomon Islands, and captured Manila, Kuala Lumpur, and Rabaul. After being driven from Malaya, Allied forces retreated out of the Johore Straits and joined defenders in Singapore, the linchpin of Her Majesty's power in Southeast Asia.

They attempted to resist the Japanese during the Battle of Singapore but surrendered on February 15, 1941. Approximately 130,000 Indian, British, Australian, and Dutch personnel became prisoners of war. Apparently the defenders outnumbered the Japanese attackers by quite a margin. The British and Commonwealth troops expected the attack to come from the sea, especially after the *Repulse* and *Prince of Wales* were sunk. Instead, they came from the north, sweeping down through Malaya like a giant, deadly broom.

While this was ongoing, Japanese air, naval, and amphibious forces were rapidly spreading south and east in maritime Southeast Asia, through the southern reaches of the Philippines, the Sulu Sea to Borneo, and south to Java and the Dutch East Indies, today's Indonesia. Naval forces of the Japanese and allied Dutch, British, Commonwealth, and Americans hopped from sea to straits to oceans like nervous fleas jumping on a dog. Fulton Lanier and his crew supported the naval encounters; he and his crew could fly from and return to safe bases in the Northern Territories of Australia. The B-17s did much better on stationary targets like airfields, troop concentrations, and military facilities ashore than moving ships.

The three main islands of the Dutch East Indies arced from the northwest to the southeast like a saucer's rim under peninsular Thailand/ Malaya and Borneo—tipping up toward New Guinea. The Dutch East Indies also curved just north of westernmost Australia; a map of the region makes the threat to that vast stretch of the large continent starkly clear. Eight hundred miles north of this cauldron, American forces were battling fiercely in what remained of their Philippine bastion. The infusion of a token handful of American bombers considerably heartened their Dutch and Australian allies, but militarily it was a pail of water tossed on a raging forest fire.

PART TWO

Crucible

CHAPTER 8

Postwar Vietnam and the United States

Four decades after Fulton Lanier's plane disappeared, our nation grappled with an outcome not expected or welcomed. The unhappy end of the Vietnam conflict prompted policy makers to seek a solution to the missing men in Southeast Asia. But the mid-1970s were not conducive to military or political institutional growth. Fortunately, there were two units left out of the residue of Vietnam, one from the Military Assistance Command, Vietnam, which had hastened its own disestablishment. (One informed and curious observer likened its rapid disappearance to "burning the remaining blankets after giving away the smallpox infested ones.")[1] This was the Joint Casualty Resolution Center (JCRC), formerly the Joint Personnel Rescue Center (JPRC), now swollen to several Special Forces qualified teams with nothing to do. They had skimmed the intelligence jewels from the rapidly disappearing Military Assistance Command Vietnam, and, of course, its predecessor, the JPRC.

As if the alphabet soup wasn't enough, the "death and identification people," US Army Central Identification Laboratory, Thailand (CILTHAI) had washed up in Utapao, and later Samae San, Thailand, as an adjunct organization. At this time, the organization was made up of no more than a commander, a few grave registration soldiers, probably one or two clerks, and an office administrator with perhaps many other assigned and implicit duties, a few civilian morticians, and Thai contract workers. This Army organization had been the backbone of two major military mortuaries; one, run by the Army in Saigon and the other run by the Air Force in Da Nang. CIL's mission was to recover the bodies/remains of military members and return them to the respective mortuaries for identification and preparation for return to their families.

As a matter of fact, the JCRC was shedding its Special Forces officers and NCOs in the invariable Reduction in Force following the ultimate conclusion of the conflict in April 1975. They had shifted their focus onto searching crash sites, but with the bamboo curtain down over all Indochina, there was nothing for them to search. The only organization leaning far forward was the Defense Intelligence Agency. Their POW/MIA analysts were puzzled.

They had long maintained files and intelligence on two known stay behinds: McKinley Nolan in Cambodia, a known deserter and perhaps collaborator with communist forces, and Robert Garwood, a Marine whose circumstances of loss were difficult to understand along with his refusal to be released with the other prisoners of war. The entire Department of Defense appeared to have lost insight on the numbers of deserters that may have remained behind; the Marines claimed they had been engaged in firefights with a white and a black combatant, dressed like Viet Cong. Plus, hundreds of airmen and a number of MACVSOG strikers, US and indigenous, lost in Laos didn't turn up when the POWs were released; if things kept going this way, the DIA decided they were going to need more analytical manpower and more linguists and knowledgeable Indochina hands and surveillance/reconnaissance platforms. They were more than glad to be shaped and hardened in the crucible of analytical discovery, recovery, and identification, along with the JCRC and CILHAI.

In the summer of 1987 I finished command of a tank battalion in the Republic of Korea and was reassigned to the Joint Casualty Resolution Center (JCRC) in Barbers Point, Hawaii, as deputy commander. My pre-Korea agreement with the J3 and the US Army Personnel Command was that I would serve the first year of the three-year tour as deputy commander and then assume command of the JCRC when Lieutenant Colonel Joe Harvey went on to another assignment or retirement.

The most extraordinary event in my first few months in the JCRC was former Chairman of the Joint Staff General Vessey's appointment as presidential emissary and his visit to get us started. General Vessey brought along a very good friend, General Robert Kingston. US Army.

Long ago, he was Second Lieutenant Bob Kingston of Task Force Kingston, Thirty-Second Infantry Regiment, when the Chinese entered the Korean conflict in November 1950. General Kingston had also been the first commander of the JCRC in 1973 in Thailand. Now, in retirement, they had rejoined the final outcome of the Vietnam War for Americans—to get them all home, or at least to find out what happened to them. Account for them.

There was also one of the infrequent repatriation of remains in Hanoi, the Vietnamese had "unilaterally discovered." For me, it was enlightening—I accompanied Paul Mather, and observed and liked his unassuming, quiet and experienced handling of the repatriation. He had been involved in the issue well before the war's end and had been one of the last to evacuate Saigon during the collapse of April 1975. At the end of a week's tutorial with him in Bangkok and Hanoi I understood the complexities and history a little better, I thought.

I also better understood the requirements of handling administrative requirements such as visas from the Socialist Republic of Vietnam (SRV) embassy, just up the street on Wireless Road, billeting for JCRC and Central Identification Laboratory, Hawaii (CILHI) recovery teams and delegations and the Air Force crews usually from C-141s.[2]

These aircraft and crews were tasked with the repatriation of remains recovered from Hanoi or unilaterally (usually "found by a Vietnamese citizen" with an unusual "humanitarian" spirit). All this was done by the Bangkok office with a skeleton crew of personnel already working hard on refugee reports and interacting daily with Headquarters and DIA's Special Office, as well as their daily contact with American Embassy (AMEMB) Bangkok. Paul Mather also handled the démarches passed unofficially to the Vietnamese concerning the warehousing of remains by the Vietnamese, exacerbating China's fears of being surrounded on both their north and south flanks. The Vietnamese felt the isolation and geared up for a third expanded round of fighting, including with a power much larger than they were.

In the late 1970s the number of Vietnamese also swelled with the inclusion of Vietnamese of Chinese descent. The Sino-Vietnamese, some citizens of Vietnam for several generations, were "urged" to move on by the Vietnamese in a burst of nationalist xenophobia and irritation by China's less than tacit assistance to the Khmer Rouge, now viewed by Vietnam as a hostile force. By then, facing a two-front war with both Cambodia and her patron, China, the SRV signed a pact with the Soviet Union.

During this period a strange phenomenon occurred. A Vietnamese of Chinese descent slipped, or was eased out of, Vietnam with a strange tale; he maintained that he'd been a mortician in Hanoi. This was an open secret—a "mortician" of Chinese descent, allowed to immigrate to the west, testifying before a congressional committee on the process of storing remains in Hanoi. He claimed there was a "warehouse" of stored US remains there with as many as four hundred, he observed. After vetting by the highest US intelligence personnel and equipment, including a polygraph, he became a source with insight into the workings of the issue of remains from a Vietnamese perspective.

Speculation was rife on the motive; was the bureaucracy so backward that they'd let a "big fish" slip through the net?[3] Was this another Kafkaesque twist the Vietnamese were putting on the issue? Everyone had an opinion, and it became a primary intelligence and negotiation topic, but it did little to move the issue forward except anger American citizens and decision makers.

CILHI anthropologists had already discovered preservative effects on unilateral turnovers of remains, and this became a topic broached in negotiations. The US position was the unequivocal turnover of all remains in their hands with details on their acquisition, but the two nations were not that far along with a mechanism for the kind of joint sleuthing that would be required. Basically, it heightened the tension between the US side and the Vietnamese side; few Americans would doubt that it wouldn't. Still, it was considered a significant underpinning to the vital cases that were the JCRC and DIA's highest priority—those cases of Americans known to have been alive in their hands, but who were not released from captivity in 1973 or who had their remains turned over.

Despite high hopes, the subject of "stored" remains wound up having very little effect on resolving cases, but it became a contentious point mentioned in the CILHI briefings during the late 1980s and was viewed as a point to keep the issue alive and stirring. These, plus the "Last Known Alive" cases, would be preeminent when General Vessey took the helm.

The Bangkok detachment was a busy office with requirements that were rarely forecast; occasionally, when the budget allowed, JCRC headquarters would send one of the linguist-analysts over to Bangkok on a short, temporary duty assignment to help out. Joe Harvey and Paul Mather, close friends for a number of years, talked on a daily basis, so Headquarters was up to speed on the various matters and rumors going on around Bangkok. Joe was a Thai Foreign Area Officer, and his language was almost native, save for the soft Texas accent. He loved Thailand with almost the same affection he felt for the beautiful Texas Hill Country.

Unlike Laos, which never lost or broke diplomatic relations with the United States (they downgraded the ambassador to a consul general after the ascendancy of the Pathet Lao in 1975), the Vietnamese had no presence, diplomatic or otherwise, in the United States, except as a UN member (admitted during the Carter administration), with a diplomat in residence at Vietnam's UN office in New York City. Thailand was an important US ally, just as they'd been overtly in Vietnam, covertly in Laos, and sometimes in Cambodia.

Paul Mather was virtually the only American who could walk the few hundred yards up to the Socialist Republic of Vietnam's embassy and get a message to their ambassador, and thus to the SRV leadership.

As I settled in to the JCRC the summer of 1987 I found the two dozen or so men and women from across the spectrum of services professional, dedicated, and very good at what they did. Most were intelligence analysts with long experience in the region and Vietnam. It was definitely "Joint"—a multiservice, or "purple"—organization, representing the traditional service colors blended together. The good analysts working for Colonel Joe Schlatter, a range of military intelligence officers who also wore Ranger tabs, seemed to be weary to the point of collapse, but when they focused on the areas I was interested in, they sharpened up and gave articulate and reasoned answers and explanations. It was easy to see why there was so much angst between the US government and its citizenry. The situations were very confusing.

If the JCRC was the repository of the history of the missing and the nexus of where to search, CILHI was a significant portion of the operational mechanism that recovered and identified missing servicemen. Slightly smaller than the joint service JCRC, it was an Army organization with direct ties to the Adjutant General of the Army, also commanded by a quartermaster lieutenant colonel with an unusually long tenure of command.

In the summer of 1987 the staff was a mixture of Army graves registration personnel, a few archaeologists, and one Japanese American physical anthropologist with long experience in forensic identification. Barely twenty personnel, total. Their office and laboratory was in the rundown section of the Honolulu docks. I remember stepping around coiled ropes, spring lines looped over stanchion, and the occasional remains of an unfortunate fish the first time I visited.

CILHI was also the conduit of funds from the US Army's Care and Disposition of Remains account, the source that paid for the recoveries and many of the attendant expenses, including the meetings in Hanoi, Vientiane, and Washington. The CILHI of 1987 was the offspring of other Central Identification Laboratories established during the era of World War II.

These laboratories, usually in specific theaters of war, helped identify the hundreds of remains that arose out of the graves registration efforts during and after the conflict. Small teams of grave registration personnel scoured battlefields and crash sites in all theaters where US forces fought, died, and were unrecovered. If these searches were unsuccessful, the administrative and legal processes of declaring the missing deceased but unrecoverable moved forward, directed by Title 10, the US Code. This was the law and essentially the primer on military-civil responsibilities and the Missing Persons Act that laid out the path for the administrative handling of the dead—or the accounting for the missing and the determination of death.

Like the JCRC and almost everything associated with Vietnam, CILHI suffered heartless neglect, not only from its parents, the US Army, but also from the Department of Defense and the US government. It languished almost forgotten on the Honolulu docks, underfunded, underutilized, and undermanned. When the inevitable backlash associated with perceived misidentifications occurred, it became one of John F. Kennedy's "trumpeted failures" of unsung government. That was still nearly a decade in the future after the war's end in 1975. But it was coming.

So the topic stalled from the time of the communist victory in April 1975 through the Carter administration and into the mid-1980s. The United States and Vietnam continued to talk past each other and spar warily, the Vietnamese hoping for diplomatic recognition but stifled by their own bureaucracy, competing ministries, and other political impediments but mostly by a lack of progress on the problem of missing American servicemen.

In the early years of the Carter administration, with increasing criticism of the US government's lack of activity in the question, a policy statement was formulated that said:

> Although we have thus far been unable to prove that Americans are still detained against their will, the information available to us precludes ruling out that possibility. Actions to investigate live sighting reports receive and will continue to receive necessary priority and resources base on the assumption that some Americans at least are still held captive. Should any report prove true, we will take appropriate action to ensure the return of those involved.

Thus the US government at the time delivered a nebulous, puzzling statement, unwittingly confusing the citizens of the United States. Did, or did not, the government have evidence of Americans still being held in captivity?

There were constant streams of refugee and citizen reports that came in with the same misspelled dog tag names. They told the same stories; the same search for rewards, in part due to the 1.5 million US dollars raised and publicized by believing congressmen and citizens, and the same scams frequently pulled on the displaced in refugee camps or in country. Animal and ancestral bones were sold and brought in as American servicemen.

Refugees reported alleged sightings of whites held, raising the sensitivity of the matter considerably, particularly those citizens who fervently believed—or wanted to believe—that Americans were still held in Indochina. A series of films with Sylvester Stallone and Chuck Norris portrayed as Vietnam War veterans returning to rescue American POWs further inflamed the public.

People wanted to know why the military wasn't doing the same thing, unaware that a dedicated unit with far harder people than Rambo had launched over one hundred searches while the war was ongoing. All were unsuccessful at rescuing even a single US POW, except one POW who died from wounds his VC captors inflicted on him during the raid. Several hundred Army of the Republic of Vietnam (ARVN) POWs were rescued, including some Vietnamese civilians. This fact, once it was pointed out in the Senate Select Committee hearings of 1991–92, would, like the US POW situation in Laos, be one of the two greatest wartime mysteries.

Our JCRC parent and historical antecedent, the Joint Personnel Recovery Center, (JPRC), was an operation within the highly classified and supposedly secret and tongue-in-cheek Military Assistance Command, Vietnam Studies and Observation Group (MACVSOG). It was established in late January 1964, when President Johnson acknowledged that clandestine and covert operations should be used against Hanoi's forces.[4] Sometime thereafter, with more POWs in enemy hands, the small staff section known as the JPRC slipped into the classified ether as OP 80, or Recovery Studies. Colonel Heine Aderholt, a noted Air Force expert on air crew survival and rescue plus air commando experience, would be the leader, but the mission entailed more than the innocuous job title suggested, or the little staff section that consisted of a dozen or so soldiers. Much more.

In the pre-1973 JCRC days when the Indochina war was raging, there were mostly Army Special Forces teams doing the reconnaissance and "Direct Action" missions—ambushes, raids, calling in air and artillery strikes—but there were also Navy SEALS, a scattering of Marine Force Reconnaissance Personnel collecting intelligence for their forces, and

USAF Commandoes also assigned, particularly in the air and maritime branches. Other operations included OP 34-A, activities in North Vietnam; OP 35 and 36, ground activities; Psychological Operations and 'dirty tricks,' like booby-trapped ammunition; and various other clandestine operational activities highlighted by cross-border "Over the Fence" operations in Laos and Cambodia.

These were long-range reconnaissance patrols ordered to find concentrations of NVA personnel and equipment then to call in air strikes on them, to locate wiretaps, prisoner snatches, and sometimes other direct action missions—such as going in to capture Soviet or Chinese equipment, and the prize jewel, to rescue American prisoners of war—under the overall bailiwick of OP 80, the JPRC, the JCRC's antecedent. During the six years of its existence, JPRC was totally unsuccessful in releasing US prisoners of war—save for one, who died a few days later due to a prison-inflicted blow to the head with a heavy blunt instrument. Their efforts did release a number of Army of the Republic of Vietnam prisoners and civilians.

When General Hunter Harris, commander of the Pacific Air Forces (PACAF), talked to Aderholt, longtime air commando and Survival, Evasion, Resistance, and Escape (SERE) subject matter expert, he talked of post-SAR (search and rescue) efforts and offered him the job as first commander. Aderholt took it on with these insights—at some point, SAR is going to be an active, massive aerial search with ground insertion if required. When everything possible has been done with no recovery it eventually morphs into a passive phase, monitoring emergency rescue channels when operating in the area, then finally, termination of efforts. This also included ground and sea losses, pilots and crew known to be KIA in the incident but couldn't be recovered at the time of loss, or in subsequent recovery operations.

Aderholt's JPRC mission was to be the focal point for the recovery of prisoners, the central office for POW/MIA intelligence, for incentives such as "rewards in kind" for information, or even ransom payments. The JPRC would coordinate the "post-SAR" missions, that is, after the active search and rescue efforts were unsuccessful, the JPRC would take over. Aderholt wanted his own forces—notably, a contingent of Army rangers who would train and stand by for a prisoner rescue.

The Army turned him down. This was classic "tell us what the mission is, but don't tell us how to do it or who to use."

The JPRC punched above its weight in terms of clout, but it was still a small, usually a dozen persons or so, staff section of a secret organization. Plus, it had an overt and clamoring side in their psychological operations (psyops) program that publicized their role in getting POWs or detainees (or remains) back, and it also had a highly secretive one in its OP 80 role of enemy prison camp raids. This kind of overt and covert mission did not lend itself well to the same organization. "I'm a Top Secret organization and here's our address and phone number," in effect.

Additionally, the military bureaucracies and normal "rice bowls" were lined up for their share of the action, requiring the permission of the American Province Senior Advisor (who probably had an inevitable leak to the Vietnamese Province Chief). Dependence on the largess of the Air Force (Aderholt, a longtime Air Commando, was a propeller guy—he flew C-47s, T-28s, A1Es, B-26s—all the slow but loitering, capable aircraft. They could stay overhead for hours; the F-4s and F-100 jets sometimes only a flash with a "bingo" (short on fuel and ordnance so use us immediately) status and were soon gone. In this case, his intuitions were correct.

He had asked for the low and slow A-1s, which could loiter over the troops for a morning or afternoon, choosing the ground commander's choice of ordnance with a flick of his gloved finger—napalm, strafe with machine guns, cluster bombs—a connoisseur's choice of ordnance to change the odds on the ground. In the six months from their organization in April, there was a constant quibble over who the ground forces would be. Aderholt's force of Army Rangers for the ground component was continually stymied by the Army planners in the Pentagon. Similarly, the jet-enamored US Air Force gave Aderholt the same answer for his request for A-1s: "we'll determine the aircraft." This was to be a tragic mistake. The propeller colonel was up against the jet-fixated generals. The "fast mover" gunfighters. MIG killers.

Ranger-qualified soldiers and officers were a small elite force and usually wound up in unit reconnaissance platoons, like junior MACVSOG recon runners. They brought back valuable intelligence. *Perishable* intelligence that an aggressive battalion commander could jump on with an air mobile raid or multicompany sweep. Perishable, rapidly acquired and just as rapidly disintegrating intelligence needed to be acted on immediately. Ideally by the unit that acquired it. This was the key to success in something so valuable to the VC, NVA, and Pathet Lao: US prisoners of war. The JPRC mission was important, but so were operational units fighting the VC and NVA. Rangers were a rare, scarce asset. Rangers wouldn't be dedicated to single missions until successive decades later—a Ranger force standing at the doorway to back up other Special Operators as they conducted their operational mayhem in South Asia or the Levant.

Even this early in the game, the JPRC would use their own, and later, self-strangling, would use available US, or South Vietnamese, or even both, in what would be known as combined operations. Initially, this required the seventy-two-hour SAR period to be concluded or turned into a passive search before the JPRC became responsible for subsequent actions—rescue from a camp, or better, rescue en route to a camp. These involved multiple clearances starting at the top and generating their own request to US Pacific Command (USCINCPAC), the theater command. If the US Army and Marines worked together it was joint. If it included allied forces, it was joint-combined. Each additional participant increased the planning and logistics factors considerably. If a unit could obtain the intelligence and act on it immediately, that was as good as it gets. Rapid collection and analysis, sometimes no higher than the field level, was important. Today it is called operational intelligence, capable of going from acquisition and rapid analysis to direct action. Anything less, with VC, NVA, and Pathet Lao captors who put so much importance on US POWs, would have little chance of success. Even a whiff of danger and they would be whisked away.

Captain Frank Jaks realized this as he finally got to his stage field in the Mekong Delta on October 18, 1966, ten days after Colonel Heine Aderholt, the JPRC commander, overflew the target area in a light plane. Aderholt flew the aircraft himself while a sergeant took photographs with a handheld camera in back. Operation Crimson Tide was about to become a much-belated—thus more dangerous—reality. The high-speed reconnaissance photos were unable to depict the camp that a young VC rallier named Teo had described with information about American prisoners held in the facility. But the disaffected VC could readily identify the camps from the low and slow oblique black and whites Aderholt and his photographer obtained. In addition, Teo was polygraphed and the results were: no deception noted. All this took time. Valuable, critical time.

Jaks, a Czech national who had escaped the communists, to become an American citizen was now a company commander out of Forward Operating Base 2, MACVSOG, in Kontum, company commander of a tough bunch of Americans and Nung strikers. They were of Chinese descent, recruited out of the *tongs* of Cholon, and they hated the Communists. They weren't too friendly to the non-Communist Vietnamese as a matter of fact. They were hard-edge mercenaries, and they and Jaks respected one another. But they were operating in the tangled highlands of the border and inside the short arc of Laos proclaimed by Ambassador Sullivan in Vientiane. This delta was flat and flooded, unusual terrain for the Nungs and Americans.

Any unplanned tactical successes in Vietnam generally were the result of actionable intelligence being acted on quickly. Depending on the "kindness of strangers" for its troops—American conventional units—naturally tied them to a lengthy recitation of the mission to US decision-makers along with their Vietnamese counterparts. They even needed permission from the province senior advisor whose Corps Area the operation was occurring in. Many hands wanted to help—aerial photos to moving in artillery to support operations. Appreciated, but this was a case of plan on the fly and execute violently and, most important, quickly. But the shortcomings were ingredients to this first mission, a near disaster.

When the ceiling lifted sufficiently to fly, Crimson Tide lurched forward and quickly turned into a near disaster when two helicopter loads of men were split up and separated. They survived the night in a tight defensive perimeter trading hand grenades and tracer rounds under the flares of "candlestick" c-123s and forward air controllers.

Jaks's forces were evacuated the next morning. No prisoners were rescued. Two Americans were KIA as well as almost one platoon of indigenous Nungs. The long delay and faulty intelligence landed them right on a VC main force battalion.[5]

Citizens and refugees sought them out for rewards rumored to vary from "going to America" to modest monetary amounts ($50–$100) depending on the veracity and timeliness of the information. Still, informants sometimes led rescuers into camps, resulting in ARVN prisoners liberated. But during the seven years of its existence, before being folded into the Military Advisory Command–Vietnam (MACV) J-2 as analysts with a lot POW knowledge, their results were not that spectacular.

Their responsibilities were liberating POWs—Americans, Vietnamese, and civilian third country nationals, missing in action, missionaries, contractors and aid workers, kidnapped and detained.

Their overt side entailed bringing back the remains of the dead. Many of these raids resulted from their area of operations in Laos, where US and North Vietnamese presence was prohibited by the Geneva Convention. Teams crossed the border into Laos by foot, helicopter, or, later in the war, by "stand-off" parachute operations—high altitude low opening HALO insertions, used later in the war, were the stealthiest but also were rife with danger, particularly in problematic weather or falling into jungle or mountainous terrain.

Laos, called "Prairie Fire" through much of the war, would also become the code word for teams in danger of becoming completely overrun. Whispering these words into an FM radio in a hasty defensive position in a bomb crater resulted in air coming in from all directions. On the ground, back-up teams lay on their rucksacks at airfields by helicopters, ready to bail out their brother strikers.

The strikers' "Bright Light" missions wound up with heavier forces going in to pick up their KIAs, those that couldn't be recovered when the teams had to fight their way aboard the helicopters retrieving them from being overrun, captured, or killed.

Operations in Cambodia were similarly called "Daniel Boone" initially, then "Salem House" when SOG and conventional units' recon teams began operating more frequently and the name became compromised by the press. The May 1970 limited incursion into Cambodia became a politically contentious issue, almost rivaling the Tet Offensive. Bright Light was the original code name for a POW recovery, but to the SOG'ers and their indigenous soldiers, a Bright Light mission was mostly the recovery of known comrades KIA whose recovery at the time would have probably doomed the survivors.

The JPRC's job was to also alert the populace, friendly, contested, and enemy alike, about Americans who might be in captivity in their area; villagers were also notified about a grave or crash site with American dead; had they heard or knew about them? Firsthand information was the goal, although many village people had heard second- or third-hand gossip concerning American POWs or remains of Americans.

The subject of missing Americans was a prime gossip topic for native and tribal peoples, and particularly refugees. It was difficult to have an overt and covert side to their mission. The double-edged blade of rewards migrated into rumors of entry into the United States and large monetary awards. There was heightened traffic in animal and ancestral bones.

The JPRC's awareness and information program was done with posters, leaflet drops (aerial and artillery delivered), loudspeaker broadcasts, and debriefing US and Army of the Republic of Vietnam (ARVN) field troops after operations. They were also the clearinghouse of all POW/MIA intelligence gathered in country. When this indicated prisoners at a specified location, US, ARVN, or combined operations were launched to rescue them. Their analytical side was much more effective than their operational results—over 120 POW liberation missions resulted only in ARVN soldiers and civilians. The single American soldier liberated died of wounds inflicted by his Viet Cong captors during the raid.

They were also authorized, or took it on themselves, to pay rewards—or ransom, but didn't call it that—for prisoners. A JPRC officer had a tense meeting with three rough and armed Cambodians, allegedly with firsthand knowledge of U. S. POWs, in a seedy Phnom Penh hotel. The officer had a canvas pouch with $10,000 in it and discretion to pay part or all of it if the information was authentic. It was not, and things almost got out of hand until the officer flashed a Browning Hi-Power 9 mm pistol and backed out of the room with the satchel over his shoulder.[6]

The intelligence was sometimes quite accurate, but outdated. Special Forces Captain Nick Rowe escaped by killing his guard and waving down a helicopter supporting a Bright Light POW rescue mission based on intelligence depicting Americans in a specified location in the Mekong Delta of South Vietnam, but they'd been moved. The search for the camp with the Americans had been terminated, and the door gunner almost shot him before they identified him as an American. He would go down in Vietnam lore as the only American who was successfully liberated by the JPRC. But in reality James Nicholas Rowe, US Military Academy class of 1960 would be one of thirty-five known US escapees from captivity in Vietnam. Only two would escape from the Pathet Lao or North Vietnamese in Laos. Nick Rowe would be assassinated by the New Peoples' Army in Manila in 1989.

As American ground forces left in the bow wave of Nixon's "Vietnamization" of the conflict, MACVSOG was drawn down and the JPRC became a MACV J-2 (intelligence) section. As part of this, as early as 1971 USCINCPAC recognized the potential in the vast air crash-site losses sprinkled over the remoter sections of Vietnam, Laos, and Cambodia. Some of them were resolved, but many of them still had associated losses. Accordingly, CINCPAC put together a contingency plan, 5100, that would shape one of the primary missions of its follow-on organization, the Joint Casualty Resolution Center (JCRC). Out of over two hundred crash sites, only eleven had been inspected by the summer of 1971. With the continuing drawdown of forces, soon ARVN troops would be picking up recon missions over the various "fences" and crash sites, such as the Blassie crash site search.

Without knowing it, or of its future existence, the JPRC, with its crash site program, had just instituted the basic architecture of its successor organization—the Joint Casualty Recovery Center (JCRC).

With the signing of the Paris Peace Accords in late January 1973, a cease-fire was established and quickly broken. American troops left the battlefield and returned to a largely unwelcoming reception from everyone except their families and loved ones. On January 23, 1973, the JPRC was disestablished and the JCRC replaced it, but it was moved to Nakhon Phnom, Thailand, to reduce the presence of uniformed Americans in country. The first commander was Brigadier General Robert Kingston, he of Task Force Kingston renown and later as General Vessey's companion in nine high-level negotiations in Hanoi. The JCRC became the operational arm of the US part of the Four Party Joint Military Team (FPJMT).

The low personnel ceiling imposed in Vietnam included only authorized Department of Defense personnel, largely in support roles for the American embassy, and the FPJMT, consisting of the United States, RVN, and its antagonists from the Democratic Republic of Vietnam (DRV) and the Provisional Revolution Government (PRG) or Viet Cong. The FPJPT was the operational organization arising out of an earlier sixty-day authorized Four Party Joint Military Team commission that set the groundwork for a further end of hostilities. During this period US POWs were released in Hanoi and the Republic of Vietnam, with a disappointing nine POWs from Laos also released in Laos. This was a major shortcoming and source of frank disbelief on the part of the American side.

The JCRC, unlike the tiny JPRC staff, had two hundred authorized personnel billets and envisioned a sweeping postconflict casualty resolution process, with many search and recovery teams recruited from the Special Forces.

They merely changed hats—from green berets to floppy jungle hats and bright orange pockets and bands on their arms. Their helicopters, all RVN flown, had orange bands around the fuselage. The live prisoner issue was envisioned as a diplomatic process, although the JCRC had ample analytical and intelligence personnel to hopefully keep the process to glean information and intelligence and simultaneously adhere to its humanitarian mission of resolving the fates of the missing.

The greatest inheritance the JCRC realized from its predecessor organization was the detailed case folders the JPRC produced. The 1,700 plus files on the 2,300 plus unaccounted for included photographs of the individual (included in the so-called capture book used for witnesses and sources to view), circumstances and locations of loss, along with the date and subsequent information that included intelligence and source reports. In later years, this information was updated with refugee reports and intelligence from the many camps located across Southeast Asia and the Pacific.

These would be used as source or negotiation folders in subsequent meetings with Vietnamese, Lao, and, after 1991, Cambodian delegations. The entire trove was taken back to Nakon Phanom, and the JCRC struck an accord with the US Army Central Identification Laboratory, Thailand (USACILHI), which set to work proposing cases for recovery and identification.

CHAPTER 9

A Bloody Shirt

In December 1973, an unarmed US and South Vietnamese investigation team was ambushed south of Saigon by a Viet Cong force, killing Special Forces captain Richard Rees and an ARVN helicopter crewman and wounding another American graves registration specialist. Other helicopters were shot up. Rees was killed when he stood up and shouted they were unarmed. The next day, the outraged commander of the FPJMT, the Four Party Joint Military Team, Colonel William Tombaugh, threw Captain Rees's bloody shirt on the desk of the PRG delegate, who, shaken, offered only his own recriminations.

A Vietnamese helicopter was destroyed and the South Vietnamese contingent suffered wounded personnel.

Communist forces were clearly making search and recovery operations too dangerous for unarmed teams, and the JCRC turned over in-country searches to South Vietnamese forces. They did manage to locate and recover some remains, despite difficulties.

After Saigon fell in April 1975, and with the region-wise politically astute Thais hurriedly closing bases where the US operated from, the entire JCRC, Joint Casualty Resolution Center, a successor to the Joint Personnel Rescue Center, and the predecessor of the Central Identification Laboratory, Hawaii, CILTHAI, were relocated to Hawaii. The JCRC moved to the naval air station at Barbers Point, and CILTHAI, now CILHI, to their facility on the docks in Honolulu. The JCRC also established a small detachment at the embassy in Bangkok to serve as liaison in the region and conduct refugee interviews at "first asylum" camps in Hong Kong, the Philippines, and other maritime locations in Asia.

Lieutenant Colonel Paul Mather, USAF, by now an old Vietnam and JCRC hand, led the Bangkok office in the American embassy on Wireless Road, just a few minutes' walk to the Democratic Republic of Vietnam embassy up the street.

It was the last vital and almost elusive link with the Vietnam War.

At Barbers Point, the Naval Air Station up toward the north shore, the main body of JCRC, settled in and began the coordination with their counterparts at the DIA Special Office in the Pentagon and USACILHI on the docks. The effort was eventually led by Lieutenant Colonel Joe Harvey, a graduate of Texas A&M University and the University of Hawaii. Joe, like Paul Mather, was an old Southeast Asia hand and Foreign Area Officer who spoke very commendable Thai.

Observers noticed the enthusiasm of those in the organizations—they seemed to be refining records and collating refugee reports with enthusiastic zeal, waiting for the "breakthrough." That moment when negotiations would begin, and they'd be on the trail of crash and battle site inspections and remains recovery again. CINCPAC and US Army Pacific visitors shook their heads in amusement. As far as they, and virtually everyone else, assumed, the war was over.

And it was, except for the families of the missing, and for this little band of dedicated men and women, it wasn't over; not by a long shot.

The number of refugees changed from a trickle to a virtual flood by the late 1970s; they were seeking asylum in camps in Hong Kong, Thailand, the Philippines, and various other countries—not all of them warmly embracing the newcomers.

The few CILHI linguists operating out of the forward detachment in Bangkok (the other detachments would not be established until the early 1990s), traveled around the camps like circuit-riding preachers. They interviewed refugees and gathered information about possible American POWs remaining behind or unaccounted-for Americans whose remains were not recovered in the tumult of the US withdrawal from Vietnam in April 1975. This also included virtually every non-Asian from missionaries, merchant seamen, and various adventurers that washed up on Vietnam's long coastline; all non-Asians were included to account for possible sightings of Americans. Predictably, many turned out to be Russians or Eastern Europeans from the Communist bloc.

For the next two decades, both organizations would be understaffed and in the backwash of the receding conflict in Indochina. There were a few recovery attempts in both Vietnam and Laos supported by CILHI in those intervening years, and CILHI continued to respond to World War II recoveries in the Pacific when a crash site or remains were found by indigenous people, or in a few cases where the theater mortuary was uncomfortable in identifying remains found, in Europe.

The JCRC maintained the database of losses inherited from its predecessor organization, the JPRC, and honed and refined case files with the assistance of refugee reports and interviews, intelligence reports, and NSA intercepts, while the Special Office for POW/MIA Affairs in the Defense Intelligence Agency analyzed and sought threads of commonality, verification of facts, or simply sifted fiction from truth.

Political and family interest plus that of Congress was energized by the burgeoning interest of POW/MIA families, particularly those associated with the National League of Families of the Missing in Southeast Asia. As years passed, this energized interest turned sharply critical and vocal. Soon, a different war had broken out, this time between bereaved families and the US government.

At the end of my tutorial year and trial breaking-in time, I would take over from Lieutenant Colonel Joe Harvey as the commander. Joe was highly thought of by the CINCPAC command chain, and I had agreed it was a good idea to take over this command when I had talked to the J3, a Marine major general, the year before I left for Korea in 1986.

A month after I arrived in the summer of 1987, President Reagan appointed retired General John Vessey, former Chairman of the Joint Chiefs of Staff, as his Presidential Emissary for the POW/MIA topic with Vietnam. The president wanted the fullest possible accounting for those missing in Vietnam and recognition of those soldiers who'd fought in this long, frustrating conflict. There was no finer choice than this well-respected four-star retired general officer, at one time the senior uniformed figure of all the services.

General Vessey came into the military through the Minnesota National Guard. He enlisted as a bugler in 1939, fudging his age a bit since he was sixteen, and eventually was assigned as a motorcycle courier in the Thirty-Fourth Division in a field artillery battalion. Later, he served in North Africa during the early campaigns of World War II and quickly rose to the rank of first sergeant. As a lieutenant colonel he commanded an artillery battalion during the Vietnam War and had been awarded the Distinguished Service Cross, the nation's second-highest award, for actions during the battle of Suoi Tre in the sweeping Junction City operation in Tay Ninh province. As a brigadier general he commanded the Military Assistance and Advisory Group, Laos.

He was well-versed in Indochina, and the Vietnamese knew he was lionized in the US military and highly respected in diplomatic circles, both US and foreign. General Vessey, with his good friend General Robert "Barbwire Bob" Kingston were a particularly effective combination—General Vessey with his low-key, quiet demeanor and General Kingston radiating tough combat experience. Good cop and bad cop, they displayed the velvet glove of diplomacy and the mailed fist of war. Kingston was a twenty-two-year-old lieutenant in the Korean conflict. His Task Force Kingston bought time marauding and raiding to cover the withdrawal of US and Korean forces when hundreds of thousands of Chinese "volunteers" entered the war in November 1950.

General Kingston became Special Forces qualified then bounced back and forth between conventional infantry units and command positions at Fort Bragg, North Carolina, home of the Special Forces. This was the only way—and a career hazarding one at that—for an officer to survive in the 1960–80 time frame. Special Forces, like Aviation, would ultimately get their own branches in the early 1980s and mute this career hazard considerably. When Vietnam fell and the JPRC became the JCRC, he was the first commander as a brigadier general.

Prior to General Vessey's appointment, the rescue concern had stalled, despite a promising combined US-Vietnamese operation in 1983 to excavate a downed US aircraft in a village just north of Hanoi. Both the United States and the Vietnamese were looking for avenues to resume dialogue, and General Vessey called us together to describe his method.

"We owe it to our citizens to provide them answers to the questions that have gone unanswered since Operation Homecoming. . . . And we have got to furnish some questions the Vietnamese should be able to answer. They should be able—and willing—to answer, what happened to our people that we know were in their hands after their capture."[1]

These cases were the most sensitive and fractious incidents in our files. We called them "discrepancy" cases since there were glaring discrepancies in the photos of pilots alive and in relatively good shape while obviously captured. Eventually, they were called "compelling evidence" cases or "compelling" in negotiation narratives to soften the meaning, which hardened the many critics of our efforts.

News photos showed pilots in captivity shortly after shoot down, in some cases with flight helmets still on, hands tied behind their backs. They were usually depicted in news photos guarded by women in pith helmets armed with bayoneted 1891 Russian carbines. These weapons were manufactured and used by Soviet troops through the World War II sieges and battles in their cities and then were passed to their Communist acolytes. These images were visible evidence that the Soviets and Chinese were also in the hostile mix facing our servicemen, at least in armament. The Chinese in road construction and active air defense.

In September 1988 we conducted the tentative beginnings of operations in Vietnam with three, three-men recovery teams in the field (a team leader, a linguist/analyst, and a CILHI Graves Recovery NCO), and the lab director, Dr. Ellis Curley, a noted physical anthropologist, and Dr. Sara Collins, a CILHI staff and field anthropologist, leasing and consulting with their Vietnamese counterparts in Hanoi from their Medical department of their Ministry of Defense. Dr. Peter Miller went along to assist in the field if the need arose, and I went along to assist everyone, if required.

Two of the three teams would visit two crash sites in northern Vietnam and a third would visit the most promising in the Hue-Phu Bai corridor of the narrow waist of Vietnam below the 17th Parallel and the wartime DMZ. Then we had the Son Tay crash in reserve as an opportune case.

This would be Vietnam Joint Field Activity (JFA) number one (actually Joe Harvey and Johnny Webb would conduct one earlier, in 1983). Theirs was the excavation of an alleged B-52 at a village named Yen Thuong, near Hanoi. One of the team members required medevac'ing by a USAF C-9 Nightingale after being struck by the excavator. No remains were recovered.

Joe Harvey remembered the hole in the ground as very deep.

The September 1988 operation and their successive iterations spread, multiplied, and were more expansive each time they occurred. They were notable for the successes they demonstrated by US and Vietnamese operators working together in September 1988, albeit cautiously this first time. Subsequent operations dissolved much of the tensions between the Vietnamese and Americans, and soon both sides were committed to the mission and had developed working relationships.

Young men from the Vietnam Office of Seeking Missing Persons, an ad hoc office that trained young diplomats from the Ministry of Foreign Affairs, and mufticlad officers from the Ministry of National Defense with Ministry of the Interior were the political officers lurking about. They all improved their English skills and learned how to work with Americans. And we learned how the Vietnamese worked, eventually what they thought and why they thought that way. After a while we understood them much better than we had during the war, a sad fact, I realized.

The recovery Pete and I attempted at Son Tay was notable for two reasons—Vietnamese flexibility at letting us into a sensitive area—the site of the famously executed but unsuccessful airmobile POW raid that ransacked an empty POW camp in November 1970. The second reason was the smooth way the Vietnamese lured us—me—into the Public Affairs ambush, even though it turned out positively in the United States' favor.

Two noted American journalists from the war, George Esper, the Associated Press bureau chief during and after the conflict, and Nick Ut, the Vietnamese photographer who had earned a Pulitzer Prize for the picture of a young Vietnamese girl wounded in a napalm attack, greeted me with Nguyen Can, my counterpart for this first operation. The once elegant but now decrepit courtyard of the Governor Generale du Tonkin residence was the scene; the two journalists wanted to accompany the team operating in the south, the one we considered the most likely to turn something up and certainly the most sensitive one. The victorious northerners considered anybody below the DMZ during the war as "puppets" of the American forces.

Worried about the press interest before we deployed, I called our actual boss at the National Security Council, the Asia specialist and one who had survived the political wars of the Nixon administration. I asked him about Public Affairs guidance and he snarled back, "If any press show up, stiff arm them!"

"Sir, how about Q's and A's?" Questions and Answers were staples to reporters, not as good as interviews or witnessing something but they provided the gist of the operation and also intimated to the public the reporters had been in touch with participants in an event.

"I don't want to tell you again. Have nothing to do with the press! You can't survive in this business by having *them* looking down your neck. Like I said, '*NO COMMENT*!' I sure as hell don't have any problem avoiding them and I don't want to hear any more about it. Understand my guidance?"

"Yes sir. Avoid the press."

My counterpart Ngyuen Can was a canny and suave diplomat; his modus operandi was a no expression inscrutability. Esper made his pitch to accompany the southernmost team and Ut stepped back to take a photograph of all of us. I resisted holding a handout antipaparazzi fashion but this was Nicholas Ut, who probably had as many Pulitzers as I had "Barely Qualified" marksmanship medals.

I kicked an imaginary pebble and looked down when the flash went off but looked right back up into the camera, hands in my pockets, when his motor drive whirred and the flash went off again. Now I visualized an 8 x 10 glossy of my deer in the headlights sliding over Dick Childress's desk in the East Wing. He was growling and honing a razor edge on his gold letter opener.

When Esper finished his tour de Hue/Phu Bai du horizon proposed press itinerary I began all the reasons I could think of not to do it: there were family sensitivities and sensibilities; this was a critically sensitive mission and the first one should be allowed to proceed without distractions.

There were bound to be some unforeseen hazards and we couldn't guarantee their safety. (I cited the 1983 mission and the medevac flight required that Joe had assured me was exceedingly difficult for both the Americans and the mid-level Vietnamese who couldn't make the necessary decisions on the spot; I embellished those difficulties as much as I could.) I threw in every reason I could think of and probably included a couple I made up on the spot.

When I finished, Esper turned to Nguyen Can, who had stood with his arms folded across his chest during my diatribe, maintaining a barely discernible amused but bored expression.

"What's Vietnam's perspective on this Mr. Can?"

The diplomat shrugged and replied, "Well, Vietnam is a free country so of course we'd have no objections, but we must defer to the U.S.' wishes in this case."

Esper turned back to me, and I noticed the small tape recorder running under his notebook.

"Well, Colonel? I can assure you it's going to be reported—one way or another," he said with an engaging grin. Ut snapped another picture.

I took a deep breath, "Look Mr. Esper, if you'll leave the team down south alone I'll see if Mr. Can might be able to let us investigate another case we were holding as an alternate; if he and you are in agreement I'll let you watch that one."

Esper looked up from his notebook while Ut stood off a few yards fiddling with his camera.

"Where is it?"

"Son Tay . . ."

They both snapped their heads up, eyes wide.

"*The* Son Tay?!" Ut asked incredulously.

"Yes, it's only about . . ."

"Oh, we know where it is," Esper interjected, his interest aroused.

"What kind of loss?" Esper asked, in full reporter mode.

Now I had to hesitate again, but I knew I was pretty far out in dangerous waters anyway.

"An F4B; I think there was one crewman lost, but I'm not sure." Actually, I was sure, and I assumed they were too, because I had a copy of the negotiation narrative locked in my briefcase and it had been discussed with the Vietnamese; I was very sure because I'd read all the cases for the fourth or fifth time on the C-141 flight to Hanoi, between nappings in the rear seat of one of the Jeep Cherokees that were strapped down in the cavernous fuselage. The details had been broached to the Vietnamese several times in "technical meetings," so named because we had no diplomatic discourse with the Socialist Republic of Vietnam, so naturally they wouldn't be called negotiations.

And they were unclassified but considered for official use only (FOUO), which was a laughable protection from the press or prying eyes. The Vietnamese might or might not share them with the press, but I suspected this was certainly a case where two veterans of the information wars, Nguyen Can and George Esper, might collude to get a juicy, notable news item on the AP or Vietnamese wires, or possibly US or international broadcast channels.

I was sure the Vietnamese had set this up, or at least not objected and perhaps had dropped enough hints to get two top journalists interested. I knew that Esper was a tenacious and respected reporter and bureau chief. The Associated Press' Saigon office in his case—he had remained in Vietnam after its fall in April 1975 and then was ushered out of the country afterward with all the Americans that had remained behind.

I also knew that Son Tay, the spectacular raid by Army Special Forces supported by a sky filled with Air Force and Navy aircraft supporting it, had landed in Hanoi's backyard. Despite the lack of US prisoners being found by the US Army raiders, they had a spectacularly successful firefight with somebody, probably some of China's People's Liberation Army (PLA) soldiers supporting the PAVN. Or, as some speculated, Russians.[2]

Whoever they were, they reportedly were bigger than Vietnamese. All but a handful of US soldiers shooting that night had shot at North Vietnamese before, much farther south or in "neutral" and off-limits Laos or Cambodia, and even in North Vietnam to rescue downed pilots. There were no US killed in action (KIA), but one Army Special Forces soldier was wounded in the thigh and one helicopter crewman suffered a broken ankle.[3]

When I heard about the raid as I trained at Fort Bragg, North Carolina, for my second tour in Vietnam, it buoyed us like Doolittle's raid on Japan had done to an earlier generation.

I knew Son Tay would be of high interest. I assumed, like most soldiers talking to the press, that it would probably also be bad, perhaps as slanted as the Tet Offensive reporting.

"OK, we agree to that, and we'll stay out of your way. We will be asking questions, though."

"I can't guarantee any answers," I replied.

"I guarantee we'll be talking to more people than you." Esper smiled, then slapped his notebook shut, turned off the miniature tape recorder he had running and slipped it in his pocket. We both turned toward Mr. Can and I asked if he could assist us on the Son Tay recovery; he shrugged again, replied that he'd try. I thought he probably already had the civilian labor crews standing by.

That night I called Joe Harvey and told him what transpired. His reaction was a sigh: "you're probably going to be fired; I understand why you had to do it, I probably would've done the same, but you heard the guidance."

Nguyen Can and I drove out to Son Tay the next morning. I had Dr. Pete Miller with me and we had enough equipment to do the excavation. Just as I thought, there were plenty of Vietnamese scurrying around with shovels and hoes.

We had a whole battalion of workers ready to go. When we arrived there were a few journalists from the East bloc press lurking around the headquarters. The Vietnamese had VNN, their counterpart to CNN, we guessed, complete with a young, female on-site reporter and a good English speaker; her cameraman nodded good-naturedly at us.

They both wore black baseball caps with a familiar insignia—the JCRC's black and orange patch: a map of Indochina, a white cross with stylized lightning bolts symbolically across all three countries. Her cameraman similarly was young, westernized, and a good English speaker. We chatted and I asked him if he'd spent time in America.

He replied "No, but he'd met many famous Americans during the war—Tom Hayden, Jane Fonda . . ."

Pete chatted with the young woman who told him about her family all being killed by the "constant bombing."

We listened stoically while they related the party line history of Son Tay and how the brave Home Guard had driven off the invaders, but not before the landing force had killed some "elderly villager." We both nodded at the right places, and Pete even managed to avoid rolling his eyes and huffing.

There were some hard-eyed older men and women standing around in Russian dress, and a man dressed a little better was quietly translating their remarks. I guess the Party faithful had arrived—the Peoples' Committee, who had the final say on anything diplomatic, commercial, and maybe military, if it had anything to do with Party principles, at least to a certain extent. Marx and Lenin were still preeminent in those days, but Deng Xiaoping's black-and-white mouse-catching cats were starting to gain a little traction, at least in China. And Vietnam was thinking about it.

My spirits, never high since the press ambush, plummeted lower. Esper and Ut arrived; their spirits were as high as mine were low. The excavation did not turn out well. An elderly man and woman arrived; they had the "exact knowledge of the grave site." Another witness arrived with the same exact knowledge, only his gravesite was a couple of hundred meters away. An argument ensued and Can arbitrated, but I could see he was getting irritated. I was harboring dark thoughts by now.

We wound up digging at both sites for a while; there would be no laying out of tape or marking off a square as large as a high school campus, things I'd seen done in Laos. We found nothing after digging test holes at both sites, with no evidence of burial (or even prior disturbance of soil as Dr. Miller pointed out) and the VNN crew covering with the anchor explaining and gesturing. Esper and Ut watched quietly for a while and then began to talk to locals gathered to watch the operation, Ut translating.

"So what do you recommend, Dr. Miller? I asked Pete. "Now I believe he could be anywhere in here." This was a field about the size of a major league football stadium—including the seating. More witnesses had arrived, all with different burial locations. Another one claimed to be here when the plane crashed, but there was no pilot's body recovered. Another live sighting report if he ever emigrated.

"If we could get that bulldozer we could maybe scrape the surface and turn something up. We could both stand on either side and go along watching what he turned up. If he hit something with evidence or some disturbed soil we could do a trial excavation there. That's all I know to do."

The Vietnamese crew was videotaping all this and Ut was photographing it. Can had been translating for the newscaster but he kept himself off camera, a wise move I thought.

The Russian bulldozer was huge. Before Can briefed the Vietnamese operator I asked Pete if he'd ever seen or done anything like this in his years as an archaeologist. I was a neophyte but I'd been on a few recovery excavations, and a bulldozer was a far cry from a PhD anthropologist on his or her knees whisking dirt away from an object with a small horsehair brush. He scratched his chin thinking, then he held his left elbow with his right arm across his chest and peered at me through his round glasses. This was a gesture and response I'd see again and again over the years, but I certainly didn't realize it at the time.

"Nope, but I think it'll work if the operator is briefed carefully to go slow and not too deep with the blade."

We're going to be looking at the dirt curling off the blade for uniform fragments, cloth, anything out of the ordinary and signal him to stop." He gestured back, out to the huge field.

"That's the only way that I can think of to do it. If he's even here. This whole area is heavily populated and I'm sure all the wreckage was carted off years ago."

Pete and I dutifully walked along each side of the blade, watching dirt curl away from the bite of the huge implement. Occasionally, Pete would hold up his hand to stop, and he and I would examine something that caught his eye, usually a rock or clump of grass or weed that might have been a fabric. Nothing but dirt mainly.

At one point the female reporter and her cameraman jogged alongside me with the microphone stuck practically under my nose; she asked me what we were doing. I made what I thought were some halfway sensible sounding but inane replies. It's hard to tell someone what you're doing when you're not sure yourself. Later back in Hawaii, when I saw the footage from network television, I cringed. It wasn't as bad as I thought—it was worse.

The operator was skilled but we continued to see nothing. Pete had done probably hundreds of excavations in his career, and in the two I'd been on in Laos I remember standing over a screen and sifting the dirt carefully by the handfuls if I caught a glimpse of something tantalizing—a piece of cloth, metal, or anything light colored or appearing different from the soil we examined.

Pete and I carefully walked the path cut just below the ground's surface, but nothing turned up that indicated anything that might depict a burial. The driver hopped down from the dozer and we asked Can to instruct him to cut another furrow parallel to this one back across the field. Then we began on the opposite side of the field and made one more over and back swath, each one about the width of the eight-foot-wide blade. I felt like a medicine man casting animal bones into a fire, watching for a sign but with no results, nothing but the rich soil of the Tonkin Plain.

When we were finished and back at the Son Tay headquarters, Esper and Ut had vanished. Ngyuen Can appeared with one shoe off, lost in the mud. He looked like he'd taken a tumble into a tar pit, but he was upbeat, and we both laughed. I guessed the public affairs gambit was successful, and he and what I guessed were members of the Peoples' Committee, the hard-core Communist political leaders, older men and women, seemed happy.

The bulldozer operator was in the back of the room drinking a cup of tea and smoking a cigarette. I shook hands with him, passing a ten-dollar US bill into his palm, hoping he wasn't a deep agent of the US Department of the Treasury. He smiled and pocketed the bill quietly and expertly with a smile, like we were old friends. I was sure I was probably breaking another US federal law. I had the curious, derailed feeling that my decision-making had torpedoed all General Vessey's hard work of the previous year.

That night I called my wife from the post office. The postal clerk pointed to the only one of three booths with a door that shut completely. She seemed sad and appeared to have been crying recently; this did not help my overall feeling, almost on cue she broke out in racking sobs. My wife Janna was excited, though. She said my mother had called her to report I'd been on the national evening news. Expecting the worst, I asked Janna how my mom had characterized the news.

"She said it was fine. Just fine. She wished your dad had seen it but he was outside with the new calves."

The post office/telephone young woman, still sobbing, with her back to me, didn't respond to my gentle call that I needed to make another phone call, she just nodded, her crying now a pitiful mewling.

I called Joe Harvey and reported the day's events but didn't mention the news report. We hung up, I looked at the flimsy bills for what appeared to be hundreds of thousand *dong* for the two calls. I murmured *cam on and xin loi, Co* (thank you and I'm sorry, Miss) and left. Apparently Joe hadn't seen or heard any of the newscast, but later it appeared that Esper and Ut had turned the Son Tay exploratory excavation very positively paraphrased into a difficult operation, with aging witnesses who couldn't agree on a burial location, but the Vietnamese and Americans were slogging on together. . . . They were resolving problems as they arose and dogged in their determination. . . . It was a gentle underhanded marshmallow toss—a rarity in anything the press reported about the POW/MIA issue. Despite this I felt that my "nine lives of Indochina" had been diminished considerably on this operation.

But for once, it was an honest, objective story that basically underlined and highlighted the yearlong diplomatic campaign successfully waged by General Vessey with the help of General Kingston. It must have been positive, to the moderate Vietnamese at least, because Ngyuen Co Thach was put out to diplomatic pasture at the next Politburo conclave, and someone more in line with Party "standards" was emplaced.

Now we were ready to exploit the good beginning—spread out to cases we knew were difficult but would be solvable with our analysis and their open channel to witnesses and knowledgeable local officials. But pretty quickly the analysts and the field operators were going to need backup; CILHI especially was going to have to do the "loaves and fishes" with anthropologists and graves registration personnel.

Things weren't that easy in the United States either. Despite our highest national priority and a presidential pass carried by the most respected general officer since Pershing, it appeared we were frequently tiptoeing around the dreaded in the military "off-line activity." Which essentially means illegal. The new vehicles we sent in on the first operation ran into the first obstacle. Dealing with Vietnam got us cross-wise with the US Department of the Treasury—Vietnam was an embargoed country still under the Trading with the Enemy Act. We had planned to use Mitsubishi Pajeros, because maintenance on them could be done in Vietnam, but we had to use American vehicles. So with a check drawn on the US government, we purchased four new Jeep Cherokees, necessitating that maintenance would have to be performed in Bangkok. To the best of my knowledge, it never was.

The salesman at the local jeep dealer was extremely happy. Hugh Klipp, our dynamo operations officer with the little mustache and round glasses, masked a very shrewd major formerly of an Eighty-Second airborne parachute brigade, delighted in spending CILHI's money in a hefty cashier's check. When the obviously pleased salesman asked him what colors, Hugh waved a "no matter" indifferent hand then rethought it.

"Get four different colors if you can, so we can go with green team, blue team, etc."

"You got it, Bro. Bro Sir, I mean."

Hugh was never out of his rumpled battle dress uniform, sporting his expert infantry badge and senior parachutists' wings.

Right now the JCRC analysts and augmentees from around the island of Hawaii were reinforcing the teams. The Explosives Ordnance Disposal people, medics, and occasional doctor that could be spared from Pearl Harbor were all great assistance, but train-up with the recovery teams and deployment would effectively take them from their busy commands on island for a month to six weeks.

I had worked the vehicles through a helpful GS-13 at the Department of the Treasury who said he'd send it up through his bureaucratic chain of command. Ultimate fixer Major Art Gorman, USMC, had set it up, slicing miles of bureaucratic red tape with him, apparently a former rugby player. Our colleague in Treasury gave me wording for the cover memorandum that would obviate any notion that we were turning over something with a military "dual use" to the still enemy Vietnamese. He also implied he was running this in an unusual channel and please don't put his name on any message traffic.

"Ah, Jesus," I thought. Things were about to degenerate into a cavalry melee and me being visited by agents of the field office of the FBI, Honolulu.

There were several headaches like these, despite General Vessey's overarching prominence and positive public affairs launch, but there was still an almost impenetrable strata of bureaucracy in the Departments of State and Defense, and we knew it was also immensely difficult with the Vietnamese, whose bureaucracy made ours as smooth as a bland slice of cheese.

They had formed the Vietnam Office of Seeking Missing Personnel, the VNOSMP, and their civilian-clothed young men might have been junior officers from an Air Defense regiment or an infantry division. Others were from their Ministry of Foreign Affairs or Interior, some junior, some mid-grade. I never asked Joe, Paul, or Lew Stern who had a couple of thousand gigabytes of Vietnam knowledge and lore compared to mine, but I guessed the VNOSMP was a way around some of their bureaucratic hurdles.

It depended on who it reported to and who that person answered to, I suppose, but I couldn't see anything as line-crossing, cost-cutting, and rapid-acting (comparatively speaking) as coming out of any ministry unless it had plenty of clout, and coming out on top of two wars as underdog military to two powerful nations, I would guess the Ministry of Defense (MOD) would have sufficient clout. But maybe the Ministry of Foreign Affairs (MOFA) had edged them out just because of that.

We dealt mainly with foreign affairs people in policy meetings, although senior defense personnel were also there, seemingly in an advisory role. In the field, the Defense representatives were pretty much always there, and the real stakeholders, the Peoples' Committee officers, were probably nearby, and certainly read in on everything. You rarely saw a "suit" from MOFA unless he was coming as part of a delegation. We never, or at least I never, had any interaction with the real stakeholders, the Peoples' Committee.

The senior persons we dealt with were certainly from the Ministry of Foreign Affairs or Defense, and assuredly the Ministry of the Interior was there, with the gentle kind faces that were probably pretty effective in an interrogation room, or others who looked to be muscle, fast on their feet, stone-faced, and pretty athletic. They'd keep the peace and do the counterintelligence, if required—it never was, from the Americans. We were serious about the humanitarian aspects.

We had to be. Getting booted out of country, or worse—jailed, for photographing something they considered sensitive or secret would have stopped what we were doing and probably set us back to *Year Zero*, a phrase gaining popularity when the Khmer Rouge closed the shutters in Phnom Penh and began their pogrom of anyone caught with eyeglasses or a ballpoint pen. The senseless slaughter there made the Rape of Nanking look miniscule in comparison.

Their Ministry of Defense and Ministry of Foreign Affairs seemed to function about like ours did, and of course their personnel in the Ministry of the Interior—their counterintelligence arm—were probably lurking in the background most of the time, much more invisible than their counterparts in Laos, who, if there, were lurking in a hammock under a shady tree.

By the time I arrived back in Honolulu, my firing had been held off, apparently. I expected the desk I was sharing in the admin area to be emptied into a couple of cardboard boxes. Instead I got a world-class verbal reprimand from our minder on the NSC. But I understood the knife across the throat threat of "next time you better do what I tell you to do." He didn't have to add "or else."

The operation's wide publicity and genuinely good results advanced the cooperation between us and the Vietnamese and portrayed an honest picture of both sides trying to do the best they could to find missing Americans. Threaded through it was the fact that cooperation and the operational tempo were increasing immeasurably, but the personnel and funding were not.

Generals Vessey and Kingston were unsure of their position four years later in the new Clinton administration; my small band and I were in the arcane policy world inside the beltway in a "five-sided building with a hole in the middle Pentagon"; no one in the White House had even contacted Vessey and Kingston, but both offered assistance if my team and I needed it. Colonel Frank Libutti, General Vessey's go-to source on the Joint Chiefs Staff, was exceedingly helpful—always a gung-ho marine who was willing to cut the red tape if the need arose.[4]

Dr. Lewis Stern, my office mate and the Vietnamese desk officer in EAPR, the fount of all things Vietnam, still provided him timely and accurate information through Frank Libutti (who would, in our opinion, deservedly become a lieutenant general, USMC) and sometimes directly.

Vessey and Kingston stopped by occasionally when we were at the Pentagon and later at the Clarendon Building. Their visits reinforced our morale considerably, and we'd back-brief them on everything going on with us in policy, and with the field operators—now the Joint Task Force–Full Accounting and the US Army Central Identification Laboratory. I had no idea that I would be back in the field myself soon.

Lew, Frank Libutti, Joe Harvey, and I frequently accompanied Vessey and Kingston on many of their nine negotiation missions to Hanoi (General Vessey's mission did not include Laos, but it was obviously linked to Vietnam; he and General Kingston knew the connection, thanks to our friends at DIA and probably, at Langley (keepers of the real secrets).

I proudly took a picture of General Vessey's large white Boeing 707 with absolutely no national markings save for a small American flag on the tail. It masked the Russian MiG 21 fighters on the flight line (the most photographed MiG 21s in the world, we joked). We only saw them fly once, during a quiet dignified repatriation ceremony. Four of them in what almost looked like a flyby then a 360 degree overhead and spaced out fairly well for landing, it was startling at the time. They passed behind us, canopies open, engines burbling. Almost like they were defiant, celebratory. A couple of our US transfer case bearers thought they could also be honoring fellow airmen, finally going home. Something very important to any Vietnamese, American, or military man anywhere.

The families were still very vocal and critical of our efforts, understandably so—their loved ones were still missing. This was demonstrated graphically to the new commander of such an expanded JCRC it would be nearly unrecognizable.

CHAPTER 10

Politics, Policy, and Follies

June 1990–July 1993, Washington, DC, Hanoi, Vientiane, Beijing, Honolulu, Phnom Penh

I arrived at the Pentagon in the summer of 1990 and by the winter of 1991, straddling two jobs, on the Korea desk and simultaneously and uneasily bearing the rather useless title of Principal Advisor to the Secretary of Defense on POW/MIA matters. President George Herbert Walker Bush, former ambassador in Beijing, director of the Central Intelligence Agency and vice president before becoming president, had led the world—with US forces as the spear's "tip"—through a thoroughly satisfying "just war"—quick, decisive, and significant. We, along with Assistant Secretary of State for Public Affairs, Pete Williams, handled all policy matters for US and enemy prisoners of war.[1]

The Gulf War had restored (everyone thought) the status quo in the Middle East. The Iraqis had pulled out of Kuwait in disarray and their Army, with the exception of the carefully husbanded and loyal Republican Guard units, was decimated. Now the world reverted to its previous state, led by men and women elected and appointed; run by staffers in Congress; and action and desk officers at Defense and the Joint Chiefs Staff, State, Treasury and the rest of the Cabinet departments. They were led by their bosses in a rarified atmosphere; that is, one that is hard to breathe in sometimes.

If you had business at Twenty-First and C Street, the Department of State, things were friendly and collegial. The Department of Defense and everyone inside the five-sided building seemed to be a little more combative.

When meetings grew tense and disagreement reigned, staffers invariably invoked the name of their two- or three-star bosses or Cabinet principal—often apologetically, like Old West lawmen or gunfighters casually pulling their coats back to reveal their holstered weapons. Sometimes this turned into "my boss is bigger than your boss" harangues between antagonists who might grab a beer somewhere after work and work it out with compromises their "super-bosses" could buy. Meetings that were contentious or left recriminations smoldering like unexploded ordnance, although they were generally smoothed over by experienced leadership.

The Office of the Secretary of Defense was the "white collar" policy establishment of the "blue collar" Department of Defense—some said the largest firm in the world; probably a hundred or a thousand times larger than Walmart—all the services, military schools, agencies as disparate as the Defense Advanced Research Projects Agency all the way to the Defense Commissary Agency. It was high stakes poker in an arena where different directorates, services, and missions competed in some cases, cooperated in others.

To some it was a fascinating place to be, shaping policy. "Face Cards" that might become more powerful in the next administration, or sit out four to eight years in "Think Tanks," until the next Populist election. To operators and outsiders of the fast track, a category I fell easily into, it was an uneasy environment. It seemed like you were entrusted with assignments that required detailed research and recommendations that would be disastrous if you weren't absolutely correct.

The last time I had to think fast and make critical decisions that were gut churning was when I was flying as command-and-control officer putting in airmobile insertions and coordinating tactical air support and artillery simultaneously sitting in the open door of a UH1-Huey. At least there was noise—sound and fury—that seemed to guide your decisions.

That wasn't the problem; all officers and senior noncommissioned officers were required to do that—except in the Pentagon you had to provide solutions in minutes. Sometimes only finding out about it as their principals were shrugging into suit coats and telling their subordinates to scurry along with them while they briefed the subordinates on questions they needed answered before the meeting finished.

The action officers galloped back to their cubicles and made frantic phone calls, taking notes and speeding back to the meeting with the notes. The officers hoped the secretary could pass them into the meeting. This type of action was called "an emergency call for fire," or more plaintively "scratching at the door to get in."

It wasn't that their bosses were callous, indifferent, or being cruel to action officers. I only met a few that weren't bright, well read, articulate, and demanding. The Pentagon was a very busy place, as was every government agency in Washington.

Prizes were awarded "by name requests" for sensitive jobs, a sure sign of a Knight Emergent or eminent grise being assigned a difficult project or task that would elevate him or her to the highest realm, maybe brigade command, or general officer, or a challenging promotion to the Senior Executive Service (SES) ranks. Or that jewel in the crown, zipped into the White House—the NSC—by circumstance.

That was happening frequently when I hesitantly arrived in June 1990. I had been plucked out of an assignment as the Staff Asian Foreign Area Officer at the Army War College to come to the Pentagon. You swallow assignments you wanted and those you didn't with the same cup of coffee.

I had been in the Asia business for well over two decades, as both a combat arms officer commanding units in Vietnam and Korea or dealing with Pol-Mil issues there and keeping track of what was going on in China, Taiwan, the two Koreas, Japan, Mongolia, the Russian Far East, and sometimes Southeast Asia, especially Indochina, since my previous assignment, two years in the JCRC. I subscribed to the then-weekly *Far Eastern Economic Review* and *Foreign Policy* as well as *Foreign Affairs*. Old habits from graduate school at Georgetown.

One of my professors opined that *Foreign Affairs*, with its feathered and ruffled end pages, at least made somewhat adequate toilet paper when necessitated, and we all laughed, particularly the few military students sitting goggle-eyed with fatigue after a day of military madness with the colonels and captains furious with rage they weren't poring over tactical map boards in the back of some armored vehicle or afloat on a carrier redolent of jet fuel.

Eventually, the tenor of the magazine changed. The Council on Foreign Relations booted some of its octogenarians and hired younger editors and staff personnel (at probably a third of the salary), and it abandoned its "Foggy Bottom squinting through pince-nez glasses" pedantic message-writing format and began sporting well-edited, thought-out pieces from more contemporary and dynamic authors.

Now young Hill staffers, temporarily out of office assistant secretaries of something or other, recently embedded combat correspondents, and the occasional over-the-hill foreign area officers, were contributing articles. It's pleasurable and instructive to read and ponder the publication today.

I frequently pulled the cover envelopes off the weekly *Review* (which habitually arrived two weeks late anyway), stacked them chronologically, and read them all in two or three sittings. Nayan Chanda and Bertil Lindner occasionally had a jewel packed away on Southeast Asia, the excesses of the State Law and Order Restoration Council (SLORC) in Burma, or of the never-ending bubbling Pol-Mil kettle of the Philippines, particularly in the Sulu Sea.

I kept a wary eye on the maritime nations—Singapore, Malaysia, and Indonesia—the second and third Muslim, although largely secular but subject to infiltration and coercion. At their embassies they were friendly and hospitable people, as they were in their countries, and it was instructive to watch their reactions as we prepared to wage a destructive war on a seemingly secular Sunni nation with a distinctly Shia majority population. They seemed to ignore those distinctions; Saddam had committed an outrage on a popular kid sister nation that had no idea how to fight a bully.

On my "walkabout" after my separation from active duty in Vietnam in October 1968, I hitchhiked through Malaysia, Singapore, and Indonesia and down into Borneo—Kalimantan and Sarawak, before moving on to Indonesia. I dropped off in Johor Bahru with a train full of Australian and New Zealand infantrymen bound for a course where they'd learn to track armed men with the aid of dogs in the trackless rain forest.

But in 1990 we were all keenly aware that we might soon have to fight not-so-hospitable Muslims. I just glanced at happenings in Oceania—Australia and New Zealand, the latter somewhat frosty over the fact that our ships calling in their ports were reputed to sometimes carry nuclear warheads.

It was a good place to ply my trade and learn something new, but as we all pronounced at the end of a fourteen-hour day, strange things happen in a building with five sides and a hole in the center.

Even though I had spent some time in Washington, DC, not in the Pentagon, I liked the city and I liked our little 1926 Sears house in Arlington, which we had owned and rented out for a decade. Clarendon was a nice neighborhood, less than two miles straight line distance to the Pentagon. It was also a Vietnamese enclave with excellent restaurants.

Arlington's moratorium on building heights ended soon after and the Beltway Machine quickly gobbled up the Mom & Pop restaurants, giving way to the more elegant and expensive restaurants, stores, and high rise residences of the young and affluent. Some of my lieutenants, with small children and working wives, were spending two hours in traffic from the less expensive suburbs of northern Virginia or Maryland.

There was some humor in the fourth floor, second corridor, C wing, but it was mostly macabre, sympathetic, or pointed. Action officers and division chiefs swirled around acknowledging introductions with a nod, both hands clutching documents. You felt like a jutting rock in a rushing stream.

In the East Asia Pacific Region, commonly abbreviated OSD/ISA/EAPR, we were in the International Security Affairs (ISA) department, headed by Assistant Secretary of Defense Henry Rowen. He was an older, well-respected academic from the West Coast, originally coming out of the Rand Corporation decades before.

From early and earlier mornings until we locked our safes and walked to the parking lot in the moonlight, problems became thornier and more complex—because the world of rough neighborhoods is thorny and complex.

While our small staff was genuinely pitied because of the ambiguous and often hateful nature of our POW/MIA work, there was genuine curiosity from the other members of my office.

This is how a friend on loan to State described our POW/MIA mission: "The sheep don't know why you're here and don't like it; you guys deal with unsavory characters in back alleys sometimes it appears." (I had come back from a frustrating mission in Bangkok involving a charlatan named Jack Bailey who'd met the Secretary of Defense and convinced him he had the picture of a Special Forces Captain riding in an aircraft that was downed over the Ho Chi Minh trail. The picture was of a German national working as a bird smuggler conned into the scheme.)

"Why is the POW/MIA section in East Asia and Pacific?" was a frequent question from our office colleagues. We could only shrug and reply "that the wars with POW issues were Korea and Vietnam." The Gulf War would change all that, and we handled the policy questions on that conflict with a happier ending than Korea and Vietnam had left.

When I naïvely suggested that the policy could be more effectively dealt with by the office of the Assistant Secretary of Defense for Special Operations and Low Intensity Conflict, I was quietly rebuffed. This was a sexy issue the man with two stars counseled. Tricky, challenging but dangerous, he admitted. A real Gordian knot. Work it harder.

In the Army War College they had described the higher levels of the

Pol-Mil world with another military abbreviation: VUACA—Vague, Uncertain, Ambiguous, Confusing, Antagonistic. The professors were right; it was all of that and more.

Then we spent several months getting ready for a war. Desert Shield began its buildup then turned into the operational phase, Desert Storm in January 1991. It was mercifully short with casualties that were minimal, at least in contrast to the vast number of servicemen spread out over the Middle East. But in the run-up to Desert Storm the Indochina POWs were still a ripe, festering policy topic, like a suppurating wound that wouldn't heal.

Some activists and interested citizens familiar with the POW/MIA topic assumed the photos of the three white individuals holding a sign that allegedly said they were still in captivity from the Indochina War had prompted the changes, manpower increases, and organizations, particularly the Joint Task Force–Full Accounting. That wasn't true. We had been struggling for months before the "Three Amigos" surfaced. When the original photo was unearthed from a Russian magazine of the 1920s, the telegenic family and former congressman who had fronted it drifted off after the Three Amigos proved to be a fake.

Operationally, we had been looking for a more robust organization and plan to capitalize on the Vietnamese desire to move forward, and the Gulf War was the nudge we needed. We had sent a paper forward up to the undersecretary for review sometime before Christmas in 1990.

USCINCPAC had vowed to take over and supervise many of the operational details with the still unshaped and un-named JTF–FA. One of our POW/MIA officers, a sharp Marine major naval aviator turned lawyer Charlie Gittins, who had served in the desert, and our two-star Navy boss, Mike McDevitt, an expert on China and the entire Pacific, had sketched it out and it sounded good. We put it on paper and staffed it up the chain of command as Desert Shield morphed into Desert Storm. We had sent the proposal up our ladder, over to the Joint Staff and out to the JCRC and the Pacific Command.

In Hawaii the USCINCPAC staff and the JCRC had knocked the rough edges off, added their operational wisdom from years of operating with the good and bad actors in the Pacific, and it was approved for planning followed by the congressional look that hopefully would be approved and funded. But first we had a war to fight. We would, with other sympathetic nations, join in a coalition, and liberate a smaller, peaceful Muslim country from a larger, stronger, rapacious one.

NATO and the US Central Command were looking over the horizon at Muslims in Croatia, Kosovo, and the rest of the Balkans, countries in breakaway freedom mode, and heard the military muttering of the rough Serbs. They were probably already planning to conduct ethnic cleansing that rivaled that in Uganda. Or Cambodia. VUACA in its most virulent, evil garments.

Asia was a cauldron that bubbled south to north, east to west, affecting all the regions that touched its watery shores. In our office at EAPR we toiled singly or sometimes with one other person, wrestling with these problems and preparing courses of action up the chain; rarely did they go up unfestooned with changes or *see me*! scrawled in vivid ink. These scrawlings would prompt quick review by the writers, sometimes cross-checking with other regions or action officers: "Got any idea what he means by this?"

Only the half dozen or so members of the POW/MIA section added manpower, and it was fleeting—a reservist here and there or on occasion an intern dropped in for a project.

When I worked Korea, the annual Military Consultative Meeting was a preeminent task, the yearly meeting of the Secretary of Defense and the Minister of Defense of the Republic of Korea. There were schedules to clear up through deputy secretaries of defense to the SecDef himself. Then his opening remarks were drafted; they went to his speechwriter to put into his words. A lot of time was spent with this until the third or fourth draft. A lot of it was me convincing my Joint Staff counterparts that the secretary and chairman of the Joint Chiefs of Staff *really* didn't want to try a traditional greeting in Korean.

Position papers on everything from force levels to weapons and equipment sales were required. You wrote politico-military assessments and coordinated requests through Defense Intelligence Agency for Intelligence assessments. Certain actions had to be coordinated with Department of State, or Treasury if it strayed into their turf. The Republic of Korea attachés at their embassy helped immeasurably, although they tried to pry information out of us on anything contentious or sensitive that might be broached. Naturally we tried to do the same. You had to be open, honest, and secretive all at once.

If one of your foreign contacts were "burned" either inadvertently or by something they deemed as deliberate they didn't just get angry—you might never hear from them again. We called that East Asian Purgatory. A month before planning for the Military Consultative Meeting (MCM) began, I'd drop by their offices at the Korean embassy with a small gift for their children and a bottle of their favorite American whiskey in a gift bag.

Then there was the press. Some of the reporters had spent years in Korea. Most followed politico-military events religiously, and some were as well informed as military officers or NCOs that had spent a decade there. Some of them were courteous; some came at you like they were sharpening knives and brandishing forks.

Best to learn as much as possible, know where the minefields are, and answer their questions earnestly, honestly, and with as few words as possible. Early on we sought Public Affairs Guidance (PAG) and Qs and As—we routinely memorized Qs and As on the way to meetings with the press, and many of the sharper, more experienced officers and NCOs could predict follow-up questions from sharper, more experienced reporters. Some of these follow-up questions could lead you down dangerous paths, so a follow-up question raised all the questions and answers to a little higher alert level.

I remembered my own press experience with George Esper and Nick Ut, pulse quickening at the memories of being cross-examined in the ornate but crumbling courtyard of the Résidence du gouverneur General du Tonkin in Hanoi two years earlier by three experts in public affairs, one of them a mid-level Vietnamese diplomat who ran circles around me, but our really contentious moments were rare.

Then you were writing cables. For Korea, if it was an armistice matter, something that might be raised to the baddies at Panmunjom, it would be addressed to CINCUNC, the Commander in Chief of the United Nations; if it involved combined forces—Republic of Korea and United States, it would go to CINC, Combined Forces Command or CFC. Or if it was a purely military matter dealing mostly with US forces such as training or force levels, you'd address it to COMUSFORK, or Commander, US Forces, Korea; the same four star American Army general, at least that's how it worked in the two decades or so I worked Korean issues, from 1973 until 1993.

Our admiral or Deputy Assistant Secretary of Defense Carl Ford, or sometimes the Undersecretary of Defense Paul Wolfowitz, would sign the message out, depending on the sensitivity of it. You had to answer a lot of questions or you'd take it back for a rewrite with additional guidance, and sometimes with a little flesh off your backside.

All this preparation that unfolded into the Military Consultative Meeting between the two countries' Secretary of Defense and Minister of Defense preceded the annual Security Consultative Meeting, which addressed it from a Politico-Military stance and regional ramifications of foreign policy. A couple of my shanghaied from the POW/MIA issue action officers and I worked it at night, daytime in the Republic of Korea.

A GS-15 worked the Philippines; she had gained some cachet by helping negotiate a complex agreement with the Philippines under the supervision of Rich Armitage, the talented former Assistant Secretary of Defense for ISA. She would be on the NSC staff in a few years. Two talented specialists worked Japan, an important ally in the Pacific that the United States eyed as a significant contributor to the upcoming conflict with the Iraqis who had brazenly annexed Kuwait.

The principal Japan desk officer was Torkel Patterson, an Annapolis graduate Navy lieutenant commander who had opted out of an advanced degree at a distinguished Ivy League school in Japanese studies for a rigorous two-year course in the Japanese language at Japanese institutions. He amazed all of us, especially me, at his ability to free translate the Japanese of our admiral's counterparts from the land of chrysanthemums and rising suns.

"Can you do that in Korean or Chinese?" one of my guys whispered.

"I can order a beer in Korean, and I can order dim sum in Chinese, by saying *dim sum*," I whispered back.

Commander Patterson also would be on the National Security Council in a few years.

Torkel's "wingman assistant" was General Powell's son, Michael, who had his US Army career ended in Germany in a rollover Jeep accident that badly damaged his back. He would be the chairman of the Federal Communications Council in a few years.

There were a lot of brilliant military and civilian area experts in EAPR during the 1990s, before and after. It was a heady finishing school for me, and I vowed to learn as much as possible. When we finished the day's work on the MCM we'd have a quick roundtable on POW/MIA Affairs. We'd deal with any "flaming duck" problems immediately.

The jewel in our office was China, though. Despite the problems we were having with sanctions and diplomacy resulting from the Tiananmen incident in the spring of 1989, China would get the message, we felt. Two smart sinologists—Ed Ross and Eden Woon, retired Army and Air Force colonels, worked it.

Everyone from the president on down realized the giant of Asia would come back and become a powerful friend or a worrisome and formidable problem for us in Asia. Everybody worked, worked hard with long hours then flew to their regions overnight from work when necessary, lugging their suitcases they'd brought into the office.

Cold coffee cups were found days after returning from meetings, sitting on top of a safe somewhere (a no-no—you might spill something on the daily "safe locked by ——" column with a date, mated with a "safe checked by ——" column next to it). It was usually curling, yellowing, and out of date anyway. Days were a paper-strewn frenzy of briefings, phone calls, and hurried lunches or hurried runs.

Officers were frequently pulled out of the Pentagon gym by a phone call to the sign-in desk; there was a penciled list with a time on it: (Rank and Name) CALL YOUR OFFICE with a date-time group under the telephone. It was not uncommon to see an officer, usually Marine or Army, trotting along still in sweaty shorts and T-shirt and his office uniform on a hanger in one hand, his shoes in the other. Scratching at the door to get back to some crisis that had messaged him out of the Pentagon Officers' Athletic Club (POAC), a dated misnomer in the years of egalitarianism when anyone who paid the fee could join.

In the early mornings everything and everyone hummed along quietly as all Pentagoners walked in at dawn and read the classified messages and sipped morning coffee from mugs that were colorful, chipped, and usually streaked with a tour of coffee stains. Quite a few of them, mine included, were emblazoned with battalions, squadrons, or ship's numbers, reminders of easier times with genuine soldiers, sailors, marines, or airmen.

In growing daylight it was a whirl of action officers moving smartly out to meetings with the Joint Staff or up to the subprincipals at the deputy assistant secretary level or urgently banging out memorandums for their bosses, who were typically waiting at the printers to rip them out and read them hurriedly as they scurried to a meeting.

Our "engine room" was the office of the Deputy Assistant Secretary for East Asia, Carl Ford, but we were getting guidance through the Assistant Secretary of Defense/International Security Affairs from the Undersecretary of Defense for Policy, a lodestone position occupied by Paul Wolfowitz, a veteran statesman. He bounced up the ladder between the DOS (the Department of State) to DOD, Department of Defense, or in our case, OSD.

When our guys switched on their POW/MIA personas (changing hats we called it) the Interagency Group we were counterparted with was the Department of State, overseen, albeit loosely, by the NSC. It steered the course through the ROADMAP that nominally would lead the Socialist Republic of Vietnam to diplomatic recognition with the United States.

Ms. Griffiths was the godmother, and a principal player. Ken Quinn, Carl's counterpart at the Department of State, was just as talented. Even though there was always a little contradiction in their view, and sometimes words back and forth with a little sophisticated bite, they respected each other as professionals.

Ironically, Carl would wound up a distinguished career that had started with him as an infantry private from Arkansas who served in Korea during a period in Korean history when the Cold War was warm there, who became an infantry officer, and who, after service in Vietnam, returned to undergraduate and graduate school. From there he returned to the US Army as an intelligence officer serving another Vietnam tour in that capacity. He returned to the Defense Intelligence Agency in Washington as the senior China desk officer.

He resigned his commission and joined the CIA, again working China issues. He interned on the staff of Senator John Glenn on a CIA fellowship as an arms control and foreign policy advisor, later serving as his foreign policy advisor on the senator's presidential campaign. Carl eventually had honed his knowledge and experience to return to the CIA as National Intelligence Officer on China—the top China specialist in the agency.

We action officers didn't meet with the NSC, but we got the guidance, sometimes such that it was.

When I donned my "Korea hat," there was very little policy guidance on Korea, virtually every response I wrote was to answer a question or support or thwart an action from State focused on relative power between the Republic of Korea, our allies, or the Democratic Peoples' Republic of Korea. I had my personal opinions, like everyone, but I always supported the CINCUNC proposals when I could. I habitually checked with the Joint Staff officers responsible for Korea.

It was a small world—I had attended forty-seven weeks of language school with the principal staff officer of the Joint Staff, my counterpart there, and had served two tours in the Second Infantry Division as a recon troop commander and tank battalion commander. I had served a middle tour as an FAO operations officer in the Combined Field Army, where we worked side by side with good Republic of Korea officer counterparts.

I monitored meetings at Panmunjom, was the liaison officer to the ROK Special Warfare Center at Songnam, and also the US Special Forces Detachment, Korea. We were responsible for any kind of bubble in security in the Demilitarized Zone, always a tense, spooky area. About a decade and a half later I'd be deep in North Korea as the CILHI commander with an OSD delegation and the Department of State North Korea liaison officer. It was also a tense, spooky area.

But three years after I left Korea, two years at the JCRC at Barbers Point and one year at the Army War College, Carlisle Barracks, Pennsylvania, when I put on my POW/MIA hat in the Pentagon, we had questions, issues, and problems to deal with from all areas. These included, but were not limited to, the Press, Congress, Veterans' Groups, and the National League of Families (Ann, the spark plug of the league, had been granted a secret clearance and I usually talked with her a couple of times a day.)

On rare occasions a family member of a missing service member would appear who just wanted to talk to someone knowledgeable about their case. Since we had no conference room (except the admiral's office), we'd sweep off the small desk with our one telephone on it and sit there. One of our officers would bring a hastily wiped out spare coffee cup for the visitor and we'd look over the visitor's case and the documentation from their service casualty officer.

If I could, I'd tell them what I remembered of the case, with the proviso the Vietnam mission was only just starting when I was assigned to the JCRC. It hadn't blossomed into the much larger task force that was now reexamining cases with surgical precision, putting some on the shelf for reinvestigation, and tackling the next ones. Anything besides policy or operational considerations arising out of it, I referred them back to their service casualty sections.

In technical meetings in Hanoi, the Vietnamese and our side would go over what they knew about the case from the capture incident or their acquisition of remains and we'd provide them subsequent information, Search and Rescue information, order of battle intelligence (what enemy units we suspected of opposing our forces), and other information that might help them locate citizens or soldiers who might have had information.

Generally, I found that mid-level civilian bureaucrats, like the ones in our office, sympathized with our mission but were a little puzzled by its origins and the manpower and funding the job required. These were seasoned policy officials varying in ages from "wunderkind" mid- to late twenties to GS 14s and 15s in their forties and fifties who'd fought the bureaucratic wars with advanced degrees and years of work in similar efforts.

They'd begun as congressional staffers, or in different Cabinet branches right out of their university, the best "Mr. Smith goes to Washington" types that had a self-vested interest in participating in good government down their career paths.

They wanted to know what we did exactly, what was the desired end state, how did we go about it, get started in this effort, and how might it affect their own jobs and missions—all these were the water cooler questions asked. They knew Hanoi and Vientiane were exotic but rough neighborhoods, and every person there, military or civilian, had been thoroughly force-fed Vietnam through their evening meals, or a few of them, fighting in Vietnam. It was, as we said, a limited war with universal American participation.

Our job was to support General Vessey's efforts and shape the best policy we could to continue the increasing cooperation the Vietnamese were putting forth. We also had to develop and shape the best mechanism in manpower, expertise, and equipment to support the field activities of the JTF-FA and the identification efforts of USACILHI.

In our view—the Office of the Secretary of Defense—full cooperation on the POW/MIA issue by the Socialist Republic of Vietnam was paramount.

State tended to be more liberal and often politely questioned our definition on cooperation between our field operators and their colleagues from the Vietnam Office of Seeking Missing Personnel, the VNOSMP, as they worked with the teams in the jungled mountains of Vietnam.

In Laos we worked primarily with Department Two, the North American Division of the Ministry of Foreign Affairs. Since it was no secret that Vietnam had thousands of soldiers in Laos during the war, we instituted trilateral meetings with Vietnamese and Lao officials. My estimation was the Lao cooperated grudgingly and minimally; our counterparts and "minders" were generally a captain or major, probably from the Ministry of the Interior, the counterintelligence operators.

We were shut out of Cambodia until 1991 when a tripartite, or more correctly, quadripartite arrangement of government was ratified after the Paris Peace Agreement of that year.

Even in the clubby atmosphere of International Security Affairs, what some called the "State Department of the Defense Department," the angst and atmospherics were far more similar to a gang fight than "collegial interaction within the interagency milieu." (This uncharacteristically florid phrase was coined by Art Gorman, my deputy, a streetwise New York City Marine, who, his colleagues insisted, "normally couldn't spell CAT if you spotted him a C and an A.")

A lot more would happen in EAPR, but a kick start from three photos alleging to be Vietnam POWs still in captivity would ultimately help propel the issue. The photos galvanized and helped make the Senate Select Committee a reality and eventually put us into a windy, cold mountain valley in Tibet. We wouldn't have been able to do that just three years before, looking back on it.

I picked up General Needham at National Airport, and we both went directly to the annual National League of Families meeting in a nearby hotel. We wended our way through security personnel and took our seats as the host prepared to present the honored guest, the president of the United States. Neither Needham nor I had ever seen him in person.

As President Bush began speaking, members in the audience began standing up and turning their backs on the Commander in Chief of the most powerful armed force in the world—the one that beat the Nazi Holocaust in the west, just as the Russian one slaughtered them in the east.

This was the nineteen-year-old man who'd bailed out of his tumbling dive bomber then was plucked from the trackless ocean by the behemoth that had broached like a giant whale, shedding water like the leviathan it was.

He had given the raft's line a seaman's professional toss to the deck and hands had pulled him above. Not until his death would the citizens who'd elected him and the rest of the world see the photograph—film, actually—frozen for a second, short hair plastered down with wet saltwater. A Mae West, the name given the now deflated yellow life jacket, framed him, like a period black-and-white portrait, showing the dazed, joyous grin of the boy who'd just become a man, a warrior.

Heckling broke out in the crowd, like a low hum, growing louder and more distinct. The president continued to try to speak over it but quickly angered. He said something indistinguishable then pleaded for quiet. Amid the shouts of "No more Lies, No More Lies!" the crowd noise grew frenetically. The meeting broke up in a frenzy and the press moved in like sharks. The president disappeared in a scrum of big men in suits and earpieces.

General Needham leaned over to me as the uproar grew louder and asked, "This is pretty bad, isn't it?"

"Sir, this is as bad as it gets," I replied into his ear, like the whispering of two Ranger students on a patrol in the dark.

We were picking our way through the melee when I spotted Ann Mills Griffith, the chairman of the League, circulating, trying to restore some semblance of order. She was calm but moving quickly and resolutely. I hailed her and introduced Brigadier General Needham as the designated new commander of the Joint Task Force–Full Accounting. She turned on a hundred-megawatt smile and shook his hand.

"Sorry to welcome you like this," she said engagingly.

"It looks, uh, exciting," he replied. Needham, an ex-Special Forces NCO and paratroop officer who had fought at Dak To and wore purple hearts, had probably seen some excitement along the way.

"Well, you've just seen some of the League members' frustrations with the government's handling of this issue. Every one of those members has husbands, fathers, sons, or brothers missing, and apparently very little is being done about it. We certainly hope you can get things rolling."

General Needham listened quietly while I bristled; if very little was being done about it, at least it was occurring during fourteen-hour days. "Colonel Jordan has been filling me in; I'll try to get up to speed quickly as I can," he replied.

"We'll talk later," she replied as a Secret Service agent and West Wing aide beckoned to her; she nodded goodbye and was swept away into the throng. A loudspeaker blared something indistinguishable,

"So that's Ms. Griffiths, huh. What's she go by?"

"Sir?"

"What do you call her?"

"We call her Ann."

"Bark worse than her bite?"

"No Sir. Her bark's bad, but her bite is worse."

"Hey, worst they can do is send you back to Vietnam with a bad haircut."

"They're doing that, too, Sir; save me a seat if you would."

We both laughed; probably the only laughing in the hotel then. But it appeared to me that for General Needham the Vietnam War had restarted that day.

The policy through the Johnson administration was keeping a tight rein on intelligence and administration knowledge of what was happening in the Missing and POW circles of the Vietnam conflict. A very bad policy.

Withholding important information from the wives concerning their incarcerated husbands or sons in Vietnam and Laos was a terrible mistake. Just how terrible it was became apparent after Melvin Laird took over the reins as Nixon's first Secretary of Defense in 1969 and was immediately besieged with the Vietnam conflict.

He was a Hawk, but he was also realistic about the Vietnamese issue and probably saw the nationalistic underpinnings of it more from a heartland of America viewpoint than an ideological "us against communism" view. He convinced Nixon to tell the families of the missing virtually everything the administration knew or imagined about the POW/MIA issue—illuminate it with the press while backlighting it against the war. But also bring the beginning of the end by turning over the fighting almost totally to the Army of the Republic of Vietnam.

The National League of the Families of the Missing in Southeast Asia became a potent political force during this time. More important information was coming out of North Vietnam by leftist American visitors than CIA intelligence. Vietnam courted the American left ruthlessly and effectively. When US Navy seaman Doug Hegdahl was released to a US antiwar group with US Navy and Air Force pilots in August 1969, their knowledge was an important intelligence and morale booster. Hegdahl had memorized all the names of the POWs in the Hanoi Hilton and imbedded them in song. Reciting "Old Macdonald" released the names of some two hundred plus men held in captivity in the Hanoi Hilton.

The flames that erupted in the1960s and '70s were still burning when my family and I moved back to our little 1926 Sears house in 1990. I had finally been snared in the Pentagon.

The incident with the president occurred during the second year of that assignment in Washington to the policy office in OSD for POW/MIA Affairs, the East Asia–Pacific Region of International Security Affairs. During this period a number of incidents would influence the issue. They were mostly positive; a few were severely debilitating.

General Vessey's "shuttle diplomacy" was opening the Socialist Republic of Vietnam's eyes to the importance their assistance in moving closer to their goal of normalization with the United States, and I went along on several of these. At first, Hanoi seemed to be the rundown semimetropolis it had been in the late 1980s. The only "westerners" we saw in the streets were Russians and eastern bloc Europeans with their distinctive clothing, haircuts, and hairstyles. Once, finishing with our negotiations earlier than anticipated, one of our Vietnamese colleagues—or opponents—invited us to the Thursday afternoon "tea dance" at a fairly modern hotel a few miles outside of Hanoi. It was shabbily elegant, Eastern European diplomats waltzing with Aeroflot flight attendants while a Vietnamese string quartet played Schubert and Mozart very competently. Outside were cages with some bored bears in them. Always a study of contrasts in Hanoi in those days.

When I switched hats to my Korean and Desert Shield role we were responsible for cajoling our respective countries in the Pacific to join the coalition and fund the effort, now going into serious billion dollar amounts. Korea was one of the hottest situations we worked, but the POW/MIA issue was a close second, with an overtone of letting the families of the missing down always on the print media horizon.

In addition, the Senate Select Committee for POW/MIA Affairs that had begun the summer of 1991 was ongoing and would terminate in January

1993. The witnesses that were dug up and testified were like a living encyclopedia of the issue.

When Desert Shield morphed into Desert Storm with air attacks on January 17 and termination in a cease-fire later on February 28, 1991, the western world was elated, particularly that part containing the thirty-five-member nations of the coalition the that the United States led.

Iraq had been ejected from Kuwait by forces that included even representation from some of the more virulent Islamic states—some we would be fighting barely two decades later, including Syria and Niger. When the US and coalition POWs were released, including two female captives, roughed up but alive and happy to be home, the nation and the world were elated.

Additionally, the Senate Select Committee in 1991 and 1992 had talked to all the luminaries and historical figures in the POW/MIA issue—activists, former principals including Dr. Roger Shields, the Department of Defense principal for POW/MIA Affairs, a well-respected and familiar face, and his counterpart at State, Frank Sieverts, an articulate and well-informed member of many delegations to Hanoi.

Distinguished policy officials like Henry Kissinger and former secretaries of Defense James Schlesinger and Melvin Laird, the latter who rightly argued for bringing the POWs' plight into the open, also testified. President Nixon submitted a letter answering questions posed by the committee. Others included analysts in the Defense Intelligence Agency and National Security Agency.

Family members and prominent members of the League of Families testified, as did many of the activists, including the obvious frauds (who were never indicted or faced with any legal action that resulted in returning the money from their schemes). Significant sensitive cases were discussed, sometimes in closed sessions, as well as testimony in December 1992 by Admiral Larson, USCINCPAC.

Chuck Trowbridge, the professional and effective head of the DIA special office and lightning rod and punching bag of the fervent activists, also testified. It was a thorough wash, rinse, and dry of the issue, and it would conclude there was no evidence of POWs left in Indochina but pointed out several perceived faulty practices of the US government's POW/MIA community.

The decision to declassify the bulk of the reports, interviews, and intelligence with the sources and methods redacted was one of the great benefits of the hearings. The resulting December 1991 McCain Bill, known as Public Law 102-190, specifies files maintained by the Secretary of Defense be made available to the public concerning Missing in Action files with emphasis on reports containing elements of the treatment, location, and condition of the person unaccounted for. It was later amended to include the Korean Conflict and Cold War MIAs also.

This eighteen-month hearing coupled with the successful conclusion of Desert Storm and the return of US and coalition prisoners held by the Iraqis, broke the fever. More than that, it carried through the long-standing objective of additional funding and personnel slots to form a policy arm in the Defense Prisoner and Missing Office (DPMO), including a Deputy Assistant Secretary of Defense for POW/MIA Affairs, and the birth of the JTF-FA. This would be the third incarnation of MACV-SOGs Joint Personnel Recovery Center, and notably the rebirth of the US Army Central Identification Laboratory, Hawaii (USACILHI), with an impressive addition of qualified people, equipment, and missions.

This included creating more personnel for the increasing tempo of recoveries in Indochina and increased physical anthropologists and forensic dentists, plus sufficient staff and support personnel. Secretary Dick Cheney's notation in the margins of our approved request indicated something very important—the JTF-FA's mission was the resolution of those still missing in Indochina.

CILHI's mission was of all America's conflicts—a few years later we reaffirmed that this included those in the theater of China during World War II.

Even in one of its distant, restive, and disputed regions. Disputed by Tibet, at least.

PART THREE

Maturation

The youths of America were diverse and individualistic, some say the rigors of the Depression molded them thusly, but now each had to be blended in a crucible of training, judgment, and cooperation . . . war was now a province of individual riflemen acting in concert drilled in obedience. Aircraft were flown by pilots, but waged war with crews . . . similarly, vessels were sailed by hundreds of sailors, no longer iron men in wooden ships but corporate seamen with steel fiber, searching the sea's skies, surface, and depths for the enemy . . . they were all part of teams, tribes, brotherhoods, families. And they were enraged.

CHAPTER 11

Antagonists

The American spirit is historically and geographically afflicted with international shortsightedness. We are wrapped securely between two vast oceans and two mostly friendly countries (we had battled both, Canada to a standoff as a result of the war of 1812, but we had better military fortune in the Mexican-American War that preceded our own Civil War).

This now-friendly security and comfort belt fuels our frequent misunderstanding and lack of cultural knowledge about our friends. Other nations point out our past history of racism; no surprises there either. We are a monolingual society actually isolated from most of the world. At least we were in the ancient predigital age. This historical isolation also means we tend to unfortunately underrate our adversaries. While we had a nominal respect for the fighting ability of the Germans in World War II, we had disdain for the Japanese, particularly their airmen. The change in that attitude by the naval pilots of the Marines and Navy was part of the maturing process of the combatants—on both sides.

We had a similar disdain for North Korean and Chinese Peoples' "Volunteers" in November 1950, until they started coming in waves in the flickering light of mortar and artillery flares over snowfields, some without weapons until they could find one on the battlefield. We also underrated the will of North Vietnam and their military abilities—at least initially.

One of Japan's best pilots, Saburo Sakai, was a descendant of a family of Samurai. Born in 1916, he enlisted as a seaman in the Imperial Japanese Navy in his teens, eventually going on to flight school and becoming a fighter pilot—a naval aviator who never flew off a carrier, and never was an officer.

During the war with China in 1938, Sakai was flying an A5M Navy Type 96 fighter and was slightly wounded in the following year—two years before the first American pilot died in aerial combat. Pilots from many allied or neutral nations flew in the RAF, including eight Americans, some claiming to be Canadians, since the Neutrality Act imposed severe penalties, including imprisonment, for fighting in foreign forces. Six of those Americans died during the Battle of Britain.[1]

In Oct 1939, Sakai shot down a Russian-built DB-3 bomber over China, and a few months later in 1940, he was among those chosen to fly the new A6M Zero fighters in field tests in combat against Chinese forces.

On December 8, 1941, as a member of Tainan Air Group based in Taiwan, he flew one of the forty-five formidable A6M Zero fighters from his unit against Clark Airfield in the Philippine Islands, downing a P-40 Warhawk fighter during that mission. Two days later he shot down the B-17 Flying Fortress piloted by Captain Colin P. Kelly, the first B-17 to be lost in aerial combat and an American loss that galvanized the American public.

With his ship crippled by Sakai's relentless firing passes, Kelly ordered his crew to bail out then remained at the controls to try to save the precious bomber; he died in the ensuing crash. Kelly received the second highest award for gallantry, the Distinguished Service Cross, and provided another furious incentive for the American people against the Emperor of Japan and his forces.

In early 1942, Sakai was transferred to Tarakan Island in Borneo and fought in the Dutch East Indies, by now a familiar area and target for the bombs of Fulton's bomber. In one incident the young Japanese aviator allowed a Dutch DC-3 passenger aircraft to pass unharmed after he spotted a woman with a child through one of the passenger windows, despite orders to shoot down all allied aircraft, combatant or not. These acts of humanity and kindness were rare in early 1942.

In the months of carnage beginning with the Nanking Massacre in 1937, Japanese brutality knew no limits, as British forces and civilians in Singapore and Hong Kong soon discovered. The code of Bushido, the Samurai code that drove the Japanese military to view any prisoners as subhuman, demanded that its practitioners die in combat. Surrender was unthinkable. Prisoners to the Japanese, particularly at the campaign level, were chattel used to build railway bridges under inhumane conditions in Thailand and to be used for bayonet practice in Nanking.

The United States was well aware there were monsters at the edge of the map.

National mobilization was transpiring frenetically and effectively, in both personnel and materiel. Passage of the Selective Service and Training Act in September 1940 showed that the United States was ready to match its mobilization materiel with manpower, even in an election year.

The Army reached its intended strength of 1.5 million midway through 1941 and had thirty-four divisions. (Just after Pearl Harbor, Congress amended the draft law, lengthening the term of service from one year to the duration plus six months and extending registration to all males between eighteen and sixty-five, with those between twenty and forty-five eligible for the draft.) All the while, final goals for recruitment became interim goals. By the end of 1942, the Army's strength was at 5.4 million.[2]

Lags in cantonment construction forced the War Department to slow enlistments and delayed the federalization of the National Guard. Only in the Soviet Union was the pace this furious and chaotic, although the Soviets easily beat our chaos as they were fighting Germans hand to hand near Moscow.

But American fighter pilots were coming on strong, initially Navy and Marine in the Pacific, then as the twin-engine P-38 Lightnings, P-51 Mustangs, and P-47 Thunderbolts arrived in theater, Fulton's brother Army Air Force knights came to cross lances with the airmen of the Rising Sun.

Edward "Butch" O'Hare, flying an F4F Wildcat fighter near Rabaul off the carrier *Lexington* would be an early ace and the first naval aviator awarded the Medal of Honor for saving his carrier. The young Naval Academy graduate downed five Japanese bombers and damaged another en route to the *Lexington* and its battle group. A year later he was shot down and died in combat, probably by a friendly airplane.

One of America's major airports—O'Hare Field in Chicago—was named for the young lieutenant, and the type of plane he flew, the Grumman F4F, hangs from the ceiling in one of the airport's corridors.

Ironically, O'Hare's father was a lawyer consigliere to Al Capone, and died violently himself, shot to death in his car probably by Capone's mob for furnishing information to authorities that put America's most notorious gangster in jail.

O'Hare's squadron commander, Lieutenant Commander John S. Thach, had worked out a maneuver to dampen the effectiveness of the new Zero that basically changed three planes in loose combat formation into two deadly ones, flying a continuous weaving pattern that turned the second "enemy" plane into the trailing "friendly" shooter. The "Thach Weave" was highly effective and was used throughout the Pacific war from shortly after Pearl Harbor to VJ Day.

The fabled shortcomings of Japanese pilots were just that, fabled. But the ingenuity of a few Navy and Marine fighter pilots coupled with their legendary courage sent many a Japanese fighter and bomber plunging into the sea aflame.

Army Major Richard Bong, America's highest scoring ace of any war, also flew in the Pacific. Flying the twin-engine P-38 Lightning, Bong downed forty Japanese aircraft and received the Medal of Honor before dying as a test pilot in a P-80 jet at the war's end. His aircraft flamed out and crashed in downtown Hollywood, California, after his fatal ejection.

The capture of Henderson Field on Guadalcanal in August 1942 would see more American aces—Joe Foss, executive officer of Marine fighter squadron VMF 121, and Gregory "Pappy" Boyington, later commanding officer of VMF 214, the famed "Black Sheep" Squadron. Both Marine fighter pilots downed nearly thirty Japanese aircraft apiece and were awarded the Medal of Honor.

Gregory "Pappy" Boyington was one of the legendary "Flying Tigers"—American pilots who had resigned their commissions to travel to China and fight under Claire Chennault, one of the iconic figures of the China Burma India Theater. They had drawn and tasted Japanese blood a few days before Christmas 1941, breaking up a bomber attack probably aimed at Rangoon.

The American Volunteer Group (AVG) was a surreptitious attempt to bolster China's morale by allowing American combat pilots to fly as civilians against the Japanese. Boyington, of northern Cheyenne heritage, was a drinker and brawler from the Pacific Northwest. He "resigned" his Marine commission in August 1941 to join the Central Aircraft Manufacturing Company (CAMCO), which was the cover corporation for President Roosevelt's quietly sanctioned band of volunteers who were paid $600 a month and a $500 bounty for every Japanese plane destroyed. Boyington was credited with downing 3.5 Japanese planes over Burma and China as a Flying Tiger, flying P-40 Tomahawks that had been transferred from a batch destined for lend-lease to the British.[3]

US pilots also had flown for the Spanish Republican Air Force (called Communist, or Left Wing, Socialist, and such to distinguish it from the General Franco's Fascist-leaning opposition force), but without US government backing. The "Yankee Squadron" rapidly fell apart and the mercenary pilots returned to the United States in a wave of lawsuits for pay.

The British didn't complain—the United States promised them a one-for-one replacement of the P-40 Tomahawk with the advanced model due off the assembly line soon. With lend-lease in full swing since March 1941 and FDR getting his sea legs as the nation drifted toward war, FDR issued an unpublished presidential Executive Order calling for the establishment of a Special Air Unit consisting of three groups—initially a first group with 100 P-40B fighters, a second bomber group with approximately 120 light bombers evenly divided between Lockheed Hudsons and Boeing DB-7s, which would later gain fame in the Pacific theater as the A-20 Havoc. The third group was envisioned as another fighter group, but Pearl Harbor curtailed all but the fielding of the first group, and it was short-lived. The group's overall effect on the Japanese Army and Navy air forces was probably less than the morale boost it gave for the American and Chinese people.

The commander of the AVG was retired Army Air Force captain, Claire Chennault. During the interwar period he was famous for his single-engine fighter enthusiasm and his flying skill. His enthusiasm was a little too much for senior bomber mavens in the AAF, and he was medically retired, for among other things, hearing loss—hardly surprising from being in open cockpit, high-powered fighters. As an advisor and trainer to the Chinese Air Force, Chennault won over Chiang Kai-shek and Madame Chiang as an apostle for airpower for China.

The Flying Tigers consisted of about eighty pilots and the same number of P-40B aircraft, plus a strong maintenance support team, as 1941 ended with the surprising Pearl Harbor attack.

The aerial Tigers mauled a Japanese bomber force coming from their base in Indochina to bomb Rangoon on December 20, 1941. Shortly after the Japanese bombed Pearl Harbor, the AVG was now combat ready. Chennault moved a squadron (Hell's Angels) to Kunming to defend the Burma Road on December 20. The Japanese sent a force to bomb Rangoon, and the AVG shot down four aircraft with no losses of their own while breaking up the attack.

On the twenty-third, the Japanese struck again and the Tigers shot down eight more of the enemy while losing three of their own.[4] On Christmas Day 1941, the Japanese Air Force sent sixty-three bombers escorted by twenty-five fighters to attack again; they were met by a force of just fourteen P-40s. The AVG ripped into the Japanese formations, shooting down a combination of thirty-five bombers and fighters with a loss of five of their own.

The combat continued into 1942 as the AVG found itself consistently outnumbered by the superior Japanese, and although the Chinese and Allies were pushed back, the AVG took a toll from the attacking Japanese pilots. The AVG maintained a superior kill ratio to the enemy and far beyond anyone else in the theater. Chennault had trained them well—not to tangle with the nimble Japanese Zeros in dogfights. In their lighter, unarmored aircraft they could outturn the heavier American "War hawks." Instead, the US pilots were taught to get above enemy formations and dive through them, use their superior weight and speed, then pull away, perhaps into a cloud bank and climb back above them and repeat the deadly procedure.

Nineteen AVG pilots became Aces while in the service of the Chinese. They were probably among the first American military contractors, employed by the Chinese air force and flying, by then, obsolete P-40Bs with Chinese air force national insignia. They destroyed 297 Japanese aircraft, both in the air and on the ground, before they were disbanded and reverted back into their previous service as pilots or going directly into Chennault's new command, the China Air Task Force. Some went to work for the China National Aviation Corporation (CNAC), a commercial Chinese company with their American partner, Pan American Airlines. Sixteen "Tigers" were lost in aerial combat, to bombing raids, and to training accidents.

The American Volunteer Group was in combat from December 1941 until their disestablishment in July 1942; they gave the Japanese their first taste of American airmen's courage and skill.

By May 1942, three months after Fulton's B-17E joined the aerial dual, the battle of the Coral Sea exploded, an event that put the Australians very much on edge. In terms of a naval slugging match it was strange. It was the first naval battle in which the combatants were carriers and the weapons were aircraft. The US pilots' newness to combat showed—they bombed destroyers they thought were cruisers and reported them as such.

The Coral Sea covered the Great Barrier Reef in far northeast Australia, the aerial "stomping ground" of all those "scattered quail" fleeing the Philippines, getting fuel wherever they could and eventually coming back into MacArthur's Southwest Pacific Command (SWPAC); Fulton Lanier and his crew were now part of them.

While the Tigers were giving the Japanese an aerial bloody nose, Fulton Lanier and his crew and squadron were striking targets in occupied Java, Papua New Guinea, and the Solomon Islands, paving the way for the seaborne invasion of Guadalcanal, Tulagi, and other vital islands that would provide coral airfields—earthbound carrier decks. Another aerial strike would come from a fictional mountain abode: Shangri-La.

April 18, 1942, midmorning, 33 degrees north, 154 degrees east, central Pacific Ocean about 750 miles from Japanese mainland targets

The US Navy carrier *Hornet* turned into the gale as sailors pushed the aircraft into position. One of *Hornet*'s escorts, the cruiser *Nashville*, had sent the *Nita Maru* fishing-vessel-cum-picket-scout to the bottom, but the flotilla was still nearly 200 miles short of her goal—another hour of flying time not counted on with aviation fuel shoehorned into their tanks and recovery airfields in China barely within reach. Unsure if the fishing boat had managed to radio back to her Japanese Navy bosses (it had) and with another suspected enemy combatant surface vessel spotted, Admiral Halsey radioed Captain Mitscher to immediately launch the aircraft.

A Japanese pilot would have been dumbstruck at the sight—sixteen B-25 medium bombers on a crowded American carrier deck. Now the landing signal officer (LSO) signaled the first aircraft piloted by Lieutenant Colonel James "Jimmy" Doolittle into takeoff position on the crowded carrier deck. The president had decreed, almost while the below deck ammunition was still exploding at Pearl Harbor, that bombs should fall on Japan as quickly as possible, and possible was a bold plan about to be executed on April 18, 1942.

The LSO's flag spun overhead in increasingly frantic circles as Doolittle and his copilot stood on the brakes and pushed the throttles and propeller controls forward to the stops. All sixteen B-25s were cranked by now, thirty-two Wright Cyclone R-2600 engines developing over 54,000 horsepower, their thunderous roars drowning out the pitching wind and booming waves as they ran down their pre-takeoff checklist. They couldn't quite drown out the screaming, hat-waving cheers of the thousand *Hornet* sailors or so waiting—hoping—for them all to get safely airborne. They were watching them from every place on the ship they could squeeze into. Officers and sailors on her escort ships were doing the same. Others were silently, intently watching the radar that would signal aerial trouble lurking above or on the horizon.

Then, as the keening wind and waves pitched ship and deck to the optimum angle, the flag snapped down. The LSO and his radioman dropped to a knee as the first plane gathered speed, the wing passing over them, and Doolittle's bomber suddenly cleared the ship, pointing nose first into the sky.

Barely seconds later, World War I combat and test pilot, winner of numerous air and motor races Doolittle made a 180-degree turn and screamed over the ship's bridge at masthead level, climbing to wait for the rest of his covey of revenging bombers to join up. The sailors screamed louder. One by one the remaining fifteen aircraft lifted off and joined up into elements to strike Tokyo, Nagoya, Osaka, Yokosuka, Yokohama, and Kobe.[5] The commander in chief's "bombs falling on Tokyo" raid was underway.

The second aircraft had dipped precariously out of sight then emerged flying a few feet above the waves. He had forgotten to drop his flaps. Militarily speaking, the raid was a pinprick, although the bundled incendiaries in their small bomb loads would give the Japanese a foretaste of what was to come. The unexpected launch caused the planes to run dry short of their intended recovery fields, some crash landing, some crews bailing out into a driving storm.

One crew landed in Vladivostok and was interned by the Russians temporarily, before "escaping." Three of the captive crew died by a Japanese executioner's sword. The un-nerved Japanese looked at some of their island objectives and nervously relooked for the phantom American carriers. The *Kempetai*, the Japanese police, did their cruel work, and there was an orgy of destruction in the areas where the population assisted the crews, particularly along the crowded southeast Chinese coast. Possible airfields were razed, a lesson the Japanese learned well and used later in Burma to counter Chennault's Air Task Force.

A puckish Roosevelt responded to the question of where the mysterious but welcome raiders launched their attack: Shangri-La, the setting for James Hilton's 1933 novel and 1937 film, *Lost Horizon*.[6]

More than military planes plowed the Asia-Pacific skies; the Chinese American airline mentioned earlier, CNAC, China National Aviation Corporation, with 45 percent ownership by Juan Trippe's Pan American Airways, had established passenger routes through northeast and southeast Asia for nearly two decades before war between Japan and China. CNAC would also play a large role in the later China-Burma-India Theater.

From its inception and launch in the 1920s it did a lion's share of passenger and cargo movement throughout with minimal equipment, especially aircraft, rarely having more than two dozen flying, and not all flying at a given time. Some would be in maintenance, waiting to get back into the sky. With American, Chinese, and Chinese American pilots and maintenance personnel, CNAC left a footprint in Chinese aviation history much larger and more significant than its size. They were first to fly the Hump, then they pioneered routes both north and south across Burma into southwest China, where the Nationalists of Chiang Kai-shek had steadily retreated after their capital, Nanking, fell to the Japanese in 1937.

Significantly, the Tenth Air Force moved into India from staff remnants, crews, and aircraft from the Philippines and took military control of the airlift; the first "Hump" mission was the delivery of fuel into China for Doolittle's sixteen B-25s, which were slated for turnover to the Chinese Air Force.[7] The fuel was flown by Pan American pilots from the Africa run, but they were wearing CNAC uniforms, and the B-25s had vanished into southeast China, wrecked along the coast or farther inland, while the Soviets pored over the one interned in Vladivostok.

More than one aerial route was required, they felt, because the Japanese were flowing northeast. If sufficient Japanese forces, particularly motorized and light infantry coupled with armor backed by air support, struck and held central Burma, there would be military chaos in the entire CBI. Central Burma was like the center of a clock face, they could go east into Yunnan, seize the capital and squeeze Chiang for a negotiated settlement—highly favorable to the Emperor's forces. They wanted all of Burma, so they could cut the precarious allied supply chain that delivered goods into the Bay of Bengal. Here it could travel by air, rail, or poorly maintained roads to the northeast Indian state of Assam. Then across Burma to the embarkation point of the Burma Road at Lashio. Then, and only then, they would have the Kuomintang forces of Chiang encircled.

Passengers and cargo largely traveled by air, and since roads were rudimentary in China, much of CNAC's earlier passengers flew on Amphibians or Flying Boats, using the rivers as airports. CNAC pioneered airmail with small single engine planes, including the ubiquitous Cessna 195s, for getting in and out of short, rough fields in the interior of China, and the latest Douglas twin-engine passenger DC-2s and DC-3s for up to fifteen passengers to the major cities of China, Indochina, and Hong Kong.

Much of this was due to CNAC dynamic and farsighted vice president, William Langhorne Bond. Once Bond came aboard CNAC in 1930, he immediately started familiarizing himself with aviation (he had civilian pilot experience but never to the level of air airline qualification) and Chinese business practices. The airline's "dragon" sobriquet came from Chinese peasants likening the aircraft to "flying dragons."

Rarely numbering more than two dozen aircraft, CNAC employed native Chinese pilots and crews; Chinese American pilots (who despite being born and raised in America, were paid the same lower salaries as their native Chinese counterparts), and American pilots with a flair for adventurous flying. Any flying in China was dangerous after the Japanese initiated hostilities in 1937. The Kweilin incident in 1938 was the first airliner ever shot down.

A CNAC DC-2 named the *Kweilin* with fifteen passengers was fired on by Japanese planes shortly after leaving British Hong Kong and entering Chinese airspace. The pilot, Hugh Woods, who would go on to become chief pilot, skillfully put his plane down in the only level place possible, a river. The Japanese continued to strafe the aircraft, killing everyone aboard. Woods, the only swimmer on the aircraft, had made his way to the bank to get assistance and survived by ducking under the water as the Japanese continued to target him by strafing. The Japanese later apologized and paid indemnity, claiming they had mistaken the *Kweilin* for a military aircraft. They had used the same excuse a year earlier when they sank the US gunboat the *Panay*, paying indemnity and saying they hadn't seen the American flags clearly identifiable on the plucky craft. War chased CNAC from city to city, initially during Japan's war with China.

Shanghai fell in 1937 and CNAC's existence and movement throughout the 1930s and 1940s might be divided into segments depending on the base of operations. It started in the international city, Shanghai, with its Bund, of European-styled buildings, and remained there until mid-1937 when the Japanese invaded China. The next base was in British Hong Kong until Pearl Harbor, December 1941; shortly afterward Hong Kong was occupied by the Japanese. During the war years of 1942 through 1945, Calcutta was headquarters. The move back to Shanghai was made early in 1946, where it remained until the Communist takeover.

As more men, materiel, pilots, and airplanes flowed into the southwest Pacific, the exhausted Ninety-Third Squadron of the Nineteenth Bomb Group was alerted that they would be ferrying the airplanes back to the United States. It was fall in America, sweaters and football season approached North Carolina as Fulton packed his B-4 bag—he was going back to teach others to fly and fight the B-17E; he was a full-blooded veteran and it was time for it to rub off on pilots training to do the same as he had done. He was leaned out, weathered by combat but still possessed of an indomitable spirit, humor, and zest for life. He was particularly considerate of his crews, especially the "youngsters," even though he might fly with them only once or twice as crew rotation and duties prevented any kind of permanent affiliation.

Fulton Lanier's logbook contained a carefully maintained 580-plus hours in less than two years as a pilot, over half of it in combat, flying off dusty or muddy airfields with unsure maintenance, mosquitoes, and crushing heat and humidity. Although he didn't know it, after a short sojourn as a flight instructor, he was destined for another vital "back-water" in the war, and some of the deadliest flying any pilot would ever experience. As yet unnamed, it would become the China Burma India theater. Its aerial focal point was the "'Hump," the Himalayan chain that rose unforgivingly out of the dank rainforests to snowcapped mountains 15,000 or more feet high along a route laced with wind, rain, turbulence, and ice—a Götterdämmerung quartet of the phenomena that plagued aircrews.[8]

He ferried a B-17E from Hawaii to San Francisco, arriving just before Thanksgiving 1942; a laconic remark in the logbook: "flew completely around the world in a B-17."[9] Back in North Carolina, Fulton unwound with his buddy, D. K., roaring around the county, seeing old friends, attending football games, and generally shaking off the physical, mental, and emotional baggage of war. His prewar boyish spirit was in full throttle, with a little wilder tint—he shot the glass globes off the weathervanes on the roof of his grandmother's house, then promised to replace them.[10]

No one could stay angry at the engaging, brown-eyed pilot, and Christmas 1942 would be joyous for Lanier and his family. After a refresher instrument course and instructor training in Pocatello, Idaho, he made the long journey out to Monahans, Texas.

Construction of Pyote Army Air Field was just being completed when he arrived in January 1943. It was nicknamed "Rattlesnake Bomber Base" for the large dens of western diamondback rattlesnakes that had been unearthed in the erection of the sprawling west Texas complex; it was desolate, dusty, and nowhere—almost 250 miles east of El Paso and 400 miles west of Dallas, it offered nothing for Lanier but flying. There was evidence that he wasn't happy at Pyote—pictures of him in the right seat of a B-17 (the copilot's seat was also the instructor pilot's seat) depict him scowling, and most likely bored.

The treeless arid plains around Monahans were probably as depressing as the monotony of checking low-time noncombat flyers out in the B-17.

His logbook continues:

May 26, 1943—"bad storm, turned back . . ."

May 27, 1943—"Lost engine . . ."

Letters home probably frightened his family and friends—they were full of incidents "where they tried to kill me and them both . . ."

Ground truth was the fact that Lanier missed combat. To a seasoned combat veteran like Fulton, Pyote and Monahans must have been purgatory—he wangled another overseas assignment, arriving in the northeastern Indian state of Assam at a bare-bones airfield named Jorhat in the summer of 1943. He was flying the right seat as a copilot in a C-47. Soon he would be in the left seat, but in a land of cobras, not rattlesnakes.

CHAPTER 12

Over the "Rockpile"

The flights that the China National Aviation Corporation pioneered over the Hump in 1940 and 1941 were flown out of business necessity. The Japanese had nearly squeezed them out of the sky, so they began flying in the safety of darkness.

Hong Kong had necessitated this; the British dominion was a safe haven, and CNAC had retreated there after the Rising Sun had made China's skies exceedingly dangerous. Soon Hong Kong would be bombed on December 8, 1941. Across the International Date Line, it was December 7 at Pearl Harbor, and CNAC would move its operation to Calcutta, where their headquarters remained until the Japanese were defeated. But from late 1940 until December 1941 they lifted out of the safety of British airspace into the dangers of Japanese fighters barely twenty minutes away over the New Territories—Chinese airspace where Japanese aerial marauders made an airliner tempting bait for the Japanese fighters.

CNAC began to fly only at night when and where the Japanese Navy or Army Air Force was a threat. They swarmed out of safe havens like bats in the dark. Airfields in China were lit with low light smudge pots, marking thresholds and ends of the runways by CNAC ground crews. CNAC had a regular Rangoon-to-Chongqing route that included service to Lashio en route, but Bond worried that Burma, particularly Lashio, might be untenable with the Japanese now flying from Vichy Indochina and rapidly encroaching the Bay of Bengal and Rangoon.

Who made the first flight over the Hump depends on what source you read. A much-ballyhooed flight with CNAC executives and British and Chinese officers was purported to have made the first flight at the end of November 1941. Plating points out that CNAC executive William Langhorne Bond made a similar flight a year earlier, in November 1940, when he traveled by car from Mandalay to Lashio then on to Myitkyina (pronounced Me-chee-naw—simply called 'Mitch" by westerners), the northernmost stop on the rail line from Rangoon.

He returned to Lashio and linked up with Chief Pilot Hugh Woods, the luckless captain of the shot-down *Kweilin*, and they flew back north over "Mitch" then on to Putao, or Fort Hertz as it was known by the British. Then they'd turned southeast into China, finally landing in Chongqing, the wartime capital. They'd managed to safely hold their altitude just below 15,000 feet over the high terrain in the reasonably clear winter weather.

But both Woods and Bond were unpleasantly surprised at the inaccurate maps. In instrument conditions this would be very hazardous flying. Other CNAC pilots probed the routes also. A few months after Woods and Bond's flight, pilot Wu Shi flew a similar track, up the Irrawaddy to Fort Hertz noting the same map discrepancies and verifying this would be a hazardous undertaking in bad weather. Bond, anticipating that one day Burma might be in the hands of the Japanese, had Captain Xia Pu fly from Dinjan, a British airfield in northern Assam, to Kunming, the city that would be a major eastern terminus of the Hump route. This could also be designated as the first flight that hundreds of others would fly from bases in Assam to Kunming, the primary Chinese transit point for both cargo and passengers.

Assam would eventually be dotted with airfields as the Hump germinated and matured. Right now, there were few. Gandhi's "Quit India" campaign was making it difficult to recruit workers for construction, and of course there was the May–October monsoons, which rendered any construction problematic at best, impossible at worst. These were fortuitous, far-sighted flights, and they enhanced CNAC's and Bond's reputation with the decision-makers, particularly after the Army Air Forces were skeptical of the air route into China.

Brigadier General Clayton Bissel, Stilwell's air chief, was one of the gloomiest critics, which was not surprising in the absence of everything an airplane needs—airfields, maintenance, navigation aids, and even airplanes themselves. But CNAC proved it could be done—they had done it and hadn't lost any aircraft or crews on the Hump—yet.

By March 1942 the Tenth Air Force had been activated and moved to India; one of its first Hump missions was to fly fuel and oil to China for Doolittle's Raiders—the bombers were to be refueled, flown to safe locations, and turned over to the Chinese. The pilots were Pan Am, in CNAC uniforms.

Typically, a flight from one of the northernmost bases in Assam, such as Dinjan, Sookerating in northern Assam, or the lyrical Almanir Hat to the west, with altitudes in the Brahmaputra River valley measured in scant hundreds of feet, headed east toward China over mountains reaching nearly 15,000 feet. Rising terrain to the south formed by the Khasi and Naga hills gave way to the 10,000 feet Paktai range, marking the border between India and Burma.[1]

Continuing east over the Chindwin River valley, the Kumon range climbed to over 14,000 feet before sloping back down to the West Irrawaddy river valley leading to Fort Hertz. This British installation was a major navigational checkpoint, followed by a series of ranges approaching 15,000 feet.

Some of the major rivers of Asia, the Irrawaddy, Salween, and Mekong, originated in Tibet and flowed around and through the Sanstung range at 14,000 feet before gradually drifting down as the route arced gently to the southeast. Then, familiar Chinese landmarks such as Mount Dali and the Yangtze River appeared. Shortly thereafter, an approach was made into Kunming, sitting at nearly 7,000 feet.

So, while airlifters were not flying directly over the Himalayas, the mountain chain's presence determined the four significant weather phenomena that affected their flight—wind, rain, ice, and turbulence.[2] Together, the phenomena of terrain and weather, coupled with inexperienced US pilots and the occasional Japanese fighter, made the "noncombat" Hump a significant hazard. The brass, in an attempt to minimize the psychological danger to nervous inexperienced pilots, attempted to change the name to "the Hill."[3]

The pilots, with typical American insouciance, nicknamed it the "Rockpile."

The Himalayas, the highest mountain chain in the world, shaped the weather in a great arc from the Bay of Bengal upward through India, northern China, and on out to the South China Sea, east of Vietnam. It shielded much of India from year-round precipitation but aided in the formation of seasonal monsoons. The great Tibetan Plateau's mean elevation of over 13,000 feet blocks climactic circulation in the Indian Ocean and restricts moisture from some places in northern Asia, causing desertification, such as the Gobi.

A great altitude variation existed from the near sea level of the Assam Valley departure airfields to the higher altitudes of southwest China, including Kunming's near mile and a half altitude. Coupled with a series of high ranges barely one hundred miles north of Sookerating ("Sook") required a high degree of piloting skill to get the overloaded aircraft up to safely cross ranges 14,000 to 15,000 feet above sea level. High pressure systems coming out of Siberia affected much of western China. The south Asia low pressure fronts collided and produced spectacular thunderstorms, some reaching above the altitude capability of the aircraft flying through them.[4]

Because of the weather challenges, the C-87 could be a difficult aircraft to fly, particularly with relatively low-time crews. The aircraft had the distressing habit of losing all cockpit electrical power on takeoff or at landings, while its engine power and reliability with the less-powerful superchargers often left much to be desired. It proved to be quite vulnerable to icing conditions and was prone to fall into a spin with even small amounts of ice accumulated onto its Davis wing, long thin airfoils designed for efficiency at high altitudes. Weather could overcome the most advanced aircraft engineering techniques in the world. It could simply encase its airfoils in ice, leaving the aircraft with all the flying characteristics of a bowling ball.

Ice could do other wicked things, also. Captain Charles "Ridge" Hammel, a Pan American veteran captain, was paired as pilot to copilot C. J. "Joe" Rosbert in April 1943. They were experienced pilots. Rosbert, a former Marine and veteran of the American Volunteer Group, was an up-and-coming China National Airways Corporation executive as well as a skilled pilot, even though most of his previous time had been in single-engine fighters. Hammel was one of the famous long-distance Pan American Airlines veterans of Africa, who skillfully used the winds aloft to extend an aircraft's fuel and distance over the trackless African wilderness.

"A past master of desert flying, he distrusted this land of three-mile-high peaks," Rosbert explained.[5]

Now he was one of a group brought together by the pressing need for experienced pilots to fly the Hump, and Pan American owned a substantial share of CNAC. Only they were blown by a fierce blizzard northwest up over the Naga Hills to the border with Tibet, and ice coated their forward windscreen, growing quickly and completely robbing their vision. They had long been on instruments when Rosbert placed bare hands over the windshield, creating a small hole, just in time to see a large mountain looming. The former Flying Tiger grabbed the control yoke and banked the C-47 into a sharp turn, too late. The aircraft caromed along the side of the mountain, tearing both wings off the aircraft before it stopped. Immediately, the wreckage was struck by the swirling snow of a blizzard, 16,000 feet up the mountain.

The third member of the crew, Chinese radio operator Li Wong, died in the crash, his neck broken. Hammel was cut badly about the face and hands, his right eyed closed, his left ankle damaged. Rosbert's left ankle was severely broken—his foot lying at a right angle to it, the pain breathtaking. They shivered in the aircraft wrapped in parachutes until the blizzard played out, then ripped aluminum panels off the aircraft to fashion makeshift sleds and tobogganed down the mountain. Eventually they reached a river far below the crash site, ran into a tribe of Mishmi natives who cared for them until a British medical officer with a patrol found them and got them back to India, nearly fifty days later. They both survived to fly again, but Hammel was later killed in a crash.

CNAC pilots were not only experienced, proficient pilots, they also had good weather sense. Ice like Rosbert and Hammel experienced was inevitable. Today, icing levels are a routine item in preflight weather briefings, but in the wartime flying over the Himalayas weather briefings were not available. Still, the weather-wise pilots knew how to seek out the warmer altitudes when icing began to coat the control surfaces. They watched the outside air temperature gauges, seeking warmer air beneath layers of altitude until the ice melted and loosened from control surfaces and propellers. The thawing ice pounded the fuselage like trip hammers.

Similarly, carburetor icing could be fought with the throttles, jockeying them full open and closed, causing backfires that would sometimes break the ice loose in the starving engines. Those were techniques that came from the depths of logbooks with thousands of hours flying experience in them. But they were largely logbooks that belonged solely to civilian airline pilots.

The best chronicler of the Hump as a noncombat theater was author Ernest K. Gann. Gann was a Hemingway-like adventurer, wanderer, sailor, airline pilot, and, ultimately, best-selling author who ferried a troubled C-87 over the Atlantic, through Africa, and across the sand-storm-swept Middle East to Assam.

This project was an operation known as Project 7A to ferry American Airline pilots and planes to the CBI for temporary flying assignments. Gann ultimately wound up in Chabua, India, a major Hump base and operations center and was swept up into the military-civilian stew of pilots and crews challenging the world's highest mountains and worst weather. He flew a Hump flight as copilot to a competent Army Major Sweeney from

Chabua to Kunming and return. We pick up his story, as Gann makes the landing:

> "We break out of the overcast to the east of Chabua, pick up the Brahmaputra River . . . and I start the descent . . . by the time I signal the landing gear down we are sodden with sweat . . . now near the center of the field we can see a column of black smoke curling upward." Sweeney shakes his head and his lips tighten. "Let's get down. Someone's bought it."
>
> "I tighten the leisurely approach for the source of the smoke is unmistakably a C-47. It sprawls flat on its belly just to one side of the runway. There are flames licking at the base of the smoke. A number of men are milling about the plane. . . . we land through the smoke and roll past the burning aircraft . . ." Sweeney leaves me at once with the explanation that he must do what he can.
>
> One airplane lands through the smoke; two others take off in succession disappearing for a moment as they pass through its writhing column. Such nonchalance is hard to understand and I wonder if I could do the same if the men my known and valued comrades . . .
>
> The major returns in a jeep, smiling, "they got out all right. Everybody okay. I told those damn kids not to be in such a rush to raise their gear, but they never listen." He told me the pilots were recently arrived and were both twenty-two years old.
>
> I wondered if they would make twenty-three and asked what happened.
>
> "Lost one engine just as they broke ground."
>
> There is no fire-fighting equipment at Chabua so the C-47 is simply left to burn itself out . . . even the plane's young pilots have lost interest and left the scene.

They receive a report that another C-87 was lost earlier that morning, just after they had departed for China. Nobody knew what happened—eleven men aboard:

> Seeking a drink of whisky from Gann's friend from airline days, Major Clark, the base operations officer, they wait to cross the runway as another C-47 takes off, climbs steeply with the landing gear still down . . .
>
> Gann continues: "The C-47 approximates a steep climb; I assume the airplane must be empty . . . otherwise the pilot is asking a great deal of a C-47 . . . there is a distinct backfiring from the right engine. The sickening sound multiplies upon itself.
>
> "I know instinctively that the pilot is going to lose that engine—or perhaps he is only simulating a loss and will at once return it to power. Surely if this is the real thing he will shove the nose down and land again.
>
> "There is ample length of runway remaining and the gear has not been retracted. We watch, fascinated but not yet truly concerned. Sweeney and I

are like old medics watching critically from the gallery while an intern performs his very first very simple operation.

"The plane passes us, faltering, sinking to perhaps fifty feet. 'Come on, son! Do something!' A C-47 is the most air-kindly and forgiving of all airplanes, but you must not abuse it. You have time, but not all the time in the world!

"And then, suddenly to our horror, there is no time. The C-47 seems to swerve toward us, then banks abruptly away. It hangs in the air, the wings tilt, and it plunges toward the earth at an oblique angle. The wheels are still down. It hits the runway, bounces crazily into the air again, and comes down hard on the right wing tip. Instantly it is torn from the runway and plunges nose first into a high mud embankment on the opposite side.

"The hollow-rending carumph as it hits is an awful sound, then for an instant there is an uncanny silence.

"Sweeney and I are stunned and still disbelieving our eyes when the silence is torn by a cannonade of explosions.

"Great sheets of flame blossom from the cloud of dust. All this has taken place no more than two hundred yards from where we sit in the jeep. We could cover the distance in seconds.

"But we sit motionless and undoing, thinking of nothing but that first, frightful impact. Our mouths are open, our eyes staring. There are no obedient muscles in our bodies, and our brains are paralyzed.

"Sweeney groans—a deep, agonized exhalation of air and strangled sound from his inner being. The pilots are dead. We do not even consider the possibility of their survival because the nose of the airplane is telescoped back until the engines are smashed against the mud bank . . . the aircraft, full of ammunition, explodes.

"The pilots are dead; four of the five passengers survive the crash."

Gann and Sweeney, dispirited and full of self-loathing for not reacting immediately to try to save the crew, now badly need to see Clark and perhaps get a drink of whiskey. While talking to him a sergeant enters the office and tells them of another crash just minutes ago—a C-87 "back in the tea patch with eighteen souls on board"—all lost, for no explicable reason.

Clark silently pours a sliver of whisky each into three tumblers and announces, "Great place isn't it."

Gann: "We drink. By my count, thirty-two men gone. And four airplanes. It is only five o'clock in the afternoon. The Hump. Not to be confused with a combat operation."[6]

It is, unfortunately, the malevolent classroom of all Hump aviators in all aircraft. This includes Lanier, four other good men, and their faithful, if quirky, C-87, tail number 862.

CHAPTER 13

Breaking a Logjam

Desert Storm and the Senate Select Committee

In the summer of 1993, I finished my tour in Washington, DC, with the ostentatious but misleading title, "'Principal Advisor to the Secretary of Defense for POW/MIA Affairs." The title had come about some two years earlier during a promotion and victory party in a Vietnamese restaurant in Clarendon, Virginia.

The victory was Desert Storm's successful conclusion—one the pundits and talking heads had labeled it a "just" war; this belated celebration really marked the end of 1992 and formal conclusion of the Senate Select Committee on POW/MIA Affairs. The American and Coalition POWs—including the first female captives—had emerged, some with crutches and bandages, in Operation Yellow Ribbon. Our boss had wanted us to conduct the operation, but our hue and cry and surreptitious leaking to the Air Force by Major Gardner and Rick Gearing, our USAF tanker pilot and Special Ops navigator, got it switched to the Air Force, and they executed it with style and flair. Or as one of our guys put it, "we couldn't have done what they did. Geez, they must have had four colonels for each POW!"

I thought fleetingly of the nameless Marine's quote about the First Cavalry helicopters—"Every Private seems to have his own helicopter." The Air Force did it with style. Operationally, from the five-day conflict, there were two downed aircraft incidents resulting in lost crewmen currently listed MIA. We were uneasily watching from the policy standpoint, but the Air Force and Navy, the affected services, were working to resolve the losses through the Joint Staff and US Central Command (USCENTCOM).

Resolving meant revisiting all circumstances of the loss and moving on down the "what happened" path. Or what might have happened. Central Command and the folks in the bottom floor of the Pentagon who handled such things were watching and doubtless dusting off their plans;

one of the things that fell into the "what happened" arena was most likely a death, which would certainly entail CILHI's assistance. If it was a Personnel Recovery, it would entail other organizations. Organizations with hard men and electronic wizards.

Most observers of the issue thought the photograph of three alleged US POWs, who the Press described as the "Three Amigos," that surfaced in the summer of 1991, was the impetus for the newly organized Joint Task Force–Full Accounting (JTF–FA), but by then we, the Joint Staff and USCINCPAC, had already put the plan on paper. We had asked for augmentation and strength increases across the board, but the real impetus was the successful end of Desert Storm and the Senate Select Committee. Who, realizing we were inadequately manned, funded, and provisioned, criticized us for not doing our job properly—then gave us adequate manning, funding, and provisioning.

Admiral McDevitt and Major Charlie Gittins had recently returned from watching the teams operate scattered across several locations in North Vietnam. Charlie was also a Naval Academy graduate, naval aviator, and recent Desert Storm veteran, a smart lawyer, and along with Art Gorman, a streetwise New Yorker who'd been a New York street policeman for a year or so while waiting to enlist in the Marines, knew how to get things done.

Sometimes Lew Stern, a Brooklynite and also ex-CIA analyst with "street time" in Bangkok, pitched in, particularly if we had to talk to the Vietnamese permanent representative in New York. Their only presence in the United States was through their United Nations membership. Prestigious, but it wouldn't bring them into the global community economically—only diplomatic recognition by the United States would do that.

They were more willing to cooperate, we knew, although there were voids and dark places along the path we'd have to shine light on together—one was losses in Laos, much fewer prisoners were released than we estimated. They wouldn't have to do any soul searching or embarrassing confessions on their presence in Laos—detailed books were being written on that already. The North Vietnamese coming down the Trail had been photographed, listened to, kidnapped, wiretapped, and even sniffed, at least their urine was noted olfactorily as not being animal.

On a long C-141 ride back from Hanoi, the admiral and Charlie talked and penciled in a proposed new organization. They had everything but a command structure; would it be commanded from Hawaii, or Washington? Would it be a Field Operating Agency of the Joint Staff?

I talked to the Joint Staff representative and he agreed it looked pretty good. He called his contact in the USCINCPAC J3 in Hawaii and found they'd been working on a similar organization and were getting ready to show their proposal to Joe Harvey down in the JCRC at Barbers Point and begin formal staffing.

I asked for a copy and they complied. We all liked it and passed a copy to General Vessey, who apparently had talked to Admiral Larson, the CINCPAC four-star commander. He decided that if it was happening in the Pacific, they ought to be the principal operational commander. When a rough draft proposal went up to Secretary Cheney with a request from us to continue planning it came back with a pleasant addendum. "Have the JTF work the Indochina war with the US Army's CILHI supporting." CILHI would be expanded to cover all America's conflicts.

Additional guidance was penciled in from Secretary Cheney himself on our draft: Do not exceed the number of personnel for both organizations legislated by Congress for the Joint Staff (about 700 we thought); Major Gittins checked and confirmed that. After the organizations were formed and operating, look at a positive time frame for accounting for all those missing that were possible. Consider four years as the time frame. Do not rush the scientific work but set up a framework that would provide continuous identifications whenever possible (the Sec Def had obviously looked at De Leon's study earlier on the Blassey—Vietnam Unknown case).

What about the Cold War? We asked the Joint Staff. You could almost hear the forehead slapping from their ring downstairs. "We didn't think of that; we'll ask." The answer came back: "Yes, definitely."

We penciled in our own notation; that this will require a different historical and research skill and experience set. The end result was the eventual establishment of the US-Russia Joint Commission, ultimately with a retired ambassador with extensive diplomatic experience in Russia and a charismatic retired major general returned to active duty.

Unfortunately, the newly named former KGB ultimately refused to open the crown jewels in their archive, despite some of the best US Russian linguists and subject matter experts extant. Time and obstructive ex-KGB bureaucrats would render the Joint Commission unsuccessful, despite our and a few serious Russian counterparts' good intentions and efforts.

The party also saluted our newly organized office and location in the Clarendon Building, a warren of modern, well-lighted, and windowed offices in the first high rise office building on the Orange Metro line of Clarendon. We were settling down with more funding, personnel, and better offices—no more dodging falling asbestos-infested paint clumps in humidity-laden balls landing on your head, desk, and papers, as in the Pentagon.

The bonus part was the two-hundred-yard walk from my front door to the office's front door. Our tiny Sears house was just across the street and up a little.

In the vanishing sobriety, we were bandying about possible titles for our new office and new division of functions. For my title Major Charlie Gittins, still reasonably unaffected by the Heinekens, suggested, "Principal Advisor to the Secretary of Defense for POW/MIA Affairs." We all hooted, but my boss, the Deputy Assistant Secretary of Defense for Asia Carl Ford, liked it.

After all, he mused, we went forward after Desert Storm with new organizations, more people and funding, and the title "added gravitas to our mission and OSD's role in it." "Since Bill is the senior uniformed serviceman in the issue in OSD that would be a great title . . ."

A couple of years later, near the conclusion of our three-year tour in Washington, I was called down to the Army Personnel Center for a "consultation" with the commanding general and a rather pointed remonstration about being much too old and slow to be lobbying for a final assignment with the Joint Special Operations Command at Fort Bragg, North Carolina.

"I need you to go out and take command of CILHI." The remonstration was laced with sufficient "F" bombs from the plainspoken major general that I only nodded acquiescence, but I did have a question about the requirement for a quartermaster officer as the commander, because I wasn't one.

"You're experienced in this issue. I need somebody suitable to the JTF-FA commander. There appears to be a little startup friction between the two organizations, and I want you to straighten it out. You're a Combat Arms officer and so is General Needham, the JTF-FA commander. I think a little mature judgment and leadership will get it on track. I think you'll find this a great job I'm offering you."

Then he raised the curtains a little, the real story: "Look Bill, we've finally gotten some illumination and help for this issue. It's important; very important, especially for the families, but there's going to also be high interest across the political spectrum on how this is going to play out. If there's some kind of squabble going on about who's in charge, or has the most experience or who's been in the issue the longest, the Army is going to lose. The Quartermaster General agrees this is the best solution, and the officer following you will be a Quartermaster officer, preferably one with some Graves Registration experience." Each Army branch was normally (in the early 1990s) commanded by a senior two-star general who commanded the post, career schools, and who served as the senior officer of the branch, in this case, the Quartermaster Center, Fort Lee, Virginia.

The general leaned back and lit a cigarette, exhaled some smoke. So much for "No Smoking in Government Buildings" I thought.

"Now, do you understand what I want from this finely nuanced guidance?"

"Yes sir, I do. And I'll give it my best shot."

"Good, good! You call me anytime if there's a problem, understand?"

"Yes sir."

I saluted and he nodded, already attacking a stack of papers in his In-box.

I opened the door to leave and heard, "One other thing, Colonel . . ."

"Yes sir?"

I turned to see him, reading glasses down on his nose and cigarette smoke curling, "I don't expect to hear from you, understand?"

This time I nodded.

CHAPTER 14

CILHI

Search, Recover, Identify

In the summer of 1993 I was back in Hawaii as commander of the Central Identification Laboratory, Hawaii. Friends would scratch their heads when they came across my name as the commander of this rather strange military organization, at a rank that had been "up gunned" in command from a lieutenant colonel to a colonel.

In reality, the increase in the rank for the CILHI commander had resulted from a long look at the mission, duties, and function of the unit—and the issue—by the General Accounting Office. But the funding, will, and enthusiasm had definitely come out of a quick victory in the desert of South Asia, one where all our prisoners had emerged from captivity and the ones killed were recovered and returned with solemn honor.

The new CILHI was much changed thanks to Desert Storm and the Senate Select Committee. Their dingy lab and offices on the docks had been replaced by a sparkling new lab along the Pacific.

Now there was sufficient funding, manpower, and resolve about the entire spectrum of POWs and recovery of the missing for the American people, Congress, and the Joint Staff to support the increased tempo General Vessey and the 1988 recoveries started. The bipartisan, thorough examination of the Senate Select Committee conducted from its inception in August of 1991 through its final report in January of 1993 was a star showing of the US Senate.

It was made up of a distinguished senator who'd been a prisoner of war, another who'd seen action and was decorated as a Swift boat commander and a medal of honor Seal. Many other distinguished senators from both parties rounded out the committee. Watching it then and comparing the current disenfranchisement between parties now on the cusp of 2020 elections is startling. In 1991 there was some bickering, but on the whole it was decidedly bipartisan and sharply focused on the mission—to examine the issue closely and work toward solutions that made sense.

Just about every member had unresolved losses in the Indochina War from his or her state. The witnesses were a "who's who" of the POW/MIA issue—wives and mothers of the missing, officials of State and Defense who had worked the issue, sometimes for decades, our own DIA analysts, unfairly criticized and the focus of much of the anger, and many more. There were those who fervently believed all the POWs weren't released—we simply did not know.

The witnesses also included a handful of charlatans who took advantage of the emotions and grief, manufacturing schemes for money. It was like the Bible—good people and bad. Believers, nonbelievers, and various agnostics of any stripe.

By the time General Vessey, Admiral Larson, General Christmas, and General Needham testified at the "sunset" of the committee in December 1992, the Senate Select Committee on POW/MIA Affairs had given the entire spectrum a thorough investigation and accounting—under oath.

They did what they said they'd do some fifteen months before—a complete and thorough examination with recommendations to improve the entire issue. The examination had largely burst the bubble of myth that hung over the entire framework of unaccounted-for American servicemen lost in Indochina but raised a few bubbles of its own.

Others on the committee fell on both sides of the matter, so much so that they published a dissenting minority volume criticizing the majority conclusions. It was a little puzzling but indicative of the belief of many.

Unfortunately, the charlatans involved were not touched by any of the investigations. The Justice Department indicted none of them, even the obvious frauds.

The JTF-FA and CILHI received more trained scientists, teams, and equipment to get them where they were going and support the critical heart and brain of the mission.

The Tibet recovery and identifications might not have occurred if that hadn't happened. It was clear that Americans still wanted their boys home, from all wars.

The frustration and anger of the families and activists came out of another war—Vietnam, one that didn't have a really happy ending, unless it was the fact that it was over.

Only the Army trains graves registration soldiers to recover "ancient remains." All other services train personnel for immediate recovery of remains such as those in an observed or recent crash, but US Army graves registration soldiers are also trained to recover incidents that occurred in the past, sometime decades in the past, sometimes centuries.

These are most often referred to as ancient remains in physical anthropology parlance. The training of graves registration soldiers also includes mapping crash and grave sites, recovering and documenting the remains, identification media, and myriad other tasks that move the legal process of identification.

There was no other identification facility in the services—indeed in the world—like CILHI, and their mission spanned all of Department of Defense and on occasion, civil disasters when required. We were the scientific slice of the process that made up the POW/MIA issue, while the Joint Task Force was the investigative, operational, and negotiation arm. The Special Office at DIA handled intelligence, but it was intelligence attached to the analytical process, for most of the DIA personnel had analyzed the cases for years, or even decades.

The service Casualty offices were an extremely large part of the process—they had the unenviable job of telling the families mostly bad news; their mission was one of extreme sensitivity, and their people were superb at telling them the facts and circumstances of their loved one's death or recovery, or why there was no recovery. The Casualty office was the conduit of information from all the organs that made up the body of the issue.

At the top was the Defense Prisoner and Missing Office (DPMO), led by a Deputy Assistant Secretary of Defense. He was responsible for all policy matters. The JTF-FA and CILHI were the operators and executors, maintaining crash site information and extracts of casualty records along with the myriad files associated with losses.

The JCRC/CILHI/DIA received policy guidance virtually "stove piped" straight out of the NSC from Richard Childress, through the "state department" of the Office of the Secretary of Defense's East Asia Pacific Region of 1987, with an appreciative gesture to USCINCPAC as it passed.

Now, in 1993, the JTF-FA, commanded by a promising one-star brigadier general who would be promoted to major general during his tour, had his own teams of experts, and a solid link to his boss, the USCINCPAC—the senior four star commander in the Pacific.

The JTF-FA included linguists and investigators, both civilian and military, as well as transportation coordinators, a Public Affairs office, arrangements with the military commands on island for explosive ordnance disposal, medical assistance, and other specialties not in their Table of Organization and Equipment. This included communicators and other support experts, like the vital life sciences personnel—those who understood aircraft safety devices, ejection seats and hatches, types of flight suits with survival gear, and other technical aspects of getting safely out of an aircraft in peril.

In addition, the JTF manned detachments in Bangkok; Hanoi; Vientiane, Laos; and Phnom Penh, Cambodia. These detachments, commanded by Army or Air Force lieutenant colonels, obtained visas, coordinated with American officials of the embassies where they were collocated, and conducted liaison with the host country military. They also acted as local commanders of investigations and joint recoveries in their areas of responsibility. They were the guys the recovery teams went to for advice or when there was trouble. There was generally always trouble, and generally it was always resolved.

In the words of Ray Spock, who had been our J-2 in the JCRC and now was the spark plug of the analyses office in the new JTF-FA: "This is a 'going outfit!'"[1]

CILHI had none of this when they operated alone, on their other missions in different parts of the world and other conflicts than Indochina, but they were usually led to crash, battle site, or remains, as we would be in Tibet. CILHI personnel were responsible for the on-site recoveries that were complex anthropological and archaeological operations.

The heart of the operational expertise team were the soldiers trained in the Army Military Occupational Specialty (MOS) of 57-Foxtrot. I found these young men and women more composed and empathetic than contemporaries in other Military Occupational Specialties.

A crash site might look like nothing but a jungled hillside when the team arrived by Russian helicopter. But it was quickly cleared with the help of locals and witnesses who might have scavenged the crash site for metal decades before.

The witnesses were extremely candid and honest about what they'd seen and done, but frequently couldn't communicate accurate times or distances. "It was two days' walk in the rainy season," or something similar they could correlate from memory.

Crash sites as opposed to ground battle sites were remote and, in many cases, only had AAA units with some transient NVA infantry support passing through, particularly in the tri-border area or along the HCM Trail on the Lao side of the border. Sometimes if the locale was sufficiently remote and of little strategic advantage, some of the local populace would remain. In one instance we excavated a US Navy RF-8 reconnaissance aircraft in Laos, after our mandated ten days on site required, without finding the pilot; a local came by on the last day and reported the pilot had been buried about sixty feet from the aircraft, near a distinctive grove of trees, and that's where we found his remains.

There was nothing totally safe in the entire operation, but the team leadership made sure it was as safe as possible for both the US and indigenous personnel. Explosive Ordnance Disposal personnel, borrowed from the various commands in Hawaii, safely removed any ordnance that might be remaining. Sometimes the dull thump of C-4 explosives in the distance signaled the end of a pile that was getting too large.

Indochina's terrain, away from the coastal plains, is one of jagged, crumbling mountainous terrain. The rugged Annamite chain, the spine of Southeast Asia, creeps down western Vietnam and eastern Laos. It's much more than a geographic curtain that insulates Vietnam from its Indochinese neighbors; it marks the difference between the sinocized Vietnamese and the Hinduized Lao and Khmer peoples to the south.

The limits of what the anthropologist estimated the crash site to be was quickly staked out in one-meter squares, and initial surface searching rapidly reached the digging and washing stage. A generator pumped water from a stream or other water course. Team members turned over aircraft parts and hopefully fragmented human remains to the *anthros* who would carefully label them and put them in a Ziploc bag with the square's location marked. An Air Force or Navy technical expert in ejection systems, flight suits, and other identification mechanisms or personal equipment could generally identify what part of the aircraft the item might have been in.

Frequently, the search would have to begin again in another grid square, but the anthro and his or her team were adamant about working as hard as they could, although sometimes a supervisor had to gently remind them about safety, particularly in the baking hot dry season or the slippery endless mud of the rainy season.

The same anthropologist who served as the scientific site coordinator in the field would also conduct forensic identifications back in Hawaii. It was a system that required intricate coordination, but it worked well. It was also a crushing travel schedule, with our officers and teams typically spending eighteen to twenty-five days in country and ten to twelve back in Hawaii with the families before going "back in the barrel" again.

Our recovery teams were normally composed of ten to twelve Americans augmented by foreign workers, led by a quartermaster (logistics) captain and a senior graves registration sergeant, or noncommissioned officer (NCO). Each team had an experienced military photographer and —most importantly—a Special Forces senior NCO medic, a fact that eased my angst considerably. A recovery in Vietnam, or Laos, looked like a classic archaeological operation, something out of *National Geographic*'s black-and-white photo layouts from the late 1940s.

By the end of the Gulf War, CENTCOM had the situation well in hand, and the POWs had all returned. One of the earliest air losses was still missing under circumstances that weren't clear. His loss occurred when I was still in the Pentagon, but it would carry over into my time at CILHI. A wingman in an FA-18 carrier-launched missile radar strike going in behind the low-level Apache helicopter raids witnessed an explosion of his wing, and one of his squadron mates didn't return to the ship. Three suppositions existed: he could have been shot down by a missile; perhaps victim of a mid-air collision with an on-coming Iraqi MIG-25 detected and tracked by an AWACS aircraft; or a shootdown by the Iraqi aircraft reported (denied by the US Navy).

Later evidence would suggest a safe ejection when his aircraft canopy was found about midway between Amman, Jordan, and Baghdad, reportedly by a Qatari falconing party. Later, an Iraqi witness statement that said he witnessed the pilot being taken by truck to Baghdad and other evidence suggested proof of life. Investigators thought his statement was accurate. The Navy changed his status from KIA-BNR to Missing-HOSTILE, the new MIA terminology that no one used, except in correspondence.

In 1996 we sent a team into the wreckage site under the auspices of the International Committee of the Red Cross and under Iraqi command and control. The team found nothing at the end of the ten-day mandated operation, but on the last day some Bedouins turned over a flight suit that undoubtedly belonged to the pilot. During the 2003 incursion some Bedouins led a US Marine unit to a burial site close to the site our team had recovered. It was the missing pilot.

Central Identification Laboratory, Hawaii (CILHI) Group Portrait, March 1996, with four teams gone; approximately fifty soldiers plus four scientists. US Army, Central Identification Laboratory, Hawaii.

Author and father with a Piper Cub, which the author's father used for flight instruction for fledgling army pilots. In 1947 the newly formed USAF would train their
pilots, my grandfather's runway returned to cattle pasture, and my father would soon be crop dusting. Author's collection.

(*Opposite*) Guard duty is lonely, no matter where it may occur. Our Peoples' Liberation Army counterparts were concerned about our safety, using the border with hostile India as a reason to maintain security throughout the night. Photograph by author.

Jamyang and "Hammer." The team appreciated our packets and their mounts, since they carried our tents and sleeping bags. When we arrived at our nightly bivouac site, our tents would be set up with sleeping mats and bags unrolled. The packers and small Mongolian packhorses were obviously fond of each other, and every time they were loaded, the packers asked their forgiveness for the heavy loads they were about to endure for the next twelve hours or so. Photograph by author.

Night camp in "Avalanche Valley." The altitude here was about 13,000 feet, and this was the last level grassland for the entire pack train. A large avalanche in the distance caused great excitement for the packers and soldiers. The crashing roar and subsequent dust cloud indicated a large avalanche and a flag for the danger such events posed, as Colonel Yi and Sherap told us, with Yeti translating. Photograph by author.

The crew of the ill-fated Flight 862, clockwise, from left: Corporal Joseph Petrella, USAAF; Private First Class Eugene Beebe, USAAF; Second Lieutenant Frank Ramos, USAAF; First lieutenant Fulton Lanier, USAAF; Private First Class Bartholomew "Benny" Giacalone, USAAF. Photograph courtesy of Carl Petrella.

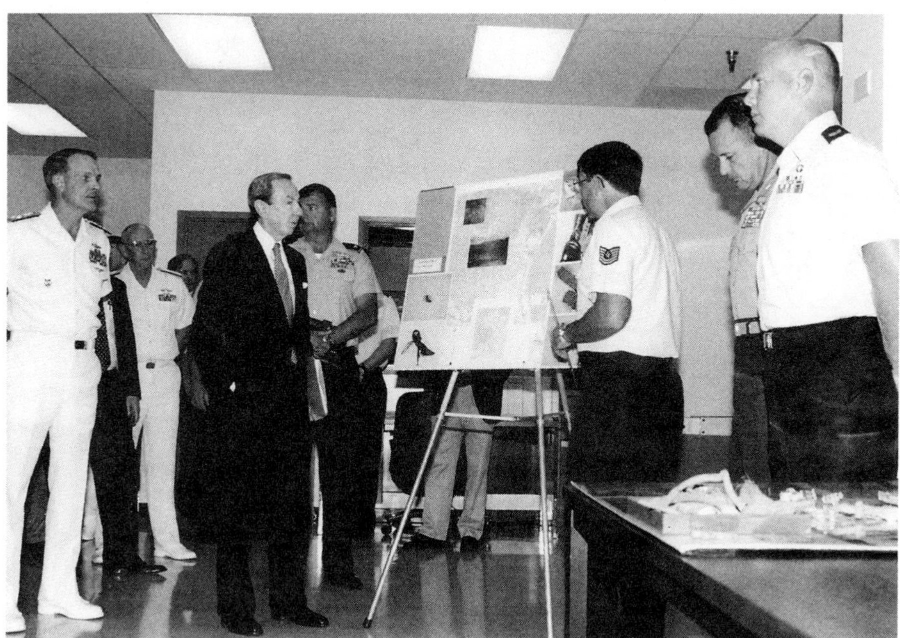

Secretary of State Warren Christopher (in dark suit and tie, viewing easel) en route to Hanoi to open formal relations between Vietnam and the United States. Christopher recognized the importance of CINCPAC's Joint Casualty Resolution Center, which became Joint Task Force Full—Accounting. Central Identification Laboratory, Hawaii (CILHI), was also central to that effort. Christopher asked to be briefed on the whole process. Admiral Charles Larson, the senior flag officer in the Pacific, brought members of his command, including his politico-military chief, J-5 Admiral Michael McDevitt (*left rear*, glasses), Author: holding notebook and JTF–FA deputy Colonel Bill Frizzell, USMC, right foreground, looking down. US Army photograph.

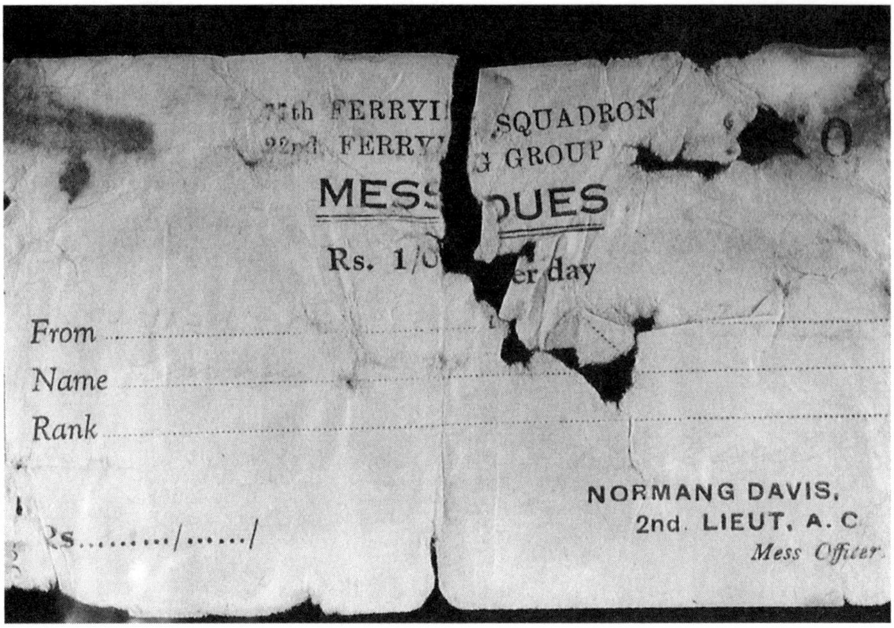

A World War II–era mess ticket, recovered from the crash site. The bearer's signature was torn off, but the relatively pristine condition of the flimsy mess receipt, even after five decades in an icy glacier, is emblematic of the preservative nature of the altitude and lack of humidity. US Army, CILHI.

AFPPA-14 (10 Apr 46) MACR NO. 2138

COPY COPY

WAR DEPARTMENT
HEADQUARTERS ARMY AIR FORCES
WASHINGTON

MISSING AIR CREW REPORT

IMPORTANT: This report will be compiled in triplicate by each Army Air Forces organization within 48 hours of the time an aircraft is officially reported missing.

1. ORGANIZATION: Location: A.P.O. 466 Command or Air Force ATC
GROUP EASTERN SECTOR ; SQUADRON STATION ; DETACHMENT
2. SPECIFY: Point of Departure KUNMING, CHINA ; Course DIRECT (TRANSPORT
Intended Destination JORHAT, INDIA ; Type of Mission CARGO)
3. WEATHER CONDITIONS AND VISIBILITY AT TIME OF CRASH OR WHEN LAST REPORTED:
OVERCAST AT 30,000 FEET; BAD ICING CONDITIONS 10,000 FEET UP.
4. GIVE: (a) Date 31 JAN 44 Time UNKNOWN ; And Location of Last known whereabouts of missing aircraft UNKNOWN
(b) Specify whether ( ) Last sighted; ( ) Last contacted by radio; ( ) Forced down; Seen to Crash; or (X) Information not available.
5. AIRCRAFT WAS LOST, OR IS BELIEVED TO HAVE BEEN LOST, AS A RESULT OF (Check only one: ( ) Enemy Aircraft; ( ) Enemy Anti-Aircraft; ( ) Other Circumstances as follows UNKNOWN
6. AIRCRAFT: Type, Model and Series C-87 ; AAF Serial No. [illegible]
7. ENGINES: Type, Model and Series R-1830-43 ; AAF Serial No. (a)
(b) (c) (d)
8. INSTALLED WEAPONS (Furnish below Make, Type and Serial Number)
(a) NONE (b) INSTALLED (c) (d)
(e) (f) (g) (h)
9. THE PERSONS LISTED BELOW WERE REPORTED AS: (a) Battle Casualty
or (b) Non-Battle Casualty X
10. NUMBER OF PERSONS ABOARD AIRCRAFT: Crew 5 ; Passengers 0 ; Total 5
(Starting with pilot, furnish the following particulars: If more than 11 persons were aboard aircraft, list similar particulars on separate sheet and attach original to this form).
Name in Full Serial
Number Status

Report of missing aircrew, noting icing conditions aloft. In the predigital world, these records provided such information as was available about missing aircraft to follow-on aircraft, ground, air, or sea forces who might effect rescue—or recovery—of aircrews. Photograph by CILHI.

Sherap Chopel, the Tibetan hunter who discovered the missing aircraft after it was released from its ice encased tomb, stands in front of a crevice, or crevasse. These are wedge-shaped cracks on an ice field, normally as deep as 50 meters. If an animal or man falls into one they normally must be rescued from above ground. There were many, but Sherap pointed them out; he was invaluable to the entire operation. Photograph by author.

Staff Sergeant Bradford (in cap, facing camera) with his beloved generator and satellite phone. Similar equipment is much more compact now, but this one provided our only communication back to Hawaii, to the American consulate in Chengdu, or to our embassy in Beijing. Tibetan packers are on left; Jon Aliosi sips tea as Lieutenant Colonel Man (in the Army sweatshirt) looks on. Photograph by author.

All the Americans plus Yeti, our interpreter and guide, who is in sunglasses, fifth from left. People's Liberation Army guards Private Chen and Corporal Hu, tough mountain troops, rotated through our tent areas each night and climbed just a couple of hundred meters behind us each day. Photograph by author.

An Air Transport Command C-46 coming in for a landing, just above the heads of a Chinese man and his draft horse. US Army Center of Military History.

Hump pilots, comparing notes between operations. Air Force Historical Research Agency.

Generalissimo Chiang Kai-shek, Madame Chiang, and General Stilwell, ca. 1943.
US Army Center of Military History.

Left to right: Staff Sergeant Mark Antal, US Army; Staff Sergeant Mike Bradford, US Army; Sergeant First Class Kevin Wright, US Army; Jon Aliosi, American Embassy Beijing. These four tough young men discuss route and dangers on the way to the crash site. Photograph by author.

Major General Tom Needham, commanding general of the JTF–FA staging out of Lai Chau in northwestern Vietnam, at crash site about halfway between Dien Bien Phu and Vietnam's border with China. He is briefed by an unknown JTF–FA investigative team leader. This is Jack Donovan's crash site, one of Vietnam's highest USAF losses: a special ops Combat Talon C-130. The entire crew was finally accounted for. Photograph by author.

Janna at Arlington National Cemetery, placing Memorial Day flowers on the Tibet crew's tombstone. She, with the working team leaders' and civilian anthropologists' wives in Vietnam, Laos, or Cambodia, would meet the as-yet unknown servicemen coming into Hickam Air Force Base on an Air Force C-141 and would also salute their departure as identified servicemen, going home to their families. Photograph by author.

Air drop at Khe Sanh, February 1968, while the Tet Offensive winds to a close in Hue. Two generations before this, the Hump combat cargo pilots and kickers started airdrops to the Chindits, American OSS officer-led Kachin guerrillas, Slim's ground forces from India, and Lieutenant General Stilwell's American and Chinese troops. The Air Force would refine airdrops based on that and further experience honed in Vietnam. Photograph by author.

C-87 crash site on Himalayan glacier, eastern Tibet. Photographs by author.

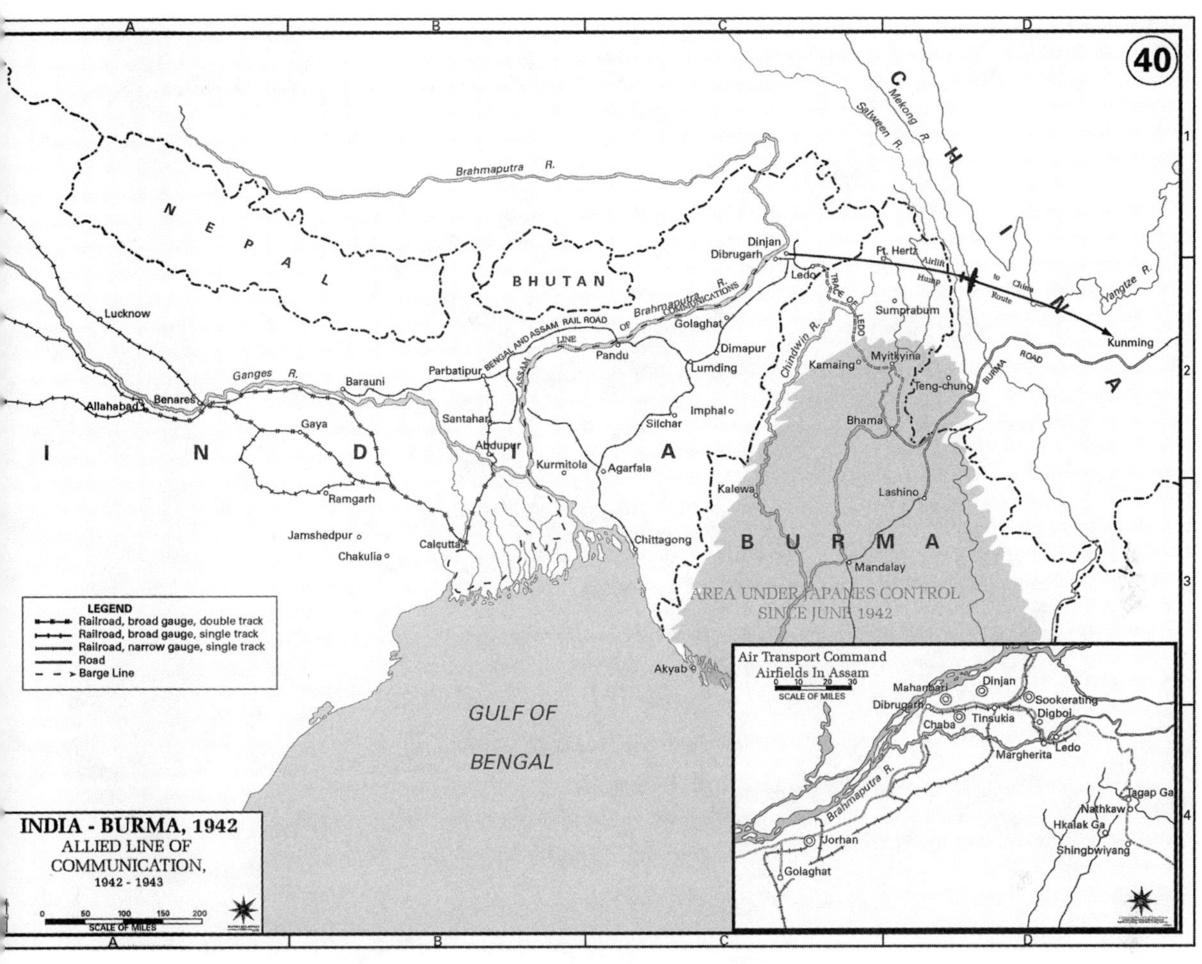

The Allied lines of communication in the China India Burma Theater of Operations during World War II, including the route flown over the Hump. US Army Center of Military History.

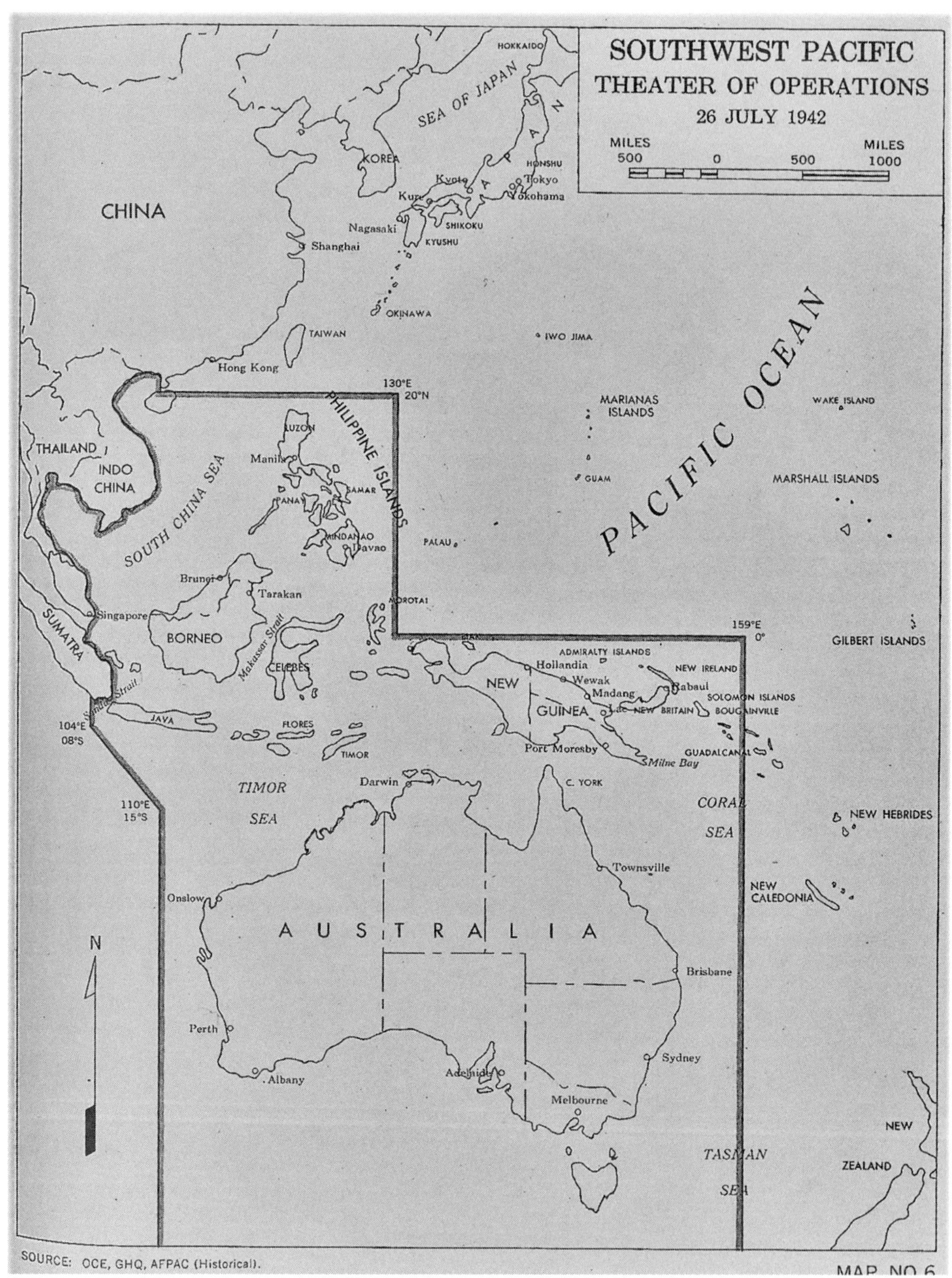

The Southwest Pacific Theater of Operations, World War II.

Napalm strike, Khe Sanh, February 1968. The Tet Offensive had been weathered and won militarily, but lost politically. Bitter fighting continued in Hue amid frenzied digging by the NVA in Khe Sanh. This was a major tactic of theirs at Dien Bien Phu: to tunnel close enough to the Marines for a concerted attack or to tunnel under their defenses and use explosives from underneath. This napalm strike by an A4 Skyhawk was directed against a secondary trench line in order to drive back enemy forces. Photograph by author.

Family photographs of Private First Class Bartholomew "Benny" Giacalone. Courtesy Giacalone family collection.

CHAPTER 15

The Third Incarnation of the JPRC—the JTF-FA

Joint Task Force-Full Accounting, in contrast to CILHI, used smaller teams, normally three to five specialists including a linguist, teamed into Investigative Elements (IEs), and a CILHI graves registration specialist. The mission of the IEs was to locate witnesses and try to form a picture of what happened and where the crash site specifically was located. They'd bring back photographs of the area, and the CILHI representative with them knew enough about recovery operations to fill in many of the blanks—distance to water sources, dangers in the area, anything significant observed, especially UXO, the much respected unexploded ordnance.

The IE team leaders were experienced combat arms captains; they knew about Landing Zones (LZs), trail trafficability, obstacles, and other Essential Elements of Information necessary to safely complete their mission. They completed and filled out our sometimes-scanty files on the incident, then proposed sites for recovery by our Search and Recovery teams. An experienced CILHI graves registration specialist accompanied the JTF IE team in nearly all cases, but if one wasn't available, they would cross check with each other.

Some of the JTF recovery teams' IE members had also served on recovery teams, so they were pretty knowledgeable; if remains were found, they were carefully cataloged, photographed, and measured, and, if they were going to be moved to an excavation site with an anthropologist present to verify whether they were human, the chain of custody would be extended. Generally, if they could be ascertained to be human, they would be of extreme interest.

There were other factors that went into the decision-making—were any of the missing Americans Asian Americans, or Afro-Americans? Were there multiple losses with combined teams, as in a US led reconnaissance team with Hmong, Montagnard, or Vietnamese members. If provenance was unknown ("someone gave these to me, but I don't remember when or who . . .") and they turned out to be nonhuman, then the information was retained, but the remains were usually returned. In the bad old days before low-orbital satellite and digital communications were the norm, "Bring everything back to Honolulu if an anthropologist can't examine it and make a determination or recommendation to the commander from the field" was the guidance.

One particular case in Laos involved an early helicopter loss flown by a Vietnamese pilot with a combined team on board. Since this was a high helo loss area and information on the number of Vietnamese crewmen aboard the helicopter wasn't known, we completely exhausted the search area, finding remains that finally included what we assumed to be the pilot and some other nonhuman bone fragments.

The grave marker at Arlington was scanty, the Americans and "unidentified Vietnamese crewmembers" were interred as X number of unidentified Vietnamese crewmen on the headstone. I'm sure their American colleagues would have absolutely insisted on the aircrew being interred with them—the VNAF pilots who flew the H-34 helos were brave and determined airmen. One American name wasn't included on the marker. Unusual, but the family member didn't agree he was in there. Unusual, but not unprecedented.

Our Search and Recovery teams, once daily work was completed (the medics and EOD personnel could swing a pick or man a shovel with the best of them), would treat the villagers for various ailments and provide rudimentary first aid and sanitation instruction to selected villagers.

Generally, a PhD anthropologist or archaeologist was the scientific director of the excavation and made the calls on the scope and pace of the remains recovery. We had a few talented ones who only held master's degrees, but virtually all eventually attained a PhD.

CILHI, like the JCRC, maintained the records of US civilian casualties as well as some foreign nationals lost during the Vietnam War and other wars, mainly missionaries and members of nongovernmental organizations. And other government organizations; there were CIA personnel lost in all three countries of Indochina. Also, missionaries. Although the State Department is the agency responsible for civilians, CILHI maintained their medical records.

Contractors were also lost, including those contractors flying or crewing on Air America or other proprietary airlines. Still, there were problems. The year 1973 was extraordinarily bad for an organization like the JCRC and CILHI, which kept a good part of their business on paper records.

In 1973, a fire destroyed many of the contemporary personnel records at the National Archives repository in St. Louis. Those lost included the five crewmembers of C-87 tail number 862, as I found out when I visited there the summer of 2001. The helpful archivists explained that the records were virtually irreplaceable, but they had requested input from family members for any pertinent military information that they could include to resurrect at least part of their personnel file (the service casualty offices and CILHI had most of the medical records, but neither retained the voluminous personnel records that make up a serviceman's military life; whenever I inquired about them the answer was, "they're archived someplace, I guess." I suspect they were archived in St. Louis.

"It was an absolutely devastating fire," an archivist lamented. All the others reflected the grief that a dedicated professional has to an irretrievable loss of their lifelong work. Apparently, after the serviceman's status review and the intricacies of Title 10, US code had determined that the serviceman was Killed in Action–Body not Recovered to satisfy legalities, awarding of back pay and insurance, and such, then the files were historically put aside for posterity. This was a generation before digitization, unfortunately.

Despite this, they dutifully brought out what they had on Lieutenant Lanier, Ramos, Giacalone, Petrella, and Beebe. Petrella and Giacalone had the only entries, a flimsy copy of an award for Joe Petrella and a handwritten list of seven or eight cities for Benny Giacalone, including a three-month assignment at National Airport. There was no heading that indicated what the cities meant. It looked like a handwritten work note, but it had been sent to the Records Center in their request for additional information the family might have.

I assumed Benny was flying/training as a radio operator for an airline, or perhaps there was a training facility there with spare seats for trainees. I explained what I was trying to do, resurrect their military and flying biographies, and the archivists somberly shook their heads when I explained that Benny was the only surviving son in a close-knit family of sisters and naturally doting, loving first-generation parents. Some thirty years after he was lost, someone, perhaps a sister, had responded with what she remembered or gleaned from letters.

Carl Petrella, who idolized his older brother, Joe, had also responded with perhaps the only thing military that Joe had sent home. I imagine Carl burned up the phone lines to NARA, St. Louis, wanting to help any way he could. I felt sorry for the archivists who seemed to share the grief of what the fire had done to thousands of families who were attempting to shed some light on what their long-gone loved ones had experienced in their military lives.

In addition, at the working, or tactical, level in Indochina, CILHI was under the operational control of Joint Task Force–Full Accounting, with many of my old unit's JCRC working there and very happy, and Joe being folded into the USCINCPAC staff as their go-to historian and subject matter expert on the POW/MIA issue. I ran into Joe at Camp Smith when I was there in January of 1993 for a conference.

"I heard from someone you were leaving for Washington this summer, but they were a little hazy on what you were going to be doing."

He chuckled, "You know I'm going to DPMO to take your job and you know I know you're coming to CILHI. But I also heard from someone you were going to Fort Bragg for a terminal tour, so which is it?"

"Well, the rumor about Fort Bragg should have been right, but that was wishful thinking. That was a rumor I started; I figured it'd be kind of like a backfire, or a self-licking lollipop; maybe something that might come true. Turned out to be more like an exploding boomerang just as you reach up for it."

"Ah, the velvet guillotine of the US Army assignments' desk."

"Who assigns GS-15s?" I asked, tongue in cheek.

"It's about time I returned to the mainland," he sighed.

"Well Joe, it's no secret you're highly regarded not only here but in Washington, and since you're taking over my job . . ."

"What's your biggest problem in DPMO, if I may ask?"

"I think they're trying to stuff too much in one bag; for instance, this Joint US/Russia Commission."

"What about it?"

"Maybe it ought to belong to State instead of Defense."

"Giving away jobs and manpower; you know that's a dangerous precedent."

"Yeah, but I'm talking about putting organizations where they belong, and this is diplomatic and historical stuff, not recovery and identification."

"But still . . ."

"Yeah, I know. You're talking to the 'original give away problems' guy here . . . did I ever tell you I tried to convince the admiral that his little pocket of festering POW/MIA sores of his directorate would be better served under Bob Andrews over in SOLIC than in East Asia-Pacific?"

This time Joe laughed, then asked seriously, "why Special Operations and Low Intensity Conflict?"

"Well, you'll remember back in the bad old days the organization you commanded came right out of the spookiest Special Operations ninjas ever fielded, the Military Assistance Command Vietnam, uh . . . Studies and Operations Group. Wink wink!"

"You could argue that point either way, I guess, but I always thought that CINCPACSOC took care of us in the old days," he said, thinking about it.[1]

"That was a case of the overcast taking care of the outcast, I think. We were lower on the whale scale than all the special operators in the Pacific," I responded.

"Or maybe it was the fact that you, I and Colonel Chambelain all wore Con Thien T-shirts.[2] I thought it would open up a buddy channel, but it didn't. I do recall he was sympathetic to us and took a lot of the flak for us from CINCPAC." I mused. "One thing he did was to protect us from CILHIs, uh, excessive Armyness. Did you know about their little escapade in the Philippines?" Joe asked.

"You mean when one of their teams was, detained I believe, by the New Peoples' Army, somewhere down island in Indian country?"

"Yeah, then released but taking their equipment, including their communications gear."

"They apparently also overlooked the requirement for an area clearance from CINCPAC," Joe added.

This was a cardinal sin. It was much worse than showing up in a non-friendly country without a passport.

"Whoa. Bet that earned them a rocket."

"Army PERSCOM should have paid attention to that, instead they bowed their back, and thumped their chest. They're doing the same thing now, only worse. They're trying to stick their thumbs in the eyes of the very organization that's giving them working space—in a very nice area, by the way—and much better housing than they'd get on an army base."

All that was true. The Lab itself was almost the last building on the base, right across the street from a trendy little beachside restaurant and bar that was part of the well-run Air Force Officers' Club system.

Joe continued, "Now, I'd stop by CILHI if I were you. They've got one of their colonels from Casualty Affairs there looking things over because the president is going to visit, and Admiral Larson is going to escort him through CILHI. I'm told that they're going to tell CINCPAC that theirs is Army turf, and the Navy isn't welcome."

"I can't believe they'd be that dense!"

"Look Bill, I know you're staying away because you're not in command yet, but you're still their policy boss. I'd take a free look to see what you're stepping into."

"You mean hold this bag—don't smell it, just hold it."

We both laughed, but it was the rueful laugh of old men, albeit not that old. But bumping up against too old for what we were doing.

Joe would be the Chief of Staff, my current real title and job at the Office of the Secretary of Defense. But he would be part of the much larger organization that it was at the time. Now, our original Deputy Assistant Secretary of Defense, a political appointee off the Senate Select Committee staff, had been dumped by the Clinton defeat of George H. W. Bush and a new one appointed. But Joe's advice was good and I took it.

The Army colonel from Casualty Affairs that called CINCPAC to tell them it would be "inconvenient" for them to inspect the unit and laboratory before the president's visit had his ears blown back by a Marine colonel I knew and respected. I had certainly stayed out of that one. When they asked my opinion I reiterated CILHI had an expensive and effective presence on their turf; there was certainly excellent housing on Hickam Air Force Base for their people: the recovery teams and the CILHI Staff. Why did they want to antagonize the Air Force and CINCPAC, who were bending over backward to help them? I pointed out that both the DPMO and the Secretary of Defense didn't want to hear about any bruised feelings. They ignored that advice and paid for it.

Retired Brigadier General Wold, an Air Force general officer, had been recommended by General Vessey as the new deputy assistant Secretary of Defense for POW/MIA affairs; Wold was a Minnesota acquaintance of General Vessey's, a lawyer, and he also had commanded the Fifty-Sixth Special Operations Wing in Vietnam. This diminutive and retired brigadier general, an uncharacteristically silent type, didn't fit the caricature of the typical Air Force fighter pilot who had commanded a Special Operations Wing, but I found him to be thoughtful, courteous, and with absolutely no ego or bluster in his manner. I thought he and the highly experienced and quiet Joe Harvey as the number two man in the organization would mesh well. Paul Mather was also a presence, this time as a senior analyst. I knew he would keep his head down and churn out impeccable work, and he did. He was a fount of historical knowledge and without an ounce of self-serving deportment.

General Needham's mission was specific and focused—resolve the fates of the missing from the Indochina War. Ours was no less—Search, Recover, and Identify—from all US conflicts—but concentrate on helping General Needham's effort to the utmost.

If anybody asked me, our primary mission was, I'd say, Vietnam, Laos, and Cambodia. And our half dozen or so non-Indochina missions during my three-year tenure as commander were accomplished with no degradation of our assistance to the Joint Task Force.[3]

We sent a Department of Defense delegation to North Korea, and I went with the nucleus of a recovery team, three people: a team leader, team sergeant, and a graves registration junior NCO—interesting, particularly for a Korean specialist, but actual operations would begin after I retired, and then maddeningly the operations stopped again. We didn't get far although we traveled north to a location near Unsan, where the Eighth Cavalry of the First Cavalry Division was wiped out by Chinese in November 1950.

Joe naturally wanted to know what everybody thought of him taking over. I was enthusiastic about it; he'd be, in effect, my policy boss. He had a long and positive history with the DIA analysts there and I knew Ann Mills Griffith had faith in his experience. The DIA leadership was good, and new talented personnel, both in and out of uniform, were swelling its ranks.

By now our staff of twelve to fifteen DPMO officers and civilians had been forecast to swell fivefold, and the JTF would dwarf our twenty- to thirty-person old JCRC; the impetus of the Senate Select Committee preceded by the first Gulf War had opened the personnel spigot. CILHI had also grown, but the increase in personnel, equipment, and technology since the Gulf War also put a new face on our mission. Now the world's nations saw the United States willing to rally countries and cultures that needed and desired stable regions in the world for their own security and safety. Desert Shield and Desert Storm had framed that effort—the United States provided the bulk of the troops for the combat operation—nearly a half million soldiers in the coalition.

There was a palpable connection to Desert Storm's quick and positive termination and the POW/MIA issue that we worked. From the start, Coalition and US prisoners of war were primary topics in the cease-fire and conclusion of hostilities negotiations. We certainly didn't want any lingering doubts, especially in the families' minds, about the safety and quick return of all the prisoners, including the two women captives, one a battalion surgeon, the other a supply specialist and assistant driver.

With Desert Storm and the Senate Select Committee, "Big Business" had come to the entire issue, just as it had in the last year of the Hump operation. By now the old mission of keeping Chiang Kai-shek supplied with every class of supplies from beans to bullets had been transformed—to shipping thousands of tons to the B-29 bases for the destruction of Japan.

In 1992 Brigadier General Thomas Needham became the first commander of the newly established JTF–FA. Needham, like most new Army brigadier generals, was welcomed into the ranks of Flag (General/Admiral) officers with difficult, often thankless initial assignments. The Army placed Tom Needham in command of the newly created Joint Task Force–Full Accounting because he was a no-nonsense officer who was strictly results oriented. A lifelong bachelor and devoted Catholic, he told me once he had grown up in a devout family and knew, even as a young boy, he was either going to be a priest or a soldier.

Major General Needham's detractors nicknamed him "Nuke 'em Needham," but his reputation for sorting out and resolving complex situations was the reason the Army leadership had charged him with this difficult task in the first place. Although CILHI's mandate was the same for all wars, when I was there most of our time was spent supporting the JTF in Indochina—Vietnam, Laos and Cambodia. But if someone found remains or a wartime crash in the Pacific, usually, but sometimes in Europe or Latin America, a CILHI team would be put in for a recovery.

But the priority task remained the JTF–FA mission in Indochina. No one seriously entertained a similar push for previous wars, although we all ruminated about it. We spent decreasing time on World War II recoveries, mainly in the South Pacific, especially in Papua New Guinea. The rugged Owen Stanley Mountains there were an unending source of crashes—a veritable aircraft graveyard. We were interested when remains were found from these conflicts, but the JTF didn't participate in them, only those losses in Indochina.

Other conflicts were CILHI's responsibility—investigation on the ground if needed or warranted; site surveys if possible; and excavation and recovery of the remains, then identification, just as we did with the Indochina recoveries.

The inability to use the Chinese helicopters was not a showstopper or deal breaker. There was a caveat, however. Wherever we were, whatever the circumstances, we had to have a plan and a method to rapidly evacuate a casualty, either US, indigenous, or host country if required. This would be a planning challenge we wrestled with when the Tibet mission became a reality. Searching for, recovering, and identifying the missing was a great mission—none better for a serviceman—but it was complex, and the command and responsibility links were more than complex—they were extremely complicated; in Tom Needham's own words, "a lotta movin' parts."

I worked for the TAG, the Adjutant General of the Army, normally a newly promoted one star who handled a crushing responsibility of administrative fiefdoms who virtually ran the personnel business of the US Army. The TAG was my rating officer because he or she also had responsibility for Memorial Affairs, all the casualty reporting and family outreach of the Army, a stygian labor in itself, but the directorate had superior people and long experience, some of them civilian. Being commanded by an agency on the mainland was a tremendously difficult challenge for both the commander, CILHI, and the TAG. Not a single General Officer from PERSCOM was able to visit a CILHI team in Vietnam or Laos, and I served under three of them.

The congressionally mandated realignment in 2002 of CILHI under the JTF–FA and creation of the new Defense Personnel Accounting Agency in 2015 straightened these convoluted command lines for my successors at least (I had retired in December 1997). Now they serve under a single agency in Hawaii, the Defense Personnel Accounting Agency, DPAA, with the DPMO, the policy arm responding directly to the Undersecretary of Defense for Policy, from their offices nestled under the shadow of the Pentagon in Pentagon City, Virginia.

Overarching all this, Title 10 is the short title of the law that governs military matters in peace and war. It outlines the role of the Armed Forces, by service, and establishes the legal basis for the roles, missions, and organization for them as well as the Department of Defense.

This is what gives each of the three service secretaries "review authority" for each of his or her missing serviceman, who is in mortal limbo—neither dead nor alive. Normally, any serviceman missing, in combat or garrison, undergoes an investigation of circumstances by a small board of officers immediately after the incident.

In a company-sized unit, normally about 140 to 150 soldiers, the battalion executive officer and two or three company-grade officers investigate the loss as quickly as possible.[4] Searches are made and witnesses give statements; the missing soldier's senior NCOs, officers, and commander also furnish all known information of the loss in statements that go forward and render a report up the chain of command. He is the "legal Next of Kin" in terms of reviewing the circumstances of his or her loss on or close to the first anniversary of it.

The secretary also has the legal authority to rule on whether to declare death because of the circumstances of the incident or continue the missing serviceman's status until further evidence is uncovered that warrants a decision of death or continuing the missing status.

These are not simple tasks, and uncertainty is threaded through much of the decision. The secretary must make that difficult decision, but he gets plenty of assistance from his staff, particularly the Adjutant General's Casualty Office of the Personnel Command and the good offices now of the higher command of the unit such as the brigade and division.

If it is a combat loss Army intelligence and professional Defense Intelligence Agency analysts may follow the circumstances of the case closely. The uncertainty of the incident is often buoyed by the grief of the families, inflamed and exacerbated by media interest in some cases; in others, years of relative inactivity may mute the emotional issue with time. Thus, the families of the luckless C-87. Their plane disappeared into the vastness of the China Burma India theater, thousands of square miles of trackless rainforest and mountains of unspeakable beauty, yet those mountains are lethal. The family grieved when the incident occurred, and the family member was notified their servicemember was missing in action. Of course, crewmembers walked out all the time, which was pointed out in letters. They sent them trunks of personal effects but reminded them that when the crewmembers showed up, the personal effects belong to them, not the persons holding them. Little tendrils of hope.

The relatives of the crew of aircraft 867, who were relative youngsters when their brothers and uncles went missing, grieved, but to every man and woman, they remembered the young men who perished in a C-87 with fondness leavened by a stab of grief—not unusual for loved ones who disappeared without a trace. Off the scope. But then the dead returned from the lost. It will happen again. And again. And that's a good thing.

Finally CILHI was a quartermaster unit, because graves registration is a Quartermaster Corps mission and responsibility, albeit a small one compared to the huge responsibility of logistics, transportation, and services to the troops. This includes everything from field showers to combat and defense of the rear areas, usually many times larger than the forward combat area. General Meigs of Civil War and Arlington Cemetery fame would likely notch grave registration a higher importance than contemporary commanders, because relatively speaking, battlefield burials and massive deaths have largely not occurred in contemporary wars, or those since Korea.

The Quartermaster General, the chief logistician in the Army, sent us the best possible officers to lead the recovery teams. He and his Chief of Staff visited the laboratory and received a briefing. Behind closed doors, I told him that the officers he was sending were excellent and what I was doing to watch out for them professionally, and Admiral Larson and General Needham had the greatest respect for them.

And that was indeed the case.

He and his chief nodded and exchanged brief glances. I knew these were questions he would have asked. I also told them that General Needham agreed with me on the question of placing our teams under the JTF's operational control in Indochina; he agreed with me that it added a safety and convenience factor particularly for the crews who most assuredly needed to get some rest after the long trip from Hawaii to Hanoi, Vientiane, or Phnom Penh—particularly Phnom Penh.

But that call ultimately wouldn't have come from him—he ran the schoolhouse for the Quartermaster Corps. The Adjutant General might have weighed in if he (or she, my second boss was a female). Although their executive officer would occasionally take the long trip out to Indochina, none of the TAGs themselves could make it, at least during my tenure. Nor would any general officer from the Army Personnel Command. Cambodia was still crime-ridden and dangerous in my opinion and we wouldn't get into it until 1991 when a complicated arrangement of government was worked out that basically absorbed three parties. Perhaps four, because Premier Hun Senn, a former Khmer Rouge, was reportedly half Vietnamese. And perhaps married to a Vietnamese.

Hun Senn personified the problems the two communist governments had—we knew the Lao and their Lao Dong party to be accommodating to the Vietnamese and perhaps a little more Stalinist in their dogmatic approach to government that did nothing for the people, particularly the tribal peoples. The tribal people likewise distrusted the government, and their attitude was, the less heard from them the better.

But the Cambodians, and the Khmer Rouge, were uneasy communist allies, distrusting the Vietnamese for their ruthless suppression and absorption of their Champa nation and culture centuries before. Now we recognized the standoff between the Chinese-supported Khmer Rouge and the Vietnamese. The Vietnamese had to fight a two-front war with the Chinese and the Cambodians, over a decade previously and not unlike the Japanese in China or the Soviets in Afghanistan, wanted to detach themselves. But ironically, they were now fighting a counterguerrilla war in Cambodia and would also fight the Chinese conventional one in 1979. I remember picking up an outdated copy of an American magazine in Korea in 1980. The cover showed two colossal elephants dressed in Chinese and Vietnamese national colors fighting each other; the headline: "When Communist Giants Clash."

"You need to check with your boss first on this?" he and Frizzel asked in one of our closed-door sessions, after a discussion of placing CILHI teams under the operational control of the JTF-FA when operating in Indochina. He and Needham were both grinning, but I knew they sympathized with my rather convoluted—but necessary—chain of command. The adjutant general was also responsible for maintaining contact with the families of the wounded, missing, and dead: Casualty Affairs.

"Why don't you just put in the task organization in the operations order," I suggested, shrugging it off.

"If somebody complains, I'll explain, take my ass-chewing and we'll agree to work something out that, uh . . . takes care of things." They agreed.

They knew I was under a complicated command structure. I thought I'd never complain about having a boss across the street—like Needham had with Admiral Larson instead of one across an ocean and continent, a pleasant dream to most people. But most of the time it had more downside than positive side.

The command relationship was never questioned, but the chain of command for CILHI and I agreed—it was still a dangerous business, particularly for those hardy men and women who might step on a piece of buried, 1968 ordnance that had lain there for decades, just waiting to maim or kill someone. I had to grin when I saw a poster in one of the team rooms—it was a picture of an M-26 hand grenade with the caption: "Once the pin is pulled, Mr. Grenade is no longer your friend." Now our mantra was "no casualties—ever." Both General Needham and I preached that nothing we did was worth the death of another serviceman.[5]

Ed Ross, the acting deputy assistant secretary, understood this all too well—he had observed CILHI teams working in Indochina and had served one tour as a combat arms officer and another as commander of an intelligence detachment.

I smiled when I hung up the phone and reflected on how government would grind to a halt if it weren't for the "informal," but careful, nonbinding or attributing coordination thousands of government employees make daily.

I had recently returned from the Lao Democratic People's Republic, where the wheels of government had rusted to a creaky near-stop because of Stalinist bureaucracy. I felt a twinge of sadness whenever I thought of prerevolutionary Laos, then known as the Kingdom of Laos before it became the Lao People's Democratic Republic.

It was a country and people I had come to admire in the late 1960s when I traveled through there on a seventeen-month meandering, hitchhiking journey around the world, on a long leave from the Army. The Hinduized Lao of the lowlands were a smiling, mañana-type people, completely different from the Pathet Lao government that emerged. Now the smiles were sometimes a grimace. The wheels of bureaucracy had almost frozen. The Lao had learned well from their Vietnamese fraternal elder brothers. Negotiating with them could be agonizing.

The gentle lowland Lao and the tough hill tribesmen who helped the CIA and the Special Forces operators prosecute the Secret War "over the fence" deserved much better than the outcome. They were a significant part of the dominoes that did fall, at least in Laos and Cambodia—especially the Khmer Rouge–dominated Cambodia. In Laos, this included years in brutal "reeducation" camps and being used as a testing ground for Soviet chemical weapons, the dreaded Yellow Rain, decades before Saddam Hussein unleashed toxins on the Kurds.

But now we focused on northeast Asia and the roof of the world. In our darkened conference room the videotape unspooled, and a tragedy from a distant, ancient war unfolded. Chinese soldiers in white gloves were gingerly picking through the recognizable remains of a catastrophic air crash.

There was a muted soundtrack with some scratchy Chinese Mandarin and some attempts at English translation. I picked up repeated references to "*Xijang*"—Tibet, straining my very limited Monterey, California, language training in Chinese Mandarin some thirteen years earlier.

"What kind of unit is that, Pierre?" I asked. The anthropologist and civilians present rolled their eyes—they were professional and, in most cases, physically tough, but tended to adopt scientific, no-nonsense personas. Why were we soldiers interested in the Chinese troops?

"Peoples' Liberation Army Mountain troops, Sir. Their mission is probably to keep their border with India secure, and of course they'll keep an eye on the Tibetans."

"How can you tell that, Pierre?" One of the team leader captains asked. More eye rolling ensued.

"Those rifles they're carrying; those are AK-74s, a newer lightweight version of the AK-47; smaller ammo, similar to our M-16; also some of the equipment includes the mules and horses. They probably have few a Tibetan and Chinese Peoples' Armed Police with them. They'll be the ones in the jungle-type hats."

We discussed the terrain and a little bit about the political situation in China and Tibet. I recounted the Tiananmen incident of five years before, since some of these officers were still in college and some of the younger scientists were finishing advanced degrees in physical anthropology, the academic discipline for forensic identification. I also outlined the helicopter problem and challenged them all to start thinking about the medical evacuation problem.

"You might be able to walk in, but you might have to fly out. Four or five days on a mule or horse with a broken leg won't cut it."

They nodded a grim assent.

CHAPTER 16

Closed States, Closed Gates, and Deadly Pyres

I was an Armor officer (technically a Cavalry officer since the branch assigned those specialties as their primary skill depended on their experience) but also a Foreign Area Officer (FAO) for Northeast Asia, specifically the two Koreas. I also was expected to maintain some expertise on China, Taiwan, Japan, Mongolia, and the Russian far east—sufficient to manage a military "situation." At least the geographic location, culture, and politico-military significance of the Russian far east gave it a geopolitical gravitas that was tremendous.

We would investigate and dig up graves in a frozen former Japanese cemetery one hundred miles north of Vladivostok for a Cold War shoot down. We were searching for US Navy fliers, US captives who were identified as dying in captivity circa 1952 in the nearby military hospital. We spent several days digging in the cemetery with the Defense attaché and Backfire bombers in the winter overcast. But the KGB files remained perpetually and frustratingly closed.

I was expected to learn about my area of the earth on my own. In my case, as a northeast Asia FAO, I had to demonstrate proficiency (which means at least minimally functional) in two languages of northeast Asia, Korean and Mandarin Chinese. I knew the tough young infantry officers, nearly all of them airborne and ranger qualified, could function well in future assignments with the Vietnamese. They understood them—and vice versa. I hoped a few of them might gravitate toward becoming Southeast Asia Foreign Area Officers as they went up the promotion and experience ladder.

As the SecDef had outlined, most of our work was supporting JTF-FA in Vietnam, Laos, and Cambodia, as was the support functions of the other arms of the Department of Defense, including the Armed Forces DNA Identification Laboratory in Maryland. These included units that could render old ordnance safe or destroyed or survival experts that could determine if an ejection was successful or not by inspecting wreckage components, divers, and the other specialists who were a scarce commodity.

But command officers also decreed that CILHI alone would have responsibility for the rest of the wars, and the rest of the world. We would do this by ourselves; our colleagues in DIA had no databases on other conflicts or governments that were applicable. In 1996 a small delegation from my old office in DPMO accompanied by a small CILHI element flew into Pyongyang from Beijing.

We were going to brief the North Koreans on our capabilities and requirements, in the hopes they had the same aspirations as Vietnam—to become a part of an increasingly affluent and free society and work with us. We had over 8,000 US servicemen unaccounted for in that tragic peninsular country.

Joe Harvey used to scoff at me when I suggested North Korea was going to POW/MIA school on us with the Vietnamese. I based this solely on the fact that whenever we arrived late at night in Hanoi, sometimes in General Vessey's unmarked 707, the DPRK ambassador's car with the emblematic flag on the bumper was the only vehicle parked in front of the Ministry of Foreign Affairs. I thought that, if true, it wasn't such a bad thing. Now we were in Pyongyang to hold "informal" discussions on the recovery of US soldiers missing from the Korean conflict. We received the "Madeleine Albright" tour; the former Georgetown professor and US ambassador to the United Nations, born Marie Jana Korbelová in Prague, the sixty-fourth Secretary of State. The tour was hosted by Kim Jong-il. We saw graceful Korean ladies pitch hoops high into the air that were caught by ladies behind them while doing a stylized, traditional Korean dance, accompanied by stringed, woodwind instruments and drums that must have been copies of period instruments of centuries past.

We were treated to a lavish musical all performed by eight- to twelve-year-old students who sang patriotic songs while depicting ancient battles that our host actors and actresses always won. The finale was boys and girls garbed in camouflage, faces camo'ed up, sneaking on stage with very pronounced stealth and hand signals from the patrol leaders while the lighting dimmed.

Ju-Che simply means "self-sufficient"—important for a rogue state with very few friends. The few friends the North Koreans had were impressive —Russia and China, who share their borders, albeit small in Russia's case.

Once Kim il-Sung departed on the Rogue State route there was no going back.

The music stopped while half a dozen miniature Special Purpose Forces soldiers established their hide positions in fake trees and shrubs that were rushed out by stagehands onto the darkened stage. Ten-year-old radio operators in the group tapped out code that a musical instrument accompanied with a *dit dah dit* sound effect, while one observed through binoculars that were seemingly focused on our party of about ten. Some of my former officers, still in DPMO, were accompanied by the current chief of staff, Alan Liotta, a GS 15 we had recruited form the CIA. The rest of us were CILHI'ers, including the team leader who had done so well in Brazil on the World War II loss.

We were the only non-Asians apparent in the audience of about 500 well-dressed Korean men and women. The tapping went on, the music returned quietly as the stage went to total darkness, then the music swelled and the lights came up. The trees and shrubs had disappeared in the brief darkness. His huge troupe did a pass in review—farmers, boys and girls, in homespun period dress, hoes, picks, AK-47s and RPD Soviet machine guns, shouldered. The female dancers in colorful *han boks*, their formal dresses; uniforms of all kinds on girls and boys.

Foreign Area Officers routinely serve as Defense attachés in embassies in their region of expertise; Foreign Military Sales officers serve as area specialists at the Defense Intelligence Agency or occasionally are on loan to some of the three-letter intelligence agencies plus the Department of State. They are sprinkled among regional staffs, with a number of my Asian FAO colleagues serving in the Pacific Command—USCINCPAC, in Hawaii, as I had previously, or USARPAC, the Army headquarters at historic Fort Shafter. This trip was especially significant to me—I'd been in the Korea business for the past two decades. We found the North Koreans intractable and even more difficult to negotiate with than the Vietnamese had been. I thought if they wanted discourse with the United States, they'd take a similar path the Vietnamese had. We were certainly too far apart in our requirements for conducting operations and what they expected of us. One of the English-speaking North Korean officers told us, unofficially perhaps, that it would be difficult for North Korean citizens who "hate the U.S. so much, to see our soldiers, even in mufti traveling on north Korean army trucks or helicopters." Our State representative, Ken Quinones, an old Korea hand who spoke excellent Korean, shook his head, but he'd been long on the receiving end of mind changes and mercurial behavior from the North Korean UN representative. Despite all this, there would be a successful recovery in Korea shortly after I retired, and a few more later, then they dried up.

In the future, as in the past, quartermaster or logistics officers—the Army branch with responsibility for graves registration—would command the US Army Central Identification Hawaii. However, the POW/MIA issue was not a career field, and its exploding growth, peaking in the early 1990s, was managed offline. I had moved laterally within the Office of the Secretary of Defense's East Asia Pacific Region from handling Korea matters to handling POW/MIA matters in that same directorate, working both portfolios at the same time. I was hired for experience, not pedigree.

This was partially as a result of Desert Storm resulting in US and Coalition soldiers and airmen taken prisoner in the conflict, and partially because of the earlier assignment at the JCRC. I was marked as having POW/MIA experience, including time on the ground in two out of three countries of Indochina working operational matters. Now in the Pentagon, we would get to expand into Cambodia as political events changed there. The color revolutions that swept the Middle East, eastern Europe, and the Balkans of the late 1990s and early 2000s were missed in Southeast Asia. But in Cambodia the Paris Peace Agreement augured a cease-fire and the introduction of a rare peacekeeping force in Southeast Asia—UNTAC, the United Nations Transition Authority in Cambodia. Soon we would be working there surrounded by a forest of armed blue berets, including some Americans with decidedly mixed feelings.

I took some time to reflect on my own career, which had included a circuitous, curious progression of jobs—what the professional development officers at the Army Personnel Command called a "checkered" career. This term was not necessarily used in a complimentary fashion by careerist military officers.

In the 1980s a former battalion commander was normally put on a "progressive" career path following a successful battalion command. These progressive career paths included sometimes not very desirable jobs that encompassed command of very important recruiting battalions or assignments to "burnishing" jobs like the Army staff in the Pentagon, where lieutenant colonels would sometime get meaningful jobs.

One way to get around this was to start identifying meaningful jobs over the horizon and showing an interest in them to senior officers who wanted enthusiasts in the jobs. This too, could be called careerist, but the officer who didn't try to at least use a little of his own rudder in job selection might find himself far afield of what was good for him or his family in terms of his expertise and background for the job itself. Or "the Lord takes care of those who try to help themselves; everybody else the Personnel Command takes care of." And that's how I got into the JCRC in July 1987. I asked for the job; the two-star Marine sniffed me and must have liked what he saw. It didn't hurt when I told him I'd fought alongside Marines in northern I Corps in 1967–68. He replied, with a slight grin, "yeah, I did too."

In the pre-1973 JCRC days when the Indochina war was raging, there were mostly Army Special Forces teams doing the reconnaissance and "Direct Action" missions—ambushes, raids, calling in air and artillery strikes, but also assigned were Navy SEALS, a scattering of Marine Force Reconnaissance Personnel collecting intelligence for their forces, and USAF Air Commandoes. Other operations included OP 34-A, activities in North Vietnam; OP 35 and 36, ground activities; Psychological Operations and "dirty tricks," like booby-trapped ammunition; and various other clandestine activities highlighted by cross-border "Over the Fence" incursions into Laos and Cambodia.

These were long-range reconnaissance patrols to find concentrations of NVA personnel and equipment; once found, calling in air strikes, wire taps, prisoner snatches. Sometimes there were other direct-action missions—going in to capture Soviet or Chinese equipment, and the prize jewel, rescuing American prisoners of war—under the overall bailiwick of OP 80, the JPRC, the JCRC's antecedent. During the six years of its existence, it was totally unsuccessful in releasing US prisoners of war—save for one, who died in a few days due to a prison-inflicted blow to the head with a heavy blunt instrument. A number of Army of the Republic of Vietnam prisoners and civilians were also released.

Reconnaissance was victimized by bureaucratic bungling before its activation—the Air Force at that time had primary responsibility for POWs in a framework that was based largely on aerial Search and Rescue and SERE—Survival, Evasion, Resistance, Escape. The Air Force had written the doctrine and run the schools.

After US ground combat ceased in January 1973, the JPRC merely changed hats—in this case green berets to jungle hats with bright orange deer hunters' vests—and became the Joint Casualty Resolution Center (JCRC) based in Thailand. This was the operational cell of the Four Party Joint Military Team, consisting of negotiation cells from the United States and Republic of Vietnam and their adversarial component, the Democratic Republic of Vietnam and the Peoples' Revolutionary Government, the PRG, or Viet Cong. The recovery teams of the JCRC, mostly Special Forces personnel, were unarmed consonant with the "humanitarian" nature of their mission, although occasionally they carried shotguns when in snake infested or dangerous animal areas.[1]

They were anointed "Joint," like their successor JCRC and its successor, Joint Task Force-Full Accounting because Marines, sailors, and airmen were also present in the Command. For linguists, analysts, and graves registration personnel, their mission continued: to account for missing US soldiers and the comparatively few civilians lost in the conflict.

CHAPTER 17

A Nation Ascendant, a Nation Eclipsed

Japan had militarized and flexed her Bushido muscles and dreamed of empire during the Meiji Restoration of the mid-nineteenth century. China moved in the other direction.

The Chinese retrenched and turned inward, quarreling and fighting among themselves while Japan was modernizing. Competing Chinese interests and factions waged internecine warfare and schemed intriguing plots while European and American commercial bullying ran unchecked.

The more China resisted the western powers, the worse its situation became. Chinese attempts to enact reforms outlawing opium sales spawned two conflicts directly attributed to British and French "free trade" efforts. These conflicts became known as the First and Second Opium Wars, the latter being an extension of the First, was also called the Arrow War, or Anglo-French effort against the Qing. "Free Trade," or enhanced mercantile advantages accrued to France and Britain, were the hallmark of both conflicts. Ultimately, Japan emerged politically and militarily powerful at the turn of the twentieth century, while China marked the end of its long period of dynastic rule as World War I and World War II shaped up.

Treaty ports gave de facto extraterritorial rights to European seafaring nations, leaving China politically adrift by the time of the Sino-Japanese War at the end of the nineteenth century. After Japan's lopsided victory over China, the Japanese destroyed the Russian fleet in the battle of the Tsushima Straits, giving great credence to peace-making President Theodore Roosevelt's admiration of the Japanese as the David who brought down the mighty Goliath of czarist Russia.

Theodore's dispatching of the Great White Fleet, the US Navy's battleship squadrons, around the globe in 1907 to emphasize America's burgeoning naval presence underscored US military capability at the dawning of the twentieth century. The 400 million Chinese saw this as another foreign invasion from the barbaric states of Europe and America. It also marked the end of the last Chinese dynasty, the Qing, or Manchu, dynasty, dating from the mid-seventeenth century. With the death of the final empress dowager, Cixi, in 1908, China began anew as a nationalist nation emerging into a modern world.

Shaking off the imperial past's view as the center of the earth in geographical, cultural, and societal terms would not come easily for China. The nation emerged chastised by humiliating defeats at the hands of the Japanese, western powers, and its own internal rebellions into the Asian cauldron of nationalism. China was now led by Chiang Kai-shek, a disciple of Sun Yat-sen; Sun Yat-sen was a Chinese nationalist who had been chosen to lead the Kuomintang's (KMT) Republican Party. He chose Chiang as the head of China's first military academy at Whampoa. Chiang had abandoned his cooperation with the Soviets and his belief that adopting Communist ideals were the well-springs of revolution.

He demonstrated good military prowess in the Northern Expeditions, or Bandit Campaigns, led to break up the warlord factions that had established themselves after the establishment of the "new China" in 1911.

Chiang also cast a wary eye on the Chinese Communist faction led by the upstart revolutionary Mao Tse-tung. He broke with the Communists completely when he realized they had no intention of power sharing or helping the Kuomintang Party as the overarching political framework of the newly formed Republic of China.

Now tended by a retinue of politically astute family and followers, China sat literally at the center of the geopolitical earth. It bordered British- and French-dominated Southeast Asia and Britain's India while China itself sprawled over Northeast Asia, from the South China Sea to Siberia. Sharing this vast region was malevolent, imperial Japan, also controlling a then-unified Korean peninsula and Formosa. China's northernmost section of shakily federated Inner Mongolia and Manchuria, home of the windy desolate plains and the Manchus that ruled from 1644 to 1921, had been "annexed" by the Japanese in 1931. It was quickly renamed Manchuko as militarily weak China looked on helplessly.

Japan had extreme geopolitical "clout" after defeating both China and Russia and joining the western nations in every military adventure of the twentieth century. This began with the rebellious Boxers up through Japan's spiritual alliance with the Americans, British, and French in World War I.

The Soviet Union was suffering purges of her military and political leadership that would leave her in perilous straits from the Axis colossus in a few years. This would spread like a great bloody stain across the Caucasus and into Russia's homeland. These would become the "Bloodlands," where millions died at the hands of Slavic Russians and Nordic Germans.

Now, political realities and prizes to be wrested from territories surrounding China changed the politico-military calculus considerably. China's vulnerability from within as well as growing potential for Japanese military action increased exponentially. This was exacerbated as the United States began a slow economic strangulation of materiel essential to the emperor's forces—particularly oil and steel.

To China's north and west sprawled Mongolia and Russia, the former just recently moved under postrevolutionary Russia's less than benevolent suzerainty and the first state to join—or be forced to join—the international Communist system. Russia's "friendship" with Japan, a political expediency to prevent fighting a two-front war with the Japanese and Germany, resulted in the Russo-Japanese Non-Aggression Pact in 1939. Now, Russia was locked in a life-or-death struggle with the Wehrmacht, and the führer's Waterloo was yet over the horizon.

Tibet was uneasily aware that Britain, Russia, and China sought its sovereignty and loyalty. The "Great Game" of empire went on mutely, submerged by the warfare surrounding Tibet and the vast Tibetan Plateau that covered the roof of the world. Tibet was also uneasily aware that it was a nation of peace and Buddhist tranquility—militarily it could do nothing to stop these behemoth powers from overcoming the nation with coercion followed by force.

British India was girding for possible invasion and preparing for the long bloody conflicts that would follow in the humid, Southeast Asian colonies of Malaya and Burma, where the Rising Sun flowed like an inexorable tide. Nationalism had swept India with the monsoon storms that worsened British problems—Mahatma Gandhi's call to "Quit India" resulted in nationwide strikes to further the cause of Indian independence.

To the south and east, French Indochina had been rendered impotent by its European surrender in 1940; it limped on under the Vichy regime, now in complete control of France's colonial states of Vietnam, Laos, and Cambodia. Japanese fighters and bombers marauded from Haiphong and Hanoi in Tonkin or northern Vietnam near China, and Tourane (Da Nang), in Annam, central Vietnam as well as southernmost Saigon in Cochin China—Saigon, the Paris of the Orient and former flower of French colonialism. Japanese coastal patrols flew out of Bac Lieu, in the Mekong Delta.

China was a weakened, newly emerged nation, still warmed by the shed cloak of millenniums of mostly benign Confucian dynastic rule. It was now just shaking off decades of war-lord-ism, watching as Communists and Japanese colluded and collided, both trying to defeat the nimble but ineffectual Kuomintang forces of Chiang Kai-shek. China was a nation rife with factions and only marginally controlled by Chiang and his advisers in western China. Inundated and surrounded by nations at war, it was virtually helpless.

The allied colonial powers in the region did not share President Roosevelt's vision of a strong but friendly China as the dominant force in postwar Asia. Their eyes were on retaining—or regaining—their former colonies. China was totally dependent on Chiang's expedient and shifty but clever diplomacy and a sympathetic United States, whose commander in chief had a long affinity for and family history with the people and culture of China. It was, like many things an American president is forced to do, built somewhat on prevarication, false assumptions, and very slick marketing. Moreover, in terms of lobbying or a public relations effort, the Chinese who surrounded Chiang Kai-shek were masters and first-class manipulators of image.

America's view of China before Pearl Harbor was veiled in racism, nationalistic hubris, and, to a large degree, the isolationism bred by large oceans protecting America's national "shoulders"—the east and west coast. Scarcely two generations prior to December 7, 1941, the US Congress enacted the Chinese Exclusion Act of 1882, the year of Franklin Delano Roosevelt's birth. For the first time since its inception, America no longer welcomed everyone to its shores.[1]

The "Exclusion" also meant vile practices of burning out Chinese communities in the Rocky Mountain West and Pacific Northwest.[2]

This was in response to the perception that the Chinese were taking American jobs by working harder and cheaper on the nation's engine of Manifest Destiny—the transcontinental railroads. Chinese immigrants had come to California in the 1850 gold rush and were grudgingly accepted as long as the gold held out and the American miners got fairly wealthy; when the gold petered out, the Chinese began laying track. The railroad barons loved the Chinese workers; they worked hard (and cheaper than the Americans), kept to themselves, and didn't cause trouble in the saloons surrounding railroad development.

America's view of Japan before Pearl Harbor was steeped in adventurism and a romance that was largely based on America's view of the "little fellow." A "David" who had slain two "Goliaths"—Russia and China—barely a generation ago. Now China, and to a lesser extent Russia, were the good guys in American perceptions.

Coupled with Germany's desire to move across Europe—most likely with a powerful war machine and "illegal" Luftwaffe, baptized in Spain with its JU-87 Stuka dive bombers, and the Messerschmitt BF-109 fast agile fighters, baptized in Spain, they sought lebensraum—living room.

Chiangs's attempts to restore China to its "rightful" place in the global community, the center of the world, economically and politically, weren't going so well. Russia's westward and southern ambitions included ice-free ports and uninhibited trade. America's desire to keep the Philippines strife free and everybody else out of this strategic hub of Southeast Asia, hardly provided symmetry of interests. America was a Pacific power now and had to counter any threat coming out of the world's most expansive ocean. And, of course, Russia was unabashedly Communist and had dragged poor neighboring Mongolia into its sphere, smashing Buddhist shrines and temples in its wake. China was the giant, but it was a decrepit, poor giant.

The change in attitude about the China of the 1880s and the late 1930s stemmed largely from Japanese belligerence and expansionism, particularly after their bloody, terrifying 1937 incursion into Nanking. Despite these easy victories nobody but the Japanese knew that, in reality, they were looking for a way out of China. Without losing face on the way out. China was the cormorant's dilemma—a tasty morsel, but too big to swallow or to spit out.

The catalysts were two cousins different as night and day. Theodore Roosevelt respected the strength and daring of the Japanese. The Japanese were the czar's navy in the Straits of Tsushima. Roosevelt viewed the Chinese as unmilitary and docile. This may have been due to the Chinese peasants' attitudes about soldiers—"just as you don't use good metal for nails, don't use good men for soldiers" was an oft-quoted Chinese proverb that was bandied about.

Somewhere in the middle was the generalissimo, Chiang Kai-shek, whose influence ring ran from the American people right on through his nationalist army (but not the Chinese Communist Party forces that were ostensibly under his command) on down to the lowliest American soldier.

Those young men would bring salvation to China in the bellies of American transport planes. This was the China Fulton Lanier and his crew had flown into on this clear last day of January 1944. Moreover, Lanier's second tour in Asia was a relearning experience for the combat veteran; he, like any newly arrived pilot, had to be recertified as an aircraft commander.

This involved flying several missions in the right seat as a copilot until he was deemed competent enough to undergo a "check ride" with an experienced and veteran captain serving as examiner. Soon he was certified as fully qualified to command a transport aircraft and immediately transitioned to an airplane that was to have a marked effect on the India-China route—the four-engine C-87.

Japan's modernization arose out of the Meiji Restoration, shortly after our own Civil War. A great deal of confidence in the Japanese psyche stemmed from the fact that since modernization Japan had suffered no military defeat. The notion of the Samurai and the warrior ethos of the military was ingrained in the populace and the government, especially the Army and the Navy. Japan had defeated both China and Russia at the turn of the century, but the defeat of the czarist navy had the most lasting effect—European powers could be defeated by modernized Asian nations.[3] As allies of the British since 1902, Japan shared in the Allies' victorious spoils of World War I by seizing German holdings in China—specifically Tsingtao and Shandong as well as the Marshalls, Carolines, and Marianas, all strategic islands in the Pacific that were also defeated German possessions.[4]

When Bushido emerged out of the seventeenth century it was a "code of conduct" for the Samurai, long a class in Japan. It melded Zen Buddhist/Confucian ideals of loyalty to their Lord and masters that transferred to the emperor in the Meiji Restoration and military modernization of the mid-nineteenth century. It drove the entire country of Japan as a national mindset.

The populations of Nanjing, Hong Kong, and Singapore got to experience Bushido firsthand. After the Nanjing massacre many assumed that the Japanese had become berserkers—gone rogue with killing fury.

Allied victories in the Great War were ratified by the Treaty of Versailles in 1919, leaving Japan as the preeminent power in the Pacific, and leaving Germany shattered by the loss of a significant portion of the young men of the country, the staggering war and damage reparations, and the seizure of its overseas holdings as well as some restoration of borders won in the wars of the nineteenth century. But there were problems and humiliations in the largely untouched Pacific area, particularly when America demanded Japan drop the "21 Demands" on her old adversary, China.[5]

The domination of China had been a longtime goal of the Japanese Army, which viewed the threat of the czar in the east, Russia, particularly, as one of the greatest threats to the emperor from a geopolitical and military standpoint.

Further humiliations ensued with the Washington Naval Treaty of 1921 that put naval limitations on Japan with ratios of battleships, also, the refusal of the British to continue the alliance between the two countries. The British decided to establish a naval stronghold in Singapore to strengthen its presence and military capabilities in the Pacific; an alliance with a belligerent Japan wouldn't be geopolitically wise. All these factors and others irritated the Japanese.

In 1940 Japan became a member of the Axis Powers and demanded the Vichy government of France allow them access to Vietnam and Laos, leaving the Burma Road as the only link to the west and supplies from the Indian Ocean and the Bay of Bengal. But now, with virtually all Burma coming under control of the Rising Sun except for the far northern part with a few British airfields and the Chindwin delta, Japan had encircled China, albeit tenuously. Japan could strike west and hit India's major cities with bombing raids or east into China but couldn't marshal sufficient troops for serious ground offensives.

Japan realized China wouldn't go away easily—Japan had been trying to ease out after taking Manchuria—Manchuko—in 1931 and regoverning China with the young Manchu heir, Puyi, the last emperor of the Manchus. That hadn't worked and Japan's preliminary overtures to a cease-fire agreement and negotiations hadn't done anything except give Chiang Kai-shek a tool to frighten the Americans and British—something to worry President Roosevelt.

The million Japanese troops permitted control of coastal China on the South China Sea and protected the Ryukus chain, which opened the door to Japan's main islands. The troops prevented China from opening a sea lane of supply and allow allies to get a foothold in the maritime region of southeast China. That was Japan's vulnerable side door.

The Japanese realized that vital islands like Truk and Rabaul ultimately would need to be protected, because surely the Commonwealth forces couldn't leave the emperor's forces to hold these vital staging points for Papua New Guinea and northern Australia. The necklace of islands stretching southeast from the Andaman Sea and the Dutch East Indies needed to be protected as well as Borneo, the Celebes, and all the approaches to Melanesia, especially Papua New Guinea.[6]

While the Battle of the Coral Sea in early May 1942 proved to be evenly matched with both sides claiming victory, the Japanese couldn't deny the loss of four carriers and other surface combatants to the fast-moving carrier battle groups the Americans had turned up. They knew the Allies, led by the American naval forces, would fight tenaciously to protect the Coral Sea's approach to northeast Australia. The Japanese knew that soon more and larger American carrier battle groups would be combing the western Pacific.

Finally, the Japanese forces had warily watched the mobilization that the United States was undertaking in both manpower and military industrial production. Japan was also fully convinced by now that subduing China had been a bad strategic mistake. Japan had to make sure the country of 400 million was shut off from supplies of war, but they didn't want to tackle another giant—India—despite the ever-increasing airlift of supplies over the highest mountains in the world, which the Americans was carrying out from bases in Assam.

The Japanese were doing these airlifts while also airlifting vital supplies to British Chindits and American Marauders battling them in Burma, coming out of the skies in gliders and parachutes. They knew they had to seize control of northern Burma and use the airfields there to squeeze the Americans out of their aerial supply effort, and also, firmly ensconced, they could swing west into Assam and seize the Hump airfields. They could also turn east and occupy the desirable airfields at Kunming and Yunnan-ni, principal aerial supply bases and ones they would use with reestablished lines of communication from the ports in the Tonkin Delta of North Vietnam. They would also provide nests for the Sentai's—squadrons of fighters and bombers.

But the Americans seemed to learn how to do difficult things very quickly.

The greatest obstacle to Hump operations was the weather. A pilot observed, "Flying weather on instruments continued to be the most threatening ordeal for pilots. Piloting a plane through the angry limbo of clouds was strange and frightening . . . flying twenty-five tons of metal, gasoline and high explosives through an unknown sky . . . in actual flight, instrument flight in bad weather was the most stressful and agonizing part of the mission."[7]

As a presidential policy or military strategy, it was sound and certainly made sense at the time—tying down one million plus Japanese soldiers on the mainland of China, without putting a sizable force of American soldiers there. But psychologically the bill to America was much higher than 10,000 tons a month, or even more. China began to cleverly foster a sense of guilt in the American people. China had been fighting the Japanese since 1937 but had initially taken their punches with the Japanese annexation of Manchuria in 1931.

The Chinese had felt Japan's wrath a *decade* before Pearl Harbor. China had Christianized (a far reach) and accepted America's democratic precepts through the missionaries who flooded her shore in the eighteenth and nineteenth centuries. Politicians and decision-makers in Washington saw Harvard-educated and fluent English-speaking Chinese with impeccable western social graces lobbying for their assistance—and military equipment and funding—with charm and wit.

China had the manpower and wisdom to defeat the Japanese. All the Americans had to do was equip and pay for the huge Chinese armies that would sweep the Japanese into the sea. The Americans wouldn't have to worry about fighting on the ground. Especially since there was no sizable force to put there. But the air was different; China needed American transport planes and fighters and bombers to conquer the space and time continuum. If the United States paid the bill with tonnage and US dollars, the generalissimo would furnish the infantry—mostly made up of members of the Chinese peasantry—armed and trained with American money and guarantors of their safety by air superiority.

As a consequence, the China Burma India theater would be largely one decided by air power, only this time—for the first time—it would be also decided largely by the allied logistics executed as a function of air power, articulated by Colonel John Plating, USAF, in his classic treatise. He was a contemporary airlifter, and the Hump airlift was in his blood. The strategic disadvantage was the relative impunity the enemy army assumed; they acted as a giant reserve force capable of reinforcing any vital island garrison, objective, or region of the Pacific. They deemed this possible assuming their sea lanes and surface transport ships remained reasonably open from the Sulu Sea through the Formosa Straits to the bleak north Pacific and the Aleutian Islands.

This was demonstrated by the massing of Japanese division-sized forces that rushed west, sweeping Stilwell's Chinese forces and his British Indian forces into India like so much spilled dust. This prompted Stilwell's famous "I claim we got a hell of a beating . . . humiliating as hell" speech. The second time in mid-1944 might be likened to the "high-water mark" of Japan's ascendancy.

There were, by the time Fulton Lanier started his tour in the Southwest Pacific Theater of Operations, over a million Japanese soldiers, marines, and airmen in China. The Pacific theater would be devoid of American combat troops for the foreseeable future, while the Arcadia Conference's inexorable decision to give precedence to Europe first, then the Pacific, would govern the priority of men, machines, and materiel. On top of that, China could only be supplied, and tenuously at that, out of British India.

The Kuomintang armies of Chiang Kai-shek were formidable in numbers on paper, and the tough three-star US general officer sent to train them was formidable on all counts. The wiry, weather-beaten West Point graduate (class of 1904) had a talent for sports, languages (a first in French), and irascibility. Officers at the School of Infantry at Fort Benning, Georgia, in the 1930s hung the sobriquet of "Vinegar Joe" on him. Stilwell liked that—it communicated that he didn't suffer fools wisely. He was clearly first choice to command a corps (a corps is made up of two or more divisions and can consist of up to 40,000 men in some instances), but this was derailed by President Roosevelt's decision, backed by Stilwell's friend, Army Chief of Staff George Marshall.

Stilwell's facility with languages led him to three tours in China, the last a four-year assignment as the military attaché, and he became quite proficient in both written and spoken Chinese. His other trait, care and the best possible training for young soldiers, came to the fore. During that tour he traveled on trains, observed Kuomintang soldiers, tapped into intelligence sources, and became attuned to the Chinese and their decision-making, from the squad level to the politics of senior leaders. He knew about the vaunted "face" and *guan-xi*, the importance of patronage. Most saw and understood how Stilwell cared very little for the effects of face if it interfered with military training, combat, or the lives of soldiers. So Stilwell, a volatile personality who internalized all stressful challenges, had no clear idea of the limits of his charter, or the actual scope of his responsibilities of command and training of Chinese troops, except that it differed considerably from the generalissimo's vision.

The price of keeping one million Japanese tied up in China was rather insignificant on the face of it. Stilwell was also enough of an old China hand to know that Chiang had several agendas, most of them covering or diverging suspicion from his real goals and objectives. Chiang had to be supplied by air from India, the only viable resupply option with the traditional supply routes into China hampered or disrupted completely—the Hong Kong–Guanzhou route, the Silk Road route out of Russia, the sea/rail route through Burma, severed by the occupation of Rangoon and southern Burma, and Indochina.

Vietnam, Laos, and Cambodia as well as Thailand were now available to the Japanese as safe and convenient launching sites for their bombers and fighters. Stilwell put more faith in the Burma Road than most, despite the calculus of burning fuel to get the fuel, ammunition, and other materiel through the provinces' skeins of corruption that took a considerable amount of cargo as toll. The Burma Road wasn't bound by the weather, could operate twenty-four hours a day, and could be cut, or harassed, by the Japanese, but it could hardly be put out of business for political reasons despite the British closing it at the request of the Japanese for a few months before hostilities to avoid a possible two-front war.

The Burma Road was back in business again. The British knew a two-front war was inevitable, it seemed, and they didn't want to upset FDR excessively.

This was the China that the crew of C-87 862 from Jorhat Air Base, Assam, India, was servicing with air-delivered cargo to Kunming, Lunnan Province, China, the afternoon of January 31, 1944.

First Lieutenant Fulton P. Lanier, USAAF, studied the sky over Kunming, China. Like most pilots, he was uncomfortable on the ground and wanted to get into the air as quickly as possible, especially as the cumulus buildup thickened to the west. By the time they arrived back over Assam in the Brahmaputra Valley of northeast India and their home base of Jorhat, weather conditions could have—probably would have—deteriorated considerably, Lanier knew. It was a toss-up—take the longer and possibly worsening weather on the southerly route, with the added possibility of running into a hunter in a Zero A6-M braving the weather looking for a slow sheep to kill. There was the dangerously lower amount of fuel to consider also. Or the shorter northern route with the higher mountains, the chance the storm wouldn't have peaked until after they'd safely passed through it. He and the weatherwise copilot Frank Ramos talked it through, because they'd have to file their flight plan soon.

Chiang and FDR's ten thousand tons would be very expensive commodities if measured in men and airplanes.

"Well, north would be safer from the Japs in the south," Ramos ventured.

"Right, even if some brave Samurai wanted to take on this front, but you seem to know a little bit about weather; better or worse south or north?"

Ramos thought a moment, eyes on the drifting clouds and the windsock, now starting to stiffen in the breeze, "it'll probably depend on when we get out of here. If we don't get hung up waiting for cargo probably better in the north, less winds aloft . . . maybe . . . I'm guessing. You've been out here longer than I have, and you've got twice as many hours."

Lanier nodded, "Yeah, I think you're probably right . . . on the other hand, higher MEA and less forgiving terrain up that way."[8]

Earlier that morning, soldiers on the ground added six tons of cargo to the 14,441 tons the C-87 would airlift from India into western China this first month of 1944. The new radio operator, Bartholomew "Benny" Giacalone, was to join the flight crew on an eye-opening first trip to China.

Lanier and his crew had been on the ground almost six hours after their cargo of fuel and aircraft engines had been off-loaded, much too long in Lanier's estimation. Lanier had probably "shopped" for weather reports from other pilots flying into Kunming that morning, and although he probably hadn't run into any Jorhat-based C-87 crews, he might have talked to a C-46 pilot from Sookerating, a couple of C-47 crews from Chabua, or a British crew flying out of Dinjan.[9]

They all related pretty much the same information—perhaps some turbulence, including carburetor icing going into Yunnan-ni, a base south of Kunming, but nothing notably good or bad. It was a normal winter weather day in South Asia and over the Hump to southeast Asia, or more accurately as the merger of southeast and northeast Aisa, as Kunming was just north of Vietnam in air miles.

So it seemed. Even with the Hump route, in existence for over two years, meteorology was still an infant technology in the China Burma India theater. It would be several months before the Air Weather Service would have reliable forecasting in place. PIREPS—Pilot Reports—were a less than suitable alternative, but they were better than nothing.[10]

Lanier knew that of southwestern China's only two "flying" seasons, winter, generally from October to May, offered better flying weather than the remaining season, summer, May to early/mid-October.[11] In Kunming and south toward the border with Indochina, fall and spring melded into winter and summer and had no special weather characteristics, except for seasonal monsoons twice yearly that could be associated with the seasons a pilot grew up with back in America. Lanier also knew that earlier in the day was likely to be smoother and contain less worrisome weather than later, when the sun had heated the air and the earth along the route.

He sighed when he reflected that just five hundred miles farther west at their home base in India's Brahmaputra River valley, there were four distinct seasons, unlike China's two, all with varying degrees of challenges and hazards.[12] First, were local conditions at the airfields, where thunderstorms, fog, monsoon rains, and wind made the usual instrument approaches and landings tricky.

This was especially true when the pilot and copilot were numb with exhaustion, cold, and were perhaps fighting turbulence and icing the entire leg back from China.[13] Second, most weather in India originated in the Bay of Bengal, which spawned tropical highs with fast-moving weather patterns. These moved northeast through the low, alluvial plains before colliding with the rising hill masses of Nagaland, Burma, and the Tibetan borderlands, turning into vicious, turbulent thunderstorms. Pilots often climbed to altitudes so high the thunderstorms were virtually impossible to avoid.[14]

Finally, the moisture in the systems, gradually rising on the platform of warmer air below, created icing and turbulence that were challenging even for experienced pilots and crews like the Pan Am veterans who had flown the African routes for years before coming to the CBI. For neophytes, like most of the newly minted Army pilots, it could be—and was—disastrous.[15]

This was one more reason to get airborne, but likely the delay was the expected transshipment of some cargo inbound from someplace, outbound to somewhere. Lanier's copilot on this flight, Ramos, seemed to have an unusual appreciation for the subtleties of weather that belied his less than 400 hours of cockpit time. Frank had flown as a copilot for a period of time with an airline as part of a contract opportunity between the Army Air Force and the Civil Aviation authorities, stemming from the broadening of the Civil Air Fleets' responsibilities as they joined the war effort.

Lanier was impressed as Ramos described the phenomena of frontal systems matter-of-factly. Fulton quipped that Ramos must have been intrigued by something more interesting that he himself had failed to note in his hurried meteorology classes.

"When you're a low-time, low-life Army student pilot flying right seat in an airliner, you're definitely at the bottom of the food chain. On a good day, the captain let me handle the flap settings as well as operate the landing gear."

"While he was flirting with the waitresses and enjoying lunch, I'd be out chasing weather charts, calling the Met guys at operations, checking altimeter settings en route . . . most captains couldn't get enough information about weather, and I learned to appreciate that.

"Occasionally you'd get a real weather pilot who'd teach me something useful; I always appreciated that," Frank noted.

Fulton nodded slowly in agreement. It seems that most of the missing crews he'd read about in rescue and safety bulletins or in preflight operations briefings had experienced encounters with weather. In just about all cases, it had been an unexpected encounter, but one viewed as an eventuality.

Crashes had been discovered that occurred years ago—gone "off the scope." In pilot parlance that meant "simply disappeared." Lanier had learned that weather patterns along all the routes were from the result of disparate weather systems sweeping across the Indian Ocean combining with the same disparate patterns coming down out of Siberia. The weather systems swirled around the Bay of Bengal in India and out of the Siberian taiga over much of central and northern China, while the South China Sea influenced much of southern China.

This latter fact was particularly true of Lunnan and Kwang-si, the rain-forested highland provinces that bordered Indochina to the south. Monsoon rains and low visibility approaches were common in India and southern China; thunderstorms and icing, including severe icing, were hazards anywhere in theater.

Severe icing was defined as icing that increased faster than aircraft systems could dispose of it. Ice could choke the engines or coat the surfaces of the aircraft until the plane staggered along losing altitude and gradually dropping from the sky in an uncontrolled descent.

As Ramos said, civilian airline captains with thousands of hours' time were especially sensitive to weather, and their copilots were charged with ferreting out details on commercial routes, something more easily done with the airlines' strong infrastructure. In three years of interaction with airline pilots, Lanier had frequently heard the copilots gripe about "chasing weather" for the "arrogant bastards in the left seat." He had also concluded that the airlines were much better informed and savvier about flying weather than their uniformed counterparts.

"Weather will kill you faster than anything; the Army hasn't figured that out, but the airlines sure have," he thought. "Plus in this Army Air Force you might be flying a plane one day and a desk the next. Might have to think about that if things go sour with the Army after the war. Guess if I had to take a non-flying job I'd probably get out and go to the airlines."

But he pushed the postwar career out of the corner of his mind. Right now, he had to get a crew over the highest mountains with the worst weather in the world.

"I'm never frightened about anything," he told himself, "merely concerned."

And right now he was very concerned about weather.

Fulton Pershing Lanier had confidence in things he could control, particularly his flying ability. His hiatus in Texas as an instructor just before arriving in India had also sharpened his skills, and he had an instinctive feel for the C-87, despite its shortcomings. It was painful to sit with his hands in his lap as a student clumsily manhandled his beloved B-17E, but he was also an excellent—if unenthusiastic—instructor, gritting his teeth in a skidding student-performed simple turn.

"Not bad, but follow me through on the controls and let's do it again."

Then he'd lightly roll the big aircraft into a graceful turn, the little black ball centered in the turn and bank indicator all through the turn, signifying perfect control between rudders and ailerons to roll-out, then back again.

"Remember, when an aircraft is loaded right and the power remains consistent it wants to fly itself. It's a comfortable feeling for an airplane, and all you have to do is be light on the controls and watchful. Never stop looking in the direction of a turn unless you're on instruments. And always get the sense of when an airplane is getting uncomfortable with itself."

His greatest moments were when a student's face lit up with knowledge and started flying more smoothly.

Lanier was skilled and proficient on instruments and habitually flew instrument approaches in clear weather to keep those skills honed.

Point to point navigation—inbound and outbound to "fixes" (known points, whether visual or electronic)—was another aviation facet that required almost as much luck as skill. That situation also came wrapped in the surly, dangerous weather and forbidding terrain; frequently you couldn't identify the radio beacons due to the static emanating from electrical discharges in thunderstorms, the high terrain blocking the signals and a host of other conditions that Lanier also couldn't control.

"Just identify the beacon for me, and I can get to it, and on to the next—following the breadcrumbs—and finally make a good approach and land safely," he thought.

He knew that was wishful thinking. A strong signal leading you to an unknown station was worse than being lost—it was a siren song that might draw you off your own map. Again, something he couldn't control. He knew that the vaunted thin Davis wing that contributed to the aircraft's high service ceiling would not carry much ice. He also knew that weather was a factor he couldn't control, so he had to plan for it. Just as he planned for the Japanese fighters that were in easy reach along the southern route and potentially dangerous along the northern route.

As Lieutenant Lanier pondered this, Private Eugene Beebe walked up and waved casually to the two pilots before turning the wave into a careless military salute.

"Did the gas groundhog see his shadow today, Gene?" Ramos asked.

Beebe, all business, laconically missed the humor. "Twelve hundred and seventeen gallons, Sir. Best I could do."

Ramos and Lanier both nodded glumly. Directives had piled up in blizzards of paper, from Air Transport Command headquarters downward to group, wing, and, finally, squadron that the airmen and their "usually" trusted aluminum steeds needed to help the war effort. The "effort" in this case was meeting the monthly tonnage requirements of aerial supplies President Roosevelt promised Generalissimo Chiang Kai-shek—the GMO—leader of the Kuomintang and all Nationalist China. All China except for of a few remaining warlords and the Communist Eighth Route Army. The mission: keep one million Japanese soldiers tied up by the Chinese, fighting since 1937 with four hard years of privation, starvation, and near annihilation before Pearl Harbor.

Neither Lanier or Ramos or the hundreds of inexperienced pilots flying the Hump could understand the logic of allotting just enough fuel to the aircraft to get it and its crew back to their home stations.

"Why don't they just drain the fuel in returned aircraft and put it in drums and ship it back?" Ramos groused. Some savvy and ambitious aviation staff officer could probably make colonel or get a desirable award for coming up with this logic.

Transport aircraft departing Kunming for Jorhat were topped off with only 1,200 gallons of fuel in their tanks. The other Chinese airfields had been similarly allotted the addition of enough fuel to get them back to their bases in Assam, with a little reserve.

Lanier, after sprinkling bombs all over the southwest Pacific, was well aware that in his B-17 Flying Fortress, you sacrificed fuel for useful load, namely, ordnance. A big aircraft like a B-17 or B-24 flew a lot better with a light load; bombs did not make for a light load, since the most common and effective bombs were 500 pounders, the B-17 could carry 5,000 pounds or ten 500 pounders. But that depended on many things—runway length and surface, altitude of the airfield, and even the temperature—the higher it was, the longer the takeoff roll.

But the weather flying out of northwest Australia, Southwest Pacific Theater, in his previous tour in 1942 could not touch this CBI route for danger when he arrived mid-1943. Everything in SWPAC occurred during daylight hours; there were plenty of landmarks to get to the targets and return, and Lanier practiced the rudimentary approaches to keep his instrument proficiency sharp.

But the number of "real world" instrument approaches he had to make were minimal in his first combat tour, usually during the infrequent rainstorms that plagued the Northern Territories of Australia, where his flights usually originated and terminated. The rugged Owen Stanley Mountains were the terrain hazard, the anti-aircraft fire coming up mainly from ships of the Japanese navy was another.

The more something in the military is disparaged, generally the more dangerous or complicated it appears, thus the more expansive the legend. Hence, the "Puzzle Palace" for the Pentagon, the "Aluminum Trail," along with the "Rockpile" and a few others, for the Hump. Ironically, the Hump had a reputation for such an aircrew killer, some senior air force leaders tried to rename the Hump the hill.

The crews scattered along the aluminum trail of aircraft wreckage wouldn't get a vote on this. Aviation gasoline—100 octane AVGAS—weighed about six pounds per gallon, and weight was the equivalent of money in the bank. Weight, more than volume, meant much to the war effort, and even Lieutenant General Stilwell, the ranking flag officer in theater, had wondered aloud about the utility of aircraft burning as much fuel as it was bringing to the fight. Stilwell's mistrust of aircraft was partially parochial—the infantryman's disdain for the elite airmen. But it was also grounded in something aircraft couldn't do without—airfields.

Airfields weren't portable, and Stilwell correctly forecast that the more effective aircraft became against the Japanese—whether fighters, bombers, or airlift—the Japanese would target their bases. Airfields had to have security. The Chinese should have been able to secure them, but he had no faith in them yet. His real trust was in their numbers. The Communists were good soldiers—but they had been diminished by time and their so-called Long March.

Stilwell saw himself as being the trainer, but the wily, political Chiang had been more convinced of the potential of air power by Chennault, a zealot who could effectively argue the point. Chennault, through Chiang, had also begun to even sway the president. With Roosevelt's predilection for the Chinese, his family roots nurtured in the China tea, silk, and, left unsaid, opium, contemporary observers might say he was "hooked."

FDR had dreams for China. He envisioned a rather Shambala world, unencumbered by imperialist big powers. Instead, it would be a more Metternichian "spheres of influence" world—with the big powers shed of imperial holdings and keeping the peace benignly, or at most with threats of intervention. China would be the stabilizing force for Asia—friendly to the United States, Christian in belief (Chiang had dropped whatever Buddhist and Confucian underpinnings of religion he grew up with, he was now a Methodist, like his wife). He typified the 'big hand, small map' type of leader. He had a vision of the postwar world—he wanted things *now* and sometimes failed to recognize and account the difficulties faced by young men cutting airfields far into the jungles, or steering carrier battle groups through storms, or wrestling to throw cargo from aircraft before throwing themselves out as well. Everything came with a price in blood.

Franklin Delano Roosevelt, like Woodrow Wilson, was a normative president—he viewed the world as it should be—conflict, discord, racial enmity, and the various social dissensions from war to alliance governed by a fair, equitable world order. All sovereign nations, indeed, all citizens, should be in agreement with all international norms and laws. His elder cousin Theodore—TR—viewed the world through an empirical, realistic lens; the world that *is* rather than a world that *ought to be*.

The allied leaders who ruled the CBI were all potentially *very* great men with many magnificent qualities. FDR and Churchill; Marshall; the impatient naval boss Admiral King; the glaring, always silently fuming Stilwell; Chennault, with his slow easy speech (somewhat like his wife, observed Chiang, when speaking English); and even quirky Wingate, who, as his punctilious British brother officers might label him: "off-putting," were all good men, with many great attributes and a few flaws.

Also Stilwell by now had realized that he and Chiang would likely never see eye to eye on anything. Stilwell taking command of Chinese forces to equip and train them, would make them Stilwell's men.

Besides that, Stilwell recognized Chennault for his leadership of the relatively small group of pilots of the Flying Tigers and the even smaller group that had formed up as the China Air Task Force and Twenty-Third Fighter Group. But with the infantryman's cynical and perceptive eye, he also knew that Chennault's charisma and genuine belief that airpower would win the war in China was an infectious illusion in the White House and the CBI.

Chennault also knew that Chiang had no inclination for Stilwell's being the go-to American. For one thing, he and the crusty, unpretentious general weren't cut out of the same cloth. He knew control of the vast Chinese armies was his sole legitimacy for likewise controlling all of China. He didn't intend to fight the Japanese in a nation-to-nation, army-to-army slugging match. His armies were destined to fight the Communists, the disease of the heart. Americans and the British could fight the Japanese, a "disease of the skin" to Chiang, but this Stilwell was going to be a problem, Chiang recognized. He knew he was a friend and protégé of the Army chief of staff, George C. Marshall.

Chiang's effective lobby in the United States was conducted by his smooth and western oriented brother-in-law, T. V. Soong. He kept an effective public affairs and lobbying effort ongoing with Congress, key Cabinet officials, especially the State Department, and of course, the White House and the key advisors to the president.

The novelist Pearl S. Buck's *The Good Earth* had depicted China in a positive light. Christian missionaries were proselytizing, not only the peasants but also their own US parishes, denominations, congregations, and the general American populace, telling about the good things going on in China.

Henry Luce, the publishing giant, was another. Luce, born to missionary parents in China and late educated at Yale, was also a devout Christian with a zeal for China. Soong soothed him along in his lobbying efforts to keep the cash and accolades going in *Time* and *Life* magazines, which seemingly all Americans read.

Chiang knew his real worth to America—keeping those one million (or maybe more) Japanese in check. They were concentrated in southeast China, dominating the coastal provinces. China was too large to conquer and too road-poor to police. Japan was like a cormorant that had tried to swallow a fish too big. It couldn't swallow it nor could it bring the fish back up. China was that big fish

Now Stilwell could present his case to Roosevelt: 10,000 tons of war materiel could be airlifted from Assam to Chinese bases in southwest China. With that, by the war with Japan beaten by the British and Americans, he could deal with Mao Tse-tung and Chou En-lai. Of course this materiel would be seen as going directly to fight the Japanese, with his Chinese troops, trained and controlled by Stilwell. Or so Stilwell thought.

Chiang knew that wasn't going to happen. Airplanes were key to the logistical, tactical, and strategic success in China. He understood that along with Chennault, his trusted confidant on aerial and strategic matters. Yes, there was a ground link from eastern Assam through Burma and on into Lunnan, but with a succession of hairpin turns and steep grades in both directions. Stilwell always kept land transportation, logistics, and ground troops' protection of their airfield in the forefront of his supply reliance. Besides, Chiang was an intelligent leader. He also had an excellent military education—at the hands of the Japanese, where he served as an artillery cadet, but he respected their discipline and attention to detail.

Weather, maintenance, and mission changes made airplanes too vulnerable for getting valuable supplies and materiel through. The requirements generated by the Chindits and the American Marauders demonstrated this, detailing several aircraft to assist the newly formed combat crews in air delivery missions.

This logistical ground artery was preeminent in Stilwell's thinking, and even Chiang Kai-shek must have realized the crusty Stilwell's belief in it. When the Ledo portion was opened, well after he'd fired the general, Chennault christened it the "Stilwell Road." But right now, Chennault had more influence with FDR than did Stilwell. Technically, the choleric Stilwell, with his rarely worn cluster of three stars, outranked Chennault with his two.

Plus, there was enhanced distrust and scrambling for position on the board between the two American generals, something that Chiang normally liked to see. Enmity between supposed allies only enhanced his position and strengthened his control over the entire theater, country, and region. After all, even though he was extremely comfortable with his position with Roosevelt, thanks to his effective lobby in Washington, he still had a hostile British presence. They certainly didn't share FDR's vision of a postwar Asia overseen by Chiang. Nor did the French.

The popular Lord Mountbatten had been interposed into the command structure in a worrisome manner, with a superlative title: Supreme Allied Commander, South East Asia Command, or SEAC, the abbreviated title.

The French wanted to ensure their Imperial holdings were intact after Japan fell; their holding of all three Indochinese states: Vietnam, Laos, and Cambodia, would ensure their importance in Asia. Unfortunately, anti-imperialist roots had taken hold in India, Indochina, and parts of North Africa. More was to come, in a differing and with a far more lasting effect, in China itself.

Air power was wondrous and wonderful, beautiful but burdensome, requiring those same muddy infantrymen that were slogging through the rain forests of Burma to attack the generalissimo's Japanese to also break off and guard those airfields. It was the ultimate zero-sum game. Air power came with a price. A very high price.

Major General Chennault fought the traditional pecking order of the United States Army as hard as he was fighting the Japanese—irony of some sort, but fighting supposedly friendly bureaucracies had been going on since MacArthur's fight with the horse cavalry clique for more and better tanks.

But in the micro sense, most would realize this was the usual grousing that went on between the infantry and the more glamorous (better paid and much more comfortable) air arm of the same service, albeit at a much higher level. At ground level, or more accurately, cockpit level, crews who were realists recognized the same argument.

Airplanes were wondrous deus ex machina magic carpets that could cleave continents in practically no time. But they needed appendages that cost more than they were worth sometimes—airfields, fuel, repair parts, and, most of all, smart people to fix and fly them.

Chennault believed that airpower alone, mainly fighters, could win the war in China. He convinced Roosevelt that with bombers he could raid mainland Japan and win the war. He had already convinced Chiang Kai-shek and Madame Chiang.

Although Stilwell functioned as chief of staff to Chiang, his actual control of Chinese troops was ill-defined. In the spring of 1942 the Americans and the British had been run out of Burma, and Stilwell had walked out of India with his staff. Eastern Assam was under the threat of Japanese air attack, but Japanese ground troops could take Assam. If that happened, Chennault would have to fight them with his now miniscule Fourteenth Air Force from China. But their airfields would probably be the first to be overrun by Japanese soldiers.

It was a puzzling quandary for the generalissimo, and it should have been. During Stilwell's walkout (him leading the unwieldy column that included indigenous nurses, from Burma), the Fourteenth Air Force aircraft had sped out of Rangoon, Moulmein, and other bases for the safety of Kunming. Stilwell had refused the aircraft because he was an infantry soldier at heart. He knew the British and Indians were struggling out in foot, and he'd share the danger. Besides, it would lose the generalissimo plenty of face, his senior American fleeing on foot from the Japanese Chiang wouldn't fight. Or let Vinegar Joe lead in combat.

Stilwell of course realized all this, he never let his emotional side overrule his intellectual beliefs (except perhaps on the subject of the generalissimo); Chiang knew that Chennault channeled his anger outward, but in logical, straightforward, convincingly understandable verbal expression. Stilwell usually internalized his, fuming inwardly and sometimes almost inarticulate in response.

Chennault was much favored over Stilwell, but he had to be careful how he played this. Aircraft could defeat the Japanese, and Chennault was much favored by FDR. But Marshall and Stilwell had ancient history, and both Marshall and the generalissimo knew that Stilwell was a fighter. A tough one.

"They had taken a hell of a beating," he said to the press. "They ought to figure out why and go back." Stilwell was also lionized by the press as a tough fighting general officer. The journalists and newsmen loved him, because a casual glance would not reveal he was a general officer. He might be a weather-beaten senior noncommissioned officer, with only the snap brim campaign hat on his head. If danger was in the vicinity, he might carry a slung M2 carbine, with perhaps a few extra magazines peeking out of a pocket. Now that wily old fox Churchill, with his untoward interest in preserving India as a linchpin possession in the region, had not only appointed the young Mountbatten as the Supreme Allied Commander, he'd also promoted him to full Admiral—four stars.

This was another problem. Mountbatten now outranked all the American generals Chiang could play; he might even outrank the generalissimo himself. Chiang had his best politicos studying the new command structure. His wife, May-Ling, and her younger brother, T. V. Soong, were his best advocates; he'd listen to what they had to say, but he'd keep his own stoic counsel. Stilwell tried to stay above all this, as much as he could. He maintained that getting the Chinese armies to fight the Japanese, alongside the Communists, was the only solution. He opined that increased airpower would provoke a retaliation on airfields.

And it did, although it was part of the renewed energy of a Japanese counteroffensive that succeeded into Japanese forces driving west all the way to the Indian border. They encircled British forces along the vital Imphal-Kohima line of communication, but the British rallied and drove them out. Fighting seesawed during the dry season's six-month fighting season, but the combined forces of the Chinese, British, and Americans seized strategic Mykitna after a long siege of back-and-forth counterattacks by both forces.

Southeast Asia Command's Lord Mountbatten, his appointment by the allies intended to pull all the disparate commands and commanders under a single umbrella, had inaugurated several plans for the seizure of the Arakan coastal region and the recapture of Rangoon. As the allied strength increased, Japanese forces got scant reinforcements and were besieged by tropical ailments, depletion of food supplies, and increasing air attacks. In their rear area, airdropped or glider-borne Chindits raised havoc, totally supplied by para drops or rough, hastily chopped out airstrips by natives or the troops themselves for C-47s diverted from the Hump.

Early 1944 saw some of the most vicious fighting in Southeast Asia, particularly Burma, as the retreating Japanese covered their withdrawals with daring defensive tactics and local counterattacks to keep the allies off balance. Allied airmen were also writing new chapters in aerial logistics, especially in "door bundles" kicked out of aircraft and into the hands of the soldiers who desperately needed ammunition, rations, and water—just as the next generation of American airmen would do at Khe Sanh over two decades later, several hundred miles to the east.

Chennault clung to his stubborn belief the war could be won from the air, an uncertain longing that Roosevelt embraced, partially because Chiang Kai-shek preached it so ardently. Chiang loathed the thought of ground combat with his troops at this point; he knew his shakily trained Nationalist armies, largely built on a bedrock of solid corruption, couldn't stand up to the tough Communists and their wily co-opting of the peasantry that hid and supported them.

Let the Americans and British grind down the Japanese, and he'd deal with Mao's comparatively miniscule forces after the war. The young Foreign Service officers observing both the Nationalist and Communist factions understood this well, as did the junior military officers.

Many of the general officers also understood this, but they were generals, and they had to somehow carry out the orders of their commander in chief, no matter how fanciful it was. Or how wrapped in ideological postwar dreams. Or perceived in a family history that didn't mention opium as a major part of the business that made FDR's grandfather very wealthy.

"Lot of flag officer egos over here," Ramos mused.

But the Americans weren't the only ones with egos combined with eccentricity—there was the commander of the Chindits, the British commando-like force that was going to be a significant part of the British ground component of the offensive against the Japanese. The American component was the 5,307th Composite Group ("where the hell are the other 5,300 Composite Groups?") Merrill's men complained. They were better known as "Merrill's Marauders," for their hard charging (and heart afflicted) commander, Brigadier General Frank Merrill.

The British Chindits were led by an ardent Zionist who'd built his reputation in the difficult post–World War I arena of Palestine. A lieutenant colonel (soon to be a brigadier), his name was Orde Wingate, and he was beyond normal unconventionality—he was a mystic eccentric who made Lawrence of Arabia look like a dull, unimaginative staff officer. He would greet visitors—even senior officers—lying on a cot clad only in his bushy beard. He vibrated with intensity, and he once pushed one of his staff officers out of a slowly taxiing C-47 and leaped out behind him, eager to get to a meeting.

Both critics and admirers would likely describe him as "mercurial," but even that shining, slippery, and dangerous element would not suffice to describe his energy and explosive impulses. These peccadilloes did not affect his tactical senses, which were attuned to the highest level. He correctly envisioned his Chindit force operating far behind enemy lines, delivered by gliders, supplied by parachutes off roughly hacked jungle landing strips. His death in a B-25 bomber crash some months later would prevent him from seeing the effectiveness of his force, along with British and Indian troops under the leadership of one of the inarguably best British generals in the war, leader of the Fourteenth Army, Bill Slim.

"Good thing it's not a combat theater," Lanier retorted.

Beebe remained silent. Some enlisted crewmembers had great fun repeating the gossip of officers to their *basha* buddies or in the ramshackle bars of Jorhat, but Beebe chose to work hard and keep his mouth closed. His dad back in Minnesota had observed "that even a fish wouldn't get caught if it kept his mouth shut."

Lanier's silent, friendly, but barely readable expression said it all: "I'm OK with the things I can control, but there's too much I can't." However, he subscribed to that old flying axiom: "The only time an airplane has too much fuel is when it's on fire."

PART FOUR

Contingent

CHAPTER 18

Chinese Winter

Beijing, Peoples Republic of China, December 1993

I had been commander of CILHI for six months.

"Is this your first trip to China, Sir?" Air Force Captain Christopher Capellas asked, looking over the seat at the three of us in the back of the embassy sedan.

"I've been to Hong Kong several times, and to Beijing twice. I always seem to be here a couple of weeks before Christmas."

"Well, you'll enjoy the coal smoke but we've been spared the yellow dust out of the Gobi so far."

The captain was out of the air attaché's office, US Embassy, Beijing. The lanky F-111 pilot had met me, Dr. Peter Miller, a CILHI archaeologist, and Staff Sergeant (SSG) Adams, a Graves Registration noncommissioned officer, at the airport.

"Normally we would have taken you directly to your hotel, but Ambassador Roy wanted a word with you if possible. He's leaving with a CODEL for a few days in Shanghai."

I smiled inwardly at the words "wanted" and "if possible," and nodded, poker faced. If Ambassador Stapleton Roy, born in China of missionary parents, a fluent Mandarin speaker who also had experienced two other ambassador posts in Asia, "wanted a word" with a travel-weary Army officer, that would be fine. I was pretty sure I knew what the subject was anyway, and it had to do with Tiananmen sanctions and American-made helicopters now sitting idle and inoperable on Chinese airfields.

"Who's on the CODEL (Congressional Delegation) or is that close hold?" I asked.

The captain glanced at the Chinese driver, almost certainly a plant out of the Ministry of Foreign Affairs with a much better grasp of English than advertised.

"Foreign relations and Trade committees, plus some desk officers and deputies off the China desk and out of the East Asia directorate. A few principals, spouses, and staffers."

I nodded again, looking out at the crowded streets and bundled-up pedestrians. No snow but plenty of swirling wind, picking up grit and street litter. A miniconvoy of three Mercedes glided by, slowed by an elderly gentleman peddling a bicycle with crates of ducks on the back, and about a dozen waddling along in front, seemingly oblivious to the noise and traffic. The luxury cars were probably a wealthy industrialist or government minister of some rank and some minions plus a few security men. The bicycle man and his ducks plodded on, without concern. The captain was also looking at the spectacle of the ducks and high rollers, and his face lit up in a grin.

"Maybe they'll be able to work in some Christmas shopping if there's time," I remarked offhandedly.

Pete's ears pricked up and the pilot turned back to the front.

"Yeah, maybe. Since Christmas is the longest holiday season, that's the best time for our counterparts to visit—the desk officers and staffers can't really travel when their bosses are busiest, so Christmas and congressional recesses are when we like to see them. Our counterparts on the service staffs and DIA too; we can really get stuff done, because we're the ones that do the work anyway, uh, no offense, Colonel."

"None taken, Captain."

"We really do get a lot of work done when they're here. We've got questions for them too and a lot of issues to discuss—it'll be long nights between us and them; we like to see who we're talking to instead of just reading and drafting cables."

"It's nice to have dinner with them, drink a beer or two."

I gathered he was also handling the CODEL; but it'd be all-hands-on-deck when they were here. Including their Chinese hosts. Military attachés told me it was important to "personalize" relations, but not to get too close to your "friends and hosts" in the host country. Nonetheless, it's far more common to hear good Chinese English speakers than American Chinese speakers. I gathered he was also handling the CODEL, but it'd be all-hands-on-deck when they were here.

Captain Capellas and I were batting this around verbally—a safe enough topic but I noticed our driver glancing discreetly in the rearview mirror looking back at us. Pete Miller, riding shotgun, turned around thoughtfully and asked, "what about your language; didn't you take a year of Korean, Colonel J?"

I looked out the window into the clutches of people leaning into the Gobi winds. I hoped to see another memorable snapshot that makes foreign travel so interesting, but there were no more ducks holding up industrialists, just uninspiring crowded, gray streets . . . albeit very wide and crowded ones.

"I was exposed to forty-seven weeks of Korean, Dr. Miller. I'm not sure anybody speaks it, even Koreans. Sure sounds different in-country than in a classroom, though."

I looked up into the rearview mirror. The driver's eyes met mine then widened and blinked once, like he was taking a photograph, with a tiny camera. Or maybe it was just my jet lag. The Chinese were intelligence sponges; they were so blatantly open about collection that some counterintelligence professionals in DIA used them as case studies in comparison with the Russians—or Israelis.

Espionage may be for economic advantage rather than foreign policy or military use; that's one of the bewildering mazes in technology transfer protocols that spawn "dual use" considerations and myriad other almost invisible consequences. Soldiers learn you have to watch what you say to anybody, especially when they are overseas.

I also knew that principals, congressmen and their staff, frequently sought facts, information, and worked on issues face to face during the holidays and congressional recesses. They really do work for their pay.

We would be an object of curiosity while we were here, and straight, factual talk rather than loose talk is better when you're dealing with the legislative branch—or any branch, except possibly the press. I learned it was far better to talk to them under controlled conditions, with a public affairs officer (from your side, preferably) and most importantly, speak the truth. If it was sensitive or classified, let them know that you can't speak about it. Far better to be the Quiet American everywhere; especially in dicey foreign nations.

There would be a lot of evenings of work for the young captain and the young Foreign Service officers on the State Department's China desk and their principals on committees dealing with China, also, the congressional staffers and their bosses, but getting to see their counterparts in the countries both worked was a welcome opportunity.

At the embassy we passed through the outside guard post manned by a Peoples' Liberation Army soldier. Across the street, we were being photographed by a long lens camera not too discreetly poised inside the lowered window of a black sedan.

"Ignore those assholes . . . they're there all the time," the captain said dismissively. Pete flashed them the peace sign; SSG Adams shook his head resignedly. Pete was a rare scientist.

After the Marine guard looked through our passports and carry-on bags, we were ushered in to a conference room stocked with coffee and snacks. The captain told Pete and SSG Adams to make themselves comfortable while we went to have a short meeting with the ambassador.

Ambassador J. Stapleton Roy was a courteous and courtly diplomat, just the kind to represent the United States in an important post such as Beijing. We retired to the "Bubble," the sound and electromagnetic safe room where we could talk securely. The political officer, the Defense attaché, a young Army brigadier general, and the Public Affairs officer, or press attaché, and I crowded into the small room around the narrow conference table.

Ambassador Roy, born in Nanking of missionary parents, had left China when the Communists took over in 1949. He was fluent in Mandarin, served in Foggy Bottom, the Department of State headquarters, and also in Moscow at the height of the Cold War. It was gratifying to see the administration had not put a wealthy but inexperienced campaign contributor in as ambassador to China.

Unsurprisingly, he was primarily interested in being reassured that the White House was not wavering about "staying the course" on holding the Chinese to the Tiananmen Sanctions and keeping their US helicopters "frozen." He knew the official State Department position from diplomatic cables, but he was interested in whether my colleagues and I had any inkling of the "atmospherics" at the NSC.

The political officer and public affairs representative volunteered a few pieces of information. The Defense attaché asked if there would be a repatriation of remains after this trip to Lhasa. I replied it would probably depend on whether or not Dr. Miller could determine if the remains were human, the aircraft was US, and a few other factors. I told him we would be glad to assist in the ceremony.

The ambassador asked if it would be prudent to send a cable back to Foggy Bottom, State Department headquarters, asking—and gently suggesting—policy decision makers start considering this. I replied it certainly would, and please be sure to include USCINCPAC, USACILHI, and Joint Task Force–Full Accounting as info addressees. I assumed that DOD and the Joint Chiefs of Staff would certainly be included.

Ambassador Roy would serve two more ambassadorships, and a posting as Assistant Secretary of State for East Asia and the Pacific and finally, Undersecretary of State for Intelligence and Research (the State Department's corollary to DOD's Defense Intelligence Agency). Canny, intelligent, and suave, he knew how the intricate diplomatic dance should be played. And he certainly understood the Chinese.

I'd met a few others with long stints in northeast Asia—Jim Lilley had graduated from Yale, worked for the CIA, but had been ambassador in South Korea and ambassador in China when Tiananmen occurred in 1989. I'd surmised they were great Chinese-speaking men for the job.

All of us, including our pilot/assistant air attaché and what forensic equipment we'd brought from Hawaii, were scheduled out of Beijing for Chengdu, the last major air-link Chinese city nearest the Tibetan frontier, the next morning. We were told that some members of the PRC Ministry of Foreign Affairs in Beijing would link up with us in Lhasa, probably at the airport.

The consul general in Chengdu met us at planeside and waltzed us through the arrival formalities. One of his consular officials coordinated our tickets and baggage transfer for the flight the next day. He then checked us into the hotel and returned later to take us to lunch and a "windshield" tour of the city. He explained that there was only one flight a day into Lhasa, and if the weather was bad, flights had to return to Chengdu. There was no lighting on the single runway so there were no night flights.

I passed on the kind offer for dinner at his residence as I was starting to feel the effects of jet lag, and with the Lhasa airport at an altitude exceeding 11,000 feet I knew we were in for a couple of rough days in a tense atmosphere.

The midmorning flight to Lhasa was uneventful save for a few unforgettable vignettes: the first, after boarding all the non-Asian passengers in Chengdu (the three of us Hawaii dwellers and our Air Force captain, who was also on a first time visit to Tibet).

I watched a flight attendant collect the knives of a group of hard-looking Tibetans dressed in a red-scarf-like headgear. She put each knife into a woolen-appearing wrap, with numbered sheaths. The Khamba handed over his knife, and another attendant handed him a wooden disc with that number on it. Both flight attendants were nervous around the tall, broad-shouldered weather-beaten Tibetans.

"Good guys to have in a bar fight," I noted absently.

"I hear there's a couple of Tibetan bars in Chengdu that serve *chang*, Tibetan barley beer, in pails. After a few of those there's always a Pier 9 brawl."

"If the Chinese police show up it gets pretty serious, according to the staff in the consulate," Captain Capellas continued.

"So you get a bar on Hotel Street in Honolulu and fill it half with Samoans and half with Khambas and get both fired up on *chang* and good old Fosters lager from Australia, who you going to bet on, Colonel J?" Pete asked, taking in the knife confiscation.

"I'll bet I'm gonna get my country ass out of there, Pete," I answered. Adams and the Captain grunted assent.

Pete stole another glance as the Tibetans shouldered their way down the narrow aisle to the back of the plane.

"Yeahhhh . . . probably a good idea;" he answered, "They do exhibit a little attitude."

"If you've got any doubt, Dr. Miller, just ask any Chinese infantryman that might've been hanging around in the winter of 1950," the captain said quietly, settling back in his seat and closing his eyes.

Then another vignette: after quickly climbing to altitude the majesty of the Himalayas was visible; the most forbidding peaks in the world pointed up at us in the clear December sky. It was simply breathtaking. I thought back to the majestic mountains of the Hindu Kush looming over the Khyber Pass that I'd ventured down in a rickety, garishly painted Jingo bus a quarter century earlier—they were the most significant mountains I'd ever seen. But they were terraced with fields and brown runs of loess and scree punctuated by huge boulders, the combination of small, rounded rocks and house-sized rocks that made climbing so difficult and tactically dangerous for our soldiers campaigning in Afghanistan some years distant. In contrast, these mountains seemed built of ivory, jagged ice.

My face was plastered against the window for most of the trip, and at about the halfway point in the flight I guessed somewhere below us was the crash site. It wasn't a reassuring view or thought. Everything about this terrain suggested beauty. *And violent, frigid death.*

The aircraft greased into a landing on the longest runway I'd ever seen in my life—it seemed to stretch miles into the mountains. The Tibetans on board broke into a loud cheer and laughter. Boarding in Chengdu they were sullen and subdued. Here they were home—an invaded and violated home for almost a half century, but one they loved fiercely.

The Tibetans filed off ahead of us and haughtily lined up to take their knives; the last one was a tall, good-looking youth of about twenty-five who lingered and returned the smiles of both flight attendants. They exchanged a few words and the young man waved good-bye and ran ahead to catch up with his compatriots. The two young ladies giggled demurely, hands over their mouths, and welcomed us to Tibet.

Over the shoulders of our reception committee, I saw a couple of helicopters of a type I didn't recognize, plus a type I did—two Pilatus Porters, or the pirated Chinese copy, complete with Peoples' Liberation Air Force markings. This was the ubiquitous, rugged little Swiss turbo prop short takeoff and landing airplane. Although US supplied helicopters were ruled out if a subsequent recovery was called for, our lifelines out of the mountains would be short takeoff and landing (STOL) fixed-wing aircraft if life-saving medical evacuation became a necessity. I mentally made a note of that.

A group of Chinese and Tibetans awaited us and hustled us through the arrival formalities; one Ministry of Foreign Affairs official took our passports. Some Tibetan officials were mixed in with them. They were, an English-speaking MFA official said, ranking members of the Tibetan Autonomous Region, and there were English speakers among the Tibetans as well as the Chinese.

Lhasa was an hour or so ride away. and halfway back we stopped for a short rest, meaning to go pee discreetly, which we all did. Then our MFA English speaker took us over to a rock wall with some archaeological drawings of men and animals. They apparently looked to the distinguished archaeologist for his opinion, and Pete stood all alone in front of the paintings, separated by a chain link fence. The ends of his white silk scarf, which we'd all been presented, hung down beneath the waist of his leather jacket.

A Tibetan custom, the white scarves represented a safe and peaceful trip while the wayfarer was in Tibet. Our friend elaborated, "I'd carry one as a return gift for them also." A cultural officer in Beijing who gave us a current overview of things in Tibet had explained the custom prior to our landing in Tibet.

"You can buy them down at the market, but make sure it's a plain, simple white one and not one of the embroidered ones. The scarves they give you will be the simple ones and I'd pass the one you have to the person that gives you your scarf."

"So how do the Chinese and the Tibetans get along?" Pete asked innocently.

"Beats me; I've never been there," replied the cultural officer, just as innocently.

He looked awfully fit and a little weather beaten for a diplomat. Pete observed the same thing afterward, "You reckon that guy is something other than a foreign service officer?"

"Pete, for purposes of this exercise I'd reckon he is a loyal, toiling member of the foreign service of the Department of State, and I don't think I'd speculate any further, particularly when any of our Chinese friends are around."

Our little crowd all waited for the esteemed Dr. Miller to provide his thoughts and comments, for any PhD archaeologist from America would surely know something of ancient hieroglyphics in China.

"Interesting, very interesting," Dr. Miller proclaimed, owlishly peering through his round glasses.

Soon the "skyline" of Lhasa was apparent, with the Potala, the Dalai Lama's palace, overlooking the Brahmaputra River and the white block buildings that made up the original ancient city. In the distance, contemporary buildings and signs blazed in the sunlight, indicating the portion of the city populated mostly by Chinese, a number that grew rapidly, as we had been told back in Beijing.

Our hosts took us to the Holiday Inn, Lhasa. Pete looked around the reception area and whispered, "You reckon this is a knock-off or the real thing?"

Then I was at the desk. Our baggage had appeared before we had, guarded by a couple of Tibetans overseen by a tough-looking Chinese man in a suit. A few Europeans—from the former Eastern bloc by appearance, and one backpacking younger couple, Canadians, with the distinctive red maple leaf flag on both their packs, waited patiently behind us. While we were waiting I asked them where they were from and where they'd been.

"We're from Alberta and we've just come overland from Xinjiang in a truck," the young man replied.

"Tough trip in the back of a truck through all that desert," the young woman offered.

"But interesting," interjected her mate, eyeing all the muscle around us.

"Yeah, *very* interesting," countered the female wearily.

"Pretty desolate," the young woman amplified. She and her partner were as dusty as soldiers coming in from a field exercise in the desert.

"But interesting," the young man added again, noting the unsmiling suited Chinese in our party.

I mentioned that I had enjoyed fly fishing the Bow River that flows through Calgary a few times, and they both perked up.

Our escorts were behind us, some sitting, some standing. The standers were from the Ministry of the Interior; I figured they might be white collar armed security guards. A couple of them spoke excellent English, and their small briefcases never left their hands.

In Vietnam and Laos the familiarity between our "minders" and us grew with every mission, and we would frequently ask them, jokingly, what they carried in the bags that were never far from their hands: "please show us your gun so we know we're protected from the 'bandits.'"

The response was nearly always a nervous laugh, followed by a demurring hand wave, but once a bored Lao major opened his gym bag and showed the team a Czech Skorpion machine pistol; the stock of the deadly little weapon folded snugly. The word went out to quit badgering Ministry of the Interior personnel carrying bags, even in the muddy, jungled, and sometimes boring terrain of Southeast Asia.

Now it was my turn to check in and the young female receptionist was all business, with my accommodations envelope ready and my instruction sheet for the oxygen bottles in my room on top. I thanked her with two more words of my ten-character Chinese Mandarin knowledge. Even though her name tag had a Tibetan nom de plume on it, she was clearly Chinese and spoke flawless English.

I pocketed my key and asked, "Is this hotel part of the American chain?"

Without missing a beat she replied, "Even we Tibetans and Chinese take holidays, Colonel Jordan. I hope you enjoy your visit to Lhasa."

We walked up the corridor followed by our two Canadian friends.

"Well Pete, there's your answer," I said quietly.

"Yeah, but what was it?"

"A clear case of intellectual property theft on our part; they had Holiday Inns in China during the Ming Dynasty."

If the Canadian couple overheard this sotto voce exchange they managed to keep relatively quiet about it as they trudged with us to the elevator. It was the last lighthearted exchange we'd have in Lhasa.

Our Chinese and Tibetan hosts gave us some suggestions for dinner and some things to see for the remainder of the afternoon and said they'd bid us farewell until in the morning, when we'd go to view the remains and the articles the PLA had recovered from the crash site. Some of the Beijing-based Chinese were sick with headaches, a common malady coming from the lowlands of China.

We Americans had started taking Diamox, a relatively mild blood thinner that eased you into the rigors of high altitudes like the 11,000+ feet of Lhasa. I offered some to our Chinese hosts, but all politely refused.

Pete and SSG Adams checked in and reported they were going to the market to see what kinds of souvenirs they might find; our captain said he'd just "wander around and see the sights," a euphemism for his work as the assistant air attaché.

Two oxygen tanks and masks were on my bed. The instructions were in Chinese and French. They didn't appear much different from my diving tanks, and I really didn't think I'd need them anyway, so I changed into Levi's and sweatshirt and pulled on a hooded jacket and green ball cap with CILHI emblazoned across the top. I added a pair of sunglasses and some lip balm. It wasn't that cold for December, but it was sunny with a brisk wind blowing down from the Tibetan Plateau.

I left the hotel and just wandered, occasionally snapping a photo with my Nikon. I was careful not to photograph anything modern that might have been a government building. It was a colorful, photogenic environment.

The streets were full of pilgrims, the women in their colorful and practical *dhobis*, a woolen sweater worn to the fingertips over a colorful ankle-length skirt, their hair turbaned with silver jewelry and ornate necklaces. The men wore everything from nondescript trousers and sheepskin and stout shirts. Virtually all carried prayer wheels and whirled them, tassels standing out. The Tibetans' wind-roughened high cheekbones were a stark contrast to the countenance of the Chinese, who scurried back and forth in casual and business clothing, their soft, rounded faces sometimes peering at me curiously through black horn-rimmed glasses. Occasionally you'd see one or two tall Khambas with the red sashes around their head, knives tucked discreetly down in their waistbands. They did exude a proud authority. They never gathered in groups of more than two or three, and they seemed as alert as policemen. Or soldiers on patrol.

I checked the tourist map I had picked up in the lobby and saw I was near the Jokhang, probably the most sacred Buddhist site in the world, so I turned toward it. It is an ancient structure. Monks, young and old, milled around the entrance and on the sidewalk.

I looked for an entrance among the half dozen open arches, and one of the monks led me gently inside and turned me over to a saffron-robed elder who was half-heartedly charging admission, even though pilgrims streamed by him into the interior, prayer wheels spinning. He asked me a question and I heard the word for Chinese and shook my head. I pointed to my chest and said, *Mei Guo*. American. He cocked his head quizzically, and I said it in a rising and falling tone, then I reversed the tones. No luck.

"Parle vous Francais?" He asked hopefully.

I shook my head again. Another burst of Chinese, followed by Tibetan. I held my hands palm up and gave another helpless negative head shake. Finally, I showed him the English on my map and dredged, from the depths of my Monterey, California, classroom, *shi meg-uo*, even getting one of the tones accidentally right, I guessed.

He barked a command in rapid Tibetan to the monk who guided me in. Another rapid burst of back and forth Tibetan and the elder monk pointed into the interior. My young escort scurried off into the gloom. A moment later he came back with another young monk, a novitiate I guessed from his brown robe, rubbing sleep from his eyes.

"You English tourist? Maybe from Can-uh-duh?" he asked.

"American."

"Ah. This morning I guided Can-uh-duh man and woman. They speak English and French; much English *prac-tis* today. My blessing." The older monk gave him some instructions and motioned with both hands for us to go in.

He steepled his hands and bowed to the monk overseeing the interior and led me into the darkness, some hallways lit by electric lights dangling from open bulbs. Candles of burning yak butter were everywhere, filling my senses with their unforgettable smell. We stopped at alcoves with statues of the Buddha, benign but imposing. Some were a foot high, some life size or larger. All serene and silent, one hand raised in benediction, perhaps for hundreds of years.

These were holy men's resting places in the walls. One held a scant collection of bones and he explained who they were, when they lived, "very old, maybe two thousand years old," he intoned respectfully. I nodded, also respectfully.

It was a fascinating and compelling place. If you mark the ascent of Christianity, Buddhism, and Islam, the appearances of all three are roughly equivalent. Both Jesus and Mohammed appeared in what is now the troubling crescent of the Red Sea within a couple of hundred years of each other and Gautama Buddha appearing in India perhaps a little later. Or earlier, as the case may be.

As I stood in the cool darkness, which was illuminated by the flickering yak butter candles, I was transported back to my youth, listening with my father to Lowell Thomas on the Philco radio, telling of strange, beautiful places. I remember as a preteen reading a Roy Chapman Andrews library book, my milky cup of cocoa cooling, that described dangerous travels in far-off north China and Mongolia.

My dad would stir several hours before dawn. He would dress in his coveralls, still coated white with the poison that comes from the tank beneath his Stearman biplane.

Like all pilots, he knows the flying is easier in the coolness of dawn, especially over the south Texas and Louisiana cotton and rice fields in this spring of 1949; on the other side of the world, Communist forces circle the remaining Kuomintang forces of Chiang Kai-shek—the ones who haven't defected to the Red Hordes just yet.

I am enchanted—and conveyed—to a place centuries earlier in this dusty warren of history and worship to a deity that exists; a man they can see and touch. This is a land, religion, and way of life that never deserted its secular and ecclesiastical leader and won't as long as Tibetans exist. He is a man not that much older than me who escaped to a hill town in India through snow-covered passes on horseback in 1959, protected by the loyal red-turbaned Khambas.[1]

They dodged Chinese ambushes and aircraft, and when he was safe in Dharamsala, the Khambas returned to Tibet to train and fight, many of them on Saipan and in a remote section of Fort Carson, Colorado, then parachuted back into the high restive plains of Xijang, the land of the Lotus. Thanks to friends in a "three letter" agency. This created a model for a similar event in Vietnam, barely a decade later; only their parachuted agents wouldn't fare so well.

Finally the monk led me out into the winter sunlight and I offered my thanks and a handful of Chinese yuan with a few dollar bills in the mix.

Back at the hotel, music seeped through the heavy doors of the Hard Yak café; I recognized Blue Oyster Cult and went in to eat dinner.

I ordered a Heineken beer and a yak burger, well done. Just cheese, no lettuce or tomatoes, I emphasized to the Chinese waitress with the Tibetan name tag.

Naturally, the burger came adorned with lettuce, cabbage, tomatoes, and a few vegetables I didn't recognize. I scooped them off the burger. In Asia, you learn to eat meat well done and avoid things you haven't actually seen washed. I ate half the burger—it was good, but I was getting tired.

As I was paying the bill, the waitress brought the remains of my meal wrapped and in a carryout container, the beer standing upright and capped with a small cork. A nice touch, I thought.

In my room I gazed out at the dim lights of the city, many of them yak butter lamps. The lights defined a proud people and their spiritual ruler, a man who still guided their souls even though he had been forced physically away from them decades earlier, his temporal presence was still strongly with them. The lights also defined the mountains surrounding the dusty plain of the city. The highest mountains in the world. The deadliest mountains in the world.

When I awoke in the morning, the bottle of Heineken beer and the yak burger were both sitting dejectedly on the nightstand where the unused oxygen bottles stood. I felt well rested. No headaches. I was a little apprehensive and had lingering doubts, though.

Time really does stand still. There is not a sound, which is unusual for a crowd of four Americans and about thirty or so Chinese and Tibetans. No chair scrapes, no muted coughs or whispers, or even the sound of the ragged breathing of those of us who didn't live above 12,000 feet. Even our frosty breaths in the super-cooled room refused to move.

We were in a basketball-court-sized concrete block room a few miles outside Lhasa and up a dirt road. The room was stark white and shared functions of a medical lecture hall and a cold storage room. I was sure there was probably another smaller, sterile room somewhere in this building or in the compound, with modern equipment, ventilation, and stainless-steel equipment including medical saws. A facility where autopsies were performed.

We were in a military compound on a plateau overlooking the placid Brahmaputra River, just now beginning its long trek downward from springs in eastern Tibet toward the arid plains of India, snaking on into Southeast Asia. Dr. Pete Miller, SSG Adams, our pilot captain from AMBEMB Beijing, and I were here to see what the Chinese brought down from a glacier halfway across Tibet from where we are now.

Earlier we crunched over a frosty dirt track in Chinese military four-wheel drives through the chilly morning fog. We passed a monastery where monks gathered outside in the cold and stared at our passing with expressionless eyes. This compound, ringed with a steel fence, concertina wire strung along the top and guarded by a detail of armed PLA, was ominous. It was a military medical facility, and inside the largest of the buildings, the sticky sweet buns and tea seemed out of place, for we're told we were in a morgue.

Just about everyone on earth, from a young age, is familiar with death. As a child, I saw relatives in caskets in somber funeral parlors; they looked like they were lying peacefully asleep. My own first experience with seeing a dead person was when I saw my dead grandfather, a blacksmith in the hardscrabble, poor Mississippi Delta. I remembered his little brown fox terrier that would joyfully jump waist high into the air, a seemingly graceful levitation, whenever I approached the front gate of the picket fence. But this time he slunk, whining pitifully, carrying the grief of events that dogs seem to fully understand. That was over seven decades ago, but I can remember it as clearly as what I had for breakfast.

Children in lands of conflict are familiar with violent and horrific deaths from war, sometimes the deaths of their own siblings or friends, in unfortunate regions where youth doesn't protect the innocent. All soldiers, particularly combat arms soldiers, are painfully close to friends and fellow soldiers who fall in battle, sometimes performing the battlefield recovery of buddies whose bonds are almost transcendent.

Only in the movies do the survivors, usually a hardened sergeant, rip the dog tags from a corpse. At least one tag and optimally both should stay with the serviceman until he gets to a casualty clearing station where his death can be confirmed and his identity established.

In the seven years I'd been involved in the POW/MIA issue, death had been an abstract concept visible only in small bits of aircraft wreckage or battle artifacts, with the occasional bone fragment examined by an anthropologist who declared it human or animal. Occasionally, a single tooth or part of dental bridgework would soar spirits. The highly acidic soil of Indochina is not kind to human remains, but teeth are some of the most durable parts of the human anatomy.[2] And dental records, especially for pilots and air crewmen, had been carefully maintained by the time of the Vietnam conflict.

One of the afflictions for everybody doing this type of work was guilt. Self-criticism for not doing enough to find them; not finding enough to identify them; not knowing enough to furnish the families anything definitive or uplifting, in written reports or in person, although they tried very hard. The ones charged with that most difficult task were the Service Casualty Officers. The ones manning the office itself were likely to be retired NCOs who were extremely knowledgeable about casualty and personnel matters, to include human emotions and grief. These latter two were learned painfully, usually in the modest living rooms of small-town war-torn America, now newly riven with grief.

Still, there was a clearly definable link between the anthropologist sifting through a crash site with bare hands, a soldier wielding a shovel, a tired-eyed analyst peering at a computer screen, and the ones in the final link who will gradually convey the results to their loved ones. The strongest link is to their loved ones; also the most fragile. Then the mixed emotions of finally knowing overlaid by the facts of what they had hoped they wouldn't face—the unknown missing becoming something irrevocably and visibly taken from them.

Casualty officers and noncommissioned officers described and articulated information on missing loved ones in situations where information is sometimes heartbreakingly absent. There were, in a few very rare cases, factors and locations of deaths and sensitive classified information that denied and blocked the answers they sought—answers that were doubly difficult because the system required telling them everything the case entailed, except when it couldn't. Unless highly classified information was involved, the mothers, fathers, sisters, and brothers knew everything their loved ones' armed service knew, everything we the operators in the field knew. Or didn't know.

Sidetracking: Even we didn't know the mission of the mysterious C-130 loss in North Vietnam. It wasn't until several years later we discovered the mission could be declassified, but the aircraft known to its small, tight-lipped community as a Combat Talon, couldn't, and these "Blackbirds" were still doing their magic in ongoing conflicts.[3]

Every one of us struggled to do the best we could; the DIA analysts were especially sensitive to the fact that any one of them who turned up a shred of analytical evidence that an American was still in captivity would be instantly lionized. Instead, they were called "debunkers"—a term that infuriated them when their efforts were criticized by those who got their information from scam artists, lurid novels posing as fact, ridiculous films, or people who replaced rational reasoning with unreasoning hope.

The worst were those who maintained government was incompetent or committing criminal conspiracy, but likely they believed that long before 1973, when 591 POWs returned to the United States. In reality, the government perpetuated the myth with the best of intentions but disastrous consequences. It happened by letting the public and the press manipulate and repeal established law and ignoring the fact that servicemen may suddenly vaporize in a fireball of jet fuel or suddenly disappear, go off the scope—never be seen again, in life or their mortal remains.

The heroic commander of Forward Operating Base 3 at Khe Sanh, Major George Quamo, disappeared in the same circumstances; his South Vietnamese piloted light aircraft that was last seen on radar over the South China Sea would be found crashed on an inland mountain some seven years later. These totally understandable circumstances raised families' and friends' hopes and expectations and crashed them back to actuality when realities of time, faulty information, or a host of other factors meant only their loved ones had not been found. All these recollections and musings passed in a microsecond in this super-cooled facility near the top of the world. A far cry from Shangri-La.

Back in the reality of this moment: Sadness at the loss (from Americans, Chinese, and Tibetans) but exuberance and thankfulness at their discovery from everyone looking on. We were one race of human beings who celebrated living. We detached ourselves from our familiar tribe and coalesced into another—one that celebrated discovery, even of the saddest kind. For a moment we were one race, a single polity that couldn't have remembered why we bludgeoned each other nearly senseless in a North Korean winter a near half century before.

The crew was lost, in their albeit temporary tribe. Now they were found, in another—tenets of Buddhism, Confucianism, Judaism, Christianity, Islam. This was a blessing of almost unbelievable proportions. Fantastic circumstances of weather and a rugged elderly Tibetan hunter had permitted a crew that had "gone off the scope" and in all likelihood was forever lost, to be found Their recovery had been managed well but in difficult circumstances of terrain and weather by former friends, later enemies, now maybe just hesitatingly friendly.

After the introductions to the lab-coated staff and polite nibbling at the snacks and chitchat, we were seated in four slightly forward chairs; Captain Capellas, Pete, SSG Adams, me. A semicircle of about forty folding metal chairs was arrayed behind us in several rows on the polished concrete floor. All were occupied, and several people stood along the back wall. Some were in suits—with briefcases.

A distinguished looking gentleman in a white lab coat and spectacles, obviously the director, read a prepared statement in English that described the "very, very preliminary findings of their forensic scientists upon preliminary examination of the remains and some of the artifacts therein."

He used the word "preliminary" several times in his statement, and "welcomed the American experts" so we can confirm what they believe, "preliminarily." Even though the word sounded like *prerimerrery*, it was easily understood in the high-ceilinged, cavernous room; his English was excellent.

Their findings and conclusions indicated three individuals were found and recovered at the crash site, and they believed the individual remains were all non-Asian.[4]

Again, in this very superficial examination, they appeared to be young men who expired violently in the crash of the airplane, where—again, superficial examination indicated it was highly likely the aircraft was of military origin and the crash probably dated from the war with Japan.

They didn't speculate on the nationalities of the crew.

Next came something surprising, even though the initial reports of it strained credible belief—an official explanation along the lines of aliens landing in Roswell, New Mexico. The aircraft had crashed into a snowfield along an extended glacial line with a reference to the Siachen Glacier. I had read about the glacier somewhere but couldn't place it in location or context. I drew a line under the notation and starred it with an asterisk in my notebook. I knew less than nothing of glaciers, nor did I have anyone in the unit who knew anything about glaciers. I had farm boy Graves Registration, on-loan infantrymen and hardened Special Forces sergeants who could discourse on burned-over loess mountain fields in Laos, or triple canopy jungle—rain forests actually—in Vietnam or Cambodia. I had a couple of archaeologists who could also discuss karst outcroppings, and the effects they might have on our recoveries. Of course they were also beautiful, the ones just off the coast of Hanoi and Vinh are beyond beautiful. I had no one who was into terrain running, bouldering, or assisted climbing harder than Ranger or Jungle Operations in Panama.

Over time, the snowfield had itself glaciated, and the aircraft and luckless crew were entombed and preserved in the ice. They were ejected when the glacier broke apart and scattered the aircraft and its contents down a slope into a narrow valley between two mountain ranges. The peaks hemming in the valley from both sides exceeded 20,000 feet in places, over seven thousand meters, they emphasized.

They didn't speculate on how the crew perished, whether in the crash, or whether they had died outside the wreckage, or were entombed soon after, or later. Only three non-Asians, they thought, in a military airplane in the war with Japan.

The director concluded his remarks and nodded toward the four of us. Every eye in the room was on us. On the walls two large portraits stared out at the room: the Dalai Lama, spiritual and temporal leader of all Tibet, and Mao Tse-tung, the chairman, the one who carried the day against the Kuomintang and ran them out of China to Taiwan.

Mao was no surprise. During the mid-1990s, leadership of China was still largely controlled and directed by the Chinese Communist Party—the CCP, despite Deng Xiao Peng's patient prodding toward a more democratic and pluralistic model for China's economy.

That model had to mold itself carefully and pragmatically around the

Marxist precepts of the Party, and not around an individual leader. There were no pictures of the current Chinese leadership, either military or civilian.

No chain of command photos so prevalent on American bases—pictures of the president as commander in chief right on down to the officer commanding the facility. What is surprising is a picture of the Dalai Lama posted prominently in this military facility. When you look at his picture it is difficult not to smile. I didn't recall seeing any in my walk around Lhasa and logged a mental note to ask Captain Capellas about this.

Chairman Mao helped engineer the split with the Soviet Union and presided over two social movements that devastated China—the Cultural Revolution and the Great Leap Forward, but he also promoted détente with the United States, truly an astonishing range of political acts.

The Dalai Lama's eyes followed me with a beatific smile, and for a moment I thought about him, in exile across the border in Dharamsala, India, with his large retinue of followers, an entire government in exile since his harrowing escape over snow-choked mountain passes in 1959. Mao Tse-tung also gazed down at me with a smile; a malevolent one.

Mao Tse-tung was responsible for our presence with an amazing reversal of thought, ideology, and policy that led to conciliation with the world, but most importantly with America. He was a hostile and inimical leader of the world's most populous nation, with an acute sense of foreign policy. What Mao didn't know about foreign policy, his longtime friend and colleague, Chou En-lai would.

FDR had a dream of a powerful force in Asia that would hopefully continue a peaceful coexistence with the West and help to ensure peace and stability in Asia. At least half of that would come to pass—China would become a powerful force in Asia but seemingly not interested in a peaceful coexistence with the West.

But then there was Richard Milhous Nixon, a Quaker president who put his faith aside for a while to wage war in the most savage terms in Vietnam. But he was also the visionary architect of an uneasy peaceful coexistence with China. He was the solitary, lonely man who, as leader of the nation, would hold the responsibility for the consequences—good or bad. His National Security adviser and later Secretary of State Henry Kissinger would make the arrangements, much like Chou En-lai did for Mao.

Despite Kissinger and President Nixon's success in China and in ending the Vietnam war, the American people and Congress couldn't—and wouldn't—excuse the excesses of Nixon's office. Nor would they excuse his successor, Gerald Ford, who pardoned him. Soon President Nixon would be gone; his vice president would take his place and preside over the last battle of the Vietnam conflict, the seizure of the US container ship *Mayaguez* in May 1975.

When the dust settled from that confusing, violent battle, three more US Marines would be missing in action in the Gulf of Thailand on a deadly island called Koh Tang. The military efforts were less than spectacularly successful, despite the heroic efforts of Marines Air Force helicopter crewmen thrown onto the island with faulty intelligence. The administration touted it as a viable effort. China's helping the Khmer Rouge wasn't a factor of the larger Sino-Soviet confrontation. It was to keep the keen combat edge of the Vietnamese military knife slightly dulled. After all, the north's victory over the south gave them the by-far-largest military in Southeast Asia, also its most effective. China's long-term strategy was to normalize and establish trade relations with the United States (finally achieved during the Carter administration) and then manage the Soviet Union somehow, without ever slipping under their subservience again. The Russians helped by creating their own Vietnam—in Afghanistan.

Twenty years after the desperate battle on Koh Tang Island a Navy chief bosun's mate and I swam out to the wreckage of a USAF CH-53; rotor mast still sticking out of the water, barely one hundred yards from shore. It had been shot down along with several others in that violent engagement. By then, the Chinese were probably the last friends in the international community the Khmer Rouge had.

But that recovery was still a couple of years in the future and I couldn't possibly foresee it. Now in Lhasa, these reminiscences of war's end and Nixon's resignation ran through my consciousness in a microsecond and I was back in December 1993. Pete Miller and SSG Adams stood by silently, motionless and solemnly reverent in white lab coats and rubber gloves, face masks pushed up on their foreheads. Our task was to determine if the remains were possibly US airmen, and if we could determine anything from the considerable amount of personal and material effects from the aircraft the PLA admirably and professionally recovered.

A large number of British, Indian, and Commonwealth airmen and soldiers also perished on the Hump. If something incontrovertible indicated these remains were not American airmen in an American aircraft, the diplomatic cards would be reshuffled and dealt again. This would incur new players, decisions, and a host of other factors, something that would be loath to the Chinese, who wistfully hoped to stanch the wounds they incurred in the Tiananmen incident. But I didn't sense any of that in this group; only genuine curiosity of how these men got to this place and who they were. Did they still have brothers or sisters or sons or daughters waiting for their return?

Politics, cultural and language differences disappear in large groups about to witness and visit the dead; especially when violence and circumstances beyond the victims' control inflicted it. There is a palpable group empathy for them and their loved ones; I sensed it immediately in this crowded, cold room. These were pathologists, physicians, and scientists who had individually and collectively witnessed untold numbers of the dead. This was their avocation and life's labor; something they'd studied and dedicated themselves to.

Despite a coating of political varnish over the whole matter I sensed they'd perhaps sigh and deal with that after the probing painful question of who were these individuals, where did they come from? Their thoughts were on later generations of loved ones who may still be burning joss sticks when remembering these men. They'd worry about sanctions and the unfortunate temporary lapse of sanity by the Party and its leaders in Tiananmen Square four years before at a later time. Their traditions, thoughts, and actions began during the prehistory of the Xia dynasty, probably over two thousand years before Christ.

Then prehistory faded into recorded history during the Shan dynasty, and scholars wrote of their feelings and activities on the Oracle bones, a mere 1,700 years or so before Christ. It would be incredibly disheartening if we did not learn more about these young airmen and who might be waiting for them at home. Perhaps their own efforts might be needed; silently point us toward dental and medical records. A reshuffling of the nationality cards would be especially loathsome to the four Americans who were also about to examine the remains.

There were certainly political considerations threaded through this operation, but I also sensed the Chinese—and Tibetans—deep commitment to this affair and to a temporary shelving of old animosities beyond May 1949, when the Communist takeover of China changed the calculus of the democratic and socialist communist world.

The Chinese, like the sinocized and culturally similarly Vietnamese, are steeped in the Confucian ideals of respect for elders and the deceased. The notion of returning remains to the villages they grew up in are a bedrock in their ethos. They wanted this badly also. To them, their operation was successful—they had found the crash and satisfied the DNA heritage in the makeup and returned this portion of the crew for the Americans to identify and return to their families. Tibetans and Chinese—wanted this mystery solved and all the families reunited with the men frozen and largely forgotten in their luckless aircraft. In their mountains. In their war with the Japanese—and the Nationalists of Chiang Kai-shek.

The Ministry of Foreign Affairs interpreter, a nervous young man, stood by my side. A middle-aged PLA sergeant, stoneface ravined by lines of freezing rain, snow, and high altitude sun, stepped forward when I indicated I was ready with a nod. With white-gloved reverence he removed the top of the wooden rectangular box, about a third as large as a normal remains transfer case, used in ceremonies normally covered with the American flag. He respectfully stepped back, giving me space to look.

I gripped the side of the box and looked inside. A pair of open dark eyes peered out of a sun-browned desiccated but young face. Wispy light brown hair covered the head. I gripped the box harder and blinked; a hot wetness washed the brain behind my eyes. Visions of young Americans supporting and standing by Chinese allies fighting the Japanese since 1937 flooded my mind's eye. My youth, young manhood, and middle age all collided in the mood generated by those beseeching eyes, and I could think of only one word to describe what was in them—*reproach*.

The unfortunate airmen in front of us were discovered by hunters in a troubled but dynamic nation that struggled out of a stifling and economically disastrous ideology. With the weight of history and some five thousand Confucian years behind that, they recognized instantly, instinctively, and culturally what it meant for these mortal remains to be returned to their homeland and their families.

They had brought us here, and for that three other Americans and I were eternally grateful.

I looked up but saw only ghostly motionless figures in the dark gray-green battle dress of the soldiers and the blurred images of the Dalai Lama and Mao; I couldn't see their eyes now. My glasses had frosted over, probably from the sudden heat generated by my own eyes in the cold, remains-preserving temperature of the morgue.

I thought of fathers and mothers of these airmen now probably long gone. Younger siblings would become a much older generation in the half century of their icy entombment. Those siblings probably remembered them only as they had been as young men, at school or with older playmates, last glimpsed proudly wearing the uniform of Americans at war. The room seemed colder and darker now, almost like the opening of the box unleashed a gloomy history. Dark clouds moved in, choking the light that came in through the oval windows, high enough to let light in, but not low enough to see the normal world outside—trees, mountains, the greenery of a living world instead of the muted gray earth that seemed to have paused respectfully for the figures on the stainless-steel tables.

The soldier reverently moved to the next box and removed the top. More remains, not as starkly human as the first, but still in a remarkable state of preservation, as were the remains in the third and final box. I removed my glasses and said to the room in what I hoped was a calm, modulated voice: "These remains appear to be Caucasoid [*sic*], and from what I could see of the uniforms, they appeared to be American flight suits of the kind worn by World War Two aircrew."

Desiccation, or dry freezing, occurs in the dry and oxygen-starved freezing winter climate of high altitude. This was discussed somewhat informally with the Chinese but not mentioned in remarks in front of the assembly. We were well-seasoned by now with leaks appearing in newspapers from large, faceless groups and "the Americans said . . ." appearing. Unlike US newspapers, foreign journalists and publishers had no problems attributing statements to names. It was vitally important for the families to get the word from their parent service first, not an AP extract from a foreign newspaper.

The young translator related this in Chinese and the still room became animated, buzzing.

"Dr. Miller and Sergeant Adams have considerable expertise in these matters and perhaps they could examine them and comment further," I added.

The translation began and stopped when he consulted his jotted notes, frowning. He turned to me, "ax-part-tees?"

"Someone who is very good," I said. "The best . . . better than . . . than . . ."

Pete meandered over thoughtfully, mask now pulled down around his neck. SSG Adams moved slowly and automaton-like behind him, face white as his spotless lab coat. Pete peered down into the first box of remains and murmured a quiet "hmmmm"—he might have been a professor in a college classroom, looking at a formula or concept on a blackboard and pondering how to begin his lecture—then he looked back at his audience. His chin rested thoughtfully in his hand, elbow supported by his chest-crossed other arm, head cocked a little to the side.

Now I smiled inwardly and wondered how many times I had seen this —Dr. Miller about to announce something that might be shocking, but something he'd learned from decades of experience in remote places of death probably several hundred times.

SSG Adams glanced in and away quickly, his eyes were unfocused and he clearly was having problems processing all this. It wasn't something seen in a normal graves registration soldier's career—or lifetime, unless he or she is recovering remains from recent combat.

Pete placed his hands on either side of the first box, lifting it up gently and holding it. He had powerful arms and veins stood out in his wrists as he hefted it appraisingly a few times before gently setting it down. There were muted gasps from the audience.

"Don't worry; this isn't a criminal investigation," he said, then nodded to the interpreter, who was momentarily flummoxed. Pete noted this, and moving quickly to cover his embarrassment and the young man's possible "loss of face," he expounded.

"In America, a criminal investigation needs to be solved quickly. That requires a rapid, but absolutely correct, identification of the victim—or victims." He nodded at the interpreter again, who quickly interpreted it.

"So criminal investigations take input from all, ah, sole source experts possible." Now the interpreter was fully in sync, even unconsciously mimicking Pete's hand gestures.

"But in America, these identifications of what we call "ancient remains" are legal matters. So we need to remove any doubt that there was scientific bias introduced into the . . . he backed up to make the interpretation easier, "that no scientific bias was present in the identification."

Nodding approvingly as the interpreter smoothly translated, he began quietly to explain what they were going to do, and I realized one of Professor Peter Miller's famous lectures was going to follow.

"The desiccated remains needed to be preserved," he said, "until they were safely back in the lab in Hawaii, and until then he would not make a scientific guess at the stature, racial characteristics, or even the sex of the remains until they were examined in the laboratory. In fact, he added, a different scientist would examine them and make the identification to prevent bias."

Now, a dozen hands shot into the air, and one man, perhaps a pathologist, shouted out an excited question, which the interpreter translated as "how would this bias be perceived?"

Pete replied that the relatives would be emotional about the discovery of their recovered loved ones and might question their findings, which was expected in America, but after all, there were many Americans lost on the Hump operation.

"We've found this process reduces that possibility of worry they might have."

Then he added, "it might be easier for us to finish this process, and then if you'll write your questions down, SSG Adams and I and will stay as long as you want to discuss them with you."

He and the interpreter looked at me for guidance, and I replied we would remain as long as there were questions. A distinguished Chinese gentleman turned in his chair and said something to the room at large; a gentleman to his right repeated these instructions in Tibetan, then nodded at the interpreter, who added in English.

"Yes, please let our friends from America finish and then ask questions."

The distinguished gentleman half-turned in his seat, added a few words to the audience behind him; a grateful sigh seemed to rise out of the rest of the observers. "and then we eat and chat."

I kept a poker face; Captain Capellas shrugged almost invisibly; Pete rolled his eyes discreetly. There was a collective *ah* from the audience, and they quieted, although pens flew over notepads, taking copious notes.

Pete and Adams put their gloved hands into the box and carefully pulled the remains out, arranging them on the examining table. Adams had taken numerous photographs of the surroundings, the containers, and the remains in the boxes. Now he photographed the remains on the table from several angles also, placing a ruler and yardstick on a level base next to key features.

All three of us knew that the same process would be repeated at the laboratory, and measurements compared to measure the effects of time of transit versus the decay of the preservative process. While these were being completed, Pete and Adams did the same with the other two boxes.

I assumed that some of the best forensic pathologists in China were present in that room, but Pete was listened to as if he were Confucius parsing the Analects.

As CILHI commander I couldn't be prouder of everyone in the unit, from the young specialist or civilian receptionist who answered the phone to the chief scientist and lab director. The staff, the captains who commanded the teams, the teams themselves, who turned into one tremendous individual that did impossible things, but especially the physical anthropologists, those "sole source *ax-purts*" who could eke out an identification of an individual or crew from the barest evidence.

They were also trained in archaeology with sufficiency to pass the most stringent standards. And that was one of the problems. CILHI had about eight to ten anthropologists, but only three archaeologists. Archaeologists could find the victims, but they weren't trained to identify them, and this became a contentious issue with anthropologists who returned to Hawaii after the "finding" and recovery of the scant remains of victims, followed by the long arduous task of identifying them.

Pete and SSG Adams had wrapped up their session and the late afternoon sun had dropped, darkening the morgue to an even gloomier state. Pete had been true to his word, the questions and answers, made at least doubly as long by the translation, had taken another hour. It was now followed by the mandatory photo session of the scientists, pathologists, and various ministry officials with Pete and Adams.

The scientific courtesy, curiosity, and tough questions were evidence the Chinese were quite interested in this whole affair, and not purely from a political point of view. I kept waiting for a quiet low-level pitch on lessening the economic screws but their only interest I saw was the remains of three American airmen, imprisoned in a glacier for a half century. They were the honored ones here today; we could sense their dignity as they lay patiently on three laboratory tables. We had figured out the *what*, now we had to figure out the *who*, and the *why* was the link that framed all this.

The Chinese had been violated by an old enemy—the Japanese. They had additionally suffered the seizure of Manchuria and the installation of the Japanese puppet Puyi, after all, Manchuria was dangerously close to Russia and was surrounded by hostile nations and corridors—Mongolia for one. If the Japanese could irritate the Russians perhaps they would be defeated. Manchuko, as they now called it, was proof positive the Kuomintang couldn't survive without modern arms, materiel, and money. They asked for our help, hoping the United States would come with military might to defeat the Japanese. Their former allies, the Germans who successfully trained some of their troops and furnished arms and equipment, were now also leaning toward the Japanese, admiring their Fascist leanings. Soon the Japanese would be in the Axis powers and plotting against a major enemy, the Russians.

Meanwhile, five brave young men lay entombed, preserved and seemingly waiting for someone to find them, while China faded from clear black-and-white friendliness to the burning red of Communism in 1949. Then vicious opponents from November 1950 to the shaky cease-fire and Korean armistice in June 1953. The status quo had been reestablished with nearly 40,000 dead Americans and over 8,000 missing after the two major POW exchanges—Little Switch and Big Switch, and the Cold War had gone to freezing. Now, at least, there was diplomatic recognition between our two countries.

Those same observations would hold true ten months later when we returned to the crash site, with the same Chinese and Tibetan crew who had done such an outstanding job before.

Through it all, the Chinese soldiers remained nearly motionless along the wall. I collected another English-speaking official and asked him if I could speak to the PLA colonel, Colonel Chen Ni Yeng, who had commanded the soldiers on their unilateral recovery. As we approached, he placed an unlighted cigarette back in the pack and pocketed it. I smiled and offered my hand and he pulled his white glove off and shook hands with me. "*Ni Hao*," you are how? The greeting I spoke was as common as *qué tal/qué pasó* in Spanish, but it just about strained the limits of my Monterey Mandarin.

He smiled and replied "*Hung Hao*," very well, and added a few more words in Chinese. My shanghaied interpreter picked up smoothly, "Colonel Neng wishes you well and hope you are not tired from your long journey."

"Not at all," I began and the interpretation followed quickly again, a subtle reminder to speak slowly.

"Thank you for the fine job you and your unit did on this mission."

His weathered face creased into a smile as the interpretation flowed, and he responded, and the Mandarin turned to English again. Colonel Neng said it was an honor to recover these brave airmen who helped with the fight against Japan.

I responded, "Is it true that the crew and the aircraft crashed on a snowfield that glaciated?" This threw the interpreter, so I rephrased it in more common terms.

"Yes, apparently so, but he said he is not an *axx-purt* in these matters. Perhaps some of the scientists know more about that."

"Colonel Neng says that the last few winters have not been so cold, and in the . . . the . . . time after the snow . . ." he looked at me quizzically and I prompted, "spring and summer"?

He nodded. "The seasons"; he grasped it, rolling his eyes and tapping his head. I had done the same thing when a word in a strange language registered.

"Yes. The *sprinnnngg* and *sum-mur*! Those times were warmer with much rain." Colonel Neng started a long-detailed soliloquy, and the interpreter nodded and tried to break in to translate, but he continued. At one point he grasped an imaginary staff and lurched forward, like he was trying to find his footing in difficult terrain, but it looked to me like a fly fisherman trying to wade a difficult stretch of river.

Finally, he finished. "Colonel Neng says it was very . . ."

"Dangerous." I interjected. He nodded and added, "and deadly."

I thanked Colonel Neng again and we shook hands and exchanged salutes. I collected Captain Capellas, chatting in Chinese with one of the military pathologists in uniform, and went back to get Pete and Adams. They looked like they were getting wrung out pretty well with all the attention and questions and the translation flying around like ricocheting tracer rounds in a cave.

"Let's wrap it up, Pete. We've still got all this material evidence to examine and photograph, and maybe we can find something about the aircraft; maybe a manifest."

"Yessir," Adams replied. "And my Tsingtao beer light is starting to blink."

"I'll buy you both a couple back at the hotel. You guys did a fantastic job; I think you could get a retirement job here if you want. Pete's bushy eyebrows semaphored again, "I could handle it, colonel, but I don't think the little lady could." I had to laugh.

The first table had an assortment of aircraft wreckage, most of it small enough to lash onto a pack horse or carry in a soldier's rucksack. The PLA soldiers had done a good job; they almost all had data plates on them, but they were electrical or hydraulic in nature and could be part of any aircraft. They were all in English, though, so we were undoubtedly going to find out it was an American—or British—aircraft. SSG Adams meticulously laid out his rulers and photographed them from several angles.

The second table was more of the same, but there was one item that astonished me. I picked it up and examined it closely. "What's that, sir?" Captain Cappelas asked.

"This, Captain C, is the upper receiver group and barrel of a Thompson submachine gun."

"Wow, who used those things?

"About everybody on our side plus Al Capone's boys and some lucky Japanese who captured them, maybe. But what else about it is unusual, do you think?"

He took it from me and hefted it. "Well, it's heavy for one thing." He examined it closer. "But there's not a speck of rust on it. Looks like it just left the factory."

"Yeah. We'll have to ask one of the scientists if that's usual for something that's been laying in the open for so long up here. Also, I wonder where the rest of it went. Can you slide over and ask Colonel Neng if of his soldiers cleaned it up, and if he knows where the lower receiver group went.

"Good soldiers can't stand to see a dirty weapon, and they always reassemble them." He took the weapon—or what was left of the weapon—and went to find the interpreter. A few moments later, he, the interpreter and Colonel Neng, back from his long-awaited smoke break, had returned.

Colonel Neng and the interpreter exchanged some more Chinese. The interpreter shook his head. "His soldiers were told to photograph everything where it remained and as it was discovered. Colonel Neng examined this gun at the crash. He said this is exactly as they found it, but he thinks some of it is missing."

I nodded, but he could see I was troubled. I remembered a Thompson submachine gun I had borrowed from an advisor to the Twenty-First ARVN (Army of the Republic of Vietnam) when I was Mobile Advisory Team leader in Vietnam. I thought it would be handy to carry in a jeep since it was shorter and packed a punch at close range with its .45 caliber ammunition.

I had disassembled it with great difficulty, and later, because it was so heavy with cumbersome safeties, I had exchanged it for its successor M3 "Grease Gun," which also required the .45 ammunition but was much simpler to use, lighter and handier. I didn't think the gun would come apart in the crash; there was no sign of crash damage on the upper part of the weapon. It, in all probability, had to have been partially disassembled, but I could see both the colonel and the interpreter were sensing my doubt, so I shelved it as a mystery—one that remains to this day.

I also asked if it were unusual for weapons not to rust at altitude. This went through a couple of versions of English with the word "rust" obviously the problem. The light went on in the interpreter's eyes when he replied, "rust, you mean like 'metal oxidation'?"

"Exactly," I replied with an encouraging grin. The interpreter and colonel conversed, then Colonel Neng caught the tough sergeant's eye across the room and gave him the "come here" sign all Asians seem to use: the demure little hand flap, palm facing the person called. The sergeant scooted across the room and snapped to attention in front of Colonel Neng. A three-way conversation ensued with questions asked of the sergeant who answered them quickly and decisively.

The interpreter turned to us, "Sergeant Cho says weapons . . ." he tapped his forehead a moment, dredging the word from his English classes . . .

"*freeze* in the high mountains, but they do not *oxidize* as fast as they do in low places." The interpreter fired another burst of Chinese at him and Colonel Neng to see if that was correct, and they both nodded.

I smiled at Sergeant Cho and thanked him for the professional job he did, nodding to Colonel Neng to include him in my thanks, and when it was translated they both broke out in grins. Sergeant Cho said something back and the interpreter smoothly translated: "Sergeant Cho says it was an honor for his platoon to bring back the brave airmen who helped the Chinese people in their long war with the Japanese."

Sergeant Cho added another phrase and it was translated: "he also says it was very . . ."

"Deadly?" I coaxed; he shook his head. "Dangerous. But his soldiers were very good, and no men or animals were badly injured."

"Well, dangerous sounds much better than deadly I guess." He shook his head and shuddered, "in the Ministry of Foreign Affairs, both are bad. Very bad." I guessed the political message had been delivered.

We shook hands all around. The sergeant saluted Colonel Neng and me, whirled, and departed

On the fifth table we found the piece we were looking for, a flat, aluminum panel that appeared to have been a portion of a cover for an electrical panel or access to the interior of the fuselage wall. The green finish was pristine; I scraped a portion of dirt off the lettering on it.

"I think we found our airplane type," I said softly. Captain Capellas peered over my shoulder. "C-87, what's that?"

"Thought you were a pilot," I joked.

"I fly planes that begin with an F, Colonel, not a C; I've ridden C-141s, C-130s and seen C-46s, C-47s and C-54s from the Big War, but that one escapes me."

I turned the panel over, looking in vain for the manufacturer or a serial number.

"It was the cargo version of the B-24, used extensively on the Hump as well as in other theaters of the war." He squinted a moment, remembering.

"I remember a military history course at the academy; wasn't it B-24s that made the disastrous raid on oilfields somewhere?"

"Yes; at Ploesti, Romania, although then it might have been called Rumania. What else do you remember about that class?" He furrowed his brow again.

"Well, they bombed at low altitude so they burned much more fuel than they would have in regular high-altitude strategic bombing. It seemed like there was a lot of controversy over the decision-making on that one."

"That's right. The B-24 was designed for high altitudes. The wing was called a 'Davis wing' as I remember, probably named after the engineer who designed it."

"It was supposed to be more efficient at high altitude, and as I recall they really wanted those oilfields destroyed, so they sent them in low level to ensure they got their bombs on target."

"There was a big navigation error, too, right?"

"Yes, as I recall reading about it the aircraft with the lead navigator spun into the sea and the next ship in his slot stepped up and became the navigation aircraft."

"They took a wrong turn over one of their checkpoints and flew right over the center of the thickest concentration of anti-aircraft artillery and fighter bases."

We were silent a moment, looking at the legend on the part.

"You fly in the great Libyan Raid of '86, Captain?"

"Jesus, Colonel, I was barely in high school!"

"Well, you'll probably catch the next one. You've got the genes, anyway."

He nodded. "I hope so."

Another small box had papers and bits of records in them. There was a maintenance log with some dates visible but indistinct. Pete held up some faded trousers and peered at something inside the waist. He took off his glasses and pulled out a small pen light and illuminated it on something.

"Got some writing on here, Colonel J? Can't make out what it says, though."

Our F-111 pilot and I peered over his shoulder as he framed it with his hand and played the light over it.

"You make anything out there with your fighter pilot's eyes?"

"No, Sir. But it sure looks like two names, see the break in the letters or numbers I guess."

"Yeah, maybe a last name and the last four numbers of his serial number, if they did it like we did back in the horse cavalry."

"You were in the horse cavalry, Colonel J?" Pete asked incredulously. I glanced at him to see if he was kidding. I decided he wasn't.

"Yeah, Pete. Me and your great, great granddaddy fought the Yankees, or was it the Confederates? I kind of lose track of time."

Pete laughed, "I was just kidding, Colonel. I know you're ancient but not that old."

SSG Adams snickered, "No you weren't, Pete. That's exactly the kind of question I'd expect you to ask. Hell, I've heard *you* ask questions like that in all seriousness."

Pete danced around, "hey, I found the trousers, didn't I?"

"Yeah, you and Sergeant Adams did a fine job, Pete. I was proud of both of you. You too, Captain C. You've been a great help."

"I don't know, Colonel. You seem to know more about airplanes and Air Force history than I do," he said ruefully.

"I grew up in an aviation family, Captain C.; my dad was a crop duster and flight instructor . . . actually he taught me to fly before I could drive. My mom had to drive me to the airport to solo, because I didn't have my driver's license. He also contracted to the Army to train aviation cadets for their initial flight instruction and ground school before they got into the military training."

"And for you, Dr. Pete, that's because it was the Army Air Force back then. Besides, I was in the horse cavalry, don't forget."

Adams snickered again, and I looked at Pete. "No you don't, Colonel. You can't get me twice. That's the rule, but SSG Adams and I appreciate your words and I'd also appreciate it if you let my boss know I didn't screw anything up."

"I have, Pete. And I will again," thinking of what it took to keep the anthropologists and archaeologists both happy, or at least, not overly unhappy.

"Now, let's finish and secure and seal this stuff. We've got chain of custody slips to fill out for all of them."

"I found these, Sir," Adams said, sliding over slips of paper sealed in glassine envelopes. "Look at this one."

It was a mess slip—a meal bill from an officers' mess in India. The mess officer's signature was clearly visible on it, written in a clear cursive script, a second lieutenant. But the lower half with the customer's signature was missing.

"Do you think he might have been on the plane, Sir?" Captain Cappelas asked.

I thought a minute. "Possibly, but not likely. But whoever signed that was, though."

"How many would be in the crew, Colonel J?" SSG Adams asked. He rotated it back and forth in the light, willing something to be there.

I thought again. "Well, for sure a pilot, copilot, and radio operator, and most likely a loadmaster, or crew chief or a plane captain, they were sometimes called."

"How about a navigator?" Captain Capellas asked.

"Again, possibly, but as I remember navigators were more likely to be in the European theater, the first priority." But they could have had passengers too; unless the Chinese video missed something there didn't appear to have a lot of cargo on it when it crashed.

There may or may not, probably not, have been a manifest. I've hopped military aircraft by just talking to the pilots and if they had room, they'd say "climb on."

"But we'll find out," I added. "Just as sure as the turning of the earth." They all nodded, but I didn't let them know that line was from my favorite John Wayne movie, *The Searchers*.

The Hard Yak café, Holiday Inn, Lhasa, December 1993

That night we nursed Heinekens in the Hard Yak café, and the talk turned to business, as it always seemed to do.

"Well, what do you guys think of Tibet?"

"Beer was better in Chengdu, sir," Adams offered. "At least they had Tsingtao."

"Did you know that Tsingtao is German beer, Sergeant Adams?"

"Give us the punch line, Colonel J; I'm not falling for the horse cavalry caper, again," Pete said with a wary grin.

"No, Tsingtao was a German town up the coast. The Germans had muscled into China late during the Unequal Treaties period and the Japanese acquired their holdings up there because they were on the allied side in World War I."

"I've never been to Tsingtao, but people who have been there said a lot of the houses and buildings could have come right out of Bavaria, including the cobblestone streets."

"So why are we drinking Heineken?" Pete asked.

"Well, they don't have Tsingtao here. One thing I can say about Heineken: I've drunk it all over the world, even in some, uh, unusual, places.

"Heineken tastes the same, whether you're in Port Moresby, New Guinea, Sibu, Sarawak in Borneo, or Rangoon, Burma—I know the names have been changed there, but it was still Rangoon when I was there."

"Well, tomorrow, SSG A. we'll be back in China and you can have a Tsingtao," Pete said.

"You're in China, now, Pete. The Tibetan Autonomous Region of China, and that's a Peoples' Republic of China flag flying over this hotel."

"Well, some people Adams and I ran into don't think so."

"Yeah, they sure don't," Adams added.

"Tibetans, I'll bet," I remarked, taking another sip of Heineken.

"Yep, they spoke good English and said Tibet will always be Tibet; they work in a restaurant Adams and I are going to; you want to come along?"

I pictured a dirt-floored Mongolian barbecue place and replied I was growing kind of fond of Yak burgers with cheese and said I'd pass.

"Dr. Miller just likes this place because it serves four kinds of meat: ram, lamb, mutton, and sheep," Adams laughed.

"That's right, I had lamb chops last night and they were the best I ever had," Pete answered.

"Pete, I'd have to be near starving to eat anything off a lamb. But you guys go ahead and have a good time. You did great today.

"We'll head back to Chengdu tomorrow and get the remains back with us on to Beijing. I talked to the lab about an hour ago, and they said a repatriation ceremony is laid on a couple of days they're bringing the transfer cases and flags."

"We'll work out the details with the Defense attaché; he'll be the senior US officer from Beijing. The ambassador is out of town, so his deputy and a senior representative of the Chinese will be the reviewing party, and I suppose they'll make short speeches."

"We'll have to rig the transfer cases at planeside. Lieutenant Gervais will have 'em prepped and staged with our guys for the ceremony and a general officer from PACAF [Pacific Air Forces Command] or CINCPAC as the presiding officer for the ceremony."

"What else did they have to say, Colonel?"

"Rick Huston in Casualty Data says they have over thirty Missing Aircrew Reports on C-87s in the China Burma India theater."

They were silent for a moment. "Jesus, how many aircraft went down over the Hump?" Adams asked soberly.

"About 600 total; not all the crews were lost, though. A few walked out, and a few were rescued; some went down in India or China, not over the Hump."

"We could be in business a long time here, Colonel," Pete remarked. "More crashes than in New Guinea."

"Don't say that, Pete. We've got teams scattered all over Indochina, and we're scratching another team up to go to Cambodia again."

I didn't mention that even the Democratic Peoples' Republic of Korea was making efforts to talk about the missing in North Korea. This would be a difficult issue to cope with, but the Department of State was hoping for a diplomatic solution like the one that was working in Vietnam.

"Let's hit the road, Pete. Sure you don't want to go, Sir?"

"Think I'll pass; you guys enjoy your meal, and, uh, don't bring back any communicable diseases."

"You mean like ptomaine poisoning, Colonel; gosh that's not communicable," Pete asked, in all innocence.

"Yeah, that's exactly what he means, Pete," Adams replied, and rising from the table he gave me an eye roll.

A few days later a C-141 dropped out of the gray clouds and thundered into Beijing airport. Winter had finally arrived in China. They were here to repatriate the American airmen home to the laboratory at Hickam Air Force Base. The inside of a glacier had been their resting place through the last half century and a plethora of other wars Americans had fought. The allies they had fought alongside became the enemy in North Korea just five years after they were lost, and for a long four decades afterward.

SSG Adams in civilian clothes worked with some of the other uniformed noncommissioned officers to transfer the remains to the transfer cases correctly; the heads of the deceased needed to be toward the front of the cases. As they put the three flags on the cases, the respect was evident. SSG Adams was especially somber.

Lieutenant Gervais, the ceremony commander, told the NCO in charge to inspect the uniforms of the Honor Guard one last time and get in place for the repatriation ceremony. He threaded through the small crowd behind restraining ropes to Pete and me. We were wearing coats and ties and standing in the cordoned area with the small crowd of Chinese, Americans from the embassy, and China's and the international press corps. A desultory, cold drizzle was spitting on us.

"Wanted to see you, sir, before we head back to Hawaii."

"It's good to see you, Flounder. How are things on the home front?"

"Busy, as always. General Needham passed his regards and asked me if you'd be back in time to come back brief him on this operation."

"Yep, we'll fly out tomorrow afternoon. I've got some meetings at the embassy today, but tell the general I'll see him and back brief him on everything that went on here. I'll debrief our Washington bosses also, then we'll follow up with a message. Is there any news interest on this back home?"

"Some. Johnnie Webb has been talking to the Honolulu papers and said there'd probably be more after the ceremony at Hickam tomorrow. We've been getting a lot of guidance from the public affairs people in Washington, and your wife said that things are fine on her and the families' end, except for Bear eating some cupcakes she'd baked."

"The American Kennel Club needs to change that breed's name from black lab to chow hound," I mused.

A middle-aged French Agence France-Presse reporter pushed through the crowd, followed by the embassy public affairs officer.

The PA officer asked if I'd answer a few questions for her, after he read a prepared statement. Other members of the press had pushed up within earshot. He gave me a veiled look that said, "be careful" and read the two-paragraph statement that summed up what little we knew of the crash.

A barrage of accented questions in English tumbled out of the crowd, and the PA officer deftly fielded them; most steered clear of the political implications. The how, when, and who found the crew was of interest, and the press officer consulted his notes, said a citizen of the Tibetan Autonomous Region found it on a hunting expedition and a unit of the PLA traveled to the glacier and made the recovery, aided by citizens of the village and its surrounding area.

Someone mentioned the entombment, but the press attaché deflected the question skillfully by replying that more details would be forthcoming but family sensitivity must be respected first. Another question was about the identity of the crew, and he used that to terminate the questions: "we don't know that yet and, of course, long-standing policy of the United States is to ensure the families are notified first."

He turned to me, Lieutenant Gervais, and the reporter and gave a two-fingered salute, this time his grin could be interpreted as "good luck." The public affairs officer had made this affair "unofficial" or "background," so no names or sources could be used by the reporters.

The French reporter took several shots with a motor drive Nikon, framing me and Lieutenant Gervais with the huge gray C-141 in the even grayer, gloomy background. The American flag on the tail was barely visible through the misting rain, only one hundred yards away.

"Colonel, how would you evaluate the cooperation of the Chinese on this matter?"

"Excellent and very professional."

"Did the Chinese mention some of the sanctions your government has placed on them since the 1989, er, problems in Beijing?"

Inwardly I grinned; outwardly I rubbed my chin thoughtfully, as if debating whether to release a juicy news tidbit. This was a perennial question in Hanoi from the international press concerning diplomatic recognition of Vietnam.

"No, they didn't. I believe we've discussed the purely humanitarian motives of the recovery of American servicemen in any country, from any conflict. The Chinese in Beijing and in Tibet certainly understood that and assisted us greatly."

The PA officer closed it off with the answer that we'd continue the press briefing after the ceremony, and the French reporter, hiding her frustration at having her one-on-one interview skillfully deflected by the embassy press attaché, raised her finger.

"Colonel, may I ask your . . ." She consulted her notes momentarily, "Lieutenant Flounder a few questions about the ceremony?" Naturally she'd listened in on the conversation with our intelligence officer.

"Of course, but it'll have to be short, because he needs to be in place soon. He's the commander of the troops for the ceremony."

Lieutenant Gervais greeted her in what sounded like the French of a native-born speaker. His first name was Pierre, after all.

Over my shoulder I heard her ask him, "Flounder, is that the name of a . . . fish?"

I walked over to where the two brigadier generals, the Defense attaché, Brigadier General Kevin Byrnes, and the Air Force general who rode in with the C-141 were chatting with a PLA general officer. We exchanged salutes and I shook their hands.

"Sorry you had to ride for twelve hours just to spend a couple of hours on the ground, sir," I said to the Air Force general.

"Glad to do it, Colonel Jordan. This is my first time in China, but I'll be coming back here in February or March with the PACAF commander. Riding in the jump seat watching a good crew fly was a treat too; we staff guys don't get to fly much. Lieutenant Gervais filled me in on what your teams and scientists do, so maybe I could bring my staff over for a briefing, sometime when you're not busy. Also, this is pretty special—participating in the return of Air Force guys from World War II."

He nodded to the PLA general and added, "From the war with our Chinese allies." The PLA general, an excellent English speaker, nodded, obviously pleased.

The Air Force brigadier was certainly well-briefed, probably by USCINCPAC's political advisor, normally a former ambassador or senior State Department official with extensive time in Asia.

"We'd be glad to do it anytime you're not busy, sir. Also feel free to bring your spouses. It's entirely unclassified, and the briefing and lab tour usually doesn't run over an hour or so."

The Pacific Air Force (PACAF) was good to our organization. They'd given most of our organization housing on Hickam, a real advantage since Air Force quarters were noticeably better than the Army housing scattered around Oahu. Also, Honolulu was terribly overcrowded, with choked traffic, so living on base was a significant advantage.

We had briefed the four-star commanding general and his deputy a few months previously, and we gave him a brick from the original Hanoi Hilton prison when it was torn down, with the word "Hanoi" stamped into it, a little bit of cement stuck on the brick. We also gave him the traditional gift for VIPs, a North Vietnamese helmet with the ubiquitous red star on it and a small brass plaque with his name and the date of the visit. The general had been a fighter pilot in Vietnam and was visibly moved.

Months later I ran into his deputy in the PX and he thanked me again for the briefing. "The General keeps both the brick and helmet on a little shelf behind his desk. I wonder if I could get some of the staff over for another briefing."

"Absolutely, Sir. Have them bring their spouses, also. We can comfortably brief about thirty people in our conference room."

I, in turn, thanked him for the assistance PACAF gave to CILHI. We genuinely appreciated it; housing and travel in overcrowded and expensive Honolulu was difficult, and being together on a first class base with good facilities made it much better for the soldiers and families. Now, I was headed back to Honolulu, eager to see my wife, dog, and to get back to the "real work" in Indochina.

The operations officer, burly college football player Major Eddie Williams, said there was "unfriendly fire" coming in from all directions, a good euphemism from an infantry officer turned quartermaster. As we went into the Christmas season of 1993, teams that weren't already checked out on Christmas leave were wrapping up operations in Indochina and getting ready to go again right after the New Year.

A JTF Investigative Element was returning from Cambodia, and I suspected we'd have at least one recovery mission in that blood-soaked unfortunate country in the near future. Tom Needham and I were packing for a short meeting in Laos; the Vietnamese had decided to take a breather themselves; they knew Christmas was an important occasion for Americans, especially soldiers.

And in Tibet, we'd found a C-87 without an identifying number, and three of its crew without names.

CHAPTER 19

"Reckon That's about the Size of It, I Guess"

December 1993, a late evening a few days before Christmas: General Needham's office at Camp Smith, Hawaii

"OK, as I understand this, you've got the aircraft type but not the specific one, three sets of remains, a very nice Thompson submachine gun, part of one anyway, and possibly some artifacts that may have names on them, but they're unreadable, am I right so far?"

"Yes sir, reckon that's about the size of it, I guess."

"So what's your next step, besides hounding your lab guys to keep the identifications coming?" General Needham asked. He was curious about the meeting in Tibet, and Bill Frizzel asked me to stop off the Friday night before Christmas leave began for both the JTF and CILHI.

Bill Frizzel maintained his usual Marine colonel stoicism, although a flicker of grin flashed; he was seemingly not in the room with us.

Bill was Needham's very able deputy. He was a large, fit man, but he could practically disappear in concentrated thought until he was asked a question or felt compelled to ask one himself.

I knew he was listening intently, occasionally pulling out a 3 ? 5 card and making a cryptic note as Needham talked. He definitely was an accomplished listener versus a note taker. I wished I had that ability.

"Not much we can do unless we get the names readable; we have to identify the specific aircraft in the Missing Aircrew Reports for the C-87 aircraft lost over the Hump.

Our World War II guys in Casualty Data are fiends on that stuff," I continued. "We've got one young lady who'll probably wind up as a World War II history professor someday."

"How many missing C-87s in your MACRs?" Frizzel asked, without looking up.

"In the CBI? Somewhere in the mid-thirties, I think . . . if you group type aircraft by theater, you can narrow them down sometimes. Rick Huston thought it was thirty-one initially, but just before I left this evening I heard somebody say they may have found have another one. Probably misfield in another theater or something, if they did."

"Is that why they have those floor to ceiling containers?" Needham asked.

"One of these days that stuff will be on computers," Frizzel opined.

"Never happen; paper is better, electricity goes out and you have to reset all the f*$%@&*g clocks."

"How many total losses?" Needham asked.

"Over six hundred, but that included fighters and bombers, probably well over 3,000 crewmen."

"Jesus, it wasn't even supposed to be a combat theater, was it?" Frizzel asked, obviously surprised.

"Not that I've read, no."

Needham looked up, thoughtful and interested, something had piqued his curiosity. Frizzel had noticed it too. Whatever had been uttered had started his wheels turning, and doubtless he would think about it, ask questions, and see if it was something they could apply to their own investigations.

He'd discuss it with Frizzel who would discuss it with his own subject matter experts and me, if it involved our recoveries.

The JTF and DPMO had scored a major coup when they convinced the Vietnamese to turn over a detailed log of aircraft shoot downs.

Colonel Bill Frizzel, a bomber—navigator "back seater" in a Marine F-4B, had been shot down and rescued along with his pilot near the DMZ during the war. After examining it, he found the date, time, and reasonably accurate location of the incident, along with details of his and the pilot's rescue, observed and reported with fair accuracy by the enemy anti-aircraft gun crews. It produced a lot of credibility to skeptics.

We'd all found out that it did no good to argue with those who were skeptical—and probably would always be skeptical—of our efforts. You had to let them see the actual results of what we had wrestled out of the Vietnamese.

I used that term because the "shoot-down logs" *had* been wrestled out of them in negotiation sessions—the Vietnamese Ministry of National Defense was just as loath to surrender their secrets to the Vietnam Office of Seeking Missing Persons as the former KGB organ of the Soviet Union—now the FSB of the Russian Federation—was to release information on shoot downs to the United States–Russia Joint Commission on POW-MIAs. Or the Department of Defense with State, or vice-versa. You could forget about the CIA.

But now, in the mid-evening a few days before Christmas, Needham and Frizzel had taken a short break from Indochina and were going over the facts of a long ago and far away tragedy and the mysteries still clinging to it.

While I had been in Tibet, we had sent another team into Armenia. An American C-130 from the US Air Force had been lured into Soviet Armenian airspace by meaconing in 1958, sending a false signal that had lured the aircraft into the deadly trap the Soviets had set for it. MiG fighter aircraft shot the aircraft down with cannon fire. There were some reports of parachutes in the air, although official Soviet statements denied this, leading to one of the more speculative Cold War cases and one we were eager to investigate. The Russians agreed to help on this. The newly independent Armenia agreed as well, and we were eager to assist the US–Russia Joint Commission. This was a successful mission and the fates of the entire crew were resolved.

CHAPTER 20

Futile Hope, Quagmired Nation

The nascent war in China had been highlighted by an extremely unstable political situation for several years prior to the Marco Polo Bridge incident in 1937. Generalissimo Chiang Kai-shek had bested rivals and orchestrated the breaking of the "Warlord" faction that had dominated China since the overthrow of the Manchus, the final dynasty, known as the Qing, that had prevailed since 1644.

He and his benefactor, the westernized Dr. Sun Yat-sen, still thought of China as a "revolution" that would shake off foreign domination and lead them along a similar socialist path the Communists professed to be the best for China's four hundred million people. After all, the largest and most successful revolution in history had occurred just two decades prior in Bolshevik Russia, when the Red Russians had ousted the White Russians, killing Czar Nicholas and his entire family.

The Communist International movement, the COMINTERN, had already incorporated their neighbor to the north, Outer Mongolia, as its first member. After a period of time this unsettled Chiang. He was uncomfortable with their differing philosophy and he veered away from them, fearing they would eventually supplant his leadership.

The secretive Mao Tse-tung and the smooth and adept Chou En-lai seemingly had flourished under the banner of the Red Star, their version of the Hammer and Sickle. From their Yenan redoubt in the north they had won converts to their side by integrating them into their ideology, helping with plantings and harvests, standing up to wealthy landowners, and speaking out for the peasants. They, especially Chou, were winning converts, and while Chiang had his ruthless side, he couldn't match them. Chiang was adept but he wasn't smooth. He, like Mao, knew that someday they'd fight.

Chiang was content to let the United States fight the Japanese when the time came. He would save his foreign aid, armies, munitions, gold, and political largesse not for "the disease of the skin, but that of the heart"—the Communists. He recognized their Spartan effectiveness while he had to hold together a vast nation. The Communists recognized military and political prowess and looked on the peasants as their constituency. Chiang broke with them; either that or be absorbed by them. Now his "allies" in the revolution became adversaries.

The Manchus out of the north China area of the Manchurian steppes had quietly achieved political power by subsuming China in the mid-seventeenth century. They had wisely left their administrative architecture in place and recognized the power of Chinese culture and customs. The Manchus themselves, disciples and protégés of their Mongol progenitors, provided the muscle to a China still in need of protection but beginning to chafe under foreign domination by the nineteenth century.

In 1911, with the reign of the dowager empress ended, China emerged blinking into the international community. China was a very weak center of the world. But it was large enough, populous enough, and sufficiently poor in infrastructures such as roads (the Burma Road with all its problems was at least capable of truck traffic). The motorized, mechanized, and armored units of the Japanese could lash out on short leashes and snarl, but far-ranging campaigns like the ones used in Malaya and the Indies weren't possible on this huge land mass.

Even Mao's march, despite a circuitous route and some earlier infiltration, took a year and covered between 4,000 and 6,000 miles. The Japanese would have to control the Chinese citizens. One million Japanese against 400 million possible enemy. River networks were the most commonly used transportation for people and equipment.

But the million men of Japan had no provisions, equipment, or experience in riverine warfare. They were, in a later president's words, "waist deep in the big Muddy." Bogged down, quagmire. Like the Soviets in Afghanistan. Or as we said in Indochina about halfway through the conflict, "you can't win; you can't lose . . . and you can't quit."

There are really two Tibets. Sir Charles Bell, the leading authority on the country between the wars, drew a distinction between "political" Tibet, where the Dalai Lamas or regents had ruled more or less continuously, and the far wider "ethnographic" Tibet. President Roosevelt coyly sketched a third Tibet when he described the origin of the Doolittle Raid as "Shangri-La," the fictional land in the Himalayas described in writer James Hilton's popular 1937 novel *Lost Horizon*.

But Bell's description of two Tibets embraced not only political Tibet but also those surrounding regions where people of Tibetan heritage predominate. These include the Chinese province Sikang, parts of Chinghai, Kansu, Szechuan, and Yunnan, and Ladakh, some distance to the west. In fact, until the tenth century the warlike Tibetans were of the great imperial powers of Asia, their armies campaigning as far afield as Samarkand, Kashgar, and Turfan, and well into western China.[1] Observations like Bell's made contemporary Tibet nervous. Implications that Tibetans were scattered around China like some "guest" residents were unpopular. Also, the peaceful precepts of Buddhism had filtered in from India prior to the eighth century AD. It became, with some fits and starts, the predominant religion by about the tenth to eleventh century and marked the end of Tibet as a bellicose state that raided its neighbors and the region.

India boiled with nationalism and viewed the war, like Vietnam, as a harbinger of freedom from colonial British and French rule respectively. Gandhi's "Quit India" movement caused problems when his government tried to hire laborers to build airfields. This, coupled with the May to October rainy season monsoons, probably added to Stilwell's and Chennault's worries.

East of Jorhat and other Assam airlift bases lay Burma, where British, Indian, and American ground troops—in insignificant numbers compared to those in Europe and the rest of the Pacific theater—were campaigning against the Japanese forces that had overrun the country nearly two years before. This action cut off the western land supply route to the Chinese.

The upper three-quarters of Burma and virtually all of the southern part, including Rangoon, were still under Japanese threat and provided abundant bases for marauding fighter aircraft of the Imperial Japanese Air Force. The terrain posed far greater threats for airmen.

Directly beyond Burma, to its east and south, lay Chinese bases in the relative safety of the great breadth of the country. A significant distance separated them from the Japanese who controlled coastal China and much of the South China Sea. Even a million troops were not enough to saturate China with Japanese security forces. They had probably known this in 1931 when they took Manchuria, installed the young puppet emperor, Puyi, and Japanized the region's name into Manchuko.

Rugged Tibet lay to the northwest. This was a remote region trying to maintain a careful, neutral balance between China, Britain, and Russia.

As far as the Tibetans were concerned, they were stranded in a bad neighborhood, with only their Buddhist faith and the mountains to protect them.

Little was known of this country in the bleak stretches of the Himalayas and across the barren, arid Tibetan Plateau. Tibet is as large as Texas and Alaska combined and remained virulently xenophobic and wedded to the precepts of Buddhism's nonviolence.

Nationalistic Tibetans, brigands, and just plain garden variety Chinese haters—like the Khambas and Goloks, laid down their prayer wheels and picked up their rifles, swords, and wooden saddles without a second thought. They were highly effective but wary warriors. Just two generations had passed since Tibetans had suffered a crushing defeat—in this case inflicted by fast firing, deadly machine guns.

The largest contingent of westerners had been the mounted warriors of the British Younghusband Commission in 1903–4, ostensibly a force to conclude a trade agreement with the newly acquired Sikkim of the British with "independent" Tibet. In reality probably a show of force over an imagined Russian interest in Tibet, a neutral buffer state in the eyes of the British, shielding India. The British considered it inviolate.

Major (later Colonel) Francis Younghusband as commissioner (the political representative of the Crown in India) and Brigadier James Ronald Leslie Macdonald, a quiet Scotsman and Royal engineer, as commander led a regimental-sized unit composed of British regular troops, Nepalese Ghurkas, Indian Sepoys, Pathan tribal regulars, Sikh riflemen, and various artillery and engineers. A section of Maxim machine guns would account for almost 700 Tibetans in the first pitched battle. In addition to all these, almost a thousand porters accompanied the column. At the end of their multiskirmish column's long march into Lhasa, were negotiations and agreements that met with British satisfaction, and British withdrawal that also met Tibet's satisfaction. Tibet also deepened its xenophobia and cracked down even harder on foreign adventurers trying to run the passes. By 1939 and the occupation of Poland by Russia and Germany, there was a sole British resident and wife, his wireless radio operator, and a Chinese Amban and his small retinue the Kashag dutifully ignored as much as possible.

Four years later Lhasa's non-Asian population swelled with two American OSS officers, Ilya Tolstoy and Brooke Dolan, trying to find a possible route for war materiel and supplies delivered to China. Tolstoy was the grandson of Leo Tolstoy and must have been quite impressed by *War and Peace*. Both Tolstoy and Dolan were characters suited for the "loose on rules" OSS, but both had good Asia credentials. Brooke Dolan was a central Asian explorer with old money and a disdain for boredom. Tolstoy and Dolan looked for an ancillary route into China from Russia, an extension of the old Silk Road artery that trucks took from the Russian Far East, but they felt the snow-choked mountain passes effectively put an end to anything resembling a reliable route. Their visit and footprint was just an interesting side note to American-Tibetan diplomatic history, and the two adventuresome young men rode across Tibet back into northern China.

Two years later the enemy arrived. Two Austrian mountaineers who had been climbing in one of the India ranges would instead take a long ride across Tibet and leave the world with a view from Heinrich Harrer's *Seven Years in Tibet* after escaping from a British India internment camp.

CHAPTER 21

A Jorhat Crew's Cautionary Tale

November 30, 1943, somewhere 20,000 feet above south-central Tibet

The radio operator, Kenneth Spencer, had sifted radio signals at Jorhat asking for a directional finding "fix" so they could ride their signal into their home base there. The signal had been so distorted the bearings Jorhat gave them made no sense, and Lieutenant Crozier, the pilot, had him relay back through Kunming using their powerful high frequency radio. The skipping signals had been buried in static, as the walls of the Himalayas played their worse tricks on both the automatic direction finder on the aircraft and the radios.

Even worse, Lieutenant Crozier had flashed the landing lights figuring they were back in the Brahmaputra River valley and headed home over Tinsukia, when they got a response from the tower there in this little Assam Valley station. But Tinsukia was only a few hundred feet above sea level, and the lights below them were much higher than that—thousands of feet higher if their altimeters were correct.[1]

The storm they had endured that threatened to tear their aircraft apart had moved on. The night sky cleared momentarily and now at over twenty thousand feet, peaks higher than that seemed to surround them. Both pilots wondered where the hell they were.

William Perram steadily called out the diminishing fuel, just moments left to "tanks dry," while a hitchhiking passenger, John Huffman, frantically tried to get his parachute on, thinking about the fate that had brought him here out of his job at the Jorhat motor pool. He had just wanted to see China. As the engine superchargers began torching, indicating fuel starvation, it was time to leave an aircraft getting very uncomfortable with itself.

All of them had struggled to get the cargo door off the trimmed and now auto-piloted aircraft, as it began to die of fuel starvation. Huffman, the automotive mechanic that didn't have to be there, had barely managed to don his parachute. They hurled themselves into the frigid darkness a few miles southeast of Lhasa, Tibet. Those dim lights were what they mistakenly believed to be Tinsukia—they were nearly three hundred miles north of where they should have been.

They would survive the flight, the storm, and the bailout.

Their survival and their long walk and horse/mule ride out was an epic adventure story, and the politics that occurred between the four countries of America, Britain, China, and their unhappy host, Tibet, was just as epic.[2]

To the Tibetans, the five airmen must have been Chinese. The Chinese were the greatest threat to their sovereignty, even potentially threatening their governing body, the Kashag, a ruling body of senior clerics. The administrative body that interpreted and transformed His Holiness's directives and guidance (as much as a regent just entering his teen years could dispense) into meaningful governance action, dithered. The question of what to do with the airmen became complicated.

If the legislative bodies of the advanced American and European governments could freeze in bureaucratic malaise and standoff with efficient communications, legations, and transportation systems, imagine Tibet's. They still communicated with long ram horns, blown from the Potala or the Jokhang, to villages miles away, who relayed them in a like manner.

The Kashag had come into existence during the Qing dynasty; the Manchus from the north had quietly and efficiently assumed power in the mid-seventeenth century and had begun administrative reforms; after all, infants, even god king infants, couldn't govern a country. The Dalai Lama was the Buddhist Wheel, the all-seeing eye, the center of the spiritual Buddhist universe and keeper of the Eightfold Path. The Manchu administrators wisely left him in his role of "god-king" and let the Kashag perform the heavy lifting of both temporal and ecclesiastical management. The Kashag squirted the secular and religious grease into the bearings, translating it into instructions for monks, temples, schools, and various departments that ran Tibet's governing mechanism.

The Communists weren't the only Chinese with eyes on Tibet. Later in the war as Nationalist forces "repositioned" (ostensibly to better their tactical position for future operations against the Japanese) in Sichuan's farthest region toward the Tibetan border, FDR's advisors angrily told T. V. Soong to cease and desist. He complied and the Nationalist forces moved away.

The Kashag, organized in AD 1721, was composed mainly of elderly monks and temporal officials who knew how things worked and how to work them, sometimes with agendas of their own—perhaps visions of power and ambition worthy of a Roman city state.

Ironically, the first CIA-trained and equipped Khamba guerrillas would land by parachute in the fall of 1957 and report by hand-cranked generator radio only a few miles from the Jorhat crew's crashed aircraft, on a sand dune in the Brahmaputra River some sixty miles south of Lhasa.[3]

The eighteenth century droned on with the occasional European missionary trying to drop into Lhasa disguised as a pilgrim or cameleer and usually turned back at one of the passes that functioned just as efficiently as an ISIS roadblock. The nineteenth century saw the British shadow-boxing with the Russians and successfully sneaking in Pundits, Hindu or Muslim spies trained by British military engineers in the art of surveying. Their surreptitious instruments included prayer beads containing 100 beads instead of the traditional Buddhist 108 and carefully recording their strides to determine actual distances.

They were told to take 2,000 paces to the mile, establish altitude by observing the temperature of boiling water and using barometers; inside their prayer wheels were paper for notations instead of rolled up prayers. The entire Trigonometric Survey of India conceived by Captain Thomas Montgomerie and his colleagues of the Royal Engineers was a dangerous enterprise at best and a deadly one at worst. Some of the clandestine surveyors were captured and killed. Kipling's novel *Kim* details much of the project.

Younghusband's 1904 gate crashing violently overrode the "ejecting unwanted guests at the pass" policy of the Kashag and their regents and, at least, wakened them to the inadequacy of their defense. Their most worrisome fear, and rightly so, was China, not realizing that the end of the Qing dynasty was fast approaching, and the powerful but benign Manchus would fade away in the swirling dust of the twentieth century.

But the Pacific theater of World War II was a maritime cauldron; battleships and cruisers had determined fates of their nation by how dominant at sea they proved to be. In 1942 naval aviation changed the calculus, and enemy navies would battle each other with aircraft from carriers, with ships out of sight. The CBI was almost entirely a theater dominated and controlled with air assets. Air supremacy, as well as protection for their fleets, was vital; everything else was largely inaccessible by foot or wheeled vehicles through belts of jungles and mountains along the Assam Burma China axis.

Burma was a strategic objective to all. Allied airfields in Assam would support ground fighting by British/Indian, American, Chinese Nationalist, and OSS Kachin and British Force 136 Karen guerrillas. Safe rescue and return of flight crews were high on their list of priorities. Fighter and resupply airfields in Burma were key tactical objectives, and, as Stilwell projected, the Japanese would go after them. A strong Japanese presence in Burma could leave part of it to deal with the smaller allied columns, while heavier dismounted and mechanized forces could invade Assam and strike at Calcutta down the long flat Brahmaputra valley, a major headquarters. Or they could pivot eastward and squeeze China from its weak western flank as the majority of Japanese fighters inexorably moved west.

But now, in November 1943, Crozier's aircraft would likely not have been there if the need of an aircraft to do what China and the United States agreed was a necessity for the sovereign survival of each. The C-87 and all the other aircraft were requirements driven. They were aerial packhorses and mules put in the skies by God and Pratt & Whitney engines (as a contemporary cap patch noted).

Douglas, Boeing, Consolidated, Raytheon, and other aircraft and aerial components' companies labored for the commercial postwar market, but also for China's (and now the U.S.') war with Japan and their European allies. The original axis of evil. The companies didn't mind, they were helping the war effort in the peaceful postwar period. They looked forward to the peacetime profits of their wartime labors. Nobody faulted them for it; they were pitching in with the boys doing the fighting, and for the first time women were welding and turning the rivets, seeking and finding new roles as wage earners.

Everyone was crossing new thresholds of freedom. All this germinated from the conflict that began to simmer in 1931 when the emperor's forces annexed Manchuria and its resources. Now FDR, resonant in his role as an "Old China Hand" based on his family's history of trading with China during the Unequal Treaties period, now had to pay the Nationalist tariff. The "bill" for holding those one million Japanese in China and out of the rest of Asia was payable in money and equipment.

British officers in the Gurkha Regiments told Americans how Kukri's could not be resheathed dry without being "blooded" either from a slashing fight with a Pathan tribesman or a Japanese infantryman, or a finger lightly scored after a brush-cutting detail, producing a few drops of blood.

Kukri's could rest easily in their sheaths only after a little sip of their nectar, blood. Now Chiang hoped allied bayonets and kukri's would take Japanese blood; his soldiers would take the Communist version after the Japanese were defeated once and for all.

The simmering embers of this war burst into flame at a bridge about fifteen miles from Peking named after a famous traveler, Marco Polo, on July 7, 1937. The Japanese, searching for a soldier missing from a night exercise, clashed with Chinese troops and an exchange of small arms fire escalated into shelling. The war was now ongoing in China, and to continue it Chiang needed supplies and money from the United States. Chiang Kai-shek set the amount, and it was expensive in almost all commodities, but especially in the blood of fledgling American airmen. In theory, the supplies would also arm and feed the Communists, also in theory, they were allies against the Japanese, but that, like so many things in China, was artifice. Chiang would wage lip service campaigns against the Japanese, but he expected the Americans and British to fight the ground campaign. Perhaps next to the Communists, he mistrusted and was most wary of Great Britain.

He knew the Communists were an ideological class, probably more dangerous in the long run than a sovereign nation. Countries in the disordered world were still subject to checks and balances, alliances that shifted with the political winds and treaties that were only temporary truths.

He could deal, he felt, in that world, but the Communists had to have their backs broken and then annihilated. He pursued them into their Yenan stronghold in their "Long March" and fought several battles with them, but none were decisive. The best he could hope for now was to safely consolidate his corrupt forces and save them for the postwar battle with Mao Tse-tung's forces.

World leaders and events were bringing India, Burma, and China fully into the technological wonders of the twentieth century, while Tibet maintained its own posture, somewhere in the seventeenth or eighteenth, perhaps, and uneasily aware of the changes to the world over the giant ridgelines that would propel them further into a future they couldn't understand. America's 'bill' to keep both Chinese factions, Nationalists and Communists, fighting was keeping them supplied with equipment, supplies, and, most importantly, funding. Chiang made sure the Nationalist side got the bulk of America's supplies and funds. The Hump pilots and crews recognized the importance of what they were doing—flying to exhaustion in deadly terrain and weather.

But the real significance of the aerial lifeline and the role it would play in the war and aviation history was not part of their consciousness or the part their heroism would have in the vital role of airlift. The legend of the Hump would find full flower—articulation—after the conflict, much as a series of confusing and frightening battles twenty-four years later almost to the day. The Tet Offensive in Vietnam—the "Wider War" that the North Vietnamese wanted badly but lost militarily, then won politically. The legend of the Hump would be articulated again logistically and operationally in the Berlin airlift from the summer of 1948 to May of 1949, when the world war that just finished militarily was burnished politically by American aircrews who fed and warmed Berliners.

World War III, many believed, had just begun as the Cold War. The technology, techniques, and some of the same pilots who flew the Hump navigated the narrow corridor into the city, preventing starvation of the citizens. Moreover, they did it in proud Air Force blue. They had become a separate and distinct service from the Army in 1947.[4]

CHAPTER 22

Refining of the Pilots

By this time in mid-1943, there were a score of bases in China receiving supplies and a score or so in India sending them. Over 3,000 pilots and probably another 15,000 crewmen were braving this and other aerial highways of this region where south and southeast Asia intersected with northeast Asia, the great land mass of China.

They ranged from neophyte newly trained airmen to 10,000-hour craggy airline captains, mail pilots who might've won their wings in World War I or soloed after a couple of hours in a "Jenny," the Curtis JN4 ubiquitous World War I trainer and workhorse off a Kansas or Nebraska wheat field. Nearly 7,000 were produced and the ones not cracked up beyond repair were sold as surplus, at ridiculously low prices. Many a "barnstormer," airmail pilot, or crop duster started off in the tandem-seated 90-horse-powered engine trainer off a midwestern farmer's field.

This was also the fate of my father's planes as an Army contract flight instructor with lease-back aircraft following a postwar aviation "boom" that quickly became "bust," returning my grandfather's black Angus to their favorite runway/pasture.

Getting people and supplies from India or maritime south China, Hong Kong, to Hanoi, or Saigon to Singapore, had been ongoing for a while. But the Japanese had put a kink in this plan since Shanghai fell to them. CNAC had been flying out of Kai Tak (sometimes spelled Kai Tek) in the Crown Colony at night, escaping into the clouds of the South China Sea to Manila or across the Tonkin Gulf to Hanoi, safely, on instruments. The flights from Rangoon over the transom of the Himalayas had begun cautiously after this, with pilots feeling their way carefully around weather cells they could see, uncomfortable with the snow-clad peaks punching up twenty thousand feet or higher, sometimes hidden in the darkness.

The prelude to this phase had not been easy; it had started in memorandums and discussions at the White House, War Department, State Department, and the Joint Chiefs of Staff even before Fulton Lanier had touched down on a dirt airfield in Australia in 1942.

The president had decreed that China be supplied. At the time only British India could safely hold the departure airfields. The Burma Road was being fully motorized and improved after the British closed it temporarily before Pearl Harbor in an acquiescent nod to the Japanese. They were capable of invading India, creating a two-front war they could ill afford. Now, much of the British-officered Indian Army was fighting in the Middle East and North Africa.

This was the situation swirling around Robert Crozier, the captain, and Mac McCallum, copilot and the radio operator, crew chief, and hitchhiking ground automotive mechanic, in December 1943. They took off from Kunming en route to Yunnan-yi for the four-hour flight to Jorhat. Just a little over a year later, in another treacherous January of 1945, the night of January 6/7 was the worst weather witnessed by the Tenth Weather Squadron, the India-China division of ATC, or the combat commands.

During the 1945 night of wrecks and death, radio frequencies were alive with "MAYDAY!" calls. All told, nine Hump transports went down with eighteen crewmembers and nine passengers; CNAC lost three of their precious few aircraft, while three aircraft between the Tenth and Fourteenth Air Forces went down.[1]

During this time of crippling winds severe icing, hail, and sleet later called "Black Week," the old dictum of "no weather over the Hump" would disappear.

From then on, in General Tunner's era of "Big Business," weather was a prime consideration of flight safety for that most precious commodity, the men who flew and crewed the aircraft and the passengers they carried. Crozier and his crew would arrive back in Jorhat four months later on foot, leading tired horses and donkeys, but Lanier and his crew wouldn't know that.

Much of those early problems with the war, the Pacific, the CBI, and the Hump had now been sorted out. A series of high-level meetings had taken place at various places in the world, beginning with Arcadia in Washington, then to Casablanca, Cairo, and the Crimea—the important Yalta Conference. Even Chiang Kai-shek was at Cairo, seen as a gesture to insure China would be an important player in the postwar world.

They would be, but Chiang Kai-shek would not be their leader.

On this cold, clear last day of January 1944, Fulton Lanier was totally focused on getting his crew and aircraft back to Jorhat safely. The easy-going former college football player from North Carolina was confident in his flying abilities. Fulton was a seasoned combat pilot when he returned for a second tour in Asia in June 1943. He enlisted in the Army early in 1941 to fly, and his logbook describes a flying autobiography—an aerial journey—that began with the end of a decade-long American Depression.

For active, young, and adventurous men like Lanier, the war was a godsend. His photographs show a handsome, trim but rugged six-foot brown-haired, and brown-eyed man. Fulton's natural athleticism led him to his first combat arena—college football. He enrolled at Campbell College in Creek, North Carolina, and quickly pursued the sport of football. His quickness, wit, and a slight flair for wildness earned him the respect of his teammates.

It started in the early 1930s and was partly responsible for the two separate air forces the Japanese fielded for the Army and Navy, and the differing missions anticipated for both of them. The Army was seen as most likely to fight the Soviets in the north and the Americans in the Aleutians, so their aircraft were designed and fielded with colder, northern land missions in mind.[2]

Their naval air force was forecast to fight in the Pacific.

Most of the conflicts were limited border engagements until the early summer of 1939 when the Soviets defeated the Japanese at Lake Khasan, and later at Khalkin-Gol, resulting in the Soviet-Japan Neutrality Pact. Stalin couldn't undertake a war on two fronts, with the Germans in Russia proper and Japan in the rim lands of China. In August 1945, as promised at Yalta, they invaded Japan, right after Hiroshima and Nagasaki.[3] They didn't worry as much about this one as they did the summer of 1941.

Despite the grim fighting and flying, Fulton and his fellow airmen were still in the shadow of the "big conflict" playing out as the Japanese swept over peninsular French Indochina and British Malaya, while the British hung grimly on to their prize jewel of empire, India. Fulton's countrymen waged a life-or-death struggle at Corregidor and Bataan, a struggle that would ultimately end in the worst American defeat America had ever suffered, despite a heroic effort. And the entire Pacific War was in the shadow of the even bigger conflict, the war in Europe against the Germans and Italians.

A lost engine was no more annoying than dropping a spoon or fork off a table. Even the loss of two engines—unless they were on the same wing—was not overly worrisome, as long as the dead engine's propellers could be "feathered," the propellers turned knife-edged forward.

Lanier also realized that ten other men—most of whom had no control over the airplane like he and his copilot did—depended solely on his skill and would live or die based on it. So Fulton Lanier did not tempt fate, crowd his luck, or let his love of flying lull him into a situation that would endanger his aircraft or crew.

Refining involved things other than flying skills.

Saburo and his Zero shared the sky with Lanier's B-17E in New Guinea, Borneo, Java, and the Andaman Sea. Saburo's unit was relocated to Rabaul in New Britain, New Guinea, in early August, just days before the Americans launched the Guadalcanal campaign, August 1942.[4]

The Tainan Air Group attacked Henderson Field almost daily, and Sakai saw many engagements there.

On August 8, 1942, Sakai was victorious over a Marine fighter flown by skilled James "Pug" Southerland. After an extended dogfight where no one seemingly had a clear upper hand, Sakai was able to hit Southerland's fighter underneath the left wing root, downing the F4F Wildcat fighter, while the Marine drifted to safety in his parachute.

This was likely discussed in ready rooms and airfield mess tents on both sides as an epic duel between two master gunfighters of aerial combat.

Wounded and half blinded in one aerial encounter, Saburo Sakai would go on to down over sixty allied aircraft, making him one of the leading Axis aces to survive the war.

He would turn to religion in later years, becoming a Buddhist acolyte, sprinkling incense and murmuring prayers, not only for his own perished comrades but also for the allied pilots who died in encounters with him.

US propaganda in these hectic days portrayed the Japanese fighting men—particularly the aviators—as men who were in a war technologically far over their head. In reality the Japanese soldiers, sailors, and airmen were tough, idealistically motivated foes. They had gone to war for —in the American view—misguided reasons.

Unfortunately, despite Emperor Gojong of Korea's pleas for Teddy Roosevelt's assistance in keeping their independence, Japan assumed hegemony of Korea; in Teddy's words: "Korea was utterly impotent either for self-government or self-defense."[5]

Roosevelt thought the Koreans were strong-minded and tough enough to contain the threat posed by Czar Nicholas's Cossacks and Russian forces to the Far East and the Central Asian "Heartland of the World" espoused by academics like Halford Mackinder and Alfred Thayer Mahan.

He didn't think much of the Chinese; after all, the Japanese had easily bested China in their war in the closing years of the nineteenth century.

Teddy's younger cousin, Franklin Delano, was imbued with sentimental views of the Chinese through mercantile family connections.

His grandfather made the family fortune in the tea trade—and opium—convincing Franklin he had roots in a land he would never see.

FDR, with Wilsonian ideals, viewed China as a benign western-oriented colossus that would keep order in the Pacific in the victorious postwar years.[6]

Unfortunately, his principal allies, led by Winston Churchill and Josef Stalin, were not as enthusiastic and didn't share this vision.

Stalin, struggling desperately with the Germans, didn't want a two-front war. Japan, joining the allies in World War I, was dismayed when the League of Nations limited its navy and capital ships at the Washington Naval Conference, 1921. Japan was a maritime nation, unlike China, and they viewed this as distinctly inimical to their interests, and worse, racially motivated.

The Japanese technology and military advances were impressive; the Meiji Restoration that fostered this modernization occurred mid-nineteenth century, after the US Navy's visit by Commodore Matthew Perry.

Successful Japanese military action against China, Russia, and Korea followed relatively soon after and only an international diplomatic initiative preserved any kind of stability in the Pacific for the next two decades.

The Pacific's amphibious and aerial warfare arena were islands, beaches, archipelagos, and vast stretches of ocean.

The southwest Pacific would be the southern limit of fighting, with the all-important mission of protecting the Dutch East Indies and northwest Australia.

As 1942 closed, the Army Air Force was receiving more heavy bombers; Roosevelt, Marshall, and Hap Arnold's war machine manufacturing was now galloping, and fresh B-17Es were rolling out with the B-17F and the final B17G over the horizon. Ironically, the B-17 would become the quintessential signature aircraft of the European Theater of Operations.

B-17s flew from bucolic English bases while the technology studded B-29 would become the emblematic aerial weapon of the Pacific, raining bombs on Japanese island strongholds and preparing for the dismemberment of

Japan by fire from the sky. B-29s would only fly from European bases after the war—as Cold War "ferrets," electronic snoops.

The war year of 1943 opened with the battle-scarred Nineteenth Bomb Group flying their aircraft to a desolate strip of Texas. The town was fly-speck Pyote, and workers and inhabitants knew Pyote Army Airfield as "Rattlesnake Bomber Base" for the dens of western diamondback rattlers that had been dug up in the construction of the base.

The 8,000-foot shining-white concrete runways were a welcome treat for the Nineteenth, who now were hastily reorienting to be instructors for newly minted pilots. *They* wouldn't have to fly their first combat missions in a plane they had never flown, or at most only familiarized with. Being home was glorious—being at Pyote was not so great—there was very little to do around Pyote.

All the rest was at Pyote—bad weather, this time in the form of high-density altitudes, where the heat fools the geography into appearing to be thousands of feet higher than it actually is. Dust storms turned bright daylight into evening takeoffs that, as the landing gear came up, forced pilots to switch instantly to instrument conditions.

Lanier had written home to his father that he was seeking reassignment to India to fly the "Hump."[7] His logbook continues his aerial journey and biography, this time from the southwest Pacific to China, Burma, and India, not yet designated a "combat theater":

> "6 August 1943:
> "Co-pilot on C-47—first flight over the Hump to Yunnan-yi, China."[8]

Fulton P. Lanier was back in Asian aerial combat, but this time the military powers had decreed the newly formed China Burma India theater—a theater of intrigue, diverse personalities, and egos and the worst weather and terrain in the world—was not considered a combat theater by military and political decision makers.

They were mostly flying cargo aircraft, and the Chinese military was supposed to do the "heavy lifting" of combat with the Japanese both in Burma and China. The British would handle the security of India, and the Americans would supply everyone.

Soon Fulton P. Lanier and other men who sat in pilots' and copilots' seats realized that there were worse enemies than Japanese fighters and bombers. Despite not being in a combat theater, weather, mountains, and the inadequacy of navigation aids could kill them much quicker, particularly the new, unskilled pilots. Like most of Jorhat's pilots.

Only one thing could save them if they safely crash-landed, an unlikely prospect with the dearth of flat terrain over most of their route. Or worse, bailing out over mountains, jungle, or the raging, swollen rivers, especially in the rainy season of May through October. They had to be rescued, discovered by airplanes or jungle runners moving quickly to young British administrators in unoccupied Burma or the wilder parts of Assam.

As these events weighed on their mind, and more and more losses occurred, they paid closer attention to the safety bulletins and operational briefings that mentioned a special unit equipped with twin engine armed B-25s. They were air crewmen themselves, not infantrymen. The jungles were trackless thick interwoven carpets of green, the canopy sometimes hundreds of feet above their heads. They knew that only smoke from a burning aircraft would give aircraft hunting for them a location for an area in which they might have landed.

The aircraft from the rescue unit had garish, distinctive paint schemes—easy to spot as friendly from the ground. Little L-5 liaison aircraft, much like the Piper Cubs some had learned to fly in as civilians, could land on short and rough fields and carry one or two injured out.

There was also a strange, relatively new and unproven craft that would change the future shape of combat search and rescue, or CSAR as it's currently called—helicopters.

"Blackie's Gang," at Chabua in northeastern Assam, had come into the fight. They used light single-engine aircraft that could land and take off on miniscule fields—airfield and agricultural, or roads that were barely trails. They used the first military helicopters, making a takeoff and escape with an injured, bailed out crewman just as rescuers burst out of the jungles after days of slashing through with machetes.

In the light aircraft they placed wounded on stretchers reaching back into the fuselage. They sometimes drained fuel to lighten takeoff weight to get them to the closest place they could land with medical facilities, or a larger, longer airfield to get the wounded to a field hospital. In addition to the garish paint jobs, the rescue planes could also drop food, water, and notes in containers with streamers to give them directions.

They had fighters and heavily armed but nimble fighters and light bombers for covering rescues from hostile forces, and the first parachuting doctors and medics jumped down to treat crews who escaped their stricken aircraft but were wounded or injured on landing.

The correspondent Eric Sevareid, the State Department's John Paton Davies, Stilwell's political officer, and two senior Chinese officers of the Kuomintang were among the twenty-one passengers aboard a C-46 that suffered engine failure and crashed in northern Burma in August 1943.

The successful linkup with Naga tribesmen and their walkout and turnover to friendly forces were some of the most famous "saves" of initial rescues from a thrown together outfit whose historical offspring would be the Aerospace Rescue and Recovery Service of the war in Indochina, which saved hundreds of pilots and crewmembers.

Soon they would have lifesaving medical teams that got to downed crews more quickly than anyone could imagine—these were the lifesaving knights that fell from the sky. For the first time and forever more the rescue of downed airmen would entwine with the "Special Operators," in 1943 the rumored "society men and blue bloods of the OSS." For the first time the Switlik Parachute Company's silk escape machine—the parachute—could deliver medically trained soldiers and doctors to crash survivors.

Lanier reluctantly mentally left the sky and thought about the ground, and how he'd have to gather his crew, care for them medically, avoid and protect them from the Japanese, and ultimately walk out of the dangerous terrain they'd fallen into, leaving their stricken aircraft.

The ultimate alternative, crashing into a mountain or the jungle aboard the aircraft, was not a choice he could make. He discarded it and thought only about surviving and flying again.

Detachment 101 of the Office of Strategic Services (OSS) had been established with "safe" locations to get to if a potentially catastrophic event occurred. What if they had life-threatening injuries on the ground? Evacuation was sometimes the only answer, and sometimes two or three medical personnel would land in parachutes, particularly if there were critical patients on the ground.

Captain Raymond Peers's Detachment 101 would figure prominently in the CBI for rescues. His Kachin tribesmen would also figure prominently in combat and saving American airmen. The tough tribesmen needed little urging to perform these tasks—they hated the Japanese.

The SOE—Special Operations Executive—had an operational detachment labeled Force 136 that was a British parallel to Detachment 101 in Southeast Asia. When Winston Churchill told Minister of Economic Warfare Hugh Dalton "to set Europe ablaze" in July 1940, members of the British Intelligence Service became very nervous. They wondered when the soldiers of the SOE were going to wander into one of their clever clandestine operations.

The SOE was seen as the operational portion of the Intelligence Service. The officers went through the same training and excelled at the same tradecraft as the Commando Regiments.

General MacArthur had forbidden the OSS to set foot in his Southwest Pacific theater. By contrast, the overall commander of Southeast Asia Command, Lord Louis Mountbatten, invited the SOE into his headquarters cantonment in Ceylon. Perhaps to keep an eye on them. Between Detachment 101 and their enlistment of the northern mountainous portion of Burma's Kachins and Force 136s Karens, there were lots of allied and native eyes keeping eyes on airmen and lost soldiers.

The Kachins hated the Japanese and were very effective guerrilla warriors after being armed and provisioned by Peers and his trusty OSS officers and sergeants. The SOE operatives in Southeast Asia were clandestine, hence the cover name "Force 136." In addition to sabotage and guerrilla operations, Force 136 also knew the largely young civilian administrators of the Foreign Office that Britain always put into posts to serve the districts and villagers. Most of them could speak the languages and dialect of the tribal peoples they administered, knew what was going on in their areas, and helped the allies, including downed airmen, get to safety. Then they returned to their sparse quarters somewhere and waited for their next trip, by foot, mule, or horse into the jungled mountains. The Americans had the Kachins from the north, the British the Karens from the south and southeast.

Although Lanier's crew was largely unaware of the missions of Detachment 101 other than effecting the rescue of downed aircrews and knew even less about Force 136, they knew they would help them on the ground. A significant part of Peers's mission was the rescue of downed aircrews with their band of Kachin guerillas. Lanier was joined by Second Lieutenant Frank Ramos, his copilot.

Fulton and Frank had tested each other's aerial ability on the trip from Jorhat to Kunming, and both decided they liked what they'd seen. Frank Ramos's quiet competence was wrapped in a completely different personality than his pilot. They had bumped into each other at Jorhat in the mess hall, what passed for officers' club, and the dusty streets of Jorhat as well as in various briefings and flight scheduling, but this was the first time they'd flown together. Lieutenant Ramos was quieter, younger, and had less than half the flying time of the ebullient Lanier, but he was eager to improve his flying skill and do the best job possible. In addition, he was a family man—married with a baby boy born just two weeks earlier.

Frank had grown up in Austin, Texas, in a multicultural family and society, one that richly spanned the best of Anglo and Hispanic history and tradition, so common in the Texas Hill Country. Ramos didn't have Lanier's flying experience, but he shared his love of flying.

While Lanier loved flying as he loved life—something to be experienced, excited by, and richly enjoyed for the sheer experience of it—Frank's first love was his family—wife Doris had recently given birth to their son, Michael, and flying was essential to their care and well-being. He had not seen a picture of the baby, but Doris provided rich details about him and poured out her love for both the baby and her beloved husband in letters from Austin.

Frank Ramos, who had already flown in the right seat of a DC-3 as an airline pilot, no doubt dreamed of the day when flying would provide his family with their livelihood. He and Doris met in 1940, a year before the United States entered the war. Doris was the daughter of Charles and Emma Grace Sawyer, proprietors of the popular Union Seafood Market in Austin.

Frank Ramos was a tall, good-looking fellow who had been raised by his grandmother. He was twenty-three, selling shoes in E. M. Scarborough & Sons department store, when he spotted Doris, who worked in the manager's office. He asked the pretty nineteen-year-old to dance at a company party. They started dating and fell in love.

In December 1941, after the Japanese attack on Pearl Harbor, Frank, by then in the Texas National Guard, went on active duty. He was selected for officer training and flight school. He shipped out to Lubbock and earned his wings there in November 1942. Then the Army Air Forces assigned him to a base in Denver. That's when he asked Doris Sawyer to marry him.[9]

More training occurred in Texas and other bases, and Frank went to Midwest Airlines as a copilot in one of the training programs that melded civilian and military training. This was not uncommon in the early days of the war when the United States was trying to get airplanes built and pilots trained. The experienced airline pilots took the fledgling Army flyers under their wings and began to teach them the techniques of understanding weather and the intricacies of instrument flying.

Like Fulton, Frank was a slender, handsome, brown-haired young man, standing six two with a graceful and quiet demeanor. He was the introspective yin to Fulton's outgoing yang. Also like Lanier, Ramos had experienced the mixed blessings the war had brought—the end of a crippling decade of economic depression followed by a dizzying whirlwind of preparation for the deadliest conflict the world had ever experienced.

Everything accelerated, even love, he found, and he reveled in the role as a new husband and Army pilot. Doris's life changed too—she'd rarely been out of Texas when she found herself on a train for Denver, looking at snow for the first time in her life. They were married in the base chapel at Lowry Army Air Base the week before Christmas, 1942. In Denver, they made their tiny house a home, setting up a small Christmas tree and enjoying the winter.

Dancing, ice skating (something new for both of them), and squeezing in a honeymoon was the norm for the young marrieds, despite the war. Frank and his fellow pilots prepared to deploy for the conflict that was just beginning to show some promise for the Americans in Europe as well as other theaters, including the Pacific.

From Denver the couple went to Memphis, where Frank underwent advanced multiengine flying training, and then they went on to Florida for completion of the training. Doris returned to Austin, leaving Frank in Florida; shortly thereafter she discovered she was pregnant, with the baby due in January.

Second Lieutenant Frank Ramos left Florida in May 1943, following the well-worn aerial path down through Brazil to Africa and on to the bustling new—but austere—base at Jorhat, in the Assam valley of northeast India. Joining the ranks of copilots, he with several other pilots who came and went at odd hours, lived in the typical basha thatched roof, concrete floor, open-air dwelling. It was built above ground to minimize the presence of crawling insects, rodents, and the occasional cobra.

He checked out in the C-47 and C-87, flew in the right seat, and settled into the aerial life of the China Burma India theater. He, and hundreds of other new copilots, learned the weather, terrain, and idiosyncrasies of the aircraft he flew. When he was not flying he strolled the dusty streets and markets of Jorhat, played cards, occasionally drank with his basha mates, and wrote home. He received a loving letter from his wife, Doris, describing their just-born infant, a healthy boy. He was hoping to get a photo of them both soon.

While flying he sat in the right seat, worked the flaps and gear when the pilot gave him the palm up or down signal, monitored the engine instruments, and conducted the preflights—all copilot's duties. Occasionally, he'd make a takeoff or landing, long narrow feet gracefully working the rudder pedals to keep the aircraft straight or to bank smoothly into a turn.

Pilots took note of his smoothness on the controls, the care and consideration he took with the enlisted crew, and how he frequently stayed with the aircraft on the ground while the crew went to a mess hall for something to eat.

When there was nothing further to do, he studied the aircraft manuals, soaking up knowledge for his on-check ride to earn the coveted left seat as a pilot in command of his own crew and airplane. He also wanted to see his wife and new child—their new son; he wanted that very much.

A week after the change of command, on a hot July morning in 1993, I had my first experience in a JTF-FA-CILHI skirmish in a meeting accompanied by our captain, Al Cutler, the assistant operations officer, and Dr. Tom Holland, the lab director. Every month Brigadier General Needham had an update meeting that covered future operations and the status of identifications of recoveries. I knew this put extreme pressure on Holland and his anthropologists. But on the ride up to Camp Smith I began to glean some of the problems the commander of PERSCOM had alluded to that needed straightening out. Captain Cutler advised me not to mention the size or numbers of Americans on the recovery teams. I thought that was rather strange, and he answered my query, with more recovery teams more anthropologists would be required and that would, theoretically, slow down the identifications. I could understand a rather convoluted explanation of that logic.

"Well, let's see what comes up and we'll take it from there," I replied.

As a former Regimental Commander told all us Squadron Commanders once, "friction and function . . . always a factor in any operation. Your job is not to let the former stop the latter. Do it quietly and give the credit to all your subordinates when it's successful."

Thorne Helgesen, our administrative lab director, was already up on the giant hill housing Camp Smith, another jewel in the military crown of Hawaii, talking to Ray Spock, now the chief of analysis of Joint Task Force–Full Accounting and an old colleague of mine from the JCRC in the late 1980s. He'd see what information he could glean that would be talked about in the meeting and give us an update beforehand. Thorne was an old CILHI hand and had started as a Department of the Army civilian mortician in Saigon during the war. Years earlier, when I was at the JCRC in the late 1980s, he told me how he had ridden to the mortuary on his scooter the first day of the Tet Offensive in January 1968.

He wondered what all the shooting was about.

Ray was a retired personnel senior NCO in the Air Force, with long service in the Air Force Casualty Office. He, like Thorne, had weathered every crisis in the JCRC and CILHI since the fall of Saigon. Both literally knew just about the entire history of the issue from the time in Thailand through the present. Or, as we used to say with a hint of the macabre, where the bodies were buried.

Thorne and Ray would try to iron out problems beforehand, or at least let each other know what was coming; they were old NCO's trying to solve problems before they blossomed.

In this case the meeting was a "bloodbath," with the lab director Holland taking the brunt, and the subject was the glacial pace of identifications coming out of the lab. That was the conundrum; they were almost condemned to being agonizingly slow—reconstructing stature from bone fragments and documenting each day's progress or lack of it is a result of scientific rigidity. I knew General Needham was under the gun on identifications, and the answers were fairly evident—his investigative teams could find and determine recommendations for recoveries—and we could recover them—far faster than our laboratory-bound anthropologists could identify them.

I jumped into the breach and pointed this out, although the JTF-FA was well aware of that. A great number of his people had come out of the JCRC like I did and they had weathered the storms of misidentifications in the past, at least at a little distance, but sometimes it took years to get identifications.

I reiterated that we were looking for more physical anthropologists and forensic dentists, and while we had the funding and the encouragement of Congress and the administration, they simply did not grow on trees, but at the time we did have one or two coming in. Suggestions had been made to contract some of the identifications out to well-known universities like the University of Tennessee, whose department of Anthropology was renowned, as were its professors, but doing that effectively loosened the control of the identifications. Finally, I raised an issue that caused jaws to drop on both sides.

Perhaps we could split the teams in some cases and use a single anthropologist to shuttle between sites. When the keening and wailing from the CILHI'ers subsided, I pointed out the first recoveries in Vietnam five years before had done that with three teams, and the sole anthropologist—an archaeologist, actually—Pete Miller, was in the role of a mobile expert, driven or flown to a site.

I also pointed out that having spent three years in the policy arena, the funds and manpower gates were thrown open for the express purpose of accounting for lost servicemen, and that meant identifications. With more anthropologists in the lab, it certainly should help, but if we thought this was a possibility I'd try to sell my boss, the adjutant general at the Personnel Command.

Thus the long time required and lengthy reviews required to ensure accuracy in the identifications. A forensic identification is a process, but it also requires review and acceptance by peers as well as a separate review by an expert board mandated for CILHI. At that time, it also entailed a review by a professional board of three senior officers—colonels from the Army, Air Force, and Marines, and captains from the Navy, ideally Vietnam veterans, who would review the operational and intelligence/analytical process (but not the scientific process).

This final look was to assure the families that officers from their loved one's service and representation from land, sea, and maritime services had no doubts or misgivings about the case. This review basically verified that investigative and search and recovery procedures had been properly and correctly conducted, by senior officers who had fought on Indochina's land, air, and waters.

I thought I could see the problem from both sides, and the best I could do was reinforce what everyone in Washington and every taxpayer wanted: results—identified remains. We were trying to speed up the process by hiring more physical anthropologists and forensic dentists as well as casualty data analysts, which was not an actual career field, but the position was filled by someone with computer and research skills. They could be trained in military history, graves registration procedures in past and present conflicts, and service casualty operations. Their early training normally included a mission or two on a recovery team to give them an idea of what it entailed and how their work developed and aided the operation.

Many new PhDs were reluctant to live in a tent on a muddy dangerous hillside for sixteen to twenty days at a time and then come right back to work making time-consuming and potentially career-damaging mistakes under the threat of lawsuits. Later Congress would decree that 200 identifications per year would be mandated. I considered that requirement, nearly twenty years after retirement, a goal as elusive and impossible as Chiang's "10,000 tons per month over the Hump." I had watched the anthropologists painstakingly going over bones—some mere fragments—and assemble skeletal parts like gigantic crossword puzzles. Two right clavicles for instance, meant another lost serviceman in a crew of fifteen. The serviceman might not be identified, but if there were no parachutes visible, or no record of an enemy voice intercept indicating prisoners that might have been taken from a crash site, this narrowed the equation, which might ultimately mean all perished in the crash, shoot down, or firefight on the ground.

In 2003, with congressional assistance and funding, mandated changes realigned the clumsy command channels, and CILHI and the JTF–FA were combined into a DOD agency. I was long retired. Later in 2014, after a long look, Congress and DOD conducted a streamlining of the whole process and the Defense POW/MIA Accounting Agency emerged. It would operate under policy guidance from a deputy assistant secretary of Defense for POW/MIA Affairs.

But there was also a whiff of "we've been doing this a lot longer than you have," and neither General Needham, the Joint Task Force, the agencies in Washington, nor I, had tolerance for that attitude. In the succeeding months the atmospherics bettered, with identifications speeding up slightly and excavation sites increasing, and the teams did, out of necessity, get smaller. Also we began borrowing infantrymen from the Twenty-Fifth Division, thanks to Major General Ord, the commander. They quickly proved they could wield a pick and shovel as well as a rifle. But the times required for the identification process would be a significant problem through all of our tenures.

Another recovery coming up was one of particular interest to me, because of the circumstances and losses—Lang Vei Special Forces camp, a few miles from its big besieged sister, Khe Sanh combat base, in February 1968. It was overrun by NVA tanks the night of February 7, 1968. There were Green Beret KIAs, MIAs, and known captured. Virtually every American in the camp was wounded. I had visited Lang Vei village and the Special Forces camp in the fall of 1967, as a passenger in a Marine helicopter. The village was overrun with tanks and infantry the night of February 7, 1968, with several missing and evidence of at least one POW. The ominous second act of the Tet Offensive in Northern I Corps.

We discussed taking the retired Special Forces camp commander, Major Frank Willoughby, back to Lang Vei. He was now working as a Department of the Army civilian at Fort Benning, Georgia.[10]

We pondered that option briefly, decided we should do it, and then noticed we were all tired. Needham veered back to Tibet. How, he wondered, did we get into these World War II cases?

"CILHI's been tied in with World War II history professors and crash buffs for years—even in the old days before it left Thailand in '75. We've got an Australian point of contact down in New Guinea that's pretty good. I think he runs a museum down there and may work for the PNG government, maybe in some aviation capacity. I need to get down there sometime." Meanwhile, we've got just about all the Missing Aircrew Reports (pronounced *Mack-ers*) from the Pacific theater plus a lot of the ones going down the eastern seaboard to Brazil. We've also got most of the really high aircrew losses from all theaters.

Frizzel looked up. Needham was still thinking.

I continued. "Joe Harvey mentioned a lady named Susan Sheehan who wrote an interesting book about a CILHI recovery in New Guinea some years ago. I haven't read it, but he says it's worthwhile."

Johnnie Webb and the anthros that have been down there say it's a pristine graveyard for "warbirds."

"Great! You guys need more business," Needham deadpanned.

Frizzel rubbed his hand over his face tiredly, but I knew it hid a grin; then he laughed. Needham smiled, shook his head.

I stood up; Frizzel and I knew Needham had plenty of work left before Midnight Mass, and I said, as solemnly and thoughtfully as I could, "You know Frizzel, I've always envied you being one of Uncle Sam's Misguided Children; and then a naval aviator on top of that."

Frizzel and Needham glanced at each other, Bill Frizzel spread his arms in supplication, a quizzical "wait for it look" on his face. Needham, despite being irritated with the long meeting on the Friday before the official Christmas holidays, had an anticipatory grin.

"It's our great uniforms, right?"

I mimed three seconds of thoughtfulness and shook my head.

"Nope, that's true, but not exactly it."

"Our superb fighting ability, then."

"Ummm, yeah, but not quite it . . ."

I looked up and wagged an "I've got it" finger.

"It's your haircuts; only a dollar a side."

A flicker of silence ensued then we all burst out laughing. Needham licked a finger and inked an invisible mark in the air.

"He got'cha, Bill One."

Frizzel wiped his eyes, still chuckling, then sobered.

"He sure did, Sir."

More chuckles and the general wound it up.

"Even up, now you guys go get a beer or something and have a Merry Christmas. Tell your troops to throttle back for about ten days and be ready for 1994."

We saluted, but Needham called us back. "Hey, I really appreciate the work your people did. Your people and our people," he nodded to both of us. As deputy, Bill Frizzel had the day-to-day work of coordinating everything, especially when General Needham was gone.

Which was frequently, and I was generally with him. I was a JCRC'er and I felt a kindred connection to the evolved from the JCRC JTF–FA; I envied the manpower and expanded mission and expertise.

Some of the old JCRC had carried over to the JTF–FA when it had finally settled in a few years before, in uniform and in a post-military career as civilians.

They had been good soldiers, sailors, marines, and airmen and now they were doing the same job in mufti, as retirees.

"Tell them all to be safe and remember what Christmas really is."

"Yes sir." More salutes and we left the general to his work.

But he yelled for me one more time, this time from the doorway; I turned back toward him and Frizzel joined me.

"I was just thinking—you don't think the Chinese could have salted that crash site, do you?"

It was a good question, and Frizzel and I shared a glance—that's what he'd been puzzling over while we talked.

"No, Sir. I don't think they could with the crashed aircraft and the condition of the remains."

"Condition of the remains, Jesus, you're right. I shoulda thought of that," he wiped a hand down a tired face.

"But that crash site is going to turn up remains for a while. The Chinese think we'll see more anytime they get an unusually mild winter or spring. I think they're probably right."

I didn't know how prophetic that casual remark would be.

Frizzel and I walked down the stairs; it couldn't seem less like Christmas Eve, 8 p.m. on the Friday before Christmas, 1993.

Somewhere in the dark, Bing Crosby sang "White Christmas," as out of place at Camp Smith, Hawaii, as it was in Saigon in April 1975. The song heralded the end of the war and the code words hiding evacuation from a stubborn ambassador who refused to believe the long conflict was finally over.[11]

His indecision would underline the chaotic abandonment of Saigon and a long, unsuccessful war that would spawn more unrest and conflict in America and overseas.

On the other hand, he'd lost a son in the war. You had to see and understand where he was coming from.

There was history everywhere in this business. History was sometimes the ghost of the past.

General Needham was right. The year 1994 did start off with a gallop; recovery missions picked up in the new year as well as politico-military matters. Admiral Larson was headed to Vietnam himself, the first US senior military commander to visit since the Vietnam war.

Bill Frizzel arranged for me to ride in the admiral's Boeing 707; I was in my summer-weight uniform and already on his plane when he and his staff came aboard in sharp Navy blue and gold flight suits. General Needham would meet us in Hanoi, but we were on a different mission than his—Admiral Larson was going to the Citadel for a senior-level meeting with the Ministry of National Defense.

General Needham and I were going to visit our teams in the field. In addition, we had cracked the mystery of our C-87. The lab team, with Rick Huston's Honolulu policewoman's wife, had taken some of the uniform items to their crime lab; under enhanced fluoroscopic lighting they had made out a name on one of the flight coveralls we'd brought back from Tibet as well as on one of the mess tickets. We now had enough to match against the manifest and had discovered there were still two members of the crew somewhere at the crash site.

We were going back, but first there was considerable work to be done on the route leading to the crash site. It had been an early spring and tremendous snow melt. Streams were raging rivers, and footpaths, fords, and bridges constructed by the PLA were inundated or washed away. We were targeting end-August to go back in and get the two missing members.

PART FIVE

Resurrection

CHAPTER 23

Maelstrom

Kunming, China; January 31, 1944

First Lieutenant Fulton Lanier, USAAF, continued to study the sky over Kunming, China; this time from the left seat of C-87 862. He had expected another load of cargo, perhaps ammunition, bombs, or gas, going to another base on the "low" side, here in China. After all, that was their mission and he didn't mind that one bit. But after waiting all afternoon, his cargo consisted of empty oxygen containers palletized for return to Jorhat.

It was hardly worth waiting all afternoon for the storm to build up, and built up it had certainly become. The clouds had darkened and boiled twenty miles west of Kunming, and night now enveloped them. "At least there won't be any Japanese fighters," he thought, "and we've got almost nonexistent cargo." He was not consoled as he idled the four engines to save fuel while waiting for the takeoff signal from the tower.

Even the Hump bases in India's northeast Assam were only moderately safe. Japanese bombers had attacked the major British bases Dinjan and Fort Hertz and threatened the rest of the safe haven airfields scattered down the Brahmaputra River valley. This could serve as an invasion route that arrowed into the major city of eastern India, Calcutta. What if they were attacked on approach, low on fuel; how long could they hide in the clouds. If there were clouds.

Lanier didn't want to be jumped by Japanese fighters with reduced fuel on board. He knew the impending weather would be trouble enough and he'd burn more fuel hiding in the overcast. His copilot had turned out to be proficient on the gauges and even exceeded his skill in knowing the vagaries of weather flying. That would be a big plus when they plunged into the hairy maws of the storm he knew lay between them and Jorhat.

He had heard of the August 1943 bailout of the VIP party in the C-46 that had put Eric Sevareid, the news correspondent, down by parachute in northern Burma. The two dozen or so passengers that had jumped also included General Stilwell's political advisor, John Service, and two Nationalist Chinese colonels.

He also knew there were competent medical personnel, and he had heard of Lieutenant Diebold, also a parachutist, of the OSS attached to the rescue squadron at Chabua. They had proved their mettle jumping into the crash site with the wing surgeon to treat the injured. He and the wing surgeon, Lieutenant Colonel Flickinger, and his parachuting medical assistants had already saved some airmen, and the myth of the Naga headhunters had turned out to be alarmist rumors.

The Nagas and other tribes coupled with the missionaries and the Kachin Japanese-hating guerrillas (they were aware the OSS' mission also included recruiting them and setting up safe havens) and still the best sources of rescue. So things were getting better. "Blackie's Gang," led by Captain John Porter out of Chabua, with garishly painted aircraft that screamed "RESCUE," kept downed aircrews from melting into the jungle, fearing they were Japanese. They were probably unaware that Blackie and his B-25 had been shot down by a Japanese fighter the previous month. Blackie Porter had helped his copilot out of the escape hatch in the cockpit, taking precious seconds to free a strap on his parachute that had snagged on a projection. The plane had crashed and exploded a few seconds after the copilot cleared the aircraft. He was the only survivor. Their motto, "that others may live," was not a hollow one.

The Hump route would continue to mature, and Aerial Rescue would mature with it. A far-sighted general named Tunner would bring the operation into the era of "big business" and the Air Transport Command, an infant barely two years old, would be the largest airline in the world. Aerial Rescue would be a large part of it. Then Tunner would go on to manage the Berlin airlift, another winning score, this time against the Communists that had reddened nearly all of central and eastern Europe.

In Vietnam, Laos, and Cambodia every pilot, crewman, and wounded warrior rescued by the lumbering HH-3s or HH-53s and the Pave Hawks and Ospreys of the wars of the 1990s and the twenty-first century owe a measure of respect to Blackie's Gang and the brave airmen of the Aerospace Rescue and Recovery squadrons.

But Lanier could think of nothing quite so disquieting as wrestling the door off his stricken plane and stepping out into a howling, freezing wind, not knowing what lay below except long walks—if he survived the jump.

He felt a little better about the aggressive and successful rescue aspect and told his three enlisted crewmen to inspect their parachutes. But no, he didn't like the idea of leaving his airplane. He was a competent and experienced pilot, but any parachute was a potential broken leg, back, or neck.

Finally, the green Aldis lamp from the tower was the signal to crank and go. The ground crewman by the fire extinguisher wound his hand over his head, the signal to crank engine number three, the closest one to the cockpit next to Ramos's seat. Soon all four engines were running smoothly and the ground crewman held up two wooden chocks he'd removed from the front of the landing gear.

They taxied rapidly to the threshold of the runway, running through the before-takeoff checklist while taxiing, saving as much fuel as possible, a practice he wouldn't have done with adequate fuel aboard. Their landing lights stabbed the darkness but didn't get far as the clouds swirled around them on the runway that was already 7,000 feet up. Now military bureaucracy had added hours to 862s takeoff time and given the storm time to stretch its muscles and increase the wind velocity dragging it out of the Bay of Bengal.

They pushed throttles and propeller controls forward, and the aircraft lurched forward, all engines screaming. Ramos calling off the airspeed as it increased and the nose wheel lifted. They were on instruments immediately, and they couldn't dodge the storm cells in the darkness, heading into a witches' brew of violent shrieking weather birthed in the Bay of Bengal and moving northeast until it slammed into a developing frontal system that came out of the Siberian taiga across central Asia. They climbed into the gloomy, low-altitude wind turbulence already buffeting them. It wasn't a good beginning.

In 1994 Admiral Larson's trip had warmed whatever chill there was between the two countries' military, and things were happening rapidly in Vietnam, somewhat slower in Laos, but regularized, and we were preparing for Cambodia, but it appeared there were no alternatives to US military helicopters use there. The live-prisoner scam artists had largely gone back into their dens due to the pressure on them from the Senate Select Committee hearings on them in 1991 and 1992.

Thanks to the Honolulu Police Department's crime scene experts with their enhanced lighting, we now had a manifest as well as the complete serial number of C-87 number 41—223862. The police detectives in the crime scene department raised the name of a crewman on a pair of trousers and another from a receipt. The Missing Aircrew Report (MACR) in our files indicated it was lost on January 31, 1944, with 100 knot winds at altitude on a return flight to Jorhat, in Assam, India, from Kunming, China; there were five crewmen manifested on it, and we had their names. There were two remaining crewmen somewhere on or in the glacier or in the valley it spilled into (or possibly more, if they were not manifested). We would be returning to Tibet.

When I returned to Honolulu, message traffic had been flowing between CILHI and our bosses through CINCPAC and the Joint Staff to State and the American embassy in Beijing. Once AMEMB BEIJING discussed the situation with the authorities, the Chinese leadership embraced the idea of an American and Chinese combined effort to recover the other crewmembers. There were many considerations to work through, however.

The crash was near one of the most sensitive, contentious areas of Tibet to China—Amdo. Nearly four hundred miles of rutted mountain roads east of Lhasa's authority, Amdo is in the high, grassy mountain-bounded plain of the eastern region of Tibet. It is the geographic beginning of the Tibetan Autonomous Region, an area the Chinese link to Tibet's cultural heritage. Tibetans on Sichuan's plain lend a Sino-like veneer to Tibet's volatile east, at least to the Chinese; the Tibetans, of course, resent the Chinese encroaching on what they consider Tibetan territory

Just north was the birthplace of the Fourteenth Dalai Lama, the Khamba's ward during his 1959 horseback flight to India. Somewhat to the south was the border with India and its tenuous "Line of Control" that seems to mark all border disputes in south Asia, including the one China went to war with India over in 1962.

The area was far enough away from Lhasa with an abysmal road connection and of a sufficient distance for the religious bonds of peaceful Buddhism to be strained significantly. Nevertheless, the Potala's bureaucratic structure was quickly overwhelmed with requirements from Beijing—permission for foreigners to visit the region, security measures to be taken, coordination with military officials, then the political and Party apparatus right down to the village government. Even during normal weather patterns, the summer rains and snow melt send landslides down, covering roads and trails, and streams and rivers swell dangerously. The year 1994 experienced a particularly warm, wet summer and fall, and road repair crews came in with exorbitantly high sums to repair them and the bridges and trails leading into the mountains overlooking the crash site.[1]

Authorities in Beijing weighed in and Lhasa established a "leading" group, headed by a senior Tibetan Autonomous Region official, to negotiate a much smaller fee to expeditiously open the road all the way to the staging area. The United States agreed to pay the fees, and work began with a target date in August for the mission. The weather gods intervened once again and more landslides cut the road; the mission was pushed back to September, with September 7 set as the start of the trek. The hike to the crash site was estimated to be three to four days each way, leaving one to two days to conduct the recovery.[2]

Additionally, the detachment of Peoples' Liberation Army soldiers in the area agreed to accompany the team and arrange the logistics, including the transportation—a pack train of horses and mules for carrying the equipment. They would also handle the communications back to the base station and provide our "security."

This wouldn't be a typical USACILHI mission, and my impression was that the Chinese didn't think much time would be required because of the earlier recovery. I had the distinct impression that the Chinese didn't expect us to find much, despite the revelation of the warming and melting glacier. There would be no question that we'd be under complete control of the PLA, with the Chinese and Tibetans who made up the small civilian contingent from the TAR accompanying us. The team would be necessarily small, because operations were still ongoing full bore in Vietnam and Laos.

A recovery in Cambodia was also in the works, and DPMO and State were also cautiously testing the waters in North Korea. Major General Needham had changed command, and I briefed his replacement, Brigadier General Charles Viale, on the operation. General Viale had been briefed completely about our worldwide mission, and as long as our support to the Joint Task Force remained effective, he had no problem with it.

I started prepping my boss, the adjutant general, with updates on the planning, including the Peoples' Liberation Army planning to send a very senior officer along as their military representative and commander of the operation. My bosses and I assumed that would also necessitate my presence. Anything less would result in a serious "loss of face" for the US Army—and, stretching the point a bit, by extension, the US government.

The spring stretched into summer and our recovery operations ticked along steadily in Vietnam and Laos. I picked one of our Special Forces medics, Sergeant First Class Kevin Wright, who had been on a Special Forces A Team during Desert Storm, to accompany us. Also, I picked two infantry sergeants (about 25 percent of our team members were now on-loan infantrymen from the Twenty-Fifth Infantry Division at Schofield Barracks on the north end of Oahu), Staff Sergeants Mark Antal and Mike Bradford.

Anthropologists and archaeologists were committed in Indochina; due to the totally different requirements for this mission, we were going without either.

We hoped to do what the Chinese had done nearly a year earlier—recover the remains on the ground. We carried a few picks and shovels anyway, but nothing for straining and searching the dirt, like buckets or washing screens.

AMEMB Beijing pitched in. In addition to extensive coordination in China and Tibet, they assigned two good US Chinese speakers to the team—political officer Jon Aliosi, a young, fit Foreign Service officer, and the assistant Army attaché, Lieutenant Colonel Greg Man, a Chinese American from Hawaii, also in shape and an excellent linguist.

We departed in early September 1994 with nearly 1,300 pounds of gear, including three aluminum transfer cases to contain remains, climbing gear, an IMARSAT satellite radio that also required a generator to operate it, and a Trimble Trimpack Global Positioning System (GPS) that was anything but trim. We were still in the predigital and preminiaturization days of 1994. We purchased civilian climbing boots, mountain sleeping bags, and one-man tents.

Our tickets routed us through Hong Kong for an overnight stay. The airline told us our gear would be moved to a "sterile" customs area for security and we'd have ample time to clear customs and reboard our flight to Beijing. The American consulate's office in Hong Kong made reservations for the four of us in a moderately priced hotel in Kowloon, and we looked forward to a peaceful night's rest before arriving in Beijing. I was fascinated, as always, by the approach into Kai Tak airport, the original airport that required airliners to practically fly their final approach at near street level. The sergeants were also fascinated. "We could look into the dining room and see that family eating. They didn't even look up when we flew by," Mark Antal said wonderingly.

We hit an immediate snag after landing. Our supplies were palletized and off-loaded in the cargo area, and we assumed we'd follow a forklift with it into a secure area for overnight storage. Instead, a Hong Kong customs official arrived with a clipboard. He scratched his head as we explained the fable the airline had given us in Honolulu. "We do have a secure area for overnight storage, but it's a very small area with lockers. It's not for cargo as large as you've brought. It will be taken to the departure exit tonight and we'll do the customs procedures in the morning."

"Are there guards or security people here after the airport closes?" I asked.

"No, but it will be safe. The airport has controlled entry and exits."

We all looked at the glass doors that had no apparent locks and looked out on a busy sidewalk with pedestrians bustling back and forth. I looked at my guys. All three shook their heads.

"Why don't you head out to the hotel, sir? We'll stay here with this stuff, otherwise we won't know what we've even lost 'til we get to Beijing," Kevin Wright said. The others chorused assent.

"We'll all stay here, guys. I think you're right; this stuff might not be here in the morning."

I continued, "Couple of you go out and see if you can find somewhere we can eat, and we'll rotate out. Meanwhile, I'll call the hotel and get us cancelled, otherwise we'll be out $810 Hong Kong dollars each tonight."

There was a chorus of nonbelief, until I told them the Hong Kong dollar formula: divide it by six.

"But still sir, $130 something dollars is something we'd rather not lose."

"I'll call from that pay phone; I've got a bunch of Hong Kong change in my carry-on bag."

The hotel was sympathetic, but unfortunately the rooms had been reserved by one of the consular officers, and only they could cancel the reservations. By now, it was getting on toward 11 p.m., but I called the consular duty number and was patched through to the duty officer, who offered apologies for the mix-up and agreed to cancel the reservations. She wished us luck and said they'd continue following the message traffic and admonished us to be safe in the Himalayas.

SSG Bradford and Antal could find no restaurants, but all of us had portions of Meals Ready to Eat (MREs) in our palletized gear, so we spent a restful but fitful night, fed and watered by the local water fountain.

We were met next morning by Lieutenant Colonel Man and Jon Aliosi on arrival at Beijing's International Airport, along with some Ministry of Foreign Affairs Chinese representatives, where a customs official notified us our satellite telephone and GPS had been held by "customs control" pending "evaluation." Jon straightened that out immediately with the help of our friendly Chinese contact from the Ministry of Foreign Affairs. Our equipment was placed there for onward movement to Lhasa in a few days, this time firmly secured and guarded.

We went to the embassy and met a few more of the officials and the Deputy Chief of Mission. We were all cordially welcomed again to American Embassy Beijing then taken to our hotel with an offer of a dinner out by Greg Man and his wife, Shirley Kan, also a Chinese American from Hawaii. Shirley was an excellent Chinese linguist with a superb knowledge of Chinese history and politics; she was also an aficionado of the Dalai Lama and closely watched Tibet. She was a great help, and her knowledge of the politico-military situation filled out our readings of it.

The next day was spent going over details, cables, and included a superb tour of the Forbidden City for the sergeants on their first trip to China. The next day we flew on to Chengdu for the evening before departing for Lhasa the following day, with a considerable number of Chinese officials in tow. Unfortunately, the Lhasa airport was below minimums for landing, and we returned to Chengdu. My seatmate, a good English speaker from the Foreign Ministry, mentioned that no flights went into Lhasa at night, and Chinese airline crews didn't overnight there because of the altitude and their fear of the effects of it.

I doubted seriously that instrument approaches were used there, and, as I noted on the earlier trip, it was the longest runway I'd ever seen. Jon and Greg found another hotel for us near the airport, Jon called the consul to tell him what happened, and we were settled in for the night. They would put out the message to Beijing to inform all the agencies that we'd been weather delayed but were OK and would proceed the next day. We would get the same flight in the morning.

The Americans scattered, Greg and Jon disappeared in different directions and our crew decided to wander and see the sights again. I found a good restaurant and read some more of Kenneth Knaus's classic, *Orphans of the Cold War*, about the Tibetan resistance and the CIA's role in it. I assumed that most of the Ministry of State Security had read the translated version. I was eager to get to Lhasa.

The next day we landed in good order, and again a number of the Chinese delegation had altitude headaches and nausea, Diamox continued to keep us Americans in good health with thinned blood as we checked in and dropped our bags at the familiar Lhasa Holiday Inn.

That afternoon we met with Chinese and Sino-Tibetan representatives and a few genuine Tibetans from the Tibetan Autonomous Region offices and laid out plans for the next day, which included meeting the key officials that coordinated everything.

We were introduced to the principal official of the Tibetan Autonomous Region responsible for our mission. To the best of our knowledge, he was a Chinese citizen who had been in Tibet for many decades. He was a lean, courtly man of advanced years who didn't speak any English in our presence. Dressed in an expensive western suit, he exuded diplomatic charm. He would also accompany us on our trip to the staging area, and, after that, the translator explained, he would meet us back in Lhasa after our "safe return." This was Mr. Bai, and everyone deferred to him.

Our good Colonel Neng was also there, and we met our principal interlocutor, Mr. Luo Zi Luo, from the Lhasa Foreign Affairs office, an excellent English speaker. Mr. Luo would accompany us on our journey to the crash site; he his assistant, whose name would be lost in the flurry of introductions and handshakes all around.

As I floundered to pronounce the young man's name, distracted by his modishly long hair and western clothes, he smiled at my tongue twisting and said: "Just call me 'Yeti.' My name is hard to pronounce in English, just as it is in Tibetan or Chinese, so everyone calls me that. I'm kind of the 'fixer' here in Lhasa."

He was a healthy-looking young man in his late twenties or very early thirties with long black hair that touched his shoulders. Perched on his head were a pair of designer sunglasses, and instead of a suit he wore jeans, a Lacoste T-shirt, and a ski jacket. He was a marked contrast to the buttoned-up Foreign Service representatives we were accustomed to. If indeed he was from the Chinese Ministry of Foreign Affairs or the Tibetan Autonomous Region office.

Even Greg Man and Jon Aliosi were slightly open-mouthed to hear him. As we introduced our team, Mark Antal, ever the spark plug of our group, recognized a kindred spirit. He stepped forward in the vertical handshake so popular after Vietnam and gripped him with an engaging grin, "Yeti, I'm Mark."

"Yo, Mark. Welcome to Tibet, man."

Everybody laughed, the ice was broken, and somehow we knew it was going to be a great mission.

CHAPTER 24

Rough Road, Rough Garrison

Legend has always intertwined Tibet's history and destiny, but legend, sometimes, is also intertwined with fact. One of these is that certain monks have the ability to fly short distances. Alexandra David-Neel, a noteworthy French woman explorer, claims to have seen, a flying monk, probably sometime in 1924. David-Neel was an Anglophobe; the British had deported her from Tibet for crossing the border to the Indian frontier. She had to travel halfway around the world to reenter Tibet from China.

The term *Lung-gom* is used to describe nimbleness and extreme conditioning to travel long distances rapidly, and practitioners of this are known as *long-gun pa*.

Ms. David-Neel:

> I met the first lung-gom-pa in the Chang Thang of northern Tibet. Towards the end of the afternoon, Yongden, our servants and I were riding leisurely across a wide tableland, when I noticed, far away in front of us a moving black spot which my field glasses showed to be a man. I felt astonished. Meetings are not frequent in that region, for the last ten days we had not seen a human being. Moreover, men on foot and alone do not, as a rule, wander in these immense solitudes. Who could the strange traveler be?
>
> As I continued to observe him through the glasses, I notice that the man proceeded at an unusual gait and, especially, with an extraordinary swiftness. Though, with the naked eyes, my men could hardly see anything but a black speck moving over the grassy ground, they too were not long in remarking the quickness of his advance. I handed them the glasses and one of them, having observed the traveler for a while muttered, "Lama lung-gom-pa chig da." (It looks like a lama lung-gom-pa.) . . .
>
> The man continued to advance towards us and his curious speed began to be more and more evident. What was to be done if he really was a lama lung-gom-pa? I wanted to observe him at close quarters, I also wished to have a talk with him to put him some questions, to photograph him.

> . . . but the man who had recognized him said, "Your Reverence will not stop the lama, nor speak to him. This would certainly kill him. These lamas, when travelling, must not break their meditation. The god who is in them escapes if they cease to repeat the ngags, and when thus leaving them before the proper time, he shakes them so hard that they die . . ."
>
> By that time he had nearly reached us; I could clearly see his perfectly calm impassive face and wide-open eyes with their gaze fixed on some far-distant object situated high up in space. The man did not run. He seemed to lift himself from the ground, proceeding by leaps. It looked like he had the elasticity of a ball and rebounded each time his feet touched the ground. His steps had the regularity of a pendulum.
>
> He wore the usual monastic robe and toga, both rather ragged. His left hand gripped a fold of his toga and was half hidden under the cloth. The right held a phurba (magic dagger). His right arm moved slightly each step as if leaning on a stick, just as though the phurba, whose pointed extremity was far above the ground, had touched it and was actually a support.
>
> My servants dismounted and bowed their heads to the ground as the lama passed before us, but he went by unaware of our presence. . . .
>
> We followed him for about two miles and then he left the track, climbed a steep slope and disappeared in the mountain range that edged the steppe. Riders couldn't follow that way and our observations came to an end. We could only turn back and continue our journey.[1]

David-Neel was the first western woman to reach Lhasa, disguised as a pilgrim Tibetan mother (with her trusty revolver hidden away) and her guide Yongden posing as her son. After two months in Lhasa, she and her traveling companion/guide, Yongden, made their way safely out of Tibet.[2]

She authored several books. Feted in France after fourteen years away in Asia, she was awarded the Gold Medal of the Geographic Society of France plus was made a Chevalier of the Legion of Honor. Belgium gave her the Silver Medal of their Geographic Society. She spoke fluent Tibetan, verified by several British fluent Tibetan speaking officers.[3]

The hardy woman's own journey came to an end in 1969, at age one hundred.

If you extend your right-hand palm inward facing your eyes and tilt it up 45 degrees, you get a rough orientation of Tibet. The Tibetan Plateau and the Chang Tang region in the north central part of the country, perhaps to your first knuckle joint, generally slope down and toward your wrist, draining the northern mountains into the great rivers of Asia—the Mekong, Salween, Irrawaddy, and others. One of the most notable, the

Yarlung Tsangpo, is a deadly mountain-cutting torrent slashing downward through thousands of feet of high mountain valleys. It becomes the placid Brahmaputra in lower Tibet and Assam, just above sea level. These major rivers of Asia trickle out of the Tibetan Plateau until the land tilts sharply southeastward, then turn into raging torrents when monsoons and winter thaws carried their waters down into the flatlands of India and the rest of South Asia.

While the vicious Tsang Po in Tibet became the tranquil Brahmaputra in India, the Mekong was largely peaceful, though dangerous in the flooding monsoons—a meandering alluvial and silt depositor in Cambodia, feeding the great Ton Le Sap Lake in that much-tortured land. It divides Laos from Thailand above the Bolovens Plateau before wandering through Vietnam's delta—named for the river that spills into the South China Sea.

Nearly half the world's population depends on these Tibet-birthed rivers: the Indus, Ganges, Brahmaputra, Irrawaddy, Salween, Mekong Rivers, as they make their way across Asia before spilling into the Indian Ocean or the South China Sea. The rivers were major navigation checkpoints when the crews could see them. The mountains lining or framing them were the major distinguishing features viewed from cockpits. Dangerous and unpredictable weather lay between the scorching hot or monsoon-flooded sea-level river valleys and the triple canopied rain forests of Burma and the Outer Himalayas. The weather systems produce thunderstorms reaching nearly six miles in altitude.

"You couldn't fly over, under, or around the bastards, and the worst thing you could do was to fly into one. It would spit you out the other side with wings so twisted the props threatened to beat on the cockpit windshields. The best thing to do was to make a 180-degree turn and wait for another day. Of course you couldn't do that, either."[4]

Lhasa is on an arid plain in the central southern portion laid out along the Tsangpo/Brahmaputra River. The area along your ring finger circling around toward the base of your thumb consists of mountain chains stretching both southerly and east and west. Access—or egress—is controlled by mountain passes that were guarded and policed by Tibetan authorities for centuries, blocked by impassable snows in winter.

To the south, Nepal, Sikkim, and Bhutan were small kingdoms that traded sporadically with Tibet; large caravans coming up from the plains of northeast India, following the Brahmaputra in the contemporary Indian state of Assam also traded along the way. This was where the greatest number of World War II Hump bases were located for their proximity to Burma and China: including Jorhat.

Caravans were controlled and taxed by the Tibetans at the passes, and their comings and goings were strictly regulated. From the northwest, similar caravans came out of what is now Xinjiang, the largely Moslem state of modern northwest China, and farther north and east along the famous Silk Road. Other passes controlled the approaches from Russia through the lesser mountain chains that surround the modern central Asian mountain ranges, the Pamirs and the Tien Shan.

India was also isolated from Tibet by passes in the Patkai ranges and the Karakoram, Ladakh, and the Pir Pajnahl, the latter overlooking Kashmir. From Jammu to Kashmir melding into the northeast border with Burma the Hindu Kush nudged the Paktai's to form a lesser obstacle; it was a control point for passage and inspection at least.

Other mountainous defiles to the southwest, south, and southeast permitted traders and caravans passage through carefully monitored choke points. Only the high arid plain to the east afforded easy access. Butting against Tibet lies Sichuan, and all of China. There were a few passes, but they were mostly ineffective. There is a common grassland plateau of some hundred miles common to Amdo Province in Tibet and Sichuan. And China was the one that Tibet loathed and feared—for very good reasons.

Fighting started in this high arid mountain-ringed plain. The Khamba tribesman and the even more fearsome Goloks were also peaceful Buddhists with a tendency toward banditry when the opportunity presented itself—the Buddhist tenets of nonviolence temporarily shelved for economic opportunity and distance from the Potala. As a matter of fact, in the wild eastern regions of Tibet, many days' walk or ride from the holy city of Lhasa, the peaceful Buddhist strain of nonviolence was relaxed considerably.

The caravans carrying luxury goods to or from the fabled Silk Road were just too lucrative to resist for some of the inhabitants. Amdo and its resident Khambas and Goloks were naturals for resistance to the Chinese. They were historically horse cavalry anyway, sharpening their heritage from the Mongols who swept Asia and central Europe like a burnished, fourteen-hands-high mounted scythe in the thirteenth century.

The high, open plateaus dotted by towering snow-capped mountains of this easternmost part of Tibet was a natural place for conventional and guerrilla warfare—and brigandage. Its relatively flat terrain, backlighted by the forbidding Himalayas, permitted sightings of long armored and mechanized columns wending their way to destroy some monastery or village in the Chinese assault of 1950–51.

The forested mountains surrounding it stripped off the wheeled and tracked vehicles of their pursuers as the guerrillas fled up its steep mountain trails on horseback. The crevices of canyons provided plenty of concealment for a handful of mounted warriors, swooping down on pursuers laboring up on foot. They galloped into Chinese formations, chopped and shot their way out, taking weapons and other booty, but no prisoners. But by the winter of 1951, the PLA had largely overrun the eastern approaches and were firmly ensconced, but still wary of the Khambas and Goloks.

Decades earlier, China had insinuated itself into Lhasa with the presence of an *Amban*, a self-invited consul and staff who presumed reasons for office in Lhasa. Although this was a relatively minor irritant, for the gentle Tibetans it sufficed to keep the low flame of xenophobia burning.

Ambans had considerably more authority in China under the original Ch'ing emperors in the seventeenth century. They were reinforced with mounted troops, sometimes as many as a thousand, to protect the Amban personally and provide protection for his retinue. They were also reminders of China's military prowess and seemingly eternal presence, but as the twentieth century approached, everything changed in China.

In 1911, the last vestiges of empire and imperial rule vanished with the death of the dowager empress and the ascendancy of Japanese militarism. The Tibetans reluctantly tolerated this existence because the Chinese were the antithesis of the placid Buddhists—the Chinese were mercantile agnostics (if you discounted Confucius and Confucian ideals, something the Buddhists viewed as purely secular). The Tibetans viewed Buddhism and the Dalai Lama incarnate as the reason for existence—especially in this only temporary phase of eternal life.

Younghusband's 1903–4 mission, ostensibly a diplomatic trade mission, quickly edged toward a protectorate of India, a thinly disguised show of force to show the Russians that Britain wouldn't tolerate the colossus meddling with their greatest colonial holding. After all, Great Britain could control the military requirements from India, unlike their struggles in North America two centuries before that had ejected them from empire there. This would be the closest serious confrontation between Great Britain and Russia.

Tibetans adapted to political accommodation much like the Thais did over the centuries. When invaded and subjugated, they merely absorbed the conquerors and maintained their culture and traditions; the political rules of governance placed on them were viewed as temporary—smilingly accepted, politely ignored.

By 1644, the Manchus from the northern rim lands of China, instituted the Ch'ing dynasty. This was somewhat of a more benign Mongol rule that had already touched Tibet during the thirteenth and fourteenth centuries. The Manchus let the established Ambans build up their own forces to assure their safety and let the peaceful Tibetans get a view of armed governance.

The monasteries, government in Lhasa, and ordinary Tibetans politely took guidance and accepted the Mongol, Manchu, and Amban presence; they, in turn all let the Tibetans practice their Buddhist beliefs, took their taxes, and occasionally sent envoys or columns over the arid plains to the Potala for some reason or other. As the Qing dynasty slipped away through the Opium Wars, the various internal struggles, and emerging nationalism at the turn of the twentieth century, Tibet gradually receded into the mountainous shadows of quiet anonymity once more.

Throughout this period, Russia and Britain were engaged in the "Great Game," a struggle for influence and control in central Asia. Russia pushed south of its borders, seeking access to warm-water seaports and a buffer zone between Russia proper and the advancing British. The British pushed northward from India, trying to expand their empire and protect the Raj, the "Crown Jewel of the British Empire," from the expansionist Russians. Tibet was an important board piece in this game.

Qing Chinese power waned throughout the eighteenth century, as evidenced by its defeat in the Opium Wars with Britain (1839–42 and 1856–60), as well as the Taiping Rebellion (1850–64) and the Boxer Rebellion (1899–1901). The actual relationship between China and Tibet had been unclear since the early days of the Qing dynasty, and China's revolution pursued by the Kuomintang made the status of Tibet even more uncertain. The status may have been murky, but it was no secret that Chiang considered Tibet part of China.

The ambiguity of control over Tibet led to problems. In 1893, the British in India concluded a trade and border treaty with Beijing concerning the boundary between Sikkim and Tibet. However, the Tibetans flatly rejected the treaty terms.

The British invaded Tibet in 1903 with 10,000 men and took Lhasa the following year. To seal it politically they concluded another treaty with the Tibetans, as well as Chinese, Nepalese, and Bhutanese representatives, which gave the British themselves some control over Tibet's affairs and established a stronger "thin red line" of political and military security layered over the northern and eastern borders of their Crown Jewel, India.

The Thirteenth Dalai Lama, Thubten Gyatso, fled the country in 1904 at the urging of his Russian disciple, Agvan Dorzhiev. He went first to Mongolia, then made his way to then Peiping. The Chinese declared that the Dalai Lama had been deposed as soon as he left Tibet and claimed full sovereignty over not only Tibet but also Nepal and Bhutan, just as they lay claim to the South China Sea as a virtual mare nostrum in the twenty-first century.

The Dalai Lama went to Peiping to discuss the situation with Emperor Guangxu, but he flatly refused to kowtow to the emperor; despite this snub, he remained in the Chinese capital from 1906 to 1908.

He returned to Lhasa, disappointed by Chinese policies toward Tibet. China responded by sending a force of 6,000 troops into Tibet, and the Dalai Lama fled to Darjeeling, India, later that same year, eerily presaging the Fourteenth Dalai Lama's flight to Dharamsala, a half century later.

The Nationalist Chinese Revolution swept away the Qing dynasty (Ching in English transliteration; in Chinese it means "Pure") in 1911, and the Tibetans promptly expelled all Chinese troops from Lhasa. The Dalai Lama returned home to Tibet in 1912.

Tibet eased into quiet, self-proclaimed independence. China's new revolutionary government issued a formal apology to the Dalai Lama for the Qing dynasty's insults and offered to reinstate him. Thubten Gyatso refused, stating that he had no interest in the Chinese offer. He then issued a proclamation that was distributed across Tibet, rejecting Chinese control and stating that "we are a small, religious, and independent nation."

The Dalai Lama took control of Tibet's internal and external governance in 1913, negotiating directly with foreign powers and reforming Tibet's judicial, penal, and educational systems.

The British realized the importance of marking out the boundary lines between India and its northern neighbors. The Simla Convention granted China secular control over "Inner Tibet," (also known as Qinghai Province) while recognizing the autonomy of "Outer Tibet" under the Dalai Lama's rule. Both China and Britain promised to "respect the territorial integrity of [Tibet] and abstain from interference in the administration of Outer Tibet."

China walked out of the conference without signing the treaty after Britain laid claim to the Tawang area of southern Tibet, which is now part of the Indian state of Arunachal Pradesh. Tibet and Britain both signed the treaty. As a result, China has never agreed to India's rights in northern Arunachal Pradesh (Tawang), and the two nations went to war over the area in 1962 but with no resolution on the casus belli. The general consensus was the Chinese handily defeated the Indians in the high-altitude war.

I found out more on a train from Calcutta to Siliguri in 1969. The second-class car was nearly deserted, so the warrant officer of the Frontier Rifles and I sat across from each other, talked, and I drank my Tiger beer; the talk was of Vietnam, initially. After a few beers, it veered into the Sino-Indian high-altitude war of 1962, one that handed China a significant victory over India over a disputed boundary. The boundary dispute still has not been resolved, but one thing was clear to him and the entire Indian Army—they needed training, experience, and arms. He had been captured in the initial fighting, then released. Then wounded and captured again. It was a humiliating experience, he said.

The British had left so hurriedly and in such confusion and violence between Hindu and Moslem contingents that the new Indian Army had never really gotten any traction, nor had the Pakistani Army apparently. This resulted in the Indians beating them badly in the early 1970s and East Pakistan became Bangladesh.

China also claimed sovereignty over all of Tibet, while the Tibetan government-in-exile pointed to the Chinese failure to sign the Simla Convention as proof that both Inner and Outer Tibet legally remain under the Dalai Lama's jurisdiction. The Chinese didn't think so.

We had a final breakfast meeting with a half dozen representatives who were already there in Yigon when we arrived. It was clear that they would be the controlling element from Beijing in our village rear base, and the talk turned to the recovery at the crash site.

"So Colonel Jordan, you will remain with us in the village while your team completes their task?"

I wasn't sure if that was a question or statement.

"No, I'll be accompanying our soldiers and Mr. Aliosi and Colonel Man."

This comment troubled our Chinese breakfast mates, all dressed in casual travel clothes. There was a burst of Chinese back and forth and I noticed that Greg Man and Jon Aliosi were still holding slices of melon in their chopsticks, poised halfway to their mouths.

I realized then that this batch was unaware that Jon and Greg were pretty fair Chinese linguists.

Jon gracefully interceded and spoke to their apparent leader: "Colonel Jordan will lead the American delegation and Colonel Neng will provide his soldiers for assistance and protection of the entire party. Colonel Neng will be in command of the operation and Colonel Jordan and his 'experts' will direct the removal of the crew's remains."

"That has been the plan all along," Jon concluded.

It was a polite, unambiguous response.

"But which of our American guests will remain with us in the village?"

Now the CILHI sergeants all took notice and watched the exchange.

I spoke up. "No one from our party; was there a requirement to leave an American?" I looked at Jon and Greg for an answer, and Greg gave me a "let's talk about this privately" look.

The question was left unsettled, except in our minds. When we broke up and all agreed to meet in the courtyard of our hotel, we four surrounded both of our buddies from the embassy.

"What was that all about?" I asked Jon and Greg.

"The 2 percent who didn't get the word," Greg scoffed.

Jon amplified, "They want to keep you back with them in the village; they'll cite everything from worries about your safety to huge decisions they'll have to make in concert with the Americans, but, Greg's probably right when he says they didn't get the word."

"They don't have to worry about my safety or any of our team. We routinely handle tougher recoveries in far more remote places than this."

This was a bit of hyperbole and puffery on my part. True, mountains are mountains, whether in Laos, Papua New Guinea, or Tibet. But this hike and climb would be higher and actually farther than any in recent memory; we were about as remote as we were anywhere we'd ever been, including Siberia, the Amazon, and far up North Korea, but still . . .

Greg spoke up again, "these guys are from Jon's bailiwick in Foreign Affairs; my only counterparts here from the Defense Ministry would be the colonel and his men. They know the story and will make sure the operation goes like it was planned and briefed to our ambassador and their Vice Foreign Minister."

Greg continued, "I know he has a captain with him that must be a company commander, a political guy, or possibly a doctor and a squad or so of infantrymen with a platoon commander and a few NCOs.

"I don't recognize anybody that might be a Ministry of Defense decision maker or policy guy out of uniform."

"But these guys are probably from a division within MFA that tagged along late and aren't read completely in. They realize that a lot more could go wrong on this operation that could go right," Greg continued.

"They'll get tarred with the old success or failure brush and having an

American in their midst and control gives them and their bosses a little more clout."

"And good old American scapegoats," I added.

They both nodded, but Jon added, "We haven't heard the last of this. They're MFA guys—foreign affairs—and you're a foreigner.

"They'll be on the horn to their bosses for more guidance. Chances are this is their first time in Tibet and they're just like we are. Flying blind."

"Strangers in a strange land, even if it is China," Greg Man added.

"Ah, Robert Heinlein," Wright murmured with a grin.

Greg nodded. "Heinlein knew the drill."

Antal and Bradford nodded, and Antal added, "There it is."

I heard this phrase often in Vietnam whenever the inevitable was mentioned.

The second morning we split up into our transportation contingents for the two-day ride into northeast Tibet. We would spend the first night at a military encampment, about halfway there. The town surrounding it was call Lin Zhi and we didn't know yet that ten hours of bouncing later we'd all be ready to roll into it. Kevin Wright chose to ride with the medics and the suspected doctor or physician's assistant in their boxy vehicle. Mike Bradford and Mark Antal rode with some of the soldiers in an enclosed three-quarter-ton-appearing truck.

Greg Man yelled and gave us a confirming salute before stepping into the cab of a sturdy green four-wheel drive vehicle with some green-uniformed PLA soldiers. Colonel Neng and his command unit departed unseen, and Mr. Luo Zi Luo, a definitely friendly face, probably a Chinese-Tibetan, and Yeti came by to chat briefly and told us Lin Zhi was also the headquarters of the PLA for that region.

It was from there the original Chinese mission to the crash site was launched, and also the garrison for Colonel Neng's unit, he related. Then they too disappeared in the chaos of departing vehicles, getting their names ticked off on a clipboard held by a PLA sergeant and his assistant.

I estimated from the map that we were about 200 miles from Lin Zhi, and beyond that, perhaps 150 miles or so from the valley and village we'd use as a base, Yigon. It was nestled in the shadows of some formidable mountains and appeared to be the largest village in a cluster of them one to three or four miles apart. It looked like it was on a tributary of the Tsang Po that drained south to form higher mountains, cut by the Tsang Po

Gorge. It was a two-day trip over the rough track we were going to travel.

We would all meet at the garrison in the evening. Now we waited for Mr. Bai, the distinguished and well-dressed head of everything in Tibet. We would be riding with him and his driver, Jigme, obviously Tibetan.

Mr. Bai arrived in a late model sedan of indeterminate make but with a semblance of a luxury car. Like most official cars in China, it was black. After shaking hands all around, I had a chance to inspect Jigme a little closer. He was squat and powerful, maybe five ten with wide shoulders and big hands and a round face capping a large head. In contrast to the immaculately turned-out Mr. Bai, Jigme had on western trousers and a shirt and light windbreaker. He also wore a turned-up fedora. He immediately fired up a Chinese cigarette and stood grinning in the wind while Mr. Bai and Jon chatted in Chinese.

Soon Mr. Bai motioned to the vehicle. Jon suggested I ride in back with Mr. Bai and he could translate from the front seat. I told him I would be better off in the front, and just leaning over the back to talk to Mr. Bai. Jon shrugged off this obvious breach of protocol, and soon we were bouncing through Lhasa as dawn approached, the sun a huge orb on the horizon. The road had patches of pavement as it straightened out of town. Far ahead of us in the windless dawn we could see the faint dust of the rest of the staggered caravan traveling ahead of us.

Mr. Bai gave us a running monologue in Chinese as we wended our way out of Lhasa. He had come here in the winter of 1951 as a PLA soldier during the "liberation" of Tibet, he said. He was a strong young man, hardened by the long effort of wresting the misguided Nationalists from the evils of "incorrect thought," as John translated it. He explained that was the polite translation of teaching Chiang Kai-shek the error of his ways.

The march west out of Sichuan had been difficult that winter; he had been separated from his unit and had to lead his starving horse through a pass in a furious snowstorm. I asked if he'd recently participated in the "liberation' of Korea," but that question slid off him without comment after Jon's translation, and he continued.

He feared for the safety of both his mount and himself, and as the horse sank dying into the belly deep snow, a monk appeared out of the storm and guided him to the safety of a cave. He had lost his horse, but this kind monk had saved Bai. Now safely out of the weather and the piercing wind, the monk built a fire and gave Bai some *tsampa*, the barley staple of Tibet, and some hot tea. The kind monk thanked Bai and the PLA for providing for his safety and straightening the "misguided" authorities in Lhasa. Jon relayed all this in a straightforward manner and I took it in the same vein.

I asked what rank Bai had been when this miracle occurred, and he replied, "Colonel. Same rank as I am now," Jon translated.

Jon and I both blinked at this, and a few seconds later Jigme hit a manhole-sized pit at sixty miles an hour that pitched all of us into the ceiling. Jigme chortled delightfully and crashed back down, his porkpie hat pushed down over his eyebrows.

Jon and Bai had obviously seen it coming and braced. But I had been pulling my notebook from my pack and was totally unprepared; I bounced off the steel ceiling with a crunch and stars flew around in my vision. I growled a blue-stream curse and yelled that we needed to slow down and drive safely. Jon said something sharply to Bai, and Bai, somewhat embarrassed, relayed that to Jigme resentfully.

He was almost like a reluctant parent admonishing a child half-heartedly. I had asked Jon a couple of times before what the secret was to getting Jigme to slow down, and Jon had turned up the pressure politely with Bai every time we bottomed out. Bai was almost deferential to Jigme, and something else puzzled me.

The small picture of the Dalai Lama dangling from his mirror.

When Bai had dozed off coming out of Lhasa, I had cocked my head at it questioningly, and Jon had shrugged his shoulders and palmed up his hands. Something wasn't readily apparent in all this. But I didn't want to get smacked into the ceiling again. Keeping my butt on the seat wasn't in the mystical powers of his jiggling portrait.

Jigme sped on after Jon and I fell silent and Bai continued his lolling doze peacefully. He really did look like a parchment-skinned young athlete who only aged in the face.

Now both Jigme and I had clashed and I had lost face. Jigme fumed sullenly for a few minutes; the steering wheel looked like a black washer in his huge hands. Soon he was back to sixty miles an hour again, slamming on the brakes and pitching us forward as he approached potholes. Bai, our colonel-diplomat, seemed to be in deep sleep, his body rocking forward like a boneless rubber mannequin each time Jigme performed his pothole avoidance drill.

After a couple of hours the road leveled out on a broad plateau, and soon we saw vehicles pulled off either side of the road. Black tents were scattered about and horsemen tended sheep in a lovely pastoral setting, framed by snow-covered mountains to the north and south. Jigme said something to Bai, and the elderly gentleman shook himself awake and announced to Jon it was time for a comfort stop. We all agreed it was a good idea.

We stretched for a moment while Jigme lighted up; he called to a passing horseman in Tibetan. Jigme and the horseman spoke some Tibetan, then the horseman and Bai exchanged some Tibetan and Bai switched to Chinese with Jon.

"Bai asked if you'd like to meet a Tibetan family and look in their tent."

"Sure," I replied, nodding graciously to Jigme. Maybe he wasn't such a bad egg after all.

"He said to stay directly in front of the tent while you approach it."

"Why?"

Another shrug from Jon, then he and Bai started walking up the road to see who had also stopped. The tent was about a football field away, and I started walking dutifully toward the front. A couple of horses were picketed in back, and the front of the tent was folded back in the pleasant warmth of noon.

About twenty yards in front of the tent I noticed a pile of hides and some other things that should have alerted me, but I was drowsy from the ride and the pleasant warmth of midday. I turned back to Jigme, who was watching me intently. He motioned me forward with both hands, smiling.

I turned around, took a step, and the hides exploded with a high-pitched howl. A two-hundred-pound Tibetan mastiff launched and was jerked up with what appeared to be a logging chain around his neck. I stood transfixed for a moment, almost nose to nose with the animal, now straining forward, large feet pawing the air.

A woman appeared in the doorway a second later and snarled at the dog. He *wuffed* resentfully, dropped down to the hides and resumed his nap. She mapped a wide path around it with her hand to get to her door. I followed her instructions carefully. Very carefully.

Inside was spacious and swept clean, with several carpets on the ground. Two small children watched me wide-eyed with hands stuck in their mouths; I gave a slight head bow to the woman and a steepled Thai *wai* with my hands below my chin. She motioned me to a seat on the carpet. A picture of a monk that looked like it might have dated from the 1930s and a colored photograph of the Dalai Lama were resting in gilt frames on a chest. She poured us both bowls of butter tea and talked, cheerfully animated. She spoke purely in Tibetan and I nodded understanding appreciation at what I hoped were the appropriate pauses.

I saw Bai and Jon through the opened doorway returning and I took my leave, digging through my pockets until I found some American change. I found the shiniest two quarters I had and nodded toward the two children and gave them to the woman. She looked at them and dropped them into the front of her *chuba*, the apron-like garment Tibetans wore over a skirt. They probably would be turned into earrings, I thought.

I circled well around the dog, who followed me with his eyes, and I mentioned to Jon what had happened.

"Looks like you and Jigme are evened out in the face events of the day," he grinned.

"I suppose."

We continued to motor over the plateau, and the road eased down to a lower altitude and a single rutted lane. We began to bump through areas of hardwood.

Poverty was evident in the small built-up areas we passed through. There might be a dozen dwellings and a couple of stores or stall-type restaurants that all passed as a hamlet or small village. Frequently we saw pool tables outside on wooden sidewalks, and apparent unemployed young Chinese or Tibetan, or Chinese-Tibetan, men playing and drinking. They became more frequent as the pasture and grazing land on the distant horizon vanished.

Soon the scenery became lush and green, the mountains pressing down on the narrow road. Once Jigme had to drive carefully around a pool table in the middle of the largely unused road through the hamlet. One player crowded the table to let him scrape by. If anyone was toiling here, they were unseen by us, working herds from horseback on the northern rolling plateau.

By midafternoon we were on a narrow dirt track crawling around lush, jungled mountains. Streams that looked intermittent during drier parts of the year were swollen torrents, and the bridges, many of them ramshackle wooden affairs, were definitely rickety. I supposed we weren't too far from the "line of control" that marked one of the troubled borders with India in this region.

I mentioned to Jon that I had traveled into Assam on an interesting train ride back in the late 1960s and met an Indian Army warrant officer who had fought the Chinese in the border war of 1962. I gathered from his remarks that the Indians had taken a shellacking, and they vowed it would never happen again; he said he'd been captured twice by the Chinese, and it was humiliating.

Jon and I talked about Vietnam and US efforts to squeeze the Vietnamese into compliance for citizenship in the world, at least on US terms, while Bai continued to doze. We were of a like mind that they could be useful friends in both southeast and northeast Asia as they struggled for acceptance and normalized relations that were just now becoming a reality. And the Vietnamese and the Chinese were at odds with each other, despite the veneer of friendship and communist amity.

The Indian's and Pakistani's veneer was now thinned to the point of nonexistence, and I related my hitchhiking experiences traveling in India, Nepal, and Pakistan and then into Afghanistan and Iran. I omitted the bad times in Iraq and Syria before I squirted into safety in Turkey. India made good on that vow of a better military in 1973, bloodying Pakistan's nose and turning East Pakistan into Bangladesh, further roiling geopolitics south of Tibet. Bai was lolling in sleep and Jon and I leaned in to talk quietly.

Jon related that this part of the road passes close to the Indian border, and the PLA keeps a wary eye on it, also one of the sensitive places when foreign travelers—like us—were transiting it. Bomi County and the area to the north into the Cham Do region were also looked on as potential trouble spots with knots of Khambas and Goloks throughout the region. Some PLA units, maybe even Colonel Neng's, might have tangled with them in the past. We were going to be in—as the intelligence reports sometime said—restive portions of the country.

We had forded a couple of streams after Bai had shouted out the window at pilgrims and travelers to wait until we were across in case we needed some muscle to get us fished out and pushed over. By twilight, we had made a couple of perilous passages around rockslides, and Jon and I had both pitched big rocks down into the gorge to smooth out the passage for Jigme, who was starting to nod.

The countryside had become considerably more lush and wooded when we rolled into Lin Zhi's muddy cantonment after twilight. Jon went off to find Greg Man and the rest of the Beijing and Lhasa contingent and I linked up with two of my three sergeants. Antal and Bradford had spent the entire day with non-English speakers they said, but they got along fine.

"We're all infantrymen, Sir . . . we speak the universal infantry language."

"Yeah, and move about two and a half miles an hour as I recall."

"Right, Sir. But steady." I laughed and agreed.

You had to love soldiers, especially infantrymen. They'd walk, work, or fight all day or night on steel canteen cups of bad coffee and a smoke, although now most seemed to take their nicotine in smokeless tobacco since modernization had forced heavier loads on their backs and higher mountains to their front.

"And I love the motto of the infantry—*do something, even if it's wrong,*" I continued.

"There it is," Bradford said, grinning.

"Cavalry got a motto, Colonel?" Antal asked.

"Plan carefully, execute violently, but when in doubt, err on the side of violence."

Greg Man chuckled, and quickly added, "if it flies, it dies"—the motto of his Air Defense branch.

Sergeant Wright had gone off with Yeti and the doctor to look at the dispensary. They reappeared in the gloom and we all decided to look for some food. Yeti pointed us to the "Soldier's Cafe" within the compound.

"Cold beer and good food," he said, and sauntered off into the darkness.

"Our rooms are right next door," Wright said. They dumped our packs in there. Haven't seen their guys from the embassy."

"They're probably working to get me off the mission," I guessed.

"How are the rooms?" Antal asked.

"No lights that I could find. Wooden bunks with some mattresses on them."

"Yeti told them to throw some blankets in there, but it's completely dark, so dig your maglights out."

We were all carrying maglites, small flashlights, in our pockets—standard operating procedure for us. We'd all experienced trips and falls in the darkness of Lao, Cambodian, and Vietnamese recovery operations.

Two weathered, middle-age Tibetan ladies seated us at a large round table with a battery-powered lamp on it and brought out bowls, chopsticks, rice, and some pork, plus large bottles of warm Chinese beer.

"*Gam bei*, Comrades" Mark Antal toasted.

"Ah, it doesn't get any better than this," Mike Bradford retorted, sipping on his Coca-Cola rip-off.

"Anyway, nobody's shooting at us," I said.

"Well, we might all be shooting at some furry four-legged guests tonight, judging by our quarters," Wright said, digging in with his chopsticks.

"Ah, Jesus. I thought we'd left them all in Laos," Bradford groaned.

"Those are the smaller southeast Asia cousins," Antal joked.

Antal was notorious for his hatred of rats but utter disregard for the most poisonous snakes in the world. Wright suggested we wash out our bowls with hot tea before eating, and that seemed like a good idea.

That night I read by maglite, and just before I dropped off I thought I heard an unmistakable squeal and Sergeant First Class Kevin Wright's heavy boot thrown against the wall. Before dawn, and after a fitful night, I creeped around the sleeping quadrangle until I found the latrine and showers, with bracing cold water, just a little rusty initially.

I walked back to our quarters with the dawn breaking when I saw our car parked, and Jigme stretched out in the front seat, asleep with his pork-pie hat down over his face. He used a tattered red gym bag for an awkward pillow, and his head was partially out the window of the driver's side.

I put my face just above the hat, which reeked of rice wine *mao tai*, and gave a guttural ROWF! ROWF! There was a flurry of arms, legs, and hat and he twisted around and looked up at me. I shot him with my finger, murmured "bow wow," put the toothbrush back in my mouth, and walked off chuckling.

We rolled along a scenic, swollen river into our jumping-off place for the mission in midafternoon. The area was a cluster of neat little hamlets, rice drying on sheets on hardstand or concrete pads. We passed small clusters of houses all the way up the river, and women were working on rice and throwing wheat kernels into the air.

On the trip we had run over large white squares of canvas with rice on them, part of the stripping and pulverizing process, we all guessed. We never got a clear explanation, even though I had seen this plenty of times in other countries in Asia.

Jon asked Bai, who asked Jigme, now recovered from what must have been a monumental hangover, about the thrown rice. They talked animatedly for a moment, with Jigme taking both hands off the wheel mimicking the throwing motion with his hands. When Bai replied to Jon the answer was, "that's just the way they do it here." Those words would be another mantra for the rest of our time in Tibet and China.

We rolled up the river, Jigme now doing a stately twenty miles an hour, and passed through the gates of Yigon, and it was evident a reception ceremony awaited us. The head of the village, or township in Bomi County, as the Chinese strangely called it, was in suit coat and tie.

Sherap Chopel, the one who'd discovered the crash site, was with him, dressed in his best but still wearing the great felt cowboy hat we'd seen in the videotape the Chinese furnished of their recovery. Schoolgirls dressed in traditional costume were in front of a crowd of half the population of Yigon. There was a banner in Chinese with the flags of the Peoples' Republic of China and the USA on it.

The Ministry of Foreign Affairs delegation, six or seven, now more comfortable in sports shirts and slacks, were also standing behind the mayor, grinning broadly, with three or four "suits" with their ever-ready briefcases, standing on each end of the crowd. They were not grinning. They had arrived two days prior to ensure that everything was in order for the operation.

Mr. Bai, bathed in applause and a spray of flowers handed to him by a schoolgirl, held up his arms like Rocky and bowed to the crowd. Jigme strutted behind him, obviously in the slipstream of his boss, but enjoying it. Jigme had explained the "canine awakening" with a pantomime that Mr. Bai had obviously enjoyed before we departed dismal Lin Zhi that morning; both of them laughed until tears came. Tibetans are great storytellers as well as skilled tricksters, and they love describing something funny, even when they're the butt of the story.

We were ushered onto a platform with a microphone in front of it. The mayor introduced us to great applause. More Chinese and Tibetan speakers followed, but it was impossible to follow the English translation with the noisy milling of the Chinese from Beijing and Chinese and Tibetans from Lhasa.

Everything blurred into a cacophony, punctuated by microphone squeals that had hands over ears. We Americans stood in a knot, grinning with an occasional wave at a child or respectful nod to a bearded ancient in the crowd. A few Khambas stood in the crowd, keeping a wary watch on things. Our suits with the briefcases followed them with their eyes.

Occasionally, the speaker motioned expansively to our group, so I gathered by the applause that our mission was being explained. We all bobbed our heads in positive response and smiled again at the speakers and crowd. Perhaps they were describing something out of the CILHI mission statement: Search, Recover, Identify.

I don't believe their fraternal siblings, Vietnam or Laos, their friends, were mentioned. Cambodia, a former *good* friend, was apparently sticking its toes in the turbulent waters of democracy. They were not mentioned either.

We were quartered in the village school on cots, each of us allocated a small room. That night about 8 p.m. I heard a soft knock on my classroom cum sleeping quarter's wooden door and someone calling my name.

I slipped on my trousers and called come in, but they knocked again. I opened the door and recognized one of the Beijing English-speaking Foreign Affairs office diplomats. He was older and distinguished; I thought he'd been at the first Lhasa visit, at the PLA unilateral turnover of the remains in December 1993, but he said he'd only read accounts of it.

I invited him in but he nervously shook his head, so I stepped down and out of the door so we'd be level. In the light of my battery lantern I could see two of his younger colleagues and further into the shadows one of the larger Ministry of the Interior types, still hanging on to his briefcase; he was without a tie, but still had his suit jacket still on. I guessed they took their charges' safety very seriously.

"Colonel Jordan, we just heard you are going on the expedition tomorrow; this is not true, is it?"

Not again. I was taken aback but thought a moment before replying as quietly as I could, "why, yes; of course I'm going. That's been the plan all along and our Department of State notified your government months ago."

"We did not know this. My department has sent my colleagues and me out to be with you so you're in contact with the embassy and your government at all times."

"Mr., uh . . ."

"Just call me Hong, please. I'm the director of . . ."

I couldn't follow the rest of what he directed, but I repeated my assertion that I was sent to Tibet to lead the American representatives of CILHI the way we did it in other parts of the world. This time I specifically mentioned Vietnam, Laos, and even Cambodia. I emphasized Cambodia.

"Well, I'm sorry we didn't know this."

"I'm sorry, too, but my orders specify me to lead my men."

They shuffled off in the darkness.

"What else did he say to you?"

"That was pretty much it. When I mentioned that high representatives of our government were also going—that'd be you and Greg Man—he started to waiver, and then when I told him that'd I'd lose extreme face with my unit and bosses, he joined his colleagues and they drifted off."

Jon marked the place in the book he was reading by lamplight and thought a moment more, before replying.

"That was a good move. Losing extreme face; I'll remember that one when things get sticky diplomatically." He thought for another moment. "This is most likely just a replay of their other approach in Lhasa. They could have been genuinely concerned for your safety, of course, and probably are." "Their boss in the MFA could have scared them with stories of what would happen to them if there was a serious accident or death in the mountains, even. And he probably did." Especially if something happened to you; after all they're the designated hitters from their directorate, so they'll suffer for anything bad that happens; their bosses will get the credit for all the good that goes on, because after all he, she, or they had the wisdom to send them here.

Or they could have been the ones sent to "friendly" up to you as we work our way back to a more amenable situation because of our past history since the troubles of Tiananmen. They'll get over it."

"They'll get over that about like we got over Pearl Harbor."

He went on, "but I wouldn't worry about it. I'd be very surprised if they didn't know you were going to the crash site."

"They're secretive externally but gossip and try to get positioned better on the board internally, and if they had you here under the protection of their directorate or division or wherever they're from, they gain tremendous 'face.'"

"OK, if you don't think it's some big deal, I'll find Wright before it gets too late just to bring him and my other two guys up to speed."

Jon grinned, "We have a saying at State: 'better to beg forgiveness than denied permission.' Of course the higher you go in the Foreign Service the more divorced from that you become."

I chuckled. "I've heard that often. In the Cavalry you're either lionized as a hero or headed toward a court-martial; sometimes both at the same time."

I found Sergeant Wright re-rigging his medical equipment so he could carry it and his personal items in his walking pack.

The Chinese and Tibetan herders and porters had rigged our big packs with sleeping bags and mountain tents for horse or mule carry, and I had mentioned that I'd like to see the animal-packing process; they were mystified, but readily agreed.

Our Special Forces medic was as surprised as Jon or me at the attempt to convince me to stay in Yigon; and the reason, like the recovered submachine gun, would be a mystery forever.

Most of the Ministry functionaries were gone when we got back.

The next morning we were all at the pack rigging, horses, mules, and men were scurrying about in organized excitement. Our "cowboys" knew what they doing and the panniers and packsaddles I'd seen in American pack outfits were similar to these in that some of them resembled long flexible baskets.

In the American west the packers used long ropes crisscrossing the loads, ending in complex knots. These kept the loads on the occasional bucking horse or rear-kicking mule. These complex "diamond hitches" rigging the American packers used was completely different from our

Sino-Tibetan pack team, now all smoking cigarettes and chattering in Tibetan as they worked. Shorter ropes attached to more points on the containers and tightened down until they were firm on the girth seemed to be the technique. Their packhorses were gentle and friendly also. The older ones were saddled with lighter loads, and these frequently were treated with oats in a cut-off soccer ball that was fixed to their muzzle with bungee cords. I saw no unruly ones and they rarely neighed.

Their packers talked to them gently in Tibetan and they nuzzled human head to animal head before setting out on their trail. The pack train would set out hours before us in predawn darkness on longer, flatter trails and be set up in a meadow or relatively flat spot. They would do this every morning.

The younger animals brought our tents and sleeping bags near enough to man pack into our night camp of five Americans and two dozen or so Sino-Tibetans, a couple of squads of mountain troops plus Colonel Neng and his command group. Being American soldiers we quickly hung nicknames on both packers and animals that carried our gear.

We were especially interested in our predigital IMARSAT satellite phone and its generator. The generator had been packed in a large wooden box; it was bulky and hardly manageable.

"Don't know if it'd be a good idea to try to pack it out of its crate," Bradford observed with a worried frown.

The pack master told Yeti that he would put no more than 150 kilograms on the younger, stronger mounts. Yeti and the packtrain master were looking it over and talking about it in Tibetan, both scratching their heads almost like two students discussing a thorny calculus problem. It was one of those "not that heavy, but very awkward" situations.

"How many pounds in a kilogram?" Bradley asked.

He was the generator guru, and an all-around good mechanic as well as having considerable infantry skills. Sergeant Wright thought a moment, reaching back deep into his early training as a medic, "little over two pounds, as I recall. A hundred and fifty kilos would be an extremely large man, over 300 pounds, so I guess that'd fit."

"Let's see what they come up with; this crew seems to know their way around packhorses," I said.

"The generator packed in the box weighs hundred pounds; unpacked it's still about ninety pounds thereabouts." SSG Bradford really didn't want to unpack the generator.

One of the Lhasa-based English and Tibetan speakers said something to the packers, and I guessed that was instructions to rig the generator in the protective box. The pack master muttered something and called over two of his wranglers, who each grabbed a rope handle with two hands and lifted it appraisingly.

"Looks like he called out his top hands," Greg Man observed.

One Tibetan wrangler dug through the pile of equipment, found a large open pack basket, and started sorting out supplies and tools to fill it as a counterbalance, putting the phone in its protective pelican case about halfway down in the basket. They lifted it until it seemed roughly the same weight as the boxed generator. Soon the boxed generator was lashed tightly on the horse's left side and the counterbalancing pack basket on the right. They led the horse across the stream and joined the other serial of horses to graze.

"*Hung Hao*," Greg said to the chief wrangler, then gave a thumbs up to the Tibetans—and the horse. Very good, indeed.

The plan was for us to leave two hours after the last pack contingent, about twelve to fifteen men and pack animals, moved out. The three serials would depart with about twenty minutes spacing between each of men, horses, and equipment. We saw no soldiers with them and were told they'd use runners to our walking and climbing column if there were problems. There were eight to twelve men and animals in each of the three serials, the older pack animals going first at a little slower speed. That would keep them from bunching up and also give the herders time to warm up the animals, looking for injuries before we got too far into the mountains.

We watched the first bunch of animals and men ford the shallow stream and disappear into the light ground fog; the mountains we were headed for were sixty miles away. They were white-topped spectral ghosts overlooking everything, as they had for millennia. We drove about seven miles and crossed the last bridge over the small river that I guessed would flow south into the mighty Tsang-po River and gorge south of us. That would frame the highest parts of the Himalayas, raised up to punch Mount Everest into the clouds somewhere to the southwest.

We walked until dusk, the ground sloping up evenly until we reached a large meadow. Men and pack animals were scattered around the relatively flat valley, the animals grazing untethered. Our colorful little mountain tents had been set up, and several cook fires were burning. That night we ate the evening meal, Chinese military rations that were actually pretty tasty and coffee.

"How far up have we traveled?" Jon Aliosi asked.

I checked my altimeter and saw it read a little over 8,100 feet, others read a few hundred feet higher or lower; barometric altimeters always had an element of doubt in them. Not too dangerous for us; sometimes very fatal for pilots who had no current barometer setting to put in to ensure better accuracy. Maybe that had been one of the factors in this crash. I spread the map out on the ground and laid my compass on it evenly with the grid lines and rotated it slowly on the ground until the compass needle pointed north to the snowy mountain range in front of us.

"Looks like we're about here, I think, maybe nine or ten miles. Yigon was around 7,200 feet," I said, pointing to a spot on the map. We bunched up around it and the two infantrymen and Sergeant Wright nodded.

"So, we gained about a thousand feet in the seven hours or so we walked," Wright mused.

Colonel Neng and Yeti walked over and greeted us. We all looked at the map and Colonel Neng moved our location over a bit, just east a few hundred yards, and nodded over to Jon Aliosi, and Greg Man, saying a few words.

"The walk will be the hardest tomorrow," Yeti translated, and Jon and Greg nodded agreement, getting most of it.

Colonel Neng pointed up to the pass ahead about ten miles, I guessed, looking at the map.

"We'll send the pack train out earlier tomorrow morning than we did today, to the east of us, and they'll continue on an easier route. The animals can't get over the mountain in front of us, so they'll leave well before dawn, probably about 3 a.m.," Yeti continued.

The contour lines five or six miles ahead of us ran together, indicating very high ground rising sharply, and I winced—probably hand over hand climbing. Yeti knelt down, pointing at them with a ballpoint pen.

"There's a high . . . I forgot the English word," Yeti admitted after a few minutes.

"Cliff?" Wright offered.

Yeti thought a moment. "Cliff, yes. It's a footpath, but very narrow and dangerous, one man only and . . ."

Then, almost like a punctuation point, we heard the Tibetans and Chinese soldiers around the horses, yelling at each other and pointing up the valley at a large pall of rising dust and debris in the air about half a mile away. Then we heard the ominous noise of the avalanche, and the sound washed over us, intensifying like a squadron of jets as it gained speed and the avalanche brought down the side of a mountain in the distance. A very ominous punctuation point.

"I guess we're not in Kansas anymore, Toto," Sergeant Antal quipped.

"You were saying, Yeti, before we were so rudely interrupted by the mountain gods," Wright reminded him.

Yeti shook his head, "Don't say that, Kevin; you'll make the mountain gods very angry." Yeti was obviously upset with Sergeant Wright's innocuous remark.

"Colonel Neng is coming over to talk about tomorrow's climb."

We all looked at each other. Climb instead of walk. Serious stuff, indeed, although looking at the map we all placed bets on how high the elevation difference would be at the next campsite. All we had to do was estimate the elevation then it would be the average of all our altimeter readings, which depended on the barometric pressure.

The winner got a Tsingtao and meal from the rest of us at the restaurant of his choice. Antal immediately announced that since he was an aspiring Ranger, he'd be the winner and he wanted to dine at the Hard Rock Cafe, Beijing. Besides, he needed a couple of T-shirts; we all laughed.

Greg Man confided that his wife, Shirley, a serious student of China, also liked the Hard Rock. Best cheeseburgers in Beijing, he added.

Finally, Jon shook his head, gave us a "you guys" look and snickered.

Wright looked at Mark Antal, "you have to win first, Ranger Wannabe," he chided.[5]

We all hooted, except Sergeant Bradford—it turned out the trendy cafe was his choice also, "so what's wrong with the Hard Rock Cafe; great place I think."

I excused myself from the competition because I was ineligible for the prize, being a ringer colonel with all that experience and gravitas, and knowing all things, I told them.

But I'd be glad to contribute to the beer and dinner, I told them.

"Sounds like Colonel Neng tipped you off," Jon said. I put my hand over my heart, looked offended, and replied seriously, "no, just the natural omnipotence of the commander."

You don't get to be an old colonel without learning a few tricks.

Colonel Neng, his captain, and Sherap showed up carrying a map board that folded into four sections.

Our chief colleague from Lhasa was with him, the good English speaker that we guessed was Tibetan/Chinese, Mr. Luo. He seemed more fluent in Tibetan and had the same hard features and high cheekbones. He had accompanied Colonel Neng and his men on the initial recovery.

The section of tomorrow's climb was depicted at an estimated 1:12, 500 scale and blown up. It was very detailed and a map like that for hiking twenty miles would probably be ten by ten feet in size. The captain opened it up on a flat rock, pulled a collapsible pointer from his pocket, and stood with us clustered around Colonel Neng. As Colonel Neng briefed, he moved the pointer along a narrow trail.

"The next two days' travel will be difficult" our Lhasa English speaker translated, "and there is a difficult crossing early tomorrow."

The captain moved the pointer farther up the trail to a place where our map depicted contour lines coming together, a sign of serious and abruptly high terrain.

"Here there is a path on the side of the mountain, with a long fall on the left." The captain repeatedly moved his pointer back and forth along the defile and then tapped the left side. The abyss.

Colonel Neng continued and the translation followed.

"We will reach the difficult place after about three hours of walking, then our next camp is about nine or ten hours walking, much more difficult than today's, but not as dangerous after the—cliff."

Colonel Neng took the pointer and delivered his next burst following the trail with it, Mr. Luo translating and Yeti standing by.

"We should start walking at daybreak in the morning, cross the river on this bridge and many more tomorrow and the next day. Then we rest for a while and replenish our water before taking the dangerous path. The next day's march will bring us to the valley of the crash, and it is also dangerous there because of the . . . the . . ."

Jon said a few words in Chinese and Mr. Luo thanked him with a nod and a smile.

"Yes, the avalanches like we just experienced. And also the crevasses on the glacier."

He and Sherap had an exchange in Tibetan.

"Mr. Chopel thinks this will pose danger, also. Do you have questions for Colonel Neng?"

"How long is the fall at the dangerous spot?" SSG Bradford asked.

This threw him, and Jon helped in translation.

Colonel Neng gave an "I don't know" flip of his hand.

Jon blanched. "Maybe five hundred meters; but maybe more."

We all got very quiet. Colonel Neng continued, and the translation followed again.

"Colonel Neng will send two small soldiers across with a small radio, then a larger soldier if it is safe."

We got quieter.

"Is that satisfactory to your side, Colonel Jordan?"

I thought for a moment. Always answer a question with another question when you're dealing with the Chinese someone had taught me.

"What's the alternative if the trail isn't safe; what do we do?"

Colonel Neng made the familiar air hissing out of a tire sound the Chinese make when an unpleasant response is required.

"Then we have to go back and take a much longer route, one we didn't take in our first journey last year. The good weather is ending, possibly in the next few days, and then it will be dangerous for us at the crash site, and our return to Yigon."

I looked at Jon and Greg inquiringly. They both simultaneously shrugged their shoulders.

"Well, then . . . perhaps we should go on and hope for the best when we get there."

When this was translated, Colonel Neng merely smiled and said, "*Hao hao*"—OK. The captain picked up his map board and they departed.

We split up and went to our tents; I heard another avalanche rumble sometime after midnight.

We crossed the stream—small river actually—on a fairly sturdy wooden bridge with rope handholds, just before dawn the next day. The water was fast, clear, and cold when we filled our canteens and water bottles the next morning; in my case, the two two-quart canteens I carried in my backpack. I dropped halazone tablets into both mine, shook them each, and tucked them away.

"I think the water's safe up here, Colonel. We haven't even seen an insect," Wright observed.

"Just thinkin' about that dead Yak in the water a couple hundred yards upstream, boys. Looks like he's been in there a few weeks."

When their mouths fell open, I said "just funnin'; but there might be."

Everyone relaxed, but later up the mountain we were all popping them in when the water wasn't so clear.

The water was flowing much faster than the other streams we'd crossed; we were going to go up in a hurry, and Colonel Neng's prophecy was correct. This was going to be a rough day's climb. Barely a half mile uphill we crossed the same watercourse but without the breadth. The bridge was shakier and the water was rushing so fast the flumes were spraying off the rocks. We were definitely going up.

An hour later all our sleeves were up and I had consumed the contents of my first two-quart canteen.

We took a break, and I noticed sweat was running off the bill of my cap in a steady stream.

"Hey Sir, you're wasting water," Greg Man called.

"Yeah, I think I've got a drain valve open in my brain."

Yeti had followed us up, leaning on his walking staff and not even breathing hard. I never saw him sit down that day.

"Just a couple hours and we'll get to the interesting part," he said, grinning.

"Did you come up this way before?" Jon asked.

"Sure, it's not too bad, but I walk a lot."

"How bad is the old death drop?" Greg Man wondered.

"Not bad at all if you do it like I do," he replied, and continued.

"I just close my eyes; you don't even notice how bad it is."

"Thanks, Yeti. I feel better now."

"Look, it's not so bad and Mr. Luo was right; you don't wanna be in these mountains when the weather's bad."

He poked his stick in the trail.

"This is dry now. When it starts raining it's slick and dangerous. Going up is bad; coming down is really bad."

"OK, let's get to the interesting part," I said, rising and shrugging into my backpack.

We started up again, all of us leaning into our walking staffs. The trail got narrower, more overgrown and rougher. Antal was in front of me and walked carefully, occasionally grabbing a vine or limb for purchase.

An hour later, I called another halt while more rivulets ran off my cap bill. It was a good time to stop and drop our packs; I checked my water and found I had consumed another half of a canteen.

"Sorry I'm slowing you youngsters down," I said between gasps.

Jon and Greg were both holding their own, and Bradford and Antal were having no problem at all. I could see that Kevin Wright was also OK, but he sat down heavily as I did. I was suffering more than anyone else, and I reflected morosely one more time how soldiering was a young man's game.

"You're not slowing us down much, Colonel," Greg replied.

"We should call this stretch "frequent break" hill," I muttered.

"We need to take frequent breaks from here on, get our breathing under control and our body heat down," Wright responded. "We also need to keep stretching once we stop at the crossing point. Don't need any cramps, stiff leg muscles, or numb feet or toes."

"Amen," someone commented.

Yeti moved on up the trail to look things over; he had a small Chinese backpack and an ornate, well-used walking staff; we all had walking staffs. Wright had a huge one, taller than his head.

Yeti reappeared. "There's a rough spot of trail ahead; there's rocks on it that are sharp; we're going to have to go over it carefully," he reported.

Colonel Neng, his soldiers, and our Lhasa friend were ahead of us somewhere; maybe at the bad place already.

"See Colonel Neng up there?" Man asked him.

"Nah; they're moving slow, too. Colonel Neng and Sergeant Cho aren't early chickens, either."

"You don't mean spring chickens, do you?" Antal asked.

"Spring chickens? That's the correct term? What exactly does it mean?" He asked in all seriousness.

Sergeant Wright grinned and answered, "Spring is the season that chickens hatch their young eggs, baby chickens."

"Ah. Thanks, Kevin," he pulled a small notebook from his back pocket and wrote it all down.

Like any good language student, Yeti reinforced a new word. He murmured, "spring chickens, spring chickens . . . they are not spring chickens, we aren't spring chickens he is not a spring chicken . . ."

Wright was on the roll though, and had a keen, understated sense of humor.

"Think of these two young sergeants, Yeti. Now Mike and Mark over here are spring chickens. They're young and run around peeping, trying to get away from mama. They're full of energy and very curious, being kids, but sometimes the coyote gets them."

"Coyote?"

"Yeah, an animal that eats other animals; kinda like a wolf."

"Yes, I know the wolfs."

"Wolves in English, Yeti." Antal corrected, laying on his back, pack loosened up behind his shoulders into a pillow. He talked with his baseball cap pulled down, walking staff leaning against his rib cage.

A soldier's rest position, I thought.

I wondered if a Mongol raider, afoot for some reason, had lain back to rest in the same position, at this same little grassy, hollow bowl of a meadow sometime in the thirteenth century.

Anytime you stop, a sergeant had told me decades ago, "eat something, take a slug of water, urinate, then go to sleep if you can—even for five minutes. Keep your weapon tied or slung loosely to you." You might have to dash for cover, or crawl to it, awakened in violence from an unsound slumber that was not really sleep.

Wright gestured over toward the two young sergeants with a straight face.

"See. They're young, so they know everything, way more than their elders. If the coyote doesn't get them they grow up to become *summer* chickens and join the infantry."

"Oh, I know all about the infantry. Like Colonel Neng's men, they carry heavy packs and get yelled at all the time."

Every one of us started laughing, and Antal, with his hat on his face and lying prone on his backpack, raised himself up and said, "Yeti, that is definitely how it is."

We shrugged back into our packs, chuckling, and Wright said to me, "Lead on, chief winter chicken, Sir."

And we did, the mood lightened as we moved up behind Yeti, who was disappearing rapidly up the worsening trail.

Yeti was right. A seam of rocks ran vertically up the middle of the trail, like some malevolent center stripe. Most had sharp points. Definitely some seismological event occurred here, probably a few thousand years ago. We picked our way carefully through fifty or sixty yards of the rocks and understood why walking was slow and careful in the Himalayas. We clustered up when we were through them, leaning heavily on our staffs in a standing break.

"I hereby proclaim that portion of our journey the 'broken ankle' trail," Antal muttered.

Yeti reappeared. "The rest are up at the crossing, just a few hundred yards away. We have to do a little . . ." he mimicked hand over hand climbing.

"Marvelous," Greg said, but he and Jon were hardly winded.

I took a slug of water and waved my cap to dry it.

"Onward and upward . . ." I said and moved out. Occasionally, I wished I was a geologist; maybe then I'd understand how and why the earth formed, particularly in this stretch. Steep, with huge masses of leafy, stunted vegetation growing seemingly right out of the boulders, narrowing the path to foot-in-front-of-the-other to get through. We pushed off the boulders to lean forward and grab a handful of vegetation to pull ourselves along.

We could sense it was sheer cliff on either side of us, but the thick vegetation protected us from the edges. The trail was reasonably safe from everything but an ankle-breaking stumble. We broke through and the trail still climbed, but at a reasonable, leaning-forward walk; we dug our walking sticks into the ground. The "few hundred yards" turned into well over a mile.

We linked up with Colonel Neng, Mr. Luo, the soldiers, and Yeti, still unruffled. The view was open and spectacular. White-covered mountains dotted the horizons. Not white-peaked mountains, but snowfields everywhere with the sun bouncing off walls of ice. I walked over and greeted Colonel Neng.

Mr. Luo smiled, "you all made it up; good! Very good! Now we rest awhile and go around the mountain."

No mention of the danger, but we all gaped at the trail disappearing around the side of the steep bluff and the infinite space to the left. We grounded our packs, stretched, and drank from our canteens.

Mr. Luo moved to translate; the trail had definitely become political, not military business. Chinese from the Colonel to Mr. Luo:

"We will rest here for a half hour; you can eat lunch if you wish and drink some water or the soldiers can make tea for you."

"How wide is that trail?" Man asked in English, then in Chinese.

"Hmmm, in centimeters . . ." Luo began.

"Less than thirty inches," Wright interrupted.

"Less than twenty, I'd say," Man offered.

Yeti nodded, "less than that I think; my heels were over the edge last time."

"How'd the horses and pack train get through this?" Aliosi wondered. It was a rhetorical question; we knew the animals would be dropped somewhere to the flatter terrain east and south of us. The packhorse loads would be man-packed on.

"Another, much longer route, but easier for the animals," Luo replied.

"After we cross, the soldiers will ensure the trail is safe and we can walk on to our camp. Your tents and phone are there."

Aliosi said something in Chinese to Mr. Luo, and Colonel Neng and Luo both answered in Chinese, obviously surprised. They both knew our two embassy members could speak and understand their language, but I suddenly suspected that Jon Aliosi's Chinese language capability was good. Very good. Luo cut Colonel Chen off by overriding him in English.

"The horses will be left at a lower altitude, and their loads man packed, but they will be there when we get there," he looked at Colonel Neng and added something else in Chinese. Neng nodded.

"In about six hours. If the rains and the bridges hadn't delayed our beginning, we could have taken the longer, safer route also."

Aliosi had obviously asked him how long to the next . . . something. I assumed it was the final campsite before tackling the crash site. Six hours.

I looked at the sun and guessed it was about midday; my watch read 1240. If it was six hours—and the Chinese seemed to always understate the time—we'd be getting into our last bivouac just about sundown. Add the evening meal and overwhelming fatigue we all felt after that and any planning and preparation for the final walk into the crash site would be less than stellar.

What I really wanted to do was to take Yeti and go over and talk to Sherap—it sounded to my ear that Yeti spoke good Tibetan, maybe native fluency; I wanted to see if I could get a good feel for the safety of the three routes and getting everybody to the half dozen or so sites we'd prioritized; these sites were probably areas with remains or personal materials depending on the contour lines.

It was less than scientific, but I'd figured to have our party lead the searchers to places surface searches could radiate out from; our four men would give the starting points. Greg and Jon could do the directing. It was better than stumbling into the valley and wondering where to start.

Also, we had the good laminated map and we could show on the report visually where we searched. We were flying blind, but at least we were flying. I pushed that grim thought out of my mind, recalling the circumstances that brought us here. Flying wasn't a proper metaphor for this crew.

"I'm ready to tackle that mountain right now," Antal piped up.

Wright shot him a warning glance and he shut up; or quit peeping. Bradford had carefully walked up to the drop and looked over, hands on his hips.

"How far down?" Somebody asked.

"Not too bad—quarter mile, maybe. But maybe more," he said, grinning.

"Way to go, Staff Sergeant Mike Bradford," I thought. "We may sometimes win wars and lose the peace politically but we're still the best soldiers in the world, and sometimes it's better to joke about danger. So we fall four football fields or six, makes no difference . . . we still have to hang our heels over the abyss and Charlie Mike—Continue Mission."

We rested for about ten minutes, and all us Americans got up, stretched, and started to lift our backpacks.

Yeti shook his head, "the soldiers will carry your backpacks around the mountain."

I noticed when our Chinese colonel got up he hadn't taken off his backpack, and the soldiers had arisen with their heavy rucksacks and weapons. Ignoring Yeti, all of us shrugged into ours.

The colonel nodded at the soldiers and a smaller one started out on the ledge, rifle slung muzzle down, rucksack high on his shoulders, and moved out on the ledge. He walked carefully; close to the mountain's massive rock wall and away from the precipice, eyes straight ahead into the cliff's granite wall, about twelve inches in front of his face. When he got to the curve in the trail, he would be out of our sight; he leaned against the face of the cliff, both hands on it high above his head, and slowly edged around and disappeared from view.

I glanced around at our crew. All were watching this intently. I didn't know if I was the only one with his heart in his boots, but it definitely etched an impression in my brain.

Soon a walkie-talkie crackled and Yeti translated: "It's safe, but be slow, careful, and don't look down."

The other soldiers went over, then Colonel Neng. Antal moved to be next but I motioned him out of the way and stepped onto the ledge. Everybody has secret fears, sometimes buried deep in the heart or soul and unrecognized, but they're there.

I, like thousands of other young men, had jumped from the infamous thirty-four-foot tower in airborne training, the psychological height that separated the men from the boys, as the tough instructors in the black baseball hats had said, grinning. We had leaped out trusting our harnesses and the wire cable that would carry us to the ground. But it was a terrifying thing and I jumped with my eyes closed. While I got out of my harness the instructor snarled at me about something I really didn't hear.

The man behind me lent a little drama to the event. All eyes were turned up at him in the tower, maybe two hundred feet away, struggling in the door with the black hat's cap bobbing behind him, he tentatively stepped out then grabbed behind for the opening, body hanging out, held by his hands on the floor of the opening. The students who'd completed the tethered leap were now in a laughing uproar; before, they'd been sitting there, backs straight and hands over their knees in the simulated seating of an aircraft en route to a drop zone.

In an instant they were doing pushups "UNTIL I GET TIRED!" the black hat had boomed. I glanced up and saw both instructors grinning broadly, watching the drama unfold in the tower. The instructor's boot firmly pushed him out the door, spinning wildly. When he hit the berm the ground instructor savaged him verbally then made him join the sweating students now straining in the push-up position, including me.

He returned to the tower, made a safer exit, and later had his wings hammered into his left breast on the drop zone with me after completing five jumps. But his secret fear had momentarily taken control of him; he had successfully pushed it back to some hidden place. He had overcome it.

Just like I had to right now, around a rock face surrounded by 20,000-foot peaks.

I approached slowly but carefully and gingerly stepped onto the ledge. I moved slowly as I approached the curve around the mountain's side. I definitely did not look at the drop, even though I visualized it mentally, then pushed it out of my mind. I did as the soldiers and Colonel Neng had done, leaned into the mountain with my hands spread shoulder width above my head and sidestepped slowly around it. I thought, "Ah, Jesus . . ." but it wasn't a prayer. Now I was alone and the narrow path had narrowed more; it felt like my boot heels definitely overhung the path. I sidestepped, toes of my boot scraping slowly across the face of the rock wall I was clinging to, until the path widened and I saw Colonel Neng grinning, holding out his walkie- talkie.

"Cakewalk," I said into it. "Just be careful, go slow and keep your toes in the mountain in the turn."

When our team and the last soldier had crossed safely we were quietly elated; no fist pumping, high fives, or backslaps. We were relieved to be across safely. Many hours later, in our last camp, we would discuss it, "what if-ing" a fall from one of us. What if it was one of the soldiers? We all agreed it would take time to get the ropes and climbing gear and we would have to send two soldiers back for the stuff.

SSG Bradford injected reality into our discussion. "Anybody falling off that mountain would resemble a run-over jelly donut. I'd vote to make sure we knew who he was and report it to Lin Zhi—maybe they have experienced mountain rescue units, but we're not one of them. These mountain troops would have gotten the body out—maybe. We should have reported it and continued on."

Continue Mission . . . Charlie Mike. But three of us—Greg, Wright, and me—knew that any man—US or Chinese—falling would have ended the mission, and instead turned it into a regrettable Personnel Recovery mission.

But now Antal and Yeti both faked yawns, and when Mr. Luo suggested we rest, we all shook our heads negatively. Greg asked Yeti if this was the worst of it. Yeti replied, "definitely the scariest, but the worst of it—probably not. Lotta tough climbing ahead."

He was right. The rest of the hike was brutal with more hand-over-hand climbing and one stretch muddily slick due to another fast stream throwing flumes of water onto the trail for several hundred yards. The six hours turned into over seven.

We made it to our base camp at twilight, generator and phone already unpacked along with our tents and sleeping bags. Our hired packers had two fires going—Chinese and Tibetan—I figured. They got along OK but they'd polarize into their own groups when it was time to settle down and sleep.

We reported to our headquarters that we were close to the crash site and all safe; we'd report tomorrow on what we found, or didn't find.

We washed off as best as we could in a pool of the small river, ate some Chinese pork rations, then slipped into our sleeping bags. The valley yawned open before us and clouds rolled in. I dismissed the notion of trying to track down Sherap. It was time to get some rest. It had grown colder and windy, and we heard another distant avalanche in the darkness.

Colonel Neng's weather forecasts appeared to be correct; on our fourth and final day, a bad storm was approaching. We were tired but wired up—we were less than three miles from the site where young Americans had come to rest a half century earlier.

Tomorrow, the weather would surely worsen.

CHAPTER 25

Glaciers and Snowfields

Dawn, September 10, 1994, 2.7 miles south of the crash site

Sergeant First Class Kevin Wright, US Army Special Forces, and I studied the figures moving over the snowfield, specks in the distance even through our binoculars. The first party was approaching the rough center of the crash site down the slopes of the snowfield. They had left at 0300, flashlights penetrating the darkness, and the snowfield ahead of them shining brightly.

We had split up into three parties on three routes. Jon and Greg would take one of our sergeants, a couple of soldiers, and the now-horseless packers on their route; they also took two experienced Chinese speakers and an infantryman trained in grave registration, so if one party had difficulty or had to retrace a route, at least one recovery team could get in and start work on the crash site. Colonel Neng considered this the longest but potentially most dangerous route since it walked across the glaciated debris field with crevasses. Sherap was also included in this party. Kevin Wright would go with an advance command group with one of their medics, Yeti, the captain and two PLA troopers with stretchers and a few packers. They also had a backpacked radio. They were the casualty recovery and evacuation team if the need arose.

Colonel Neng, Mr. Luo, a good English speaker, and I would go straight up the valley with four soldiers and an FM radio. It was definitely the shortest route, probably only a third of theirs, straight-line distance, but it had a large boulder field we had to climb across, which triggered an alarm in my brain. The sleeting wind suggested there would be some ice on the boulders.

"About three hours for them to get there on their route?" Wright asked.

I looked at my watch; "probably a little longer if they crossed the river when they thought they would; maybe three and a half.

"There should be roughly an hour or so of careful walking in the snowfield of the glacier and another snowfield that had washed down into the valley."

The map indicated the sprawled wreckage was scattered somewhere between thirteen to fourteen thousand feet in altitude over several hundred yards. Jagged snow-covered mountain peaks on both sides of the valley speared the sky, topping 20,000 feet and wreathed in a milky fog.

The wind was biting, and the sun was a slowly rising blood red orb. A passing squall had dropped a mix of sleet and rain on us earlier. Now it was back, flecking us like steel insects flying. It was totally unlike the mild fall weather we'd experienced yesterday and at the beginning of our trek.

"What do you think, Sergeant Wright, you being a senior NCO, and badass Special Forces guy, and all that?"

"I really don't think you're going to make it over those boulders; he looked around for something to scale them with, the old boy scout trick of putting a man next to a tree, measuring his height with an outstretched thumb then walking his height up the tree. He squinted into the descending light of dawn coming down twin rows of peaks in front of us. He studied the boulders in front of us through the binoculars. The ones behind them disappearing into the mist and fog.

"I'd say that first boulder is probably twenty, maybe twenty-five feet. You're going to have to free climb that, which wouldn't be too hard under some circumstances."

The map showed elevations of over 20,000 feet going up the valley.

"But those circumstances aren't here. I also think, Sir, that is the coldest sun I've ever seen, and we've had that stingin' rain and sleet . . ."

"Yeah, I know. Ice on 'em. We'll take a shot because Neng is so intent on it, but I've got my wimp-out argument close at hand."

I pointed at his route on the map.

"We may be following you."

Wright's cold sun was slowly changing the light to orange from red as it rose.

"But as a medic, I'm thinking about that frozen rock garden out there breaking bones."

"Well, they're all young men and in shape . . . Sergeant Antal has been RIP-ing for ranger school back at Schofield."[1]

I knew I was groping for optimism with that remark. Our wranglers now coming behind us along an easier approach had coaxed three younger horses on until they could be hobbled and grazed in a relatively flat place with grass and water about two miles southeast of us. Our man-packing Sherpas and horsemen had set up a hasty advance camp, then some moved on up the mountain to join us near the final camp before the crash site. They were tired; they had traveled all night, with two weak flashlights for the whole party. We camped there overnight and now we were going to make the final push to the site itself.

"We've been lucky, but the old weather window's going to close soon."

He nodded. "Just like it did for those guys in the plane."

"Amen. And a lot of others, too."

The weather had been cool, dry, and pleasant when we started walking a few days earlier. The first day had also been relatively level and easygoing, but subsequent days had seen a sharp increase in altitude, with steep elevation changes in short distances. Now on the fourth day we had acclimated to the altitude and toughened up, but we were all tired, and I was definitely the tiredest.

The hand-over-hand climbing had been arduous, but so far, nothing you see on Everest, or *Into Thin Air.* Our technical climbing ropes and gear remained back, in the main base camp, largely unused but serving nicely as a rope corral and tie-down for the horses. I had told Sergeant First Class Wright to break out three 100-foot military climbing ropes and half a dozen snap links in case we had to retrieve someone from a crevasse or other hole.

I wanted him to hold all the rescue gear with him and the captain, commander of the tactical command and, potentially, the rescue team. Wright, and a few Tibetans and Yeti, would move with them until the columns were all safely in the valley. I knew Colonel Neng's plan was to keep the tactical command team on a route with good FM radio reception and fairly centrally located to all three routes.

After the teams had safely closed out in the valley, Wright and his potentially lifesaving team would move forward and join the small teams on the actual crash site. If I could have retained enough Chinese language skill to be at least barely functional, I would've let Colonel Chen know about it and my rationale—get his opinion. Instead, I studied the map and walked around thinking and studying the map again; I talked to the sergeants, and finally I lit my pipe, hoping the spirit of that crew was hovering above us, vectoring us in to take them home.

With Sergeant First Class Wright backing up the medics in the Tactical

Command party and the Chinese civilian "doctor" back at base camp, we would spread the medical capabilities as best as we could.

Now the slimmed-down pack train was laagered in a meadow a few miles back on a flat plateau, but well out of avalanche danger. We had reported in by Bradford's beloved satellite phone and cumbersome generator; we had joked that if Patch, the faithful horse that carried it, could get its hooves on an AK-74 he'd probably shoot them both to pieces. Bradford was not amused. We had all talked through the dangers of the "assault" phase, getting into the crash site itself and the dangers that we might face. The primary one was falling into a crevasse.

Some of them, Sherap warned, had been covered over with drifting wind-blown snow, which might have frozen into a thin sheet. You could unknowingly plunge into one of those. These were certainly worrisome and we had planned for it back in Hawaii. Wright's safety and rescue crew's three 100-foot military climbing ropes and snap links were the only lifelines we carried. These would be used if we had to lift men out of these crevasses.

This and most of our as-yet-unused technical climbing gear, except for the three ropes and snap links, required one of the fifteen or so horses to carry it. We had encamped near our "Line of Departure," in military terms—leaving relative safety for relative hazards. The hazards now were the car-sized boulders we'd have to free climb and weather that was threatening. I considered that hazard number two after the crevasses, but broken bones were a distinct possibility on our route.

"How far back is the remuda and the rest of the pack train?" I asked in the morning darkness, after laying out the graphics on our map with a grease pencil the afternoon prior.

"On the map, only looks to be about six clicks (kilometers) southwest, maybe four miles. But the terrain is rough in between us. The sat phone is still set up back where we spent the night; I tied tarps over the phone, antenna, and generator and weighted them down with rocks."

Kevin Wright and I were discussing the tactical control and rescue party.

"You thought the aid station with their doctor and a couple of soldiers with a radio for security was going to stay up on the glacier until we got onto the crash site, then they changed their minds?" I asked.

"Yeah, the English-speaking doctor and captain made that clear—they wanted no part of going into the valley; they'd handle bad casualties back there. The military medics could handle the rest on the crash site and evac any casualties back; they've got two folding litters. I think they might have avalanche jeebies or just want to stay away from the dead as long as possible."

"That'll probably work OK as long as they've got a working radio; if we have a casualty that's critical up in the valley on the crash site, Neng will have to order them down."

"I think the captain is their political officer; he doesn't look or act much like an infantryman," Wright replied.

"I think you're right if he and the doctor changed what Neng ordered. If he is a political officer, he'll have some clout; maybe he can probably even countermand Neng."

"The map shows a flat area just north of the pack train camp, maybe three to four hundred yards long with no apparent hills or gullies. I guess the whole level area would be suitable for a small fixed-wing plane if we had to air evacuate someone," I replied.

"It might take some clearing, maybe not. I'm sure they've got good pilots up here; fixed- or rotor-wing."

"Well, they all made it out with no calls but radio checks, so the dangerous, fast route is OK, at least so far."

"But Colonel Neng and I are going to take it slow on those boulders."

"Yeah, and the softies from Lhasa, too," he retorted with a grin.

"If you mean the 'please stay here with us crowd,' I think they dropped off after we'd driven over the bridge."

"I'd like to hear Jon and Colonel Man flesh that out a little when we get back to Yigon, if they'll talk about it."

"Might be a Thompson submachine gun mystery," I thought. "We'd never know."

"Colonel Man and I are going to take it slow, too. We're not in our early twenties either," he added.

"So nothing's changed with the plan for getting people out with serious or life threatening injuries?" He asked.

"Everything's the same; Man and Aliosi know the Chinese have helos that can get in here and we don't have to play the STOL card (short takeoff and landing fixed-wing) aircraft unless it votes as well."

"Not looking so good right now, is it."

We both looked up into the fog and mist.

"Weather's spooky up here. Like early autumn and Indian Summer in Salt Lake City all the way through the mountains, then we get up here and it's startin' to ugly up."

"Yeah, if we'd been two weeks later we wouldn't have made it this far. Definitely wouldn't have made it back, not safely anyway."

The back-up plan was suggesting to the Chinese for Nepal to send some helos like we see on National Geographic plucking climbers off the killer mountains, like Everest. The Nepalese seemed to have cracked the code on aero-evacuating European and other foreign Everest climbers.

"We uniform guys won't get drawn into the helo issue or anything political; that's Jon and Greg Man; the politico and the attaché's bailiwick."

He snorted. "Good luck with the Nepalese idea. Somehow I'm thinking 'big loss of face' with that one, but I guess . . . I think anyway that they already have a plan in place, and they all seem to be competent . . . tough. These guys are good soldiers."

I nodded. "The Nepalese plan was something we conjured up in Hawaii, talking to some of the CINCPAC operators. It was dead on arrival anyway; Jon and Greg got a laugh out of it, though." We envisioned something far different in Hawaii, looking at the rough terrain on the videotape. All of us assumed there might be assisted climbing involved. We were disabused of this notion when we got the laminated 1/50, 000 map from a friendly source at CINCPAC. The entire route was scarcely over 15,000 feet and the crash site was at about the same route. But the valley abutted some 20,000-foot peaks, and since none of us were avalanche experts, that became one of our greatest concerns.

"I think the same thing you do about the soldiers. They're good; they run these mountains like mountain goats. Colonel Neng laid it out pretty well last night with the routes and the safety and I amplified it a little bit, especially with the search areas and material and personal evidence, but especially the safety part," I added.

There had been a discussion between Neng and Yeti, and they walked off a little to conduct it with much arm waving and pointing up the valley. But Neng gave Greg Man, Jon Aliosi, and me a thumbs up sign; I guessed it had been about the routes and safety.

"I know, I talked to him about it," he didn't take his eyes from the binoculars, but I saw a flash of a grin. "They were arguing over the three routes we picked."

"Figured you might have," I answered.

"Your route is the worse, harder and more dangerous because of the boulders. Now the boulders have ice on them."

"Who said that, Neng or Yeti?"

Sergeant First Class Wright and the two PLA medics had conducted field medical clinics, with Yeti translating into Tibetan and English and conducting the English to Chinese translation as well, he had stayed closer to the Chinese than any of us.

Yeti was the major link; he was obviously subordinate to Luo, but he had a lot of influence with Neng.

He flowed effortlessly from one language to another; he was the most skilled multilanguage translator I had ever seen; he could easily have been one of the simultaneous translators at the United Nations.

I smiled tiredly. A Special Forces NCO is rarely behind anyone else; after all, officers lead the Army, but NCOs run it. Lower ranks do the running, but they're in training all the time to move up the responsibility and authority chain. Baton in the knapsack.

"Both implied it, but Yeti translated, of course."

"Apparently the suits looked at the routes in Lhasa and they determined you'd go on this one because it was safer."

"If they thought this one was safer than your routes they must've missed a few map reading classes in Chinese Ranger school."

"Well, to Yeti's credit he didn't bad-mouth them, just said they'd not realized there were boulders like barns scattered around. I'd guess Neng probably told them that maps can fool you, but face and all that . . . anyway, Yeti just said, hey man, not a problem."

"Hey man, not a problem . . . ?" I echoed incredulously.

Apparently, Sherap had warned his old friend Colonel Neng about the crevasses on his route—the largest party that contained Bradford, Antal, and Jon, and both Neng and the medical staff, had been concerned. Maybe the wiry Tibetan hunter had been teasing them with a Tibetan sharp-pointed stick, but Sherap had admitted that overall it was a safe route, if taken with care.

I glanced up at him, "Sergeant Wright, you've got to be kidding about Yeti giving you that answer."

He placed his hand over his heart and grinned.

We both burst out laughing. A Chinese-speaking Tibetan or maybe some combination thereof, speaking unaccented lower California English, and looking like a young, modish John Travolta in *Saturday Night Fever.*

Wright grimaced and stretched again.

"I guess he's right about both routes into the valley being a bear. You check his footgear last night?"

"No, why?"

"He's wearing Danner mountain boots now. I'd have a pair if I could afford them."

"Maybe they're a Chinese knock-off."

"Maybe. But they looked like the real thing to me."

"Whoa. Serious stuff for the Yeti."

"What do you think he is?"

"Oh, he's a TAR official, for sure," I replied, scanning with the binoculars, trying to make some sense of just who it was crawling onto some kind of man-made object up the valley—airplane wreckage, maybe.

We were just too far; I had to get up into that valley—so did Wright; he was the closest thing to a physician we had. He had a lot of confidence in the Chinese medical team, but they were spooked by the mountains, the coming bad weather, and possibly handling the dead—perhaps for the second time.

"No, I mean is he mostly Tibetan or Chinese or what?"

"He told Jon and Man he had a Tibetan father and a Chinese mother, kind of a reverse of what I've read, but not outlandish. He hasn't talked much to me about where he came from or his family.

"He speaks English and knows the slang like he was raised in the States or Canada, but I try to stay away from those kinds of conversation."

"What about Sherap?"

"One hundred percent pure Tibetan I'd guess. He's comfortable around Neng, and they seem to speak a little Chinese and a lot of Tibetan, so I'd guess Colonel Neng is on a long-time posting here."

"Or a sleeping Tibetan dictionary," Wright mused.

"Yeah, maybe . . . I don't think the PLA or the Party would have any trouble with him marrying a Tibetan. Matter of fact, they'd probably like that; likely be more inclined to keep him here than send him someplace like Xinjiang."

"Hell, Neng could be part-Tibetan himself, even," I replied. High cheekbones, the stocky rolling gait of a horseman; I couldn't see him in Khamba regalia, but take the uniform off and he could be any herder, or tough tradesman.

That was something I had to ask Greg Man about, I thought.

"OK, tell me again, Sir. This is Xijang, right. What's Xianjang? That's the little Muslim problem they're dealing with, right?"

"Right. Uighurs. We saw a few in Chengdu; it's even farther north and west of where we are. FAO's and attachés I've known who have traveled there say it's bad news—desert and caravan country—more like Saudi or Kuwait, I'd guess."

I continued, "Wild country, wild people, and the PLA probably has a little more of a security problem, especially after Desert Storm. Skull caps and facial features that look Kuwaiti, but I'll bet now Han Chinese are the majority."

"That's the trouble with these short, one-time missions," he said quietly.

"In Vietnam and Laos you get to know the players, but the security guys either don't speak much English or don't let you know they do," he continued, straining his eyes with the binoculars, like I was.

I was beginning to think I'd made a mistake last night when Neng was offering up his version of who should go where, and how we should make the final attack on the valley. I should have gone in the fast, seemingly more dangerous way with Antal and Bradford, I thought, keeping an eye on the lightening horizon.

Wright continued, "Yeah, the Vietnamese are formal, sometimes a little stiff; the Lao are kinda loosey goosey, but both disappear after the chow break for a short siesta; same work ethic we've got, but they approach things differently."

I related Joe Harvey's tale of seeing an elderly Hmong woman once somewhere in Thailand or Laos at a much lower altitude, while we waited for the valley to light up in Sergeant Wright's cold sun.

We were just a couple of soldiers, nervously chatting before we conducted an assault. A no-shooting assault, but dangerous nonetheless . . .

"She was having some sort of seizure, all bright colored clothes and silver, weaving around and crying. The Thai just kind of smiled, embarrassed for her, but they didn't stop to help her."

We were near our office at Barbers Point. It was close to twilight and the burning of the cane fields after harvest looked like Laos in the slash-and-burn season. This was when the wandering hill tribes, staked out another plot for planting, a couple of mountains away, generally, then move on when it would no longer bear crops.

Our small headquarters, underneath the base personnel office, had a strip-mall-like setting, far from the Waikiki glitter, probably less than twenty miles, but an hour's drive—or more.

Barbers Point, like Bellows Air Force Station, Kanehoe, and Schofield Barracks, was one of the military jewels on Oahu, a nice, but crowded, traffic-choked island.

Up the Waianae coast, traffic and crowds thinned out and Barbers Point Naval Air Station lay halfway up it. The people were nice, lived simply, and the views were spectacular.

Janna would never fall in love with Hawaii—too far from home and her bluegrass roots and family, but she loved coming up to the isolated beach with the dog.

The walls of the valley were brightening considerably, massively dark to gray, to the dullest red, and then to crimson gold, a kaleidoscope turned slowly, swiveling the dawn down vertically. The valley soon bathed the first groups in light. The sun pushed the drizzle off somewhere, maybe westward into Xinjiang's desert, where the moisture would be appreciated.

Sergeant Wright's cold sun seemed to rise from the toes of your boots in the dark to twenty degrees above the horizon in five minutes or so.

"This is the way the world began," I thought . . . "but probably not how it will end." The jagged peaks on each side stood above us a mile or more, 20,000 feet and more. The visual impression in the relatively narrow valley was strangely like entering a narrow but long cathedral-like roofless building through a wide door. The building, in this case, was being backlighted by Kevin Wright's slowly rising "coldest sun he'd ever seen."

The gradual upsloping of the valley foreshortened it even more—a wide open dangerous highway of uneven terrain. Volkswagen-sized boulders were scattered to our front, diminishing to a narrow ribbon a few miles up the canyon. Definitely a steep uphill walk for a few miles. I dreaded the climb over the boulders, but Colonel Neng insisted it was the easiest and safest, if longest, route. Undoubtedly words that he'd been prerecorded with from the suits who looked at the maps in Lhasa, but not what he'd experienced the previous year when he'd made the initial recovery.

"Remind our guys when you link up with them if there's any 'drama' at the crash site let Colonel Man and Jon handle it—that's their bailiwick and the Chinese are in overall charge of everything but the remains," I told Kevin Wright, struggling into his life-saving backpack, loaded with medical gear.

"They know that already, but I'll remind them."

"Well, good luck, chief medic."

"No, Sir. I think from now on I'm the badass Special Forces NCO."

"That'll work, too," I chuckled. "OK, let's link up and go; you get with Man and I'll find my guys."

Colonel Neng, Mr. Luo, three soldiers, and a sergeant with a radioman and I crossed the last rickety bridge and started walking. After an hour we were still only halfway to the boulder field, but they had grown from Volkswagens into Mack trucks. Also, the gradual slope had been an upward runway that was deceptive; it strained you from the back of your heel to the base of your neck.

A rising wind brought cold rain mixed with sleet that came right down the valley into our faces, but despite that, I was bathed in sweat under my rain gear. I caught up with Colonel Neng and his radio team in the shelter of the first large boulder; he was smoking a cigarette and speaking into his radio. Mr. Luo was putting a sweater he'd worn back into his pack. I drank some water and asked him how far up to the crash site.

"Once we get over these difficult boulders, perhaps a mile," Luo translated.

"How far do these boulders go?"

He and Colonel Neng discussed it for a moment, and he replied, "Maybe a half mile, but maybe further."

I stood back and looked at the top of the huge rock. Maybe twenty feet up, maybe more. Colonel Luo nodded to two infantrymen and motioned up with his chin. One formed a hand stirrup and the other clambered into it; the soldier on the bottom lifted him until he could get a hand purchase. He clawed his way up with his feet, his AK-74 sliding against the rock face as he pulled himself up. He knelt on a narrow ledge and reached down for his buddy, pulling him up until he could get a grasp.

The radio team was next; the sergeant tied a rope from the radio onto his web harness, and the radio man repeated the stirrup process, then peeled the radio off and attached his rifle to the rope now up on the rock with the sergeant. I thought he was a conscript from some metropolis in mainland China—the mountain troops rarely even set their rifles down.

The NCO pulled both radio and rifle up as gingerly as he could but they were still clattering and bouncing off the rock. Then I went up, grunting, the stirrup man staggered a little with my 215 pounds, spread unevenly over my six-three frame. I found a handhold and scrambled up to flop down by Colonel Neng, who was on one knee, fumbling out another cigarette. He offered me one with a grin, and I replied "xie xie, no . . . filthy habit." Since our translator was on the ground, he merely grinned wider.

I stood and looked around, wondering how I was going to get down. Ahead of us up the canyon the boulders appeared to be an unending stream of irregular-shaped two-story houses. The sleety rain had stopped again, but a cold wind was weaving me around on the chunk of granite. Water had frozen in crevices in the rock, as expected. I began to have serious misgivings about this route, as Mr. Luo clambered up and sat down heavily.

He wasn't grinning; Colonel Neng was about to sit down over a shallow seam of rock that edged down with a little forgiveness, if you were careful. One of the soldiers was edging down the seam gripping the surface with both gloved hands and placing his feet down, one at a time. I wondered about the hand-stirrup soldier who was the last man. I turned around and saw him free climbing the surface like Spider-Man. So that was one of the real mountain troops, I thought. He moved quickly and decisively.

His shirt had been tied around his middle and his long-sleeved undershirt's sleeves were pushed up to his muscular biceps. His rifle was lashed over his pack, its short barrel poked horizontally over his back. Soon he popped up over the top and surveyed the rocky scene ahead of us. He walked over and saluted us with a grin.

If he was winded after that fast, grueling climb, I couldn't detect it. He and Colonel Neng chatted a minute, pointing to certain features on the descent to the ground. Colonel Neng and he exchanged salutes again and Neng clapped him on the back. Then the soldier flew off the edge of the rock and landed on the face of the one below and in front of us, feet and both hands seeming to grip it like the geckos in Vietnam gripped the ceiling above my bunk. I gaped, unbelieving.

Colonel Neng and Luo gave appreciative chuckles and the soldier lifted one hand in the okay signal and slowly inched down to the fissure path. He was clearly a good soldier and experienced mountaineer; and the mutual respect Colonel Neng and he had was apparent.

Neng watched the soldier clamber safely to the ground and eased from the sitting position down until one boot was on the crevice, then he did a little butt scoot off, landing with the other foot and putting out both hands to break his fall. He picked his way down to the ground carefully, one hand never leaving the rock.

I stood looking down at the crevice seam, and being taller, stepped down with one foot and dragged my other foot down clumsily, one hand on the opposing rock face, working my way down to the ground. Luo followed me.

We repeated variations on this method three more times and the boulders still seemed to stretch on forever. On the ground once again, I suggested a little conference. My legs were vibrating like a tuning fork.

Luo, Neng, and I huddled from the wind in the rock's shelter. The soldiers sat in a cluster of other boulders, a few yards away. Some of them had their rations out and were nibbling on them in animated conversation. Break time.

I said, looking at my watch, "I think we need a safer and faster route. It's taken us nearly forty-five minutes to get this far and it appears as dangerous as any of the other two routes. We've edged closer to the west wall of the canyon. Perhaps we should get out of here and walk along it."

Luo translated all this as Colonel Neng leaned with his back behind the wall bent over and holding his knees. He grunted occasionally as Luo translated.

Then a spirited two-way conversation for a moment or two and Luo turned to me.

"The Foreign Office representative instructed Colonel Neng to take the safest route possible to ensure none of us leaders are injured."

Us, of course, probably meant me. I remembered the worried conversation about my safety with them. It was probably issued with the best intentions, but it was turning into a dangerous miscalculation.

"Perhaps it would be safer and faster for us to move to the canyon wall out of these boulders. The walking would certainly be faster and we could turn back into the valley once we get past them."

More conversation followed and Neng turned and called out for his men to join us. He instructed the communications NCO to seek a path out of the confining boulders into the east wall of the canyon, now some four hundred yards from us. Luo mentioned something to them about the avalanches; all eyes turned to the muscular young man who was obviously the mountain expert, and Luo leaned over and said something to Neng, who merely replied, "*hung hao.*" Very good.

He passed instructions to the sergeant; the sergeant said something to "Spidey" (I would love to remember the name of the soldier, but he would remain in my mind the rest of my life as *Spider-Man*, who led us safely out of the punishing boulders). Later Luo asked me about the sobriquet and I replied it was the name given to anybody who had superhuman strength and unquestioned knowledge about danger anywhere. He laughed and repeated it twice, delighted to log a new English word.

Spidey gestured to another soldier and they put their packs and weapons back over their shoulders and started to carefully pick a path through the boulders, sometimes hands out and touching boulders on either side of them for balance. We followed carefully, after the radio team, followed by Colonel Neng, Luo, and two soldiers and I "protecting" us in the rear.

Thirty minutes later we were out of the boulders, trudging upward toward the others, still a mile away from the crash site, mindful of avalanches and listening for the distinctive warning sound of them coming down to bury you forever in a Himalayan valley. Now, as we approached within shouting distance, soldiers, porters, Chinese, and Tibetans seemed to emerge from the glacier, walking down the glissading snowpack from the top of it.

The night before, we had identified six or seven locations that had a high probability of remains based on terrain. Our estimation was they'd be in the snowy path of the avalanche of the glacier coming apart.

Man, Aliosi, and Wright greeted us. They had found remains—many remains. The Tibetans scurried, pulling our guys toward remains and pointing them out but not getting too near them. Some remains were still shrouded in faded flight-suit apparel. Sergeant Bradford and Antal together with some soldiers and packers were working the west side of the canyon. Their routes had been safe and faster, and they all had found remains, thanks primarily to Sherap. He had guided them through the deep, life-taking crevasses, pointing them out with his walking staff and probing carefully, always in the dangerous lead of their column. They had walked down the avalanche pass, boots barely breaking through the crusty snow.

"Sergeant Wright and Greg have been talking about the remains; we probably ought to think about how to get them back down to Yigon."

"Yeah, we need to get them down and get them locked up and maybe find some ice. They'll still have to go through customs in Beijing before we load the transfer cases, and I imagine some of them are getting soft," I answered.

"Yeti suggested we run them back to the grazing area and put them on a couple of packhorses. We can go straight down the pack trail and get there pretty fast." Greg added.

"How long before we've covered the whole area?"

"We've still got this area that goes almost back to the boulders," Wright replied. "About a three-hundred-yard rectangle and I'd guess there'd be quite a few in there. It's a pretty steep downslope."

"We need to get those remains back as quickly as we can to Lhasa, then plan for the movement from Beijing back to Hawaii, I guess. Apart from a few instances in Vietnam I'd rather forget, I don't have any experience with fresh remains, or bodies, other than what I picked up in Lhasa with preservative powder."

"Me either," Wright replied. Jon and Greg shook their heads, "no," maybe even "no way."

But then Sergeant Wright continued, "I saw some larger remains where the flesh just kind of slid off and I remember Pete talking to a couple of anthros about the solid content and skin "slewing" or maybe its spelled 'sloughing'"

Jon and Greg were staring a little open-mouthed, but by now we'd seen a plethora of remains, although no semicomplete set like we'd seen in Lhasa the year before. I went through the ancient remains/small fragments explanation again, but they'd understood it before we started.

"Yes, he said essentially the same thing to the Chinese scientists when we were here last year. That's why he put that grayish-white preservative powder on them."

I looked at the sky, probably two hours before we needed to get out of there and make it back to our laager area, I estimated, thinking about an hour to get out and off the glacier to at least safer, level ground. Plus the entire team would be pretty tired by then.

"OK, I'll go link up with Antal and Bradford and we'll get their guys back to link up with the rest."

Sergeant Wright stood on a rock and gave out a piercing whistle (Sergeant Wright had briefed our guys on the necessity of not yelling in the valley, or creating undue noise because of the avalanche danger), then circled his arms in the air, meaning "link up," and as soon as I started toward them they began moving quickly downslope toward me, the remains bagged and carried by them and the PLA soldiers. The Tibetans formed a loose line behind them, pretty much following single file. When we'd formed up and cached the remains, we moved in a long skirmish line toward the boulders, the two sergeants on either end keeping the lines' ends curled up.

The Tibetans immediately pointed out pockets of uniform remnants, and the PLA soldiers started picking them up and placing them in the bags again, dropping them as they filled, leaving a Tibetan standing by to keep an eye on them. In about an hour we'd thoroughly searched the area, filling a few more bags. It seemed like these uniform fragments were a little more faded, had probably been there longer than the ones farther up the valley.

We took a team picture, almost complete except for the wranglers back at the pack camp. The interpreter told them the Tibetans didn't want to touch them. I found a small gauge, still preserved and compact enough to fit in my pack. Later I discovered it was an oxygen regulating gauge. I had it mounted on a plaque and gave it to Mike Stepanovich. A personnel parachute's familiar D-ring pull handle went to Carl Petrella. Yeti appeared and confirmed the information about the Tibetans and the remains. "Religion and customs," he shrugged. We continued the search and found more parts of the aircraft, and more remains, which our sergeants packed carefully.

By late afternoon we had picked up the rest of the scattered remains, and facing a long slog back to base camp, we reluctantly left the valley; there were no more remains we could find. All of us were elated and tired but saddened by the circumstances of the crash.

As we were leaving, the skies partially cleared as we started to file out of the little valley. We were all, Tibetans, Chinese, and Americans, physically and emotionally drained as we turned up the slide leading over the glacier; a route the first group had determined to be relatively safe and easier passage than our boulder-strewn route from earlier that morning. Sherap had performed his work well, leading them safely through the yawning crevasses. This time we walked back in the melting, muddy footprints they'd come in on, then skirted the danger zone of crevasses carefully. Sherap furnished a soft, melodious accounting of the dangers all along the route occasionally tracing a path up a wall to an overhang with his walking stick.

Greg Man was in his battle dress uniform (BDU), the distinctive senior parachutist's badge depicting a parachute with a star over the top, over his breast pocket. The equally distinctive insignia of a single leaf identifying him as a lieutenant colonel, United States Army, was on his collar. He had hesitatingly asked if he could wear it for the recovery, knowing that we traditionally wore civilian clothes in Indochina and other locations. I told him if we had brought ours, we certainly would have worn them.

I was walking with Colonel Neng, Yeti, and Sherap, with a couple of PLA soldiers leading and two more behind us, AK-74s dangled over their chests in case some border-disputing Indian soldiers showed up.

Jon and Sergeants Bradford and Antal had left with the remains an hour before, packing them out themselves with a single packhorse and Tibetan wrangler, they had left on foot with the remains packed in duffle bags, all three humping them back to the horse and wrangler and then headed back to the grazing area and the main party. They spent the night with heads on packsaddles and under Tibetan blankets. They made it back to Yigon the next day, moving quickly down the pack trail.

The sun had warmed the valley and the clouds were breaking up.

Colonel Neng stopped us and pointed back up the valley, and as the overcast gradually came apart, a brilliant rainbow was visible over the peaks of the far mountains and disappearing beyond the glacier. it appeared to end right over the icy path the wrecked aircraft and crew had taken as the plane was gradually pushed into the valley, probably breaking up further and strewing its precious cargo into the open.

Colonel Neng said a few words and Yeti translated: "that is a good omen for our comrades who died and your journey back to America." We continued on to the base camp, but we dropped behind the rest of the moving mass of soldiers, packers, and Chinese command group.

Mr. Luo for some reason decided it was time for pistol practice. We stopped to fill our canteens and he pulled a small Russian Makarov pistol from his pack. He aimed at a rock in the water about twenty feet out and hit low on one side. He fired again and missed, then handed the little handgun to me.

"Now you."

"Mr. Luo, I'm a very poor shot with a pistol."

He motioned me to shoot, waving both hands at me. I did. The shot sailed off somewhere unknown. I carefully passed it back to him.

"Got him, first shot," I proclaimed.

He looked at me questioningly.

"That camel I was shooting at. In Xinjiang."

"Ho Ho! Xinjiang is almost a thousand miles from us."

"Well, I had to hold over a little bit." Luo smiled politely, but obviously didn't get it. He squeezed off the last of the magazine rapid fire, splashing water and boulders. The Tibetans and soldiers looked on amused.

"I hope that won't trigger an avalanche," I said.

It didn't; we limped back to camp, elated, and exhausted.

Jon, Sergeants' Antal and Bradford, and a couple of Tibetan guides and horses took the remains back down to Yigon ahead of us and moving quickly, where a cold dark room was available.

The rest of us also took the pack train route back, and we found it much easier, but longer. We didn't tackle the narrow ledge again, to everyone's relief. The rest of the trip was anticlimactic and basically an armed camping trip, in spectacular scenery, punctuated with another spectacular avalanche for a soundtrack.

We had a small ceremony in Yigon when we returned. There were more speeches and Jon Aliosi, Greg Man, and I thanked our hosts for their great work and for keeping us all safe; we couldn't have been more sincere. I gave my civilian binoculars to Colonel Neng, who like us, was ready to go home.

We returned to Lhasa two days later, spending a long day in Yigon photographing the remains and carefully listing what they were and where they were located on the valley sketch, although there were only one or two flesh colored long bones as I remember. Plus the dentition. Dentitions are good; as are single teeth, as long as there are dental records present. The remains were secured in transfer cases. The days and nights were much colder, and a keening wind blistered the steppes and mountains. I saw horsemen, both man and mount, with backs to the wind, reminding me of fleeting visions of New Mexico winters. The riders hunched their heads down in the billowing, long woolen jackets when a gust struck them, and we progressed slowly but steadily back toward Lhasa with an occasional rockslide halt. We traveled under the cold sun, dodging potholes when we could, all bouncing off the inside roof of the car when we couldn't.

When we parted in Lhasa I thanked Mr. Bai and shook Jigme's hand, surreptitiously passing him an American twenty dollar bill wrapped around by some Chinese ren-min. He gave me a crushing bear hug. Mr. Bai took a snapshot of us both grinning into the camera.

The afternoon we returned I ran into our three NCOs in the courtyard of the Hard Yak café. They were sitting there with three Tibetans and one Chinese woman.

The Tibetan women were outdoors healthy, dressed in their long Tibetan skirts and adorned with plenty of silver jewelry. The Chinese woman was a little older and smartly dressed in a business suit. They were, Kevin Wright explained, high school teachers, and the woman was their "senior supervisor."

She spoke excellent English and the three younger Tibetan teachers spoke some, all eagerly practicing with the sun-tanned American soldiers.

Antal and Wright were enjoying a Heineken and Bradford sipped his cola. It was a pleasant Sunday afternoon in Lhasa, Tibet, under a now warm and friendly sun. We all laughed and talked, my Chinese sending our newfound companions into paroxysms of giggling, and the supervisor wiping tears from her eyes then repeating it like the teacher she was, drawing the tone marks in the air.

Soon I bade them farewell and made my way to the Jokhang again. I wanted to see it one more time; now I thought I could appreciate it even more. I did, and maybe understood a little better, also.

CHAPTER 26

Bringing Them to Life

Alexandria, Virginia; the annual Hump Pilots Association meeting in the new millennium and I was back in the China business as a civilian contractor China specialist for Army International Affairs. December 1997 wound up my thirty-two-plus years of military service when I retired. It was my MRD, Mandatory Retirement Date—thirty years commissioned service. As much as I loved it, that was enough. I reminded myself, *this is a young man's game*.

I worked in the Army Deputy Chief of Staff for Operations directorate, DCSOPS, and pronounced "dess-ops." My boss was a young infantry colonel, and we both worked, up the chain, for General Eric Shinseki, the chief of staff, the senior Army leader, and member of the Joint Chiefs of Staff.

Both he and his four-star deputy, Jack Keane, were tough, no-nonsense officers. General Shinseki and I were both majors in the Third Armored Cavalry Regiment two decades previously; I had decided with no guilt-ridden conscience to forego an assignment there in uniform years ago, despite the careerists' good advice. I was finally in the heart of it, albeit as a civilian. I liked it. I worked with young majors and lieutenant colonels, men and women, who had lived and worked in the regions and languages they studied. They might be asked to invade a country, or conversely, eject invaders some day, as virtually all of them did in Kuwait. Most likely they'd be assistant military attachés or possibly even Defense attachés, most of whom were Foreign Area Officers. Their children had taught their counterparts' children to speak English and vice-versa.

They had served in all areas of the world, including a Hispanic captain in Korea in 1986–87, a company commander in the tank battalion I commanded in Korea who was now a colonel headed for Lima, Peru, to be the Defense attaché.

But that was my day job. My night job was finding out more about that crew of young men in the pictures; men who had spent a long time in the Himalayas.

A trio of WACS in the distinctive brown uniforms and 1940s hairstyles belted out the "Boogie Woogie Bugle Boy of Company B" to the accompaniment of a zoot-suited ten-piece band. They were the Andrews Sisters incarnate; the band was period Benny Goodman, and America was still able to have a little fun despite the rigors of World War II.

On the dance floor, senior citizens, still athletic and enjoying the golden years, were dancing, and one athletic older couple were jitterbugging. My wife jitterbugged and I "arthritic bugged" as she described it to our neighbors in Clarendon, Virginia.

It was the annual meeting of the Hump Pilots' Association (HPA), an organization started after the war. Unlike the Veterans of Foreign Wars and the American Legion, the HPA was organized by a few pilots in 1946, meeting in one of their basements then mushrooming over the years.

It gave the Hump veterans a lodestone to remember their service and their buddies. The good things about the China Burma India theater were burnished, and the bad things were either laughed about or heads were shaken grimly, remembering engine fires or ice banging into the fuselage as it was flung from thawing propellers squirted by alcohol. Jan Thies, the executive secretary administrative sparkplug of the HPA had kindly seated us at the Jorhat table, with six other gentlemen and two wives. All had dodged the infirmities of advanced age with that old homegrown remedy, activity—both physical and mental. Jan kept the organization running, serving in a combination role of adjutant, first sergeant, and Mother Teresa of the organization.

They had endured the worst conditions in a mission they were barely trained for and relied on their wits instead of absent experience in the worst weather and most unforgiving terrain on earth. They also, like soldiers had done for millenniums, relied on each other.

The guy in the right or left seat of the airplane, whether it was a cargo C-47, C-46, C-87, or C-54, had endured and survived. Radio operators and loadmasters had pried cargo doors open in typhoon freezing rain at higher altitudes (pilots learned that each thousand feet of altitude decreased temperatures about two degrees Fahrenheit). They upended precious drums of aviation fuel, which tumbled into jungled mountains to lighten loads—and prevent their deaths. They had learned and skirted danger when they could, faced it when they couldn't.

They talked of the real business of flying—thousands of hours of boredom, seconds of stark terror. They also had prospered and mostly retired successfully. The lessons you learn in the Himalayas when your plane is on fire and falling are enduring. Now they looked at us curiously. My nametag had my name and Janna's and the short notation: WRITER, writing a book about the HUMP."

I told them the complete story. I started with the beginning, September 1993, when a Tibetan hunter stumbled onto the crash and some remains, right on through the September 1994 recovery and the subsequent identifications. The article in the May 1998 issue of *Smithsonian Air and Space Magazine* started it all. None of them had read it.

"Do any of you recognize these guys?" I asked, passing the photograph to the couple on my right when the band and singers had taken a break.

The men and their wives all gathered around and looked over the seated couple's shoulders; they passed the photos around. One gray-haired ex-pilot put his finger down on Ramos's picture; he thought he might have remembered seeing him but couldn't remember any details, and he was sure he'd never flown with him. It might be a logbook experience for some of the other pilots and copilots, though. There were pictures and locations for hundreds of them in the three large volumes of the Hump Pilots' Association book, *China Airlift*. But I could find no photos or bios of these five men.

Lanier never mentioned any crewmembers in his logbooks that Bill and Diane Lanier had provided, just weather, destinations, and any troubles or significant incidents—*bomb hung up at Dili*, for example, in Australia. It was all about flying and bombing.

Or, *he tried to kill us both . . .* at Pyote.

The Jorhat crews continued, "Basically we were poorly paid airline pilots sleeping under mosquito nets in a grass covered shack. We came in late at night or early mornings and quietly had a drink—or several—and went to sleep under the nets," one of them remarked.

"Most of the other crews were gone; flying or laying around in their underwear in the sun or shade, waiting to fly."

After all, we all conceded, this had all occurred sixty years ago. "Where did all that time go?" one pilot remarked plaintively. "You didn't spend it inside a crashed plane on a glacier," another observed. The other pilots and wives nodded somberly.

By then, thanks to the editor at *Smithsonian Air and Space Magazine*, I had good accounts on Frank Ramos, the copilot, from his widow, Doris Stepanovich. She remarried a CBI veteran and officer, but not a pilot, and enjoyed a long and happy life with him until he passed away in 1983. She had much to remember of the CBI and the Hump.

All the crewmember relatives that had been present at the Arlington burial of the group remains had bonded and linked for the rest of their lives. Carl Petrella had established himself and his creds by providing composite photographs of the entire crew on a single tintype page, some formal commissioning or certification photos (Lanier and Ramos), the former in helmet and pilots' high-altitude garb (expected) and Ramos, handsome in his uniform and wings, a slight smile on his face anticipating a great postwar future with his wife and infant son, and maybe a sister or two or a brother for young Michael.

Joe and Beebe were snapped almost paparazzi style, work and flying lining their faces. Giacalone was pictured in uniform with his mother, almost holding on to her son. She didn't want to lose the last one.

The CBI twice-widowed Doris's son, Michael, born just a few months before Frank disappeared with the crew, never knew his biological father. He grew up with a loving, caring stepfather. He told me that he'd "rarely thought of his actual father; now I can hardly think of anything else."[1]

Now he could hardly think of anything else, as he looked over the oxygen meter, delighted and overjoyed to touch a piece his real father might have tapped with his finger. Doris thought her second husband would also be overjoyed at the news of Frank Ramos's recovery and identification. He, like Frank, was a very good man.[2]

By March 2002, I was also compiling Joseph Petrella's history from the excellent files of Carl Petrella, and Janna and I flew to New Jersey to see him and his wife.

They were both lovely people, his wife maybe ten years younger than he. Carl was as even tempered and quiet as he was volatile and enthusiastic. He had been a senior figure in the transportation department of New Jersey and knew everybody. He reminded me of a Tony Soprano without the homicidal instincts.

He insisted we spend the night with them. He'd made arrangements for the Belleplain VFW Post to be open the next morning at 9 a.m. for our "tour." I raised my eyebrows since most of experience with VFW posts was evening openings for meetings and the bar. He winked and said, "I contribute heavily."

The commander of the VFW post met us at the door. He greeted Carl warmly; Carl was probably the biggest supporter of his post, and they were obviously good friends as well. We took a tour of his neatly arranged facility, with meeting rooms and lists of projects for Veterans framed neatly on the wall.

Their members ranged from grizzled World War II vets to those of the most recent conflicts—Vietnam provided the bulk of them, affluent citizens and men now in retirement who could pursue their projects with more time. There was also representation from veterans of Desert Storm and the peace-keeping efforts in the Balkans and Sinai.

All of us opined that, unfortunately, there would be veterans from future conflicts; the world was becoming a rougher neighborhood all the time.

We passed into a tastefully decorated room with hushed lighting and blown-up photographs of three fallen warriors. One of them was Corporal Joseph Petrella, US Army Air Force, lost in the CBI on January 31, 1944.

Artifacts from his military life were laid out in a glass case with other photographs of him during his tour at Jorhat, India. He had served in the Seventy-Seventh Airlift Squadron, Twenty-Second Air Transport Group, and after the disestablishment of these units, formed new ones in the strange system the Army used in these matters. His new unit became simply Base Unit 1335 of the India China Wing, Airlift Transport Command. Base Unit 1335 was Jorhat's nom de guerre. The artifacts, uniform pieces, and personal items were laid out neatly in the case.

I thought, sadly, some friend had inventoried these items carefully in Joe's *basha* to be sent through the military process with a letter from the personnel office. The bureaucratic language in the accompanying letter reminded the family that these were to be safeguarded by them for return to the missing person if he returned. They weren't to assume ownership of them anytime in the foreseeable future.

The future arrived in 1946, when a board of officers met in India and reviewed the facts and the work done by the Search and Rescue unit and the graves registration personnel. Major Francis M. McCullar, an infantry officer and president of the board, members Captain Lester E. Barlow, also an infantryman, and Captain Harry L. Bowen, a member of the Adjutant General's Corps, sadly concluded the men were now dead and forwarded their recommendations to Washington, where they were rarely contested.

Off the scope, without a trace. Now officially Killed in Action—Body not Recovered. KIA-BNR. Now Unaccounted For in the new lexicon.

One of Petrella's full little notebooks was also in the case, and I asked if I could look at it. The post commander obligingly opened the cabinet and gave it to me. I thumbed through it; it was, as I had imagined, finely detailed in the elegant cursive handwriting of yesteryear, with the date, type of aircraft, destinations, and the pilot's rank and name and time elapsed in the air. I especially noted the destinations and the pilots' ranks and names.

I did a quick double take and gasped; I read it again. On a date in September 1943, Petrella had been the RO on a C-47 flying a round robin trip from Jorhat to Sookerating to Chabua and back to Jorhat. Total flying time, 2 hours, 46 minutes.

The pilot was Second Lieutenant Graydon Spurgeon.

My mind reeled back to August 1970, and a hot day at Biggs Army Airfield, Fort Bliss, Texas, in El Paso. Retired Lieutenant Colonel Graydon Spurgeon, US Air Force, squatted twenty yards away from me smoking an unfiltered Camel. Despite the heat he wore a battered leather flying jacket with the CBI patch faded of almost all color over one breast. An equally faded leather nametag with his name and rank was under a faded silver outline of the wings with wreath of a command pilot in the US Air Force sewn over the other breast.

His hair was springy white and his face held the sun lines burned in well through two years in the air, staring out of a cockpit's left seat. He was lean and supple as a reed. He stood, field stripped the butt military style, and let the hot wind take it away.

I was about to get some more professional advanced flight instruction. I finished checking the fuel in the small bulb of the Beech Musketeer for the dreaded presence of water (an unlikely event in El Paso in peak summer).

"Why the big hurry for your commercial and instrument check ride?" he asked.

"My vacation's over; I'm reporting back to active duty in just over a month."

"Were you a helicopter-type fellar' in the Army?"

"Nope, just a mud dauber, goin' back to Vietnam."

"Vietnam? Thought you'd already been."

"I guess I get to go back; I don't mind."

He sighed, "Well, nothing but Japs there when I was flying in the CBI."

He told me he flew the Hump once upon a time when I queried him about the patch.

"Mostly C-46s, but a few times in a C-47, then I transitioned to the C-54. Nice airplane, a little short on service ceiling, but comfortable, fast, and easy to fly. We flew a lot of VIPs from Washington in them."

"Now I fly that tired DC-4 over there for the El Paso vacation club, mostly to Mexico full of fisherman; basically the same airplane with airline seats instead of cargo space; but it's still a good old airplane. And I get to go along free, long as I fly the airplane."

Soon we were in the air, and he smoothly demonstrated a maneuver known as "pylon eights," an advanced maneuver that I would have to demonstrate on the commercial flight examination. If successfully flown it demonstrated I could fly the airplane in a constantly moving figure eight around two towers while passing through the same points and crossing the midpoint at the same altitude. I would have to judge the wind's effect on the maneuver and defeat its efforts to move the aircraft off course.

Spurgeon was the consummate airman, and he looked the part. Even better, he was a superb instructor and was constantly encouraging, giving helpful tips. I had some trouble initially slowing or stopping the turn; this always spoiled the exit—not coming out through the entry point I came in at the same altitude, and location. I was always at a different altitude and sloppily blown downwind, missing the location marker on the upwind side of midpoint to gauge the wind on the ground.

He demonstrated it flying himself from the right seat—the instructors' seat, multiple times, rolling into the turn and constantly turning, climbing up and floating down, judging the effects of the wind on his track and adjusting continuously, effortlessly, then flying out of the maneuver, repeating it the other way. From above, the plane's track would appear as the same maneuver, superimposed over the original one.

"Remember there are two moving forces here, the airplane and the wind. So pick your stationary points carefully. Spread your pylons farther apart and pick a distinctive spot midway through it, like that big house below with the red roof and the small lake behind it. You should pass through that point in your entry and exit of the maneuver, at the same altitude and in level flight. The only time you're not climbing, descending, and turning is when you come in or out over that same point."

He demonstrated halfway through it, rolling out right over the house, and handed over the controls to me.

"You've got the controls," he said, the instructor's mantra.

"I've got the controls," I echoed, the student's response. I finished the second eight and rolled out level five or six hundred yards east of the house.

"You lost your center point when you rolled out downwind; don't forget to check the wind in all quadrants. Best indicator is smoke, but use trees, ripples on the lake, whatever you can get."

I tried it again. Better. I was sharpening my skills.

His easygoing manner moved me swiftly through the syllabus, and a few weeks later I passed both the commercial and instrument check rides and was certified to fly as a commercial pilot with an instrument rating, in an Airplane, Single-engine, Land. Then I left for Fort Bragg, North Carolina, for two months' training and returned to Fort Bliss for eight weeks training in the Vietnamese language. During that time Son Tay raiders crashed into the prison camp practically in Hanoi's backyard. After that I headed back to Vietnam.

I heard Spurgeon speaking with just a hint of Missouri twang; I was still in the skies of West Texas, the reliable little Musketeer's engine humming.

"You okay, Colonel Jordan?" the genial post commander asked, concernedly, back in the present time.

Joe had flown with the same pilot I had flown with, nearly twenty-five years later, I explained, and both his and Carl's eyes widened. "That's kind of spooky," the post commander remarked.

Indeed it was.

After we gracefully slid out of the invitation to spend the night at their home (with his wife tempering his argument) my wife and I discussed things in the motel.

I told her about the Spurgeon incident. When I finished, she said, "That's kind of spooky." I laughed.

"That was the VFW's reaction, also."

But I agreed; just some kind of a circle closing, I thought.

Janna loved and was devoted to her parents. Her dad, like most citizens in those years, went into the Army and fought with the Second Infantry Division as a basic infantry soldier—a rifleman from the beaches of Normandy, the Battle of the Bulge, and into Czechoslovakia when the war in the European theater ended. He was a good soldier, at the end trekking through Europe, finally as a hardened sergeant of infantry. Then the famed Indianhead Second Division received word they were slated, along with hundreds of thousands of other soldiers, to take a deep breath and prepare for the invasion of Japan.

Later I would serve twice in the same division—in Korea, this time—commanding a Cavalry Troop and a Tank Battalion. It was and is a great unit to soldier in.

Years later, when we were both decades beyond our combat time, Janna's dad confided to me, "you know, I was sorry to see all those poor people who had nothing to do with Pearl Harbor killed by the two bombs, but I sure didn't want to go to Japan. I knew if I went, I'd be killed. I'd used up all my luck in France, Belgium, and Czechoslovakia."

But he never bought a Japanese car; and he gave me a memory of that conflict; a Walther .32 automatic, taken from a "German gentleman" captured somewhere, Belgium, Germany or maybe even Czechoslovakia. Everything kind of ran together and he wasn't sure. Like me and Vietnam, the event dimmed, but the memories did not.

I presented all this information to the former Hump pilots that night, and added I needed to know where the other three men had trained, spent their stateside time, and what skills they acquired and how they got them.

In the late 1990s the internet was coming online, but it certainly wasn't as ubiquitous as it is now, and nobody could get information from something they carried in their pocket—the advanced technology cell phone. I explained that I'd called the National Archives, then had been directed to the service archives in St. Louis, but a disastrous fire had wiped out thousands of military personnel records in the St. Louis National Records Center. Including all five of C-87 862's crew and a great portion of every serviceman's military records who'd served between World War I and 1960.

Back at the Hump Pilots' reunion there was various head scratching, but other than going to the surviving relatives nobody had any good advice, as much as we all discussed it. They, as pilots, had all trained at different bases and they assumed schools for radio operators and flight engineers/loadmasters were similarly scattered around the United States.

These pilots all served in the 1943–44 period of "no weather over the Hump" and night flying that Colonel Tom Hardin, commander of the Eastern Sector of the India China Wing mandated. I asked them what were the biggest impediments they experienced during their time in the theater; they all agreed weather, inexperience, unreliable navigation aids, and a few other "nuisances."

That was probably the answer sixty years later to a much older pilot like Graydon Spurgeon or John Nelson; while they were young men flying the HUMP their "nuisances" would have been much more serious.

We shared a final drink as we closed the evening out. My last question to them was, "Did anything ease your concerns while you were in the CBI? If so what was it? Also, what was the most important improvement they saw in their flying tours in the CBI?"

The answer was universal from all of them: Search and Rescue.

The band started back up and Janna and I bade them farewell before "thanks for your service" became a welcome refrain to veterans of any conflict.

"You gentlemen and ladies stay safe, and remember 'needle, ball and airspeed,' the old flying axiom my dad had taught me and countless others —stay straight and level and don't fall out of the sky."

"Always," a couple of them replied, grinning. But I was thinking "search and rescue" as we walked out. "That Others May Live."

When Lieutenant Carter Harman landed his helicopter behind Japanese lines in Burma on April 25–26, 1944, he probably didn't realize his was the first helicopter rescue in history.[3]

A First Air Commando sergeant pilot, Ed "Murphy" Hladovcak had crash-landed his L-1 aircraft with three wounded British soldiers on board, and Harman was making the last of four pickups. Just as Harmon was straining his YR-4 helicopter recovering the fourth man, khaki-clad soldiers burst from the jungle. Harmon thanked his lucky stars but later discovered these were Allied soldiers who had hacked and hiked a land route to the three wounded Brits and Hladovcak.

Like many things that occurred on the Hump, things seemingly shaped and formed themselves out of requirements un-forecast and subsequently modified and refined until they worked. It was apparent that the Hump would be a junkyard of crashed airplanes (the "Aluminum Trail" would be a popular nickname, and also the name of a book self-published by the widow of a lost Hump airman. It contained the Missing Air Crew Reports of nearly all planes lost over the Hump and statistics for crashes and rescues. As accurate as any, probably).

Pilots, crews, and passengers bailing out would need rescuing. As early as 1943, the Air Transport Command alerted numerous missionaries in Burma and China, many of them American, to the probability and solicited their help. In addition, remote reaches of Burma were usually administered by young colonial officers from Britain's Foreign Office, operating as bachelors from remote outposts. They were invaluable; most could speak the local languages. The best assets were the natives. They were ubiquitous both in Burma and China, with many minority tribes that were naturally hill men dotting the jungled mountains of Burma and southern China.

Contrary to the warning about headhunting voiced in many hastily written survival pamphlets, the Naga's took many US and allied airmen to safety.

The overall mission for recovery of lost airmen and other servicemen in the CBI fell to the Office of Strategic Services (OSS), in this case, Detachment 101, under the leadership of Captain William R. Peers, US Army, a notable unconventional warfare expert with a keen sense of intelligence and clandestine operations.[4]

Detachment 101, from its British base at Fort Hertz, picked targets for the Tenth Air Force, furnished real-time intelligence on Japanese deployments and installations, and was responsible for over five hundred rescues of downed airmen and other CBI personnel. Together with the British Force 136, who provided radios and training for British citizens and subjects, they proved to be an active, effective force.

Force 136 recruited British nationals, colonials, and friendly indigenous peoples with longtime experience in Burma and knowledge of the terrain and languages as well as the customs of the tribes and clans; they used these recruitments to carry out their surreptitious missions and rescues. Peers's group of OSS operatives, less than one hundred uniformed Americans, were training and leading tribal groups in both Burma and China, especially the Kachins, as guerrillas.

Crews and individuals that who joined the "Caterpillar Club"—bailed out of a stricken aircraft, were a poignant concern to the leadership on the Hump and in other aerial units scattered around the CBI. Pilots and copilots in particular had excessive stresses placed on them due to the nature of their flying. The reappearance of a crew or remnants of a crew limping out of the jungle and mountains, bearded and emaciated after months of evading Japanese searchers, suffering wounds and injuries untreated, was joyous, but demoralizing—a visual reminder that this was the *best* that could happen in a bailout over the jungle.

In a constant and unvarying atmosphere of uncertain airplanes, undertrained crews, hundred-mile-an-hour siroccos of freezing winds overlaying trackless, deadly terrain, there were only two likely certainties—death or the inevitably of bailing out of your aircraft.[5]

Charismatic leadership in the form of the aggressive young captain, John Porter, nicknamed "Blackie," headed the first hastily organized rescue organization at Chabua. Porter stripped a B-25 down for speed and low and high-altitude searches for parachutes dotting trees or the smoke of a burning aircraft, and his organization sported C-47s with crews that might have come from the newly formed Combat Cargo organizations, expert at putting their planes into small fields to evacuate wounded.

Or unloading mules for transport, holding their breaths as they tramped through the straw put on the floor. Or dropping survival packages by parachute into tiny drop zones. Or wrestling heavy boxes of ammunition or mortars or howitzers out of the widened cargo doors. They had considerable expertise in supplying Wingate's Chindits and Merrill's Marauders with "door bundles"—kicked out or parachuted supplies of ammunition, water, and food.

There were a few light, single-engine planes that could use hacked out, short jungle airstrips to lift out one or two wounded. They were usually flown by skilled sergeant-pilots.

They also used that strange, clattering flying beast, the helicopter.

In August 1943, a new element was introduced when a C-46 carrying well-known journalist Eric Sevareid; twenty-five-year-old John Davies, Stilwell's foreign policy adviser; two senior nationalist China colonels; and others totaling eighteen passengers, developed engine problem and all had to jump from the stricken airplane. The copilot was the only fatality, but others were injured.

After one of "Blackie's Gang" located the crash and dropped supplies, another came over and three more parachutes blossomed. It was surgeon Lieutenant Colonel Don Flickinger and two more medical personnel. The wounded men were treated, the copilot was buried in a solemn ceremony, and a week and a half later a young British administrator walked in with a rescue party. These were the antecedents to the courageous PJs, the pararescue men who could parachute in or, more likely, go down a hoist to pick up wounded deep in enemy territory.

Blackie Porter was killed in December 1943, shot down by a Japanese fighter while he was en route to a rescue. Even his last act was heroic; to free his copilot, Second Lieutenant James F. Spain, who had hung up in the hatch trying to bail out. Porter untangled him and pushed him out. The copilot would be the only survivor.

But every rescued pilot and crew by a CH-53 Pave Low helicopter in Laos and Vietnam or later wars is a thankful nod to the heroism and innovations of Captain Blackie Porter, Lieutenant Colonel Don Flickinger, and Lieutenant Diebold of the OSS.

Another Hump commander, Major General William H. Tunner, brought the Hump into the era of "big business," even when it was almost overcome by events in China as America realized the aerial route "bang" wasn't worth the Chinese "buck."

Nonetheless, his command attention to rescue continued to be a key improvement in crew survivability and morale, especially on a chaotic night in January 1945, when planes fell out of the sky all over the Hump, just a year after Fulton and Frank pushed the throttles and prop controls forward and disappeared.

"Black Friday" of January 6, 1945, a year after 862 went off the scope, would end many of the innovations that General Tom Hardin decreed—

after this, there "*would* be weather over the HUMP." Air Transport Command would keep planes on the ground in dangerous weather. Pilots could make weather decisions themselves, but they had to be justified. Reliable navigation aids and weather forecasting were also now in place, and General Tunner's round robin stations of aircraft maintenance, called Phase Line Maintenance for inspections and repairs, were keeping more, and safer, aircraft in the air.

He later would go on to lead airlift efforts in the Air Force, organizing and running the successful Berlin airlift in 1948. That long effort showed the Russians the Americans could overcome just about every obstacle they put on the board.

Blackie Porter's men were truly the "Knights Who Fell from the Sky."

CHAPTER 27

Sacred Searchers

Even before the war's end, different soldiers were fanning out all over the world. They scoured the hedge rows of France and the beaches of Normandy, following unit records of battles, advances—and servicemen who were unrecovered. They went to crash sites of the mighty Eighth Air Force and their fighter escorts that spun crazily to earth, canopies intact until they exploded in a fireball as they hit the earth.

Crash locations were carefully marked on wingmen's maps while they watched, horrifyingly pleading for the stricken pilot and crew to "GET OUT!" into their oxygen-masked microphones. They probed the earth of ground battles and firefights through France, Belgium, Germany, and the lines of retreat into Eastern Europe. These were men of the Quartermaster Corps, but they weren't logisticians—they were Graves Registration soldiers—officers, sergeants, and enlisted men who largely walked and cut trails through jungle or navigated trackless deserts.

They searched sweltering South America, especially the routes to and from Belem, Natal, Amapa, and the jungles and coast around Brazil with information on possible sites of disappearance. They braved the reaches of Kiska and Attu in the Aleutians, looking for the men who had not survived or been recovered from the vicious first northern Pacific clash with Japanese forces. They visited the sites of shallow-water shot-down aircraft and talked to hundreds of witnesses of crashes and battles, many visiting the sites of firefights and reporting apparent American dead lying unrecovered. They were the first investigative elements, like Needham's in the JTF–FA.

There was one poignant story of a B-17 lost with all aboard in the Mato Grosso in 1943. It took off from Parnamirim Field, Natal, Brazil, closest point to West Africa, and went "off the scope," mistakenly mixed in to the European losses administratively and historically for some reason. The

Army Air Force had assumed they were lost after coming to Europe.

Two years after the war some natives found the wreckage in almost impenetrable rain forest. An American graves registration team with native guides was ambushed en route to the crash by hostile natives, and only one survivor managed to stagger into a government outpost to relate the tale, one of Rick Huston's World War II history buffs told us.

The aircraft lay undisturbed for another near half century to be found again, by a unit of tough Brazilian Special Air Service soldiers, modeled on the famous British unit. They were training in the area. Cables flew between Brasilia and Foggy Bottom, and again, information traveled down through the Office of the Secretary of Defense; a CILHI team was designated to link up with the unit and recover the twice lost and found aircraft.

There were no Portuguese speakers in the unit but there was one team commanded by a Cuban, Captain Mario Garcia. Mario had extensive experience with the Eighty-Second Airborne Division, wore the badge of a Master Parachutist, Ranger, and the Air Assault badge, the iconic award of the 101st Air Airborne/Air Mobile Division. He was thoroughly familiar with rough surroundings that had to be supported by helicopter. He spoke native Cubano Spanish.

Three weeks after they'd been on site, I spent the night battling mosquitoes on a jungle airfield, in a bunk in the hangar with a Brazilian lieutenant colonel. He commanded the air unit supporting the SAS detachment. He also spoke no English.

That night we had dined in a run-down *bodega* with dirt floors in the little town. The setting reminded me of the bar scene in *Star Wars.* Garcia's driver/bodyguard ate with us, his American M-2 carbine draped over his lap. He and his commander wore their sidearms displayed in shoulder holsters.

At dawn two young pilots flew us out in a helicopter and descended into a cleared landing zone, rotors almost scraping the trees. They dropped me off and *el Comandante* circled the hole twice with the pilots and flew off.

I carried the sack of mail and inevitable cookies and melted chocolate my wife had received from the spouses of the team and spent a very enjoyable day watching and digging at the excavation, the SAS soldiers helping. Mario said there was rough communication with his Spanish but he was picking up a little Portuguese every day.

"Sir, a jaguar has been hanging around the camp at night. That's why you see a few guys carrying loaded M-2 carbines; so far it hasn't been a problem, but they make an eerie noise."

"Uh, they also have plenty of beer, and we've been having one or two a night with them; we've had no problem." he said somewhat sheepishly.

We never drank beer on a crash site, but this one was certainly different and had to be treated differently.

"Not a problem, Mario, as long as the troops don't get boisterous and out of hand, and then you know what'll happen . . ."

Mario and his sergeant stared expectantly.

"Jaguars will rip your flesh."

Mario laughed. "Yessir, and I know who the Jaguar will be."

"There 'tis," his sergeant nodded.

"Don't suppose they could spare a cold *Antarctica* tonight, do you . . . ?"

"If they can't you can have mine, Colonel," Mario's senior sergeant responded.

"Thank you, Sergeant. Appreciate it but don't think it'll be necessary. I see an SAS sergeant-major over there and I assume you have communicated with him."

"We *have* talked, Sir."

"Just don't trade him anything that's sensitive or isn't replaceable, the loser paying for it after a thorough report of survey, of course."

"Understand, Sir," they both said almost simultaneously.

"Good, I've got your mail in a large plastic bag in my green rucksack; have your mail guy grab it will you?"

"Also disperse the cookies and candy, before Godzilla ants find them."

And the beat went on. Ten men were identified as a group burial. World War II had a few more of its "off the scope" heroes returned to Arlington after a year or so at CILHI. There were no problems, and at the end I was long gone from it; there was a formal ceremony when the remains were brought out in American flagged-draped transfer cases. There were speeches made, both by Mario and Brazilian military and government leaders.

The translated speeches mentioned that the American military was intensely interested in returning their dead to their homeland. I read that and silently agreed with Mario's sergeant—there it is. The airmen went home; all were identified relatively quickly, and a lingering World War II mystery was solved with the layered tragedy of the searchers being lost.

By September 1945, planning that began well before the Japanese surrender crystallized immediately in all areas of the Pacific, initially with the intention of finishing their mission in September 1946, a highly optimistic goal. At the time, American missing numbered 5,700 individuals in the Pacific theater, a number that was absurdly low, by thousands, but they proceeded on, knowing full well that in actuality their efforts would go on for years.

American Graves Registration Services had separated from the wartime combat commands that managed them and now came under the overall purview of the Quartermaster General. Areas of high losses, like the Philippine Zone, had high missing numbers from such areas as Bataan and in the waters fringing the island. Japan and Korea were designated another zone as well as the Southwest Pacific, the area Fulton flew and fought in early in the war. Then there was the CBI.

> Searchers in the "HUMP" area were men imbued with the spirit of adventure. Few white men had ever penetrated this remote and little known region of the Himalayas and the men were often exposed to unforgettable experiences in the battles with the elements and contact with the natives. In fact, many of those recalled for redeployment felt reluctant to move to more familiar and civilized scenes.[1]

This infatuation may have worn off after a couple of mountain climbs in Naga land. Their searches in the Pacific would not—could not—be as extensive or as successful as those in the European theater, however. Asia was still largely an aerial and maritime theater, with vast reaches of the Pacific and the South China Sea/Indian Ocean area that served as aerial and naval battlefields. And graveyards.

The China Burma India theater was, as cheerily described by the graves registration history, almost forbiddingly wild and unknown. But they came anyway and ventured into the vast reaches of India, the dangerous mountains of Burma, and did the best they could along the Hump.

By November 1946, however, the American Graves Registration Service (AGRS) submitted a report that indicated that searches along the coastal regions of China were far more successful, with its infrastructure of better roads, services, and facilities. Ports helped enormously with resupply and communications, also, the populace had remained largely in place so there were better witnesses to losses and adequate labor pools for porters and guides.[2] Undoubtedly it was easier and more enabling to supply services and facilities. Unfortunately, most Americans weren't lost along coastal regions—but in triple canopy rain forests and icy, remote mountains.

In these wild reaches there was even a case of Americans still held in captivity, this time in the furthest reaches of Lolo Land. This situation was more suited to the Vietnam era of losses, and it was never widely publicized, but it inflamed the searchers' imagination no less than Vietnam losses would seize them in a later generation.

The event began in the summer of 1946 when a search team departed from Chungking and was soon waved down by a ragged farmer. He told a tale he heard of Americans being held by people to the northwest who were often referred to as "Lolos." He admitted this was hearsay information—a term we became quite familiar with four decades later in Vietnam, Laos, and Cambodia; he had not personally seen the Americans or their aircraft.

The Americans were intrigued, however, and after talking to several other Chinese in the area, decided to investigate further. Another member of the search team was asked to check with the local priest, Monsignor Stanislaus Baudry, Bishop of Hsichang, who had been in the area for over thirty years. The bishop said he'd also heard rumors of five Americans held by the Lolo who allegedly were going to be sold into slavery. He'd even notified the American ambassador and asked permission to investigate. He'd received no reply and let the matter drop, though keeping his eyes and ears open.

A special graves registration team was organized under the direction of Lieutenant Colonel W. H. Wurzler, who worked under Colonel Charles F. Kearney, chief of the China Zone. The operation was considered sensitive, so the command decided it should be a "secret operation." The team set up a headquarters element in Hsichang, on the edge of Lolo territory, and posted leaflets and posters and began conducting negotiations. Circulars were also distributed throughout the area in the Lolo language. Attempts to go into Lolo territory were thwarted, even with permission from the generalissimo.

The reported problem was noncooperation from local authorities who were split on factionalism and the raging civil war now going on between the Nationalists and the Communists. Everywhere the team heard tales of the savagery of the Lolos. The Chinese sent in some teams who didn't go far or came back exaggerating the rumors of the savage Lolos. Still, the rumors of the missing Americans continued and the case remained compelling.

Eventually, two Americans decided to go in disguised as traders; Captain Edward McAllister and Sergeant John Fox found the Lolo's surprisingly friendly and helpful. After much discussion and searching, the Americans concluded the rumors were just that—rumors. The mission was concluded and the long case closed in November 1947.[3]

None would venture into Tibet until four decades later, our September 1994 mission, then another mission some years later and more discussions and recoveries in mainland China.

The second recovery was conducted by another CILHI team sometime in 2002, larger and better equipped with digital communications and

GPS's that safely rested in a pocket. They recovered a C-46. The pictures depict a hazardous operation, with the team doctor, an obviously experienced mountaineer, dangling from a Swiss seat, feet planted on a karst outcropping. This was in another location in Tibet. And the results were not published that I could find.[4]

A Chinese team went back into our crash site in 2015.[5] They found more crash materiel from the site, and more remains. They turned them over to an American official, probably the consul general in Chengdu.

I mused on this a moment as I read the account in a Xin Hua English-language release. It detailed the work of Mr. Yang Jianchao, the team leader and deputy director of the Jianchuan Museum in Chengdu; I looked at a picture taken in the valley—except for the faces it could have been us, over two decades previously.

Most surprising were the words of a Mr. Luo Song, "one of five local people who discovered the remains in 1990. "Five local people? 1990 instead of 1993? Luo Song? Had Sherap finally passed from this mortal veil and been reincarnated as a Chinese?[6]

I grinned inwardly at this thought and put it aside—just another mystery I thought at the time. I thought about trying to contact the "new" CILHI, or whatever its current name was under the restructured Defense Personnel Accounting Agency, to inquire about the status of the remains.

My wife peered over my shoulder astonished, "you walked and climbed to that crash site over twenty years ago. Mr. Chopel or Sherap or whatever you called him couldn't have done that now, could he?"

"That'd be the day," I muttered, shaking my head negatively.

"Isn't that from a John Wayne film or something?" she asked.

I decided against trying to contact the DPAA. Nothing was sadder than old meddling soldiers, poking around on ancient battlefields of their minds. Particularly when the DPAA, and the entire Department of Defense, had grown rather opaque.

After searching their website, I discovered there was no current Deputy Assistant Secretary of Defense for Prisoners or Missing; the post was currently being held by a person who I assumed was an interim director. Also there was no telephone number or other information inlet into the organization, unless you were a family member with a question on a missing loved one.

A 1-800 number. My wife and I chuckled at the memory of all manner of people having our cards with our office numbers and our desk extensions when we were in the fledgling DPMO. We might have been incompetent, devious, or debunkers but we were accessible. I thought of Joe Harvey's perhaps apocryphal tale of tour busses rolling up to CILHI on the docks of Oahu in the old days; the CILHI command briefing was good theater in those lean times.

I accused Johnnie Webb of selling tickets, but he retorted the Army still gave him adequate money to fund the JCRC's participation.

We Americans on the team—and the Chinese—had speculated the glacier would turn up more remains. I assumed CILHI was working on the identification. I worked on the book, off and on during this period. I also worked as a China desk officer during 1998–2000. I was a contract civilian for the Army's Deputy Secretary of the Army's International Affairs. We mainly worked with Taiwan and the Peoples' Republic of China in a rather convoluted arrangement.

We had no diplomatic recognition of Taiwan, since we now recognized them as part of China, but they were one of our largest Foreign Military sales customers and they had a small, but lethal, non-nuclear defense force. They also skillfully flew airplanes for us in Vietnam and maybe Laos during the open and the secret war. They were usually painted black and they were the infamously whispered "C-crews" that never appeared on an Air Task Order or ATO. They liked it that way.

Chiang Kai-shek had found things much easier on Taiwan and under the protective shadow of the Taiwan Relations Act of 1979. Taiwan flourished economically and internationally, with a booming trade relationship with their Communist adversaries across the Taiwan Straits, despite the obvious military and political uncertainties between them. It was certainly in the interests of the United States to have a friendly nation on the shores of the vital Taiwan Straits.

They, like the small nation of Israel, surrounded by foes, received the best American equipment we could sell them, all but the most secret and technologically advanced we wanted to protect. Their representation was TECRO, the Taiwan Economic and Cultural Relations Office, while ours was the American Institute on Taiwan, or AIT, in Taipei. The American official who led that would be the de facto ambassador to Taiwan, in a manner of speaking, for the Republic of China was a stateless nation to the United States. They called themselves that, we simply called them Taiwan. It existed as a part of China with special attention and *implied* protection by us, a codicil necessary for the beginning of recognition in 1972.

The official's counterpart in the United States, a stone's throw away from our Army International Affairs office in Rosslyn, was Lieutenant

Colonel Greg Man, US Army (retired), a teammate and veteran of the glacier and mountain redoubt of our C-87 and priceless, luckless crew. The best man in the world for the job.

Man transmitted US policy, albeit in a convoluted fashion, to his counterpart in Taipei. It would be like the United States recognizing Mexico as a sovereign, friendly nation but giving Sonora "special recognition" and being recognized and affirmed as a "legitimate" part of Mexico. Then selling Sonora military weapons.

Such was the power of Congress, the Taiwan Relations Act of 1979, and far-sighted legislators who realized the Taiwan Straits were a very necessary strategic seaway for America to preserve peace in northeast Asia. His Man's, Shirley, was now a GS-15 and a leading writer for the Congressional Research Service, the organization that wrote private papers for the US Congress. Her specialty was, of course, China and Taiwan—and the Dalai Lama.

"Have the 'bad' Chinese come to visit recently?" The "good" Chinese lieutenant colonel from TECRO asked me one day in 1999, two years after my retirement.

"Of course," I replied, "they come all the time because we tell them we sell you enough helicopters so that every private in your army has his own."

This was a variation on the legend that a Marine rifleman from the Twenty-Sixth Marines allegedly uttered after the famous First Cavalry Division had cleared Route 9 to permit road traffic to Khe Sanh. It was the Cavalry's Operation Pegasus launched in the late spring of 1968.

"Every f%$!@!g Private in the Cav has his own f%^$#!g private helicopter," he burst out after wave after wave of First Cavalry helicopters, with the distinctive gold sabers on their noses, flared and landed at a now relatively safe Khe Sanh.

"Excellent! Keep telling them that," the Chinese officer proclaimed.

"That's why they come to us—to complain about it," I responded.

They laughed uproariously, but I told them about the time the bad Chinese became good Chinese in a windy, high altitude Himalayan valley, protected by a massive glacier with dangerous concealed holes in the snow, shedding some of its weight in avalanches. And some of its weight had been five American heroes, lost but not forgotten.

They nodded and agreed; the bad Chinese could do some good things occasionally. The "some kind of circle" moved closer to closure.

As I write this, the Chinese recovery frames the ending of this book. The Chinese civilian museum volunteers went back into C-87 862s sad gravesite in August–September 2015, our crash site, I thought protectively and jealously, then quickly changed my mind. Finding more remains would be nothing but positive for the families, I thought.

But the remains we brought out could only positively identify four of the five crewmen, but with sufficient remains to account for all five. The unidentified crewman? Pilot Fulton Pershing Lanier.

Or would it trigger bad memories? Surely they had been told by Army Casualty that other remains might be found at a later date. I had found out about the Chinese recovery almost by accident on the Library of Congress' website, where a young fact-checking staffer had directed me toward it in a two-hour daily open forum where you could chat with expert Library of Congress "fact checkers."

The Chinese expedition was a mixed lot—researchers and students from a university in Chengdu. The archaeologist apparently represented a museum there, looking for artifacts commemorating China's long struggle against the Japanese and American and allied efforts to aid them.

I was surprised when I brought two images up, startlingly similar to our own pictures; one depicted a team of Chinese and possibly Tibetans holding up a large banner. The long valley rose up behind them; the second image showed the wreckage—the same wreckage we had photographed and crawled around looking for identifying data plates.

I was even more surprised when they said the original hunter who found the crash site accompanied them. The surprise heightened when he had a Chinese name. Could it be Sherap, who would have been possibly in his early eighties? Doubtful. Either he had finally been sinocized or the Chinese had altered the history a little.

I remembered sitting with Sherap at his home after we returned, while Thorndrup translated his story of childhood (even if I could remember his name it certainly doesn't need to be divulged). Sherap's wife sat patiently and quietly beside her dying father, brushing flies away from him.[7]

It was a mystery, and I resolved to leave it at that. The Chinese, despite my disparagement on other issues, like the mistakes they made in Tiananmen Square in 1989, had assisted us faithfully and well in 1993 and in the expedition a year later, twenty-five years ago from this September 2019 writing.

Their aggressive actions a decade later resulted in tragedy when a Chinese F-8 fighter rammed a US Navy patrol plane, forcing it down on Hainan Island in the South China Sea (we wrestled with that incident when I was at Army International Affairs, in long sessions with the Defense attaché, a very capable US Army brigadier general who happened to be an Army aviator).

Finally, their more recent actions concerning their Nine Dashed Line territorial extension of their sea boundary and their activities in the South China Sea certainly fly in the face of normal geopolitical global respect. It also flaunts Accords of Sea law; tribunals accused them of wrongdoings and violation of international laws of the sea, but China didn't back off their claims or stop their construction efforts on tiny coral and sand outcroppings in the Paracels and Spratley Islands.

It also seems logical with their common boundary with the Democratic Republic of Korea, they could exert a more positive attempt at moderating North Korea's truculent behavior that is peaking at the moment of this writing. That would be an extremely good thing the bad Chinese could do.

But these are merely musings of an old Asia hand infatuated with all things east of the 180th meridian since childhood, who once went along with some very good US and Chinese soldiers and tough Tibetans on a humanitarian military action in the mountains of Tibet. Then, as now, we admit there is only one China, and Tibet, like Taiwan, is part of it.

We thanked them for their professional and diplomatic courtesy, and I especially thanked Colonel Neng as I handed him my civilian binoculars, for keeping the US soldiers as safe as possible.

At least we urge the Chinese to treat their Tibetans better. And we've still got a wary US Congress with their hands on the sanction switch if things spin out of control again.

So I'd leave those mysteries alone; there were far better, younger, and more experienced China people in government and the military to interact with them diplomatically than I.

EPILOGUE

"This Is a Holy Place"

We finished the briefing like we always did, in CILHI's lab on this late Sunday morning in late 1996. We waited respectfully for the head of the visiting delegation to ask questions, or to comment. He continued to peer down at the table at a case that we used explicitly because of its age—the crew of a World War II and Korea era B-26 had crashed in Vietnam in 1963 and remains and artifacts had been recovered or turned in—I forget the exact circumstances of acquisition.

This was an interesting case because I always thought the B-26 Invader was an impressive aircraft, and its use in three wars confirmed its effectiveness. We had staged our unit photo (well, half the unit who was there, anyway) in front of the B-26 that rested on a pedestal at Hickam.

As I recall it was a difficult case of identification also, perhaps because of the dearth of identification media or even remains that might differentiate the race of the crew. I knew the Vietnamese Air Force also flew this aircraft, so that was the first mystery to solve—was it an American aircraft? We had to be mindful also that there were Asian American airmen and pilots.

I had been asked somewhat hesitantly by his chief of staff the week before if it would be possible for a Sunday briefing and if it would be OK if their party wore civilian clothing since they were scheduled to go straight to Honolulu International and depart on a civilian flight back to Europe.

Of course, I replied, we'd be glad to do it; two of our group were civilian and I'd probably be in a field battle dress uniform along with Sergeant Butts, our young command briefer. The principal was a respected three-star general who was soon slated for a fourth star. He was a hero of Desert Storm as the commander of VII Corps as well as having been in Vietnam, where he had lost part of a foot as a young major in the Blackhorse Regiment of the Eleventh Armored Cavalry.

He had overcome that wound to continue on as a leader in combat arms, and even back to being a fair runner. He was famous for taking his twice-annual PT test with troops under his command. His name was Frederick Franks (no relation to General Tommy Franks, who led CENTCOM in Operation Iraqi Freedom a decade after Desert Storm). Now, clad in khakis and a polo shirt, he glanced up at us, while his staff of four or five similar mufticlad officers stood back respectfully.

General Franks glanced around the gleaming lab, and I noticed his eyes were moist beneath his steel-rimmed glasses.

"This is a holy place," he murmured. "This is a holy sanctuary," he boomed spreading his arms in an ecclesiastical gesture that covered the whole lab. Johnnie Webb, Tom Holland, and I exchanged quick glances.

"That's what we consider it also, Sir," Sergeant Butts replied, the first to find his voice and always fast on his feet.

"We all get to go on a couple of recoveries so we can appreciate and understand our mission; I'm one of the junior logistics NCOs but I've served on recovery teams in both Vietnam and Laos," he continued proudly.

General Franks and his chief of staff smiled and nodded, obviously pleased; and it pleased me, also. A good soldier and general officer had recognized a good soldier and realized this was a good unit. This was also my cue.

"Sir, we always like to present a little gift that's kind of emblematic of our mission and we hope it's a remembrance for you," I said.

Sergeant Butts handed him a North Vietnamese soldier's green fiber helmet with the characteristic red star and gold wreath on the front. A small plaque with his rank and name and date of visit was affixed to the visor of the helmet.

The general took it, obviously delighted, then his staff simultaneously applauded, with "great briefing and tour" or variants coming from all of them. General Franks shook Sergeant Butts's hand and complimented him on the briefing. There were handshakes all around and murmurs of good will.

We followed them out to the staff car and van and exchanged salutes, handshakes, and good lucks. General Franks waved as he got into the staff car and we saluted again, since we didn't normally wave to generals.

In early 1994, on identification of the aircraft as a C-87 and its crew manifest of suspected identities, CILHI assembled all the medical records and began work on the identification of the remains the Chinese had turned over in Lhasa.

Mitochondrial DNA, that mysterious genetic structure passed down the maternal line, was an established fact, but was not yet used widely or conventionally, and it is a destructive process for the bone or bones involved. It was discovered in the 1960s by a husband-wife team of scientists. Once established with scientific certainty, research and development followed quickly, along with the expected court cases for identifying deceased—sometimes for years—or hundreds of years.

A reference base requires a cheek swab from a maternal relative—male or female, but it has to be a brother or sister, son or daughter of offspring down the line that originated from the mother of the victim. The maternal side.

This scientific method also requires sufficient bone material from the victim to obtain a sample for testing. The testing is also destructive, although it requires only a small sample of the bone. At that time, the Armed Force DNA Laboratory in Maryland (called AFDIL in the military lexicon) was making great strides in advancement. But it wasn't completely and confidently fielded yet.

Leaning forward, AFDIL had begun a registry for relatives with missing servicemen—mainly from World War II and Korea. Their samples were taken and carefully stored, with accompanying information also carefully logged and digitized.

It is a complicated process. When I visited the laboratory in early 1996 a biochemist explained the process slowly and carefully, but even though I have an undergraduate degree in chemistry, even her simple explanation slipped over me. I just remember gratefully that these were very smart, dedicated people and eventually this would be a great tool—another weapon in our arsenal to convince other nations we were serious about this matter of missing US servicemen.

But even in the late 1990s it was conventional forensics that held primacy—dentition, stature, race, and sex. We were elated to have dentition from some of the crew (surprisingly, none from the two pilots)—teeth are the most durable components of the human body, and their protective enamel protects them from the ravages of even the most acidic soils, like that found in Indochina.

And CILHI's two forensic dentists while I was there were among the best in the world. Using an automated database they could match teeth on their screens to anomalies in the missing relatively quickly, then carefully write their forensic evidence up under the purview of the lab director.

The remains' dentition, teeth, as I recall, matched the adequate dental records on one or two crewmembers who had dental records, ensuring their identities. As mentioned, we were equally surprised that both pilots had no dental records (medical records were not part of the devastating St. Louis fire).

Air crewmen now universally have carefully maintained dental records, and I believe the losses over Vietnam and Laos brought this about early in the Vietnam conflict. Now all servicemen and women are swabbed and dental records carefully maintained in the event of catastrophic death.

A long four years elapsed before the painstaking verification of five humans through the conventional methods of partial reconstructing of the bodies or sufficient unidentifiable remains to insure there were five personnel on the aircraft. And sufficient verification that they were who the lab asserted they were, with personal identification media (dog tags, ID Cards, personal items verifying identity, and such), which was unfortunately absent except for the marked clothes and signature on the mess chit.

Or distinctive identifying physiological characteristics (known broken bones, for example) or teeth; three had dental records, all the enlisted men. Unusual, but not unexpected. Nobody thinks they're going to die, and the Army Air Force—the one organization that should have mandated dental records were maintained at least as medical records.

Then this report and recommendation went up the chain to Army Casualty to convince every expert who reviewed them. The remains were buried as a "group burial," in Arlington National Cemetery. Portions of the identifiable remains went with the families to their cemeteries of choice. Both Fulton Lanier and Frank Ramos were sufficiently taller than their enlisted crewmen, and this was also determined by the careful segregation and analysis of the remains. But only Lanier would remain personally unverifiable from remains recovered from both the PLA unilateral recovery in December 1993 and our main recovery expedition at the crash site in September 1994.

The Chinese effort in 2015 solved this final unanswered question—the museum recovery team found a US Army shoe, still preserved with sufficient osseous remains to yield mtDNA. Also found were fairly complete skeletal remains that showed evidence of violent fragmentation, consistent with a violent aircraft crash. The crew died violently and likely instantly. They didn't freeze or starve to death in a buried C-87.

Their marker stands today in Arlington National Cemetery; my wife placed flowers on their grave every Memorial Day that we lived in northern Virginia, less than a mile from their final resting place.

The Chinese expedition from the Chengdu Museum would accept Captain Lanier from the maws of the glacier, a little over two decades later. Like any good captain, he was the last to leave his ship, and by now mitochondrial DNA was well established. The Armed Forces DNA laboratory was well equipped, funded, and manned with the best scientists in the field. They might either confirm or deny that the remains were Lanier; if the remains weren't, they would probably match one of the other samples they might have at AFDIL. One thing I thought for sure: whatever they said would be the accurate and unassailable final word.

As Fulton Lanier and Frank Ramos pushed throttles and prop controls forward in the early evening of January 31, 1944, a witches' cauldron of weather awaited them. The moving forces that Lieutenant Colonel Graydon Spurgeon had so eloquently described in 1970 to me on an airfield in West Texas were preparing an aerial ambush for the crew of the C-87 Liberator.

Theirs was an aircraft trying to get home with only a portion of the fuel the big plane could carry. The pilots might have talked to pilots who had landed earlier and listened to their grim experiences coming eastward from Assam or from other locations in China. The normally placid winter weather had been cursed by the storm.

A year later another January storm of the same magnitude, or worse, would bring aircraft down like so many waterfowl falling to hunters' guns. The airwaves were choked with Mayday calls as aircraft were hurled about like ping-pong balls. It was sufficiently bad to change the rules of flying the Hump. General Tunner decreed henceforth there *would* be weather over the Hump. Moreover, if an aircraft commander had any qualms about safety, he could, after notifying his base unit command group, delay the flight until the problem was repaired or the weather returned to minimally safe conditions.

Their sister crew, piloted by Crozier and McCallum, had encountered a similar storm on November 30, 1943, and parachuted from their aircraft. They were naturally assumed lost when they didn't return to Jorhat; now, as 862 buffeted to altitude two months later, Crozier's crewmembers were moving out on horses and mules, across Tibet to India, still tending to their bail-out injuries. The malevolent gods of bad terrain, weather, or troubled aircraft—or all three—would catch William Perram the next year. He would unfortunately perish on the Hump.

"Frank, as soon as 'Tommy King' releases us, we'll climb out on 250 degrees; I'll handle the gauges and you watch the engines for ice and breaks in the overcast."[1]

Ramos acknowledged with a nod.

"Now both Ramos and Beebe were watching the engine instruments and out the canopy windshields, straining to see any obstruction. Lanier's eyes flicked to the 'gauges' that permitted 862 to fly 'blind' through the gathering storm and darkness.

"Watch for anything distinctive you can see on the ground."

"Eugene, give Lieutenant Ramos a hand watching the engine instruments and keep an eye on the fuel gauges.

"If you see so much as a flicker in the fuel flow on any engine, call out. This might be a good night to sit it out in China," was advice Fulton would probably have given the crew. He was an aggressive, mission-oriented pilot, but not a reckless one.

"Twenty or thirty degrees farther south than our usual heading," Joe yelled to Benny, pulling his earphones away to stay off the intercom. Benny nodded. Flight 862 would be climbing almost sideways, nose pointed toward Calcutta, well to the south of their base.

All had watched the windsock standing stiffly pointed northeast at Kunming as even the surface winds quartered the runway strongly from the southwest. From the Bay of Bengal, another "belly of the beast"—the weather beast. Meanwhile, Joe and Benny were searching desperately for any signal—voice or Morse code—they could identify as a "bread crumb" along their route.

There are many variables in the fuel consumption of an airplane's engines—speed, load, altitude, turbulence, and how much the fuel is "leaned" to increase the air/fuel ratio, but planning baselines said the engines would burn between eighty to ninety gallons per hour on each engine. The health of the engines and the usable fuel made up the "bank account."

All four engines were 100 percent of the account; the loss of one engine would reduce it to 75 percent. Still flyable if the propeller controls could "feather" it—turn it knife edge into the wind to reduce the drag. However, if the "Gremlins" invaded the prop governors, sometimes they would over speed and the props would run wild, screaming before they occasionally tore off, sometimes flinging themselves through the cockpit like a giant eleven-foot scimitar. A runaway propeller governor was the inexorable beginning of initiation into the Caterpillar Club. Depleted fuel meant bankruptcy.

As 862 climbed through 10,000 feet, it was buffeted by the strongest turbulence the pilots could recall. The control yokes fought them as they struggled to keep the wings and the nose relatively level and upright. They would balloon up several thousand feet, throttled back at full carburetor heat on all engines, fighting ice buildup. After the wild climb, the bottom fell out and they would drop like a 25-ton leaf, everything pushed back to dangerous maximum power and propeller settings.

"Masks everybody," Ramos called on the intercom, and one by one the crewman felt the bladder-like rubber device fill with air and verified they were up on oxygen.

The wild ride continued. Everything not tied down was bouncing off the cockpit ceiling. Beebe was holding on with two hands as he moved back and forth to the fuel gauges then duck-walked back over to the space between the two pilots to monitor the engine instruments. He held on to Ramos's seat but felt like he was trying to ride a bull.

"Belt yourself in, Gene. We'll get out of this hopefully in a little while," Fulton called over the intercom. Beebe looked at him; the pilot was grinning. Beebe complied, wrestling himself back into the engineer's seat and buckling in.

"I think Lieutenant Lanier likes this stuff," he thought.

Lanier did like all flying, especially when it was rough and demanded the utmost pilot skill. Weather was a deadly fighter, much more dangerous than a knife- or gunfight—because weather had a dangerous unseen ally—terrain. When weather and terrain unleashed their most diabolical tactic, weather masking terrain, things could get very problematic.

Now Giacalone and Petrella were bouncing against their tightened seat belts, looking for beacon signals in the static coming through their headphones. Beebe looked over his right shoulder; the menacing fuel gauges continued to record the depletion of fuel.

In the right seat Lieutenant Frank Ramos held his control wheel firmly and monitored the engine gauges like a hawk from a high branch searching for movement below. His responsibility was to keep the airplane flying by keeping the four engines running.

Beebe also knew that Lieutenant Lanier in the captain's seat on the left was using that same hawk-like observation of the flight gauges—altimeter, airspeed, gyrocompass, turn and bank indicator, rate of climb indicator, plus radio frequencies vital to navigation and others. His responsibility was to get them back to their Jorhat airfield safely. If that wasn't possible he had to find a closer airfield he could set 862 down on. He knew there were fighter strips scattered around that the British had built and the AVG had used. He knew where they were. He only knew where 862 *should* be in this maelstrom.

He knew the two radio operators were listening to two different sets trying to contact various towers that might exist below them, establishing contact in the ferocious storm and offering them long counts to establish their relative position. Now he knew it wasn't just to land safely, but to establish their position when they leaped into the icy wind in a parachute. To give them their relative position wherever they were, India, China, or Burma. He didn't even consider Tibet.

His last thought was, "It takes all five of us to fly this ship," and then the sounds an airplane makes as it gets uncomfortable with itself; the engines started torching, one by one, and Private First Class Eugene Beebe called his last intercom message, quietly but strongly: "Guess we're dry, Sir." If the glass tube sight gauges had any usable fuel indicated in them, Beebe could have pumped the last of it into the engines from the remaining tanks.

I was a surreptitious passenger on that flight, a spectral sixth crewmember. Especially on that last tired night as we sat around a fire eating the Chinese field rations and drinking powdered coffee. We all were nursing sore, battered limbs. Snatches of a scene flashed then faded away as uneasy sleep drifted me into dreamless unconsciousness. My little tent and bag turned colder and ballooned in the wind. I never dreamed the faces I wouldn't know yet, or imagined the quietened throb of the four giant Pratt & Whitneys, or felt the mind-numbing cold in my sleep. Sometimes that would happen at short rest pauses on the mountain, where there is only breathtaking beauty in your vision.

It wasn't a particularly disturbing scene; I'd wake from a blank dreamless cold sleep. I bounced only a little with them in their tortured airplane, could hear the four Pratt & Whitneys' reassuring roar, but muted enough to hear imagined conversations unimpeded by noisy tumult or looming disaster. Instrument panels that were anything but digital—bare metal showing through painted toggles, gauges with pointers and only the radios with numbers in windows. A pedestal between the pilots festooned with handles with knobs: throttles, propeller, and fuel mixture controls. But I was wide awake, not alarmed but very curious. What were the faces disguised by oxygen masks saying to each other?

I was detached from the cold and wrenching fear they all endured, but it was clinically not uncomfortable, and most disquieting was the lack of smelling the sweating rubbery oxygen masks and the high-octane fuel and engine oil fluids. What was unrelenting was the imaginary noise—muted considerably from the actual roar—of four powerful Pratt & Whitney radial engines. It wasn't a nightmare, but it was faintly disturbing—and real. It flickered like a strobe light and then drifted away from me. Finally, I slipped into sore and exhausted sleep as if I escaped in some spectral parachute, I imagined the mountains looming before them in a grudgingly generous break in the overcast they had flown in for hours. The beautiful snow-clad peaks gleaming in a now cloudless starlight outside my tent.

Lanier flashed his last charming smile in the terminal microsecond of life in this ethereal realm now ended. He grinned not at his death but at a life well lived—albeit a short one. His time on this earth had been adventurous; he had flown and fought for his country, bringing his crew back safely each time in the southwest Pacific. He had also mastered the Hump as a command pilot, no small feat for anyone. He had an adventuresome life by anyone's standards.

The Aluminum Trail was scattered with wrecks flown by airline pilots with thousands of hours as well as the neophyte crewmen of the US Army Air Force. But Lanier's relatively brief life had been enriched by love for his family; they had loved him back equally. They would mourn his loss, but also celebrate his life well—and heroically—lived.

He had wrestled this airplane to both their deaths as bravely as anyone could have, with Frank Ramos and his three young men assisting, but the terrain and weather, worthy but deadly adversaries, had won. His crew would have thought the same. They had experienced short but adventurous lives. They had done their best also, and they knew they'd live forever as young men in their families' and friends' hearts.

Their relatives and friends would grieve but find some measure of solace in their devotion to their country in a dangerous undertaking—in a deadly, faraway and forbidden place. And they would grow old, be plagued with the illnesses and accidents of the aging, while these five men would always be young, brave, strong, resolute in their faith and beliefs.

But there was a mystery I could try to solve, and it came about through a technological advancement that would have provided us immense assistance in 1994. Someone more talented than I would have to teach me its wizardry.

It was Google Earth.

I found out I was digitally challenged. I read John Plating's well-researched and meticulously detailed account of the Hump.

It was a contemporary strategic airlifter's appreciation for his forbearers. Particularly impressive was his Google Earth autopsy of several crashes and his concise accounting of what and how these aircraft were lost. It was a look at their longtime ice-covered and unheralded graves from the unerring eye of a satellite. A friend of mine took me in hand, mindful of my digital incompetency, and we sat, me in the copilot's chair to his right in front of the flat screen of the desktop computer.

"Dinosaur," he muttered.

"My wife's. She's a traditionalist," I responded.

"Name your favorite place in the United States," he directed.

"That's easy; Ruidoso, New Mexico."

"How do you spell it?"

"You can't spell New Mexico?" I chortled.

"You wanna' learn this or not?" he retorted.

He typed in the name and the globe spun.

Ruidoso, New Mexico, focused into view, from a satellite, the legend at the bottom said, around forty miles above the earth. He panned over the familiar places, the peaks surrounding it and the airport east of there—I had landed there many times.

"Can you do that with latitude and longitude, lat/long?" I asked.

"I think so; give it to me."

I recited the numbers I had carried for such a long time and rattled them off from memory. It took half a dozen tries before 30 degrees north latitude and 94 degrees east longitude registered, then he typed in the rest. Minutes and seconds north of the equator; minutes and seconds east of Greenwich were added in decimal equivalents, but I had to look those up in my notes.

Seafarers had been measuring the heights of heavenly bodies that provided their latitude, north or south of the equator, by the sun or recognizable stars, for centuries. Longitude, those vertical lines from pole to pole, could source time and horizontal distance as the earth passed through fifteen degrees of rotation every hour.

The globe spun again and New Mexico wheeled away on the screen. Africa flew by, then the familiar shape of India slowed and it felt like we were rapidly falling to earth. Snow-covered peaks became distinctly clear and an avalanched snow slide that ended in a valley appeared.

"Jesus," he breathed. "This is the crash site?"

I nodded. It was indeed, maybe where I landed in my spectral, imaginary parachute fall. Out of an aircraft with a crew I couldn't hear.

> "No dental records available for Capt. Lanier or 1st Lt Ramos. . . . Conclusions: Several Intersecting lines of evidence suggest that Capt. Lanier, 1st Lt Ramos, Cpl Petrella, Pfc Giacalone and Pfc Beebe died when their C-87 aircraft impacted a mountain in Tibet. The remains apparently were locked in ice for almost 50 years before they were discovered . . . ID Packet CIL 1994–144 dtd 27 October 1997.

It was hot that early fall afternoon of September 28, 2017, at the cemetery in Lillington, North Carolina. The motorcycle escort of the Patriots and Rolling Thunder had led our cortege of an estimated two hundred people or so to this tidy cemetery, at the junction that leads up the road to Ervin, where Bill and Diane Lanier live.

Janna and I had met them some years ago. They graciously lent us Fulton Lanier's logbooks to copy, and Janna and I had gone to the local Walmart. I smelled the old familiar airplane dope, tobacco smoke, and airmen camaraderie as I wiped a fingernail of Australian or New Guinea mud off one of the pages. Pilot's logbooks. I explained to the young woman what they were and why we needed good copies and she complied graciously, copying several weeks' worth of entries carefully.

Now each recorded flight of individuals was meshed into a crew, thrown together by duty rosters for one flight. Although the final one was unrecorded, it bonded them together for a long time. A very long time.

The remains the Chinese had turned over now had the advantage of a quarter century of mtDNA scientific and legal maturation. A swab from a remarkable woman, Fulton's sister, had verified his identity. Fulton was blessed with a strong line of Laniers, men and women.

Mary L. Boykin, Lanier's late sister, was the matriarchal presence to both "him and me," recalled Bill Lanier, a trim retired pharmacist, although confined to a wheelchair for an injury to his hip at the funeral. "She married at age fifty," Diane Lanier, Bill's wife related, smiling. "She gave them that cheek swab with enthusiasm and hope after you, your team, and the Chinese found them and put names on them; she always knew he'd return." Bill and Diane related how she lived out the remainder of her widowhood on a large property with a long circular driveway that had always been in the family before passing away.

They asked the driver of the hearse bearing Fulton's flag-covered casket to drive around it slowly and stop for a moment.

My wife teared up.

"This is a miracle," Bill Lanier said, "this is the happiest day of my life."

Retired judge Frank Lanier, Fulton's nephew, added, "This sets a lot of things right; he said, "there wasn't any doubt what happened, but just to have him here means a lot."

About thirty members of the Chinese community from the Triangle area were also in attendance, bringing a large spray of flowers emblazoned with "thanks for helping us in World War II." Their spokesman, Minqiang Jin, echoed this sentiment, saying, "they fought the enemy together not only as soldiers, but brothers."

In 2015 and 2016, during the exacting identification, both at CILHI on the skeletal remains and at the Armed Forces DNA Identification Laboratory's (AFDIL), careful sequencing of the thirteen other samples from maternal relatives that donated swabs, everything clicked into place.

All of these thirteen failed to come up with the unique combination of genomes and matching sequences.

Fulton's and Mary's did.

Thus the exclusions of the other crewmembers' maternal donors and the verifying of Fulton's and Mary from the equation verified the remains as Fulton Pershing Lanier, Captain, US Army Air Force, lost on January 31, 1944, in the service of his country.

Fulton, previously the only crewmember not personally identified and buried as a known crewmember, was now verified with scientific certainty. Moreover, by something I had considered "a long shot" years before—AFDIL's "bank" of thousands of genetic samples, carefully taken, cataloged, and maintained. Now he remained with his crew at Arlington and with his family, at Harnett Memorial Park in Lillington, North Carolina.

Casualty assistance officer Major Robert Matthew Starcher, Infantry, of Fort Bragg, escorted Fulton's niece, Mrs. Powers, the designated Next of Kin to the covered gravesite in the heat. Halfway there she unhooked her arm from the militarily correct bended elbow and slipped her hand in his, and they walked slowly to their seats.

Seven maroon-bereted paratroopers of the Eighty-Second Airborne Division at nearby Fort Bragg, ceremonially moved the flag-covered coffin to the gravesite, spectators saluting or holding their hands over their heart. The motorcyclists held their individual national colors in an honor cordon encircling the gravesite and also rendered salutes.

The Paratroopers folded the American flag carefully into the tricornered shape and passed it to their sergeant, who slowly wheeled and passed it to their commanding officer, a captain. The NCO stepped back and brought his hand up in a slow, final salute, and the captain stepped forward, kneeled, and said condolences to the niece, Mrs. Virginia Price. He passed her the flag, then stepped back with his own final, slow salute.

Fulton Pershing Lanier, Captain, US Army Air Force, had stayed with his ship to the end—like any good captain. But now he was home, brought by the Chinese from the Chengdu Museum, who alerted their government, the American consul, the Department of State, Defense, and the Army who notified the family. Our government ordered a handful of elite American Warriors to conduct and honor his burial while consoling and thanking his family for their sacrifice seven decades prior.

And the anthropologists agreed the considerable skeletal remains of his mortal body were broken with intensity witnessed in many other high-speed aircraft accidents. So they might have been encased in the ice for a half century, but their deaths were quick and over in an instant.

Outside, seven of the Airborne soldiers shouldered their M-4 carbines and fired three volleys of blank ammunition, the final twenty-one-gun salute given to the highest heads of state and every modest unassuming serviceman and woman who died in the service of their country. After the ceremony another couple of paratroopers policed up the brass casings and gave them to Major Starcher. He would pass them to the family.

Another paratrooper from the Division band played the somber "Taps" on his bugle. Like the perfectly synchronized three volleys, it was flawless—and sad.

I will never live to see the final closing of that circle. The glacier will, in all likelihood, continue to give back the crew it claimed so violently over seventy years ago; it may take decades, and I'm no longer a young man. But it's the perfect example of human linkage and personal identification, present linked to the past, with life's ultimate outcome trumping all.

There is a distinct possibility unknowns in group burials—the only thing known is they all died together—they will come to life again as an individual, and rest with their friends and loved ones, thanks to mtDNA and a maternal relative breathing life into their long ago memories. A resurrection certainly of some sort.

I know in my mind and being that the determination of all American citizens to return our fallen would continue. Nearly all nations share this;

the Chinese and Vietnamese especially, ironically, two nations we fought in frozen wasteland and dank rain forest, and two countries I would spend a considerable slice of my life studying and soldiering in.

It also sends an unmistakable message to potential enemies: treat our prisoners humanely, and care and keep track of our dead as much as possible, remembering they are fallen warriors.

I thought of Tom Needham's final words at his change of command in Hawaii: "Soldiers don't get much in hard careers that sometimes end with their deaths in hostile lands—one thing they deserve is a final and honorable ride home."

Just as sure as the turning of the earth.

Acknowledgments

There was a marked serendipity to the timing of President Reagan's new approach to the POW/MIA issue in the summer of 1987. His appointment of General Vessey as his personal emissary insured that a visibly respected military figure represented the issue far above the relative back bench—but loyal, toiling, and unappreciated—at the operational, analytical, and scientific level it had staggered along since America's conflict in Indochina ended.

President Reagan wanted the issue solved, or at least resolved to an acceptable reasonableness that most Americans could agree on and move forward. The fact that General Vessey had Admiral Larson, General Needham, Paul Mather, and Joe Harvey in the "Forward Edge of the Battle Area," the FEBA (soldiers sometime refer to it as the Forward Edge of the Bad Asses) was an extra blessing. General Vessey and General Kingston took the time to visit me three times when I was assigned to EAPR in the Pentagon not only to discuss the policy issues but also to check on my health and my wife's. My wife hosted General Kingston at a luncheon in our quarters and she invited some of the team leader wives; it was a memorable occasion. General Kingston, despite his Patton-like reputation, was an erudite and articulate guest who explained the intricacies of the importance of Vietnam in the postconflict world, particularly with an expanding role of China in politico-military affairs.

After all, America and China had made amends. There was no reason for the United States and Vietnam to be at diplomatic loggerheads for a quarter century as we had been with the Peoples' Republic of China since 1949. Particularly with Vietnam's hopeful forecast role as an economic "tiger" instead of a militant one in the future of the region, as well as the rest of Asia.

This failure to deal with China as anything but an adversary led to divisions in our own polity, and our own citizenry. It also ruined the careers of several loyal Foreign Service officers, journalists, and other career civil servants who served long and well in dangerous regions of China.

John Service survived the parachute jump from the stricken C-46 and the long walk out to safety only to have his career ruined and his loyalty questioned; as did many others who only spoke the truth, including newsmen.

Lieutenant Colonels Joe Harvey, US Army, and Paul Mather, US Air Force, nurtured the operational negotiations and technical side of the issue along for a number of years. In Paul's case, since the war, a war for him that never really ended, and for Joe from an academic and professional background in all Southeast Asia that was matched by few.[1] This was anything but an easy, or even a definable task.

They were both patient and inspirational, and they guided me through the warrens of talking points, negotiation narratives, and operational realities carefully and well. There were also byzantine mine-strewn and booby-trapped byways in the paths of our small organizations—Joe and Paul kept me on the right side of the wire and on a safe (relatively, anyway) lane.

Johnnie Webb, an Army quartermaster officer with considerable Graves Registration experience, commanded CILHI through much of that decade, then served ably as my second in command, later in key positions as the shape and size of the organization expanded from 2003 onward. It, like General Tunner's Hump, entered the realm of big business.

Major General Tom Needham, well assisted by Colonel Bill Frizzel, with oversight from Admiral Charles Larson, sadly gone much too soon, were the finest stewards of the expanded JCRC/JTF-FA possible. Their men and women, in uniform or mufti, spent long hard hours in tandem with the CILHI recovery teams to bring back and identify those soldiers, sailors, and airmen left in Indochina's hostile mountains and rain forests.

Similarly, the analysts of the DIA Special Office for POW/MIA Affairs toiled long and hard, largely unsung and unduly criticized, but they provided the information we needed to move forward.

EAPR's Dr. Lew Stern provided numerous enjoyable chess lessons on General Vessey's white, unmarked Boeing 707 (save for the four stars on the tail) en route to Hanoi. Lou was the wellspring of all things Vietnam, and General Vessey respected his knowledge and advice highly; I'm privileged to call him a friend.

Similarly, Ed Ross, the King of China, as we knew him, was a valued colleague and boss when we formed DPMO up out of our pitifully small crew of young officers, NCOs and civilians who nevertheless attacked every problem tenaciously and with good spirit. Ed, too, also has sadly gone on—a loyal soldier and another good friend passed to Fiddler's Green, a slice of cavalry heaven.

Ann Mills Griffith was a great source of information on the entire POW/MIA issue; a tireless, dedicated colleague who could also be a ruthless opponent if you differed with her. Like the Marines: "No better friend, no worse enemy." Particularly when you were wrong and she was right. I found this was generally the case when she and I differed on things. She was, and is, a tireless worker and advocate for the families of missing Americans.

Nonetheless, when the final pages of the POW/MIA history are written, she, like Vessey, Kingston, Needham, Mather, and Harvey should each have a dedicated chapter. As should the young Army, Navy, Marine, and Air Force members and the dedicated civilians such as B. J. Andrews, who wept with many families.

These Soldiers, Sailors, Marines, and Airmen colleagues I worked with and who worked for me in the Pentagon and later in Clarendon's DIA complex were among the best officers I've ever known—patient, loyal, and always ready to go on to the next challenge, after figuring out and advising me on exactly what that challenge happened to be. I referred to them earlier and they represented the best of their Armed Services, and I thank them again for their hard work, loyalty, and friendship.

It was the greatest privilege to work with and lead the men and women of the US Army Central Identification Laboratory, Hawaii, who were proud of their hallowed mission—Search, Recover, Identify. They were—and are, simply the best. Good luck to you all on the hazardous sites where brave men died. Janna and I think of you often. Brett Hill, my neighbor, kept my computer running when I attacked it like a neanderthal, spinning it out of control. He doesn't say much, but his fingers on a keyboard are those of a concert pianist.

In reviewing the *Smithsonian Air & Space* article back in 1998, Dave Elliott, a retired Air Force fighter pilot and former Raven Forward Air Controller in Laos, and his wife Carol, a retired Air Force General Officer who oversaw many sensitive intelligence programs from Vietnam to the Balkans, thought the article was OK, "but it'd make a better book."

So Dave provided the cheers, suggestions, bourbon sips, and fly-fishing strategy in stopovers at the Big Sky Country of Montana on the way to our tiny Idaho cabin and Carol the genealogy lessons; she is a formidably skilled researcher in the arcana of American tax, census, and other public records and archives.

Finally, Johnny and Jo Rusin, one of the few husband and wife teams who went to combat together in Frederick Franks's VIIth Corps' Desert Storm attack ("this is a holy place"), both colonels, provided a great pair of objective eyes. They reviewed the manuscript for readability, accuracy, and that final arbiter of the military personnel business, accountability of the Missing.

All this some four decades after the first time they took me under wing, all of us young captains in the nation's capital, during our bicentennial year and the unmooring of a president. Our office would preside over the limited ceremony at his departure, and Johnny Rusin, the nation's ceremony officer, would preside over it on the South Lawn of the White House. Jo's advice was especially welcome; she is the author of several fine books addressing military leadership, particularly from a woman soldier's viewpoint. It is illuminating—and more than a little unnerving—to write a book for an editor with a PhD in military history, particularly to a history philistine such as me. Dr. Jay Dew showed extreme patience and great guidance throughout; it is always a pleasure to work with professionals. Finally, editor Thom Lemmons and his fantastic staff.

The House Armed Services Committee, led by Congressman Mac Thornberry, R (Thirteenth District) and his dedicated committee members and staff are the best possible stewards of our Armed Forces and their families. They work tirelessly and professionally to ensure our troops are well manned, well-armed, and well-fed and led, a stark reminder to us fossils of the times our young soldiers' families had to make do with food stamps. If anyone deserves a "Thanks for your service," you men and women of the HASC all do.

There would have been no book if it weren't for the encouragement and assistance of the ones who loved these men and encouraged the chronicling of their military lives and deaths.

Ramos's wife, Doris, and her son, Michael, and his wife Lynn, were stalwart pillars of support in providing insight into the life of Frank Ramos; years later Doris would marry another officer, albeit not a pilot who served in the CBI, and enjoy a long and loving marriage with him. Sadly, she too has gone. She had much to remember the China Burma India theater for.

Similarly, Fulton's nephew Bill Lanier, his wife Diane, and his nephew

Judge Frank Lanier, provided such rich coloring of Fulton Pershing Lanier, I decided he would have been a good man to go into combat with—or have a beer with in a dusty Outback town. His niece, Virginia Powers, is a dignified portrait of a southern lady who had seen her beloved man back from combat in honored but sad circumstances since America's most grievous war, the one we waged with each other.

I wished I'd met his aunt.

Dr. Tom Troyano and his wife similarly filled out all aspects of young Bartholomew "Benny" Giacalone's short but well-lived life. Tom also delivered a moving eulogy at his memorial service.

Joseph Petrella, the eldest, had the unflagging memory and love of all his brothers, none more than the youngest, Carl, who enshrined his memory. Now Carl and his lovely wife are with Joe, a family who gave their all in World War II. He is a perfect biblical example of brotherly love. His diligence also closed a personal circle for me—he preserved Joe's logbook that showed that a young lieutenant Spurgeon took him once on a flight several decades before he did the same for me. Now all those brothers are gone, as is Graydon Spurgeon, Lieutenant Colonel, United States Air Force (Retired).

And the incomparable Night Crosser John Nelson, who didn't quite make it to one hundred years on and above this old earth.

Finally, the young men on that airplane: Fulton Pershing Lanier, Frank M. Ramos, Joseph Petrella, Bartholomew "Benny" Giacalone, and Eugene E. Beebe. They perished as young men and that is how they're remembered—strong and dedicated young airmen who flew and fought to the very best of their ability and who never grew old. They blazed aerial trails for succeeding generations, going into a conflict with the scantest but best training and equipment an unprepared America could summons. It was an honor to help give them their last ride home.

My wife Janna, who soldiered on with me the second half of my military sojourn in this all too short cycle of life and rebirth, was an indomitable soul mate and reviewer. My mother and father set me out on the best-laid course in life, warning me of bad weather and obstacles along the route. Janna kept me safely on that heading. I've always loved her dearly and always will.

Finally, as I quoted John Masters in the Retrospective Overview, the most eloquent tribune of the allied soldiers' struggles in Burma, much of this was written from memory and recollection; time has dimmed some of it, but not the events that happened or the people of the journey.

Any errors in this work are mine alone. However, those memories dealing with soldiers, US and Chinese, especially those gone on to Therap's next cycle of life, are still as clearly and sharply defined as the battle sight on a rifle.

There will be, with my own passing, a final somber ceremony, hopefully three shots from seven rifles, followed by a mournful passage of "Taps" from a lone bugler a folded flag passed, ending with a slow salute.

Then I'll link up with them.

Notes

REFLECTIONS

1. Masters, *Bugles and a Tiger*, preface, xvi.

CHAPTER 1

1. The remains are in a tended American Battlefield Monuments Cemetery in Mexico City and are still visited by Americans, Mexicans, and foreign visitors.

2. Poole, *On Hallowed Ground*.

CHAPTER 2

1. These figures appear to be astonishingly high. That's because they are astonishingly high. They approach US servicemen's combat deaths in Vietnam after seven years of pretty much constant combat for about 10 percent of the troops. One figure that does appear pretty consistent *from all sources* is 116,000 for combined combat and noncombat US uniformed service member deaths.

2. https://www.va.gov/.

3. Poole, *On Hallowed Ground*, 142. These were combat and noncombat deaths. Different sources cite different totals for the dead, wounded, and missing from wars up to and including World War II and Korea. One internet source claims nonbattle deaths greater than battle deaths for this conflict—not surprising since the 1918 influenza worldwide epidemic devastated citizens of every nation, military and nonmilitary alike.

4. Poole, *On Hallowed Ground*, 143.

CHAPTER 3

1. A Spartan mother's parting advice to her warrior son, attributed to Plutarch. http://depthome.brooklyn.cuny.edu/classics/dunkle/athnlife/warfare1.htm, accessed August 13, 2018.

2. Sledge, *Soldier Dead*, 150.

3. Poole, *On Hallowed Ground*, 144.

4. Poole, *On Hallowed Ground*, 145, quoting Neil Hanson, *Unknown Soldiers: The Story of the Missing of the First World War* (New York: Alfred A. Knopf, 2006), 241.

5. American servicemen were interred abroad in cemeteries turned over to the United States "in perpetuity," so in the strictest sense they weren't buried in American soil. Americans working and administering these cemeteries did not enjoy diplomatic immunity or the other conveniences offered Foreign Service officers working out of embassies or consulates.

The last few lines of the poem "My Boy Jack" (a nickname or diminutive of John) illustrate the grief mixed with pride that Rudyard Kipling felt for his youngest—his only son:

> Except he did not shame his kind—Not even with that wind blowing, and that tide.
> Then hold your head up all the more, This tide, And every tide; Because he was the son you bore, And gave to that wind blowing and that tide.

Kipling was a proud Englishman and fervent nationalist (with more than a hint of racist imperialism in his makeup, an understandable experience of much of his life spent in colonial India). He was never a soldier but had covered the conflict during the Boer War in Africa, 1898–1902, and early fighting in France as a war correspondent prior to his son's death in combat. He also became the literary advisor to the War Graves Commission. Like Theodore Roosevelt, he carried the grief of losing a son to his grave. The anguish was intensified by the fact that Kipling's son was never found, although researchers found disputed evidence that placed his mortal wounding distant from where official records indicated he was killed in the early 1900s. A headstone bearing his name and also disputed rank of first lieutenant, and date of death, stands in France. Who is buried beneath that headstone is anyone's guess.

CHAPTER 4

1. Poole, *On Hallowed Ground*, 146, referencing Marie M. Meloney to General Peyton March, November 13, 1920, NARA, RG 407, Box 563, File 293.8.
2. Meloney to March.
3. Poole reference to B. C. Mossman and M. Warner Stark, *The Last Salute: Civil and Military Funerals, 1921–1969* (Washington, DC: Center of Military History, 1971), 3–4.
4. Poole, *On Hallowed Ground*, 158–59.
5. Poole, *On Hallowed Ground*, 235–56.
6. Poole, *On Hallowed Ground*, 241.
7. Poole, *On Hallowed Ground*, 243.
8. Poole, *On Hallowed Ground*, 246.
9. Poole, *On Hallowed Ground*, 247.
10. Poole, *On Hallowed Ground*, 247.
11. Poole, *On Hallowed Ground*, 248.

12. Poole, *On Hallowed Ground*, 248.
13. Poole, *On Hallowed Ground*, 248.

CHAPTER 5

1. Peiping, or Peking as it is sometimes romanized, became Beijing when China accepted the pinyin dialectal translation of the Chinese characters sometime in the 1958–59 time frame. It was variously called by all three names, gradually turning to the modern pronunciation by the 1970s, particularly after the US-China thaw during Nixonian times.

Russia supported the Spanish Republicans. Aircraft, armor, supplies, and advisers stiffened their resistance, as did the International Brigade whose American and European participants would be called "Communist" or "anti-Fascist," again depending on the political leanings of the observer. Germany and Italy supported Franco, the insurgent general who more closely matched Germany's and Italy's autocratic power model of Fascism.

So, by 1937 and the Marco Polo bridge incident, the soon-to-be Axis powers were growing and validating their training and doctrine in proxy conflicts or smaller—but no less violent—wars. During this time the world simmered toward global conflict, but the US military's ability had deteriorated to nothing. Infantrymen used broom handles to replicate rifles; placards placed on Model A Fords declared them tanks. Douglas MacArthur, chief of staff of the US Army, fought the cavalry clique that dominated the army since the Indian Wars, pressuring the cavalry to turn in their mounts for tanks—but the number of tanks in the US inventory in 1937 would fit in a small American yard.

In the Philippines, China, and Nicaragua and a few other Latin American nations, US Army, Marines, and Navy forces had experienced some combat, but it was strictly small unit actions that would be entered into the military lexicon as "expeditionary actions"—basically an expeditionary force that could be transported on a ship, or at best, a number of ships.

2. Plating, *The Hump*, 94.
3. "Only two USAAF units flew cargo." Plating, *The Hump*, 39–41.
4. Plating, *The Hump*, 94.
5. At least military aviation received a boost from the burgeoning airlines and American aviation companies, particularly Boeing, Douglas, Consolidated, and others. These companies happily developed aircraft for commercial use after the war that would be useful to the Army Air Forces, Navy, and Marines in any "possible" conflict. So would avionics and communications along with navigational aids by General Electric, Rayco (later Raytheon), and others keep the US military in the technological game.

Future enemies' militaries strengthened and learned from their experiences. America had gotten weaker and smaller. But even as war clouds burgeoned and before Pearl Harbor, positive aviation activities were taking place for China. China National Aviation Company (CNAC) was one of the emerging businesses, from the commercial point of view. With nearly half of the company owned by Juan Trippe's aggressive Pan American Airways and its smart and farsighted manager William Bond, CNAC managed with superb, if somewhat idiosyncratic pilots. The fact that another airline that would go on to fame, Lufthansa, was competing for dominance in China and the Far East provided CNAC cheering sections at the Department of State and the US military. Particularly since the blitzkrieg and Battle of Britain were ongoing.

CHAPTER 6

1. A knot is a "nautical mile per hour." It is 6,080 feet in length, 1.15 times the length of a statute mile. It has been the unit of speed for sailing ships since ancient times when a knotted rope was pulled through the water to determine the "speed over water." Aviation began using it once air navigation became a necessity. Convert a "knot" to a statute mile per hour by multiplying the knots times 1.15. It is grammatically incorrect to say "knots per hour."

2. Plating, *The Hump*, 110.

3. Plating, *The Hump*, 110.

4. Plating, *The Hump*, 109–10.

5. Plating, *The Hump*, 53.

6. Even the hard-driving Hardin would lament the losses of a series of crashes in November 1943, to the lack of suitable navigation aids in a memorandum from his Eastern Sector back to headquarters.

7. Plating, *The Hump*, 148–49.

8. Plating, *The Hump*, 161.

9. Plating, *The Hump*, 161.

10. Plating, *The Hump*, 145, 158–59.

CHAPTER 7

1. Celestial navigation is the result of precise star and sun readings and accurate time hacks to record the second, minute, and hour when readings are taken (at Greenwich Mean Time—GMT).

2. Spencer, *Flying the Hump*, 42–43.

3. Lanier, logbook entries, January–February 1942.

4. Liddel Hart, *History of the Second World War*, 221.

CHAPTER 8

1. Captain Jerry Williams, former JCRC member, to author, January 1976, Springfield, VA.

2. The USAF airlifter crews rely heavily on the reserve components, and the distinction between active duty Air Force and part-time crews disappeared (many of the pilots and copilots flew for the airlines). All crews—active duty/reserve components—were excellent and professional.

3. JCRC and CILHI Command Briefings, 1987–88.

4. Veith, *Code-Name: Bright Light*, 3–5.

5. Veith, *Code-Name: Bright Light*, 137.

6. Retired Lieutenant Colonel Fred Caristo, a tough SOG'er, recalled that mission in a discussion with some of the POW/MIA staff at the DPMO in early 1993. He also received the Distinguished Service Cross, second only to the Medal of Honor, for another attempted Bright Light POW rescue in Cambodia.

CHAPTER 9

1. If memory serves me correctly, General Vessey came to the JCRC the second week of August 1987 and then flew on to Hanoi. I also recall Joe Harvey, Dick Childress, and Ann Mills Griffith accompanying him (along with General Kingston of course). We all refined the "discrepancy cases" back at Barbers Point during his and General Kington's short stay in Hawaii; then we went on for initial negotiations with the urbane and westernized Foreign Minister Nguyen Co Thach. General Vessey would make nine trips to Hanoi during my tenure in the JCRC, 1987–89, and the Office of the Secretary of Defense, 1990–93; after the Joint Task Force was formed and his final testimony to the Senate Select Committee in December 1992 and presidential election, he and General Kingston quietly backed off the issue but remained as the éminence grise available for consultation and advice.

2. Later archival research suggested the opponents were North Vietnamese elite paratroopers from the 305th Parachute Regiment who were being trained as counterreconnaissance combatants against SOG recon teams.

3. Gargus, *Son Tay Raid*, 209.

4. Author's conversation with General Vessey, January 10, 1993.

CHAPTER 10

1. Williams, now a top NBC reporter, was no-nonsense but highly personable and good to work for during this period. Much of our work was basic escape and evasion stuff, and CSAR passed to decision-makers talking before reporters and international cameras—never release the name of an airman evading capture, as a matter of fact, stay away from mentioning active escape and evasion; the enemy loves to hear that stuff.

CHAPTER 11

1. https://en.wikipedia.org/wiki/Non-British_personnel_in_the_RAF_during_the_Battle_of_Britain#United_States, accessed December 7, 2018.

2. https://history.army.mil/documents/mobpam.htm, accessed December 18, 2018.

3. Confirming a pilot's claims of downed aircraft when fighting two on one was difficult; when two friendly pilots downed one of the enemy, witnesses determined how the "spoils" should be divided; thus, a pilot and his wingman in the incident would share a portion of the victory.

4. https://tshaonline.org/handbook/online/articles/qtf02, accessed April 24, 2019.

5. https://history.army.mil/documents/mobpam.htm, accessed December 18, 2018.

6. "The Doolittle Raid, 1942," EyeWitness to History, www.eyewitnesstohistory.com, 2007, accessed January 22, 2019. The president's retreat in the remote Catoctin Mountains of Maryland would be Shangri-La until President Eisenhower renamed it Camp David in honor of two Davids: his father and his grandson.

7. Numbered Air Forces were created before the war to manage aerial operations in a geographic area, a country, or theater (perhaps several numbered Air Forces depending on the size and geopolitical situation). They are layered between the operational units and major commands. The Tenth Air Force initially had military and civil aviation responsibility for all of India. This was easy to establish with the British "ownership" of India. The Fourteenth Air Force was eventually created in China, and the Tenth retained control of US air operations in India and Burma.

8. Plating, *The Hump*, 56.

9. "Flew halfway around the world," Lanier logbook entry, no date indicated but it was in the fall of 1942. Unit history indicates a late October 1942 departure from Australia.

10. Interview with the Lanier family in North Carolina.

CHAPTER 12

1. Plating, *The Hump*, 40.
2. Plating, *The Hump*, 56–61.
3. Plating, *The Hump*, 55.
4. Plating, *The Hump*, 48.
5. Brewer, "China Airlift—the Hump," 170.
6. Gann, *Fate Is the Hunter*, 265–71.

CHAPTER 14

1. Telephone conversation with Ray Spock, August 1992.

CHAPTER 15

1. The Special Operations Command, of all regional commands, headed by four star generals or admirals, had its own Special Operations division, usually commanded by an experienced Service Special Operations colonel or naval captain.

2. Con Thien (the Hill of Angels) was a Marine firebase almost in North Vietnam that was overrun by the NVA in May 1967. Our Army Special Forces boss, now an Army colonel heading Special Operations, Pacific Command, was the captain commander of the supporting Special Forces "A" Team at the fire-

base. Additionally, it was my platoon that was there at the time, a few months before I got to Vietnam, but they were still manning it when I arrived in the late summer of 1967. Joe had spent time there evaluating personnel radars. It was a particularly bad and dangerous place. It also was a primary target for NVA artillery hidden across the DMZ. Con Thien was the deadliest piece of terrain in Vietnam. In my opinion, it was much worse than Khe Sanh because of its small size and prominent presence almost across their border. Con Thien veterans were a small club at USCINCPAC. The few others were Marines and our Army Special Forces colonel boss who was the chief special operator in the Pacific.

3. These recoveries included the two phases of the Tibet loss, the subject of this book; a C-130 shot down over Armenia in 1958, after a meaconing false beacon drew it into their airspace; a World War II B-17 recovery in the Amazon; a World War II B-17 recovery in Papua New Guinea; and a Pacific World War II ground loss in a French-administered Pacific Island chain. There was also a mission I led with Moscow's US Army attaché in the Russian far east based on some candid and seemingly accurate intelligence, but results came up maddingly dry on that one. The FSB, successors to the KGB by merely a name change, hadn't been ready to pull the trigger on furnishing witnesses to talk to the Joint Commission. They were still the same people that were there before—different name but still the ones who'd keep the secrets.

4. Company-grade officers are second lieutenants to captains; field-grade officers are majors through colonels. Normally, a battalion has five companies and about eight- to nine hundred soldiers depending on its function: combat, combat support such as military police or intelligence, or combat service support such as logistics, facilities, and services. A missing soldier is the highest priority in a unit, and there is plenty of assistance and command attention placed on the soldier's safe return. Sometimes a little too much.

5. On April 7, 2001, a Vietnamese MI-17 struck a foggy hilltop in Quang Binh province in central Vietnam, killing all seven Americans and nine Vietnamese aboard. The dead included the incoming US Detachment 2 commander and the outgoing one as well as other members of the JTF-FA and US Army Central Identification Laboratory. Among the Vietnamese, the dead included Colonel Tran van Bien, a longtime colleague and veteran of both the French and American wars. They were advancing another recovery operation and orienting the new commander to the country. There were no survivors of this tragic event.

CHAPTER 16

1. Conversation with Lieutenant General Michael Canavan, US Army (Retired). Canavan was a captain team leader assigned to the JCRC when it was headquartered in Thailand. "It used to really piss me off to see an NVA platoon in uniform and armed get off their helicopters grinning at us. We sat on the tarmac waiting for our beat-up Hueys dressed like a bunch of *deer hunters without weapons*." April 2004.

CHAPTER 17

1. Chinese Exclusion Act, Bradley, *China Mirage*, 42–46.

2. Bradley, *China Mirage*, 42–46.

3. Liddel Hart, *History of the Second World War*, 204.

4. Liddel Hart, *History of the Second World War*, 205.

5. These demands reinforced territorial gains and concessions from the Sino-Japanese conflict. These were initially presented to the Nationalist government in 1915, four years after the Manchu dynasty's nearly three centuries of fairly benign reign ended. After World War I Japan demanded reparations from German holdings in China as one of the victorious Allies; Japan had also diplomatically—but forcefully—reasserted the demands to the Chinese.

6. Melanesia, Micronesia, and Polynesia were all island groupings in the central and southern Pacific, largely grouped by ethnography and racial characteristics.

7. Plating, *The Hump*, 56.

8. Minimum en route altitude—an altitude that gives sufficient clearance to the highest obstacles on the route. Generally 1,000 feet, but local commands could prescribe them higher. Altimeters largely depended on barometric pressure during the period, and if not set to local surface barometric pressure, they could vary by hundreds of feet. Plus, mountain wave characteristics could zoom a plane thousands of feet higher on approaching a mountain and drop it a similar amount on the other. It was one of those factors that were foremost in a pilot's mind in World War II; it still is today if the pilot is flying a light aircraft.

9. Dinjan was a British airfield in Assam. The Commonwealth airmen of Canada, Australia, and New Zealand also flew the Hump, but mainly to support their own operations in theater. They were also largely, unlike their American military counterparts, experienced pilots.

10. Accurate weather forecasting units of the USAAF would not come to the Hump until later in 1944. Again symptomatic of a theater considered secondary to the main effort in Europe.

11. Plating, *The Hump*—China's "two flying seasons—winter and summer," 56–57.

12. Plating, *The Hump*, 58.

13. Plating, *The Hump*, 56–59.

14. Plating, *The Hump*, 57.

15. Plating, *The Hump*, 56–57.

CHAPTER 18

1. As of this writing, the Chinese have "discovered" the Fifteenth Dalai Lama. He has been undergoing training in Beijing for some time.

2. Sheehan, *A Missing Plane* (dentition/teeth importance and durability), 32–34.

3. Gargus, *Combat Talons*: Gargus's two books cited in this work reveal a great deal about the Combat Talon C-130s from the epochal combat mission in

the Son Tay raid to the loss of the one the JTF and CILHI recovered in North Vietnam. Basically, the mission wasn't compartmented special access information, but the airplane was at the time. John is a formidable and tireless researcher and chronicler. He also flew in the Son Tay raid and speaks from experience.

4. Anthropologically, remains were largely categorized as Caucasoid, Negroid, and Mongoloid until the mid-twentieth century. Back then, archaeologists, anthropologists, and medical examiners seemed to use the terms as unemotionally as someone describing different tribes.

CHAPTER 20

1. Hopkirk, *Trespassers*, 6.

CHAPTER 21

1. Starks and Murcutt, *Lost in Tibet*, 25.

2. Richard Starks and Miriam Murcutt's, *Lost in Tibet* recounts the details of their flying, bail out, and trek out to India, even though some crewmembers were injured severely, and the political intricacies, particularly between Britain and Nationalist China. These are well documented by the authors and leave readers on the edge of their seats. In addition, the authors interviewed the copilot, who went on to a distinguished flying career and penned his own narrative, *Tibet—One Second to Live*; it was self-published in 1995. Curiously, he didn't dwell overly on their adventure in Tibet, and it comes across as just another exciting chapter of several in his lifetime flying career.

3. Knaus, *Orphans of the Cold War*, 1–2.

4. The Central Intelligence Agency, the National Security Council (NSC) as well as numerous changes to the national intelligence process, were also created from the same National Security Act of 1947. The Army, Navy, and Air Force intelligence departments were also merged into what would eventually be the Department of Defense, with all the services' secretaries under the purview of the Secretary of Defense.

CHAPTER 22

1. Plating, *The Hump*, 215.

2. The Japanese view was different—flush with success from the Sino-Japanese war of 1895 and the Russo-Japanese war of 1905, only the peacekeeping efforts of Theodore Roosevelt kept the Japanese from taking warm-water ports on the Russian mainland. Portions of the volcano-strewn Sakhalin chain were ceded to Japan, along with control of Korea, and Russian troops withdrew from Manchuria, strengthening the Russian presence there until they annexed it completely two and a half decades later.

3. www.en.wikipedia.org/wiki/Soviet conflicts, accessed June 5, 2016.

4. Sakai, *Samurai!*, 145.

5. Bradley, *China Mirage*, 83.

6. Roosevelt viewed China as an important postwar actor in Asia. Bradley, *China Mirage*, 300.

7. "written home to his father he was going to fly the HUMP," Bill Lanier telephone interview, May 10, 2010.

8. "over the HUMP . . . copilot on a C-47." Lanier logbook entry.

9. Author's interview, Doris Stepanovich, September 23, 1998.

10. We did take him back and searched for his command bunker without luck; there were a few bone fragments discovered around the site, as I recall, but basically it was overgrown with shrubbery and farmed. It was spooky, but gratifying, to visit Khe Sanh again and drive down a much improved Route 9 from Dong Ha, unrecognizable from 1967 to 1968—then a warren of overgrown ambush sites. No runway split the base. In fact, there was no base. Miles of German razor wire was gone, with no evidence of it ever being there. I walked back toward the southeast looking for MACV-SOG's Forward Operating Base 3, the SF and their Bru strikers headquarters, then a concertinaed redoubt with a Seabee-built bunker that legend held was air-conditioned and loaded with steaks and whiskey. I found nothing but plots of agricultural land.

Paul Mather's office in Bangkok, formerly called the Bangkok Detachment of the JCRC, or simply Bangkok by the old JCRC hands, became Detachment One; Hanoi, Jack Donovan's domain (nicknamed the Ranch), became Detachment Two; Vientiane, Laos, Detachment Three; and eventually Phnom Penh, Cambodia, became Detachment Four. One and Four were commanded by Air Force lieutenant colonels, Two and Three, Army lieutenant colonels. All were screened through their personnel commands and selected by General Needham.

11. In April 1975, the version heard was sung by Tennessee Ernie Ford; no one could find a Bing Crosby version.

CHAPTER 23

1. Aliosi, *Life in the Foreign Service*, 27.

2. Aliosi, *Life in the Foreign Service*, 28.

CHAPTER 24

1. Newby, *Travellers' Tales*, 329–30.

2. Hopkirk, *Trespassers*, 227–29.

3. Hopkirk, *Trespassers*, 227–29.

4. Personal conversation: Lieutenant Colonel Graydon Spurgeon, over a beer and a three-dollar steak in the Florida Bar, Juárez, Mexico, February 1970.

5. A decade later my wife would point out in an article in *Army Times* that Sergeant First Class Mark Antal and his Ranger buddy had won the grueling "Best Ranger" award at Fort Benning, Georgia.

CHAPTER 25

1. RIP: Ranger Indoctrination Program; units run this for their soldiers going to Ranger School, the eight-week arduous school at Fort Benning, Georgia.

CHAPTER 26

1. Author's personal interview, Mike Stepanovich, February 20, 1999; by telephone, November 26, 2017.

2. http://www.arlingtoncemetery.net/tibet.htm, "Back from the HUMP," accessed April 20, 1999, and several times thereafter.

3. https://en.wikipedia.org/wiki/Air_Rescue_Service, accessed January 4, 2017.

4. https://en.wikipedia.org/wiki/Air_Rescue_Service. Two decades later, as a lieutenant general he would chair the commission that investigated the My Lai massacre. During the Vietnam War he had commanded the Fourth Infantry Division.

Detachment 101s mission was to launch "hit and run" operations against Japanese units, a considerable threat in Burma, as their strategy had shifted to a large offensive against allied airfields in order to clear avenues for an invasion of India. They, like their Special Operations successors through subsequent wars, were also responsible for personnel recovery. See also Helo rescue, US// www.cia.gov/library/center-for-the-study-of-intelligence/kent-csi/vol4no3/ html/v04i3a11p_0001.htm, accessed January 22, 2016.

5. The Switlik Parachute Company, family owned and in business since 1920, provided testimony for bailout victims with a pin and classy certificate. They also included a letter attesting to the fact they had "hit the silk" of a Switlik parachute and survived.

CHAPTER 27

1. American Graves Registration Service History, the Pacific, 489.

2. American Graves Registration Service History, the Pacific, 489, 490.

3. American Graves Registration Service History, the Pacific, 482.

4. Later CILHI recovery of the C-46, in 2004. http://www.dpaa.mil/ Resources/Fact-Sheets/Article-View/Article/569618/chronology-of-personnel-accounting-progress-in-china/, accessed December 23, 2015.

5. Xinhua/PR News article, August 13, 2015, accessed on December 3, 2015. A conversation with a Mr. Xu? (name telephonically indistinct), PRC Embassy, December 16, 2015, revealed that he'd heard nothing about the Chinese August expedition into the crash site and recommended calling the museum. I believed he was a public affairs official. I demurred and he agreed to follow up after the holiday season. I did try to follow up with him and reached a different person who knew nothing about it.

6. January 6, 2016, conversation with unnamed official, PRC embassy; the

PRC Ministry of Foreign Affairs had put out no official word that she was aware of concerning the private and apparently unannounced museum activity at the crash site. She did not think there were Chinese laws prohibiting this, and the US consul general apparently expressed gratitude for the turnover of remains. It all turned out extremely well, she thought, all things considered. I agreed.

7. Conversation with Sherap and Thorndrup, September 16, 1994.

EPILOGUE

1. "Tommy King" was code for Kunming. Flight instruments; Airspeed indicator; Rate of climb indicator in feet (or descent) in feet per minute; Altimeter; Directional Gyro slaved to the compass.

ACKNOWLEDGMENTS

1. The US Army Command Historian, Colonel Charles H. Briscoe, PhD, a respected and decorated Special Operations veteran, interviewed Joe, Paul, and me by telephone over a period of several weeks and would later write in a special edition of the Army *Special Operations Journal* describing the POW/Missing recovery efforts in the Vietnam conflict, *Veritas:* " but the relentless work of Air Force Lt Col Paul Mather and Army LTC Joe B. Harvey, spanning fifteen years, developed the MIA recovery protocols used to this day. . . . they are the 'unsung heroes' of the JCRC," 4.

Bibliography

BOOKS

Acheson, Dean. *Present at the Creation*. New York: W. W. Norton, 1969.

Bell, Charles. *The People of Tibet*. Oxford: Clarendon Press, 1928.

Brackenbury, Wade. *Yak Butter and Black Tea*. Chapel Hill, NC: Algonquin Books, 1997.

Bradley, James. *The China Mirage*. New York: Little, Brown, 2015.

Brewer, James F., ed. *China Airlift—the HUMP*. 3 vols. Paducah, KY: Turner, 1980.

Campbell, Christy. *Air War Pacific*. New York: Crescent Books, 1990.

Carter, Carolle J. *Mission to Yenan*. Lexington: University of Kentucky Press, 1997.

Chan, Victor. *Tibet Handbook*. Chico, CA: Moon Publishing, 1994.

Chanda, Nayan. *Brother Enemy*. New York: Collier Books, 1986.

———. *Brother Enemy: Indochina after the War*. New York: Random House, 1987.

Clarke, Douglas. *The Missing Man*. Washington, DC: National War College, 1979.

Colley, David P. *Safely Rest*. New York: Caliber Books/Penguin Group, 2004.

Constein, Carl F. *Born to Fly the Hump: A World War II Memoir*. Bloomington, IN: 1st Books, 2001.

Dunham, Mikel. *Buddha's Warriors*. New York: Penguin, 2004.

Fairbank, John K. *The Great Chinese Revolution: 1880–1985*. New York: Harper and Row, 1986.

Fall, Bernard B. *Hell in a Very Small Place*. Cambridge, MA: Da Capo/Perseus, 1966.

Feis, Herbert. *The China Tangle*. Princeton, NJ: Princeton University Press, 1972.

Flanagan, Edward M. *The Los Baños Raid*. Novato, CA: Presidio Press, 1986.

Gann, Ernest K. *Fate Is the Hunter*. New York: Simon and Schuster, 1961.

Gargus, John. *Combat Talons in Vietnam*. College Station: Texas A&M University Press, 2017.

———. *The Son Tay Raid*. College Station: Texas A&M University Press, 2010.

Hopkirk, Peter. *Trespassers on the Roof of the World*. New York: Kodansha, 1995.

Karnow, Stanley. *Vietnam, A History*. New York: Viking Press, 1983.

Kissinger, Henry. *On China*. New York: Penguin, 2011.

Knaus, John Kenneth. *Orphans of the Cold War*. New York: Public Affairs/Perseus, 1999.

Liddell Hart, B. H. *History of the Second World War*. New York: Da Capo, 1999.

Masters, John. *Bugles and a Tiger: A Volume of Autobiography*. New York: Viking, 1956.

———. *The Road Past Mandalay: A Personal Narrative*. New York: Bantam, 1963.

Mather, Paul D. *M.I.A.: Accounting for the Missing in Southeast Asia*. Washington, DC: National Defense University Press, 1994.

Meyer, Karl E., and Shareen Blair Brysac. *Tournament of Shadows*. New York: Basic/Perseus, 1999.

Murphy, Edward F. *Dak To*. New York: Pocket Books/Simon and Schuster, 1993.

———. *The Hill Fights*. New York: Presidio/Ballantine, 2003.

Morwood, William. *Duel for the Middle Kingdom*. New York: Everest House, 1980.

Newby, Eric. *A Book of Travellers' Tales*. Viking/Penguin, 1985.

O'Daniel, Larry J. *Missing in Action: Trail of Deceit*. New Rochelle, NY: Arlington House, 1979.

Plating, John D. *The Hump*. College Station: Texas A&M University Press, 2011.

Poole, Robert M. *On Hallowed Ground: The Story of Arlington National Cemetery*. New York: Bloomsbury, 2010.

Prados, John, and Ray W. Stubbe. *Valley of Decision: The Siege of Khe Sanh*. New York: Dell/Doubleday, 1991.

Quinn, Chick Marrs. *The Aluminum Trail*. Self-published, 1989.

Rooney, D. D. *Stilwell*. New York: Ballantine, 1971.

Sakai, Saburo, with Martin Caidin and F. Saito. *Samurai!* New York: Ballantine Books, 1957.

Schemmer, Benjamin F. *The Raid*. New York: Harper and Row, 1976.

Shaplen, Robert. *Bitter Victory*. New York: Harper and Row, 1986.

Sheehan, Susan. *A Missing Plane*. New York: Berkley Books, 1986.

Sledge, Michael. *Soldier Dead*. New York: Columbia University Press, 2005.

Smith, Thomas T. *Until They Are Home*. College Station: Texas A&M University Press, 2011.

Snow, Edgar. *Red Star over China*. New York: Grove Press, 1938.

Snyder, Timothy. *Bloodlands*. New York: Basic Books, 2010.

Spencer, Otha C. *Flying the Hump*. College Station: Texas A&M University Press, 1992.

Spurling, Hilary. *Pearl Buck in China*. New York: Simon and Schuster, 2010.

Starks, Richard, and Miriam Murcutt. *Lost in Tibet: The Untold Story of Five American Airmen, a Doomed Plane, and the Will to Survive*. 2nd ed. Guilford, CT: Lyons Press, 1993.

Stern, Lewis M. *Imprisoned or Missing in Vietnam*. Jefferson, NC: McFarland, 1994.

Stockdale, Jim and Sybil. *In Love and War*. New York: Harper and Row, 1986.

Taylor, Jay. *The Generalissimo*. Cambridge, MA: Belknap Press of Harvard University Press, 2009.

Terrill, Ross. *Mao, a Biography*. New York: Touchstone/Simon and Schuster, 1980.

Thomas, Nedda R. *Hump Pilot*. Palisades, NY: History Publishing, 2014.

Thorne, Bliss K. *The Hump*. Philadelphia: J. P. Lippincott, 1965.

Tuchman, Barbara. *Stilwell and the American Experience in China*. New York: Grove Press, 1971.

Tung, Rosemary Jones. *A Portrait of Lost Tibet*. Berkeley: University of California Press, 1996.

Underbrink, Robert. *Somewhere We Will Find You*. Bennington, VT: Merriam Press, 2010.

Van Slyke, Lyman, ed. *The China White Paper: August 1949*.

Veith, George J. *Code-Name: Bright Light*. New York: Dell, 1998.

Willet, Robert L. *An Airline at War*. Self-published, marketed by www.booksurge.com, 2008.

Yarsinke, Amy W. *No One Left Behind: The Lt. Comdr. Michael Scott Speicher Story*. New York: New American Library/Penguin, 2002.

REPORTS/INFORMATION PAPERS

Aliosi, Jon. State magazine, *Life in the Foreign Service*, August 1995.

Autodin Message: *Office of the Secretary of Defense, Assistant Secretary for Public Affairs, Current Issues: POW/MIA Affairs* (OSD/ASD-PA); dated 292131Z July 1987.

Files, Department of State. *U.S. Relations with China*. Washington, DC: US Government Printing Office, 1949 (extracted from FRUS-1949, with cover letter from Dean Acheson).

Final Interagency Report of the Reagan Administration on the POW/MIA Issue in Southeast Asia. Washington, DC, June 19, 1987.

(FOIA) Memorandum for Commander, US Army Total Personnel Command . . . TAPC-PEZ, Alexandria, VA Z-C—SUBJECT: *Proposed Id of CILHI 0144-94 (Tibet Crew)* dated October 27, 1997.

Foreign Relations of the United States (FRUS), 1940, 1949, 1954, 1975.

Goldich, Robert L. CRS Brief for Congress. *POWs and MIAs: Status and Accounting Issues*. Updated July 22, 2003.

Jordan, W. H. (Lieutenant Colonel, USA). *Politics, Perceptions, and Prisoners of War*. Carlisle, PA: US Army War College, 1989–90.

———. *Smithsonian Air & Space Magazine*, March 1998.

Lima Sites and Landing Fields in Laos. Unclassified. Air America. Vientiane, 1971.

Missing in Southeast Asia. 94th Congress, February–March 1976.

Not to Be Forgotten. Pamphlet, United States Army Central Identification Laboratory, Hawaii, undated.

POW-MIA Fact Book. Department of Defense, July 1992.

Senate Report 103-1. *Report of the Senate Select Committee on POW/MIA Affairs*, January 13, 1993.

U.S. Congress, House, Subcommittee on Asian and Pacific Affairs. *Access to Classified Live Sighting Information Concerning POWS/MIAs in Southeast Asia—Is New Legislation Needed?* 100th Congress, April 1986.

U.S. Delegation—Four Party Joint Military Team: History, March–December 1973. Undated document.

ELECTRONIC COMMUNICATION AND ORAL INTERVIEWS

Canavan, Michael, Lt. Gen. USA (Retired).

Donovan, John "Jack," Col. USA (Retired).

Gorman, Arthur V., Lt. Col. USMC (Retired).

Harvey, Joe, Lt. Col. USA (Retired).

Lanier, Bill and Diane.

Mather, Paul, Lt. Col. USAF (Retired).

Nelson, John. November 2009–January 2016.

Petrella, Carl.

Petrella, James.

Stepanovich, Michael and Lynn.

Stepanovich (Ramos), Doris.

Stern, Lewis, Dr.

Troyano (Giacalone), Tom, Dr.

Index